Bloom's Classic Critical Views

GEORGE GORDON, LORD BYRON

Bloom's Classic Critical Views

Alfred, Lord Tennyson
Benjamin Franklin
The Brontës
Charles Dickens
Edgar Allan Poe
Geoffrey Chaucer
George Eliot
George Gordon, Lord Byron
Henry David Thoreau
Herman Melville
Jane Austen
John Donne and the Metaphysical Poets
John Milton
Jonathan Swift
Mark Twain
Mary Shelley
Nathaniel Hawthorne
Oscar Wilde
Percy Shelley
Ralph Waldo Emerson
Robert Browning
Samuel Taylor Coleridge
Stephen Crane
Walt Whitman
William Blake
William Shakespeare
William Wordsworth

Bloom's Classic Critical Views

GEORGE GORDON, LORD BYRON

Edited and with an Introduction by
Harold Bloom
Sterling Professor of the Humanities
Yale University

 BLOOM'S
LITERARY CRITICISM
An imprint of Infobase Publishing

Bloom's Classic Critical Views: George Gordon, Lord Byron

Copyright © 2009 Infobase Publishing

Introduction © 2009 by Harold Bloom

Bloom's Literary Criticism
An imprint of Infobase Publishing
132 West 31st Street
New York NY 10001

Library of Congress Cataloging-in-Publication Data
George Gordon, Lord Byron / edited and with an introduction by Harold Bloom; Heike Grundmann, volume editor.
    p. cm. — (Bloom's classic critical views)
    Includes bibliographical references and index.
    ISBN 978-1-60413-438-4 (acid-free paper)   1. Byron, George Gordon Byron, Baron, 1788–1824—Criticism and interpretation.   I. Bloom, Harold.   II. Grundmann, Heike.   III. Title.   IV. Series.
    PR4388.G44 2009
    821'.7—dc22

                            2009012454

Volume editor: Heike Grundmann
Series design by Erika K. Arroyo
Cover designed by Takeshi Takahashi
Printed in the United States of America
IBT IBT 10 9 8 7 6 5 4 3 2 1

This book is printed on acid-free paper.

All links and Web addresses were checked and verified to be correct at the time of publication. Because of the dynamic nature of the Web, some addresses and links may have changed since publication and may no longer be valid.

Contents

Series Introduction ix

Introduction by Harold Bloom xi

Biography xxi

Personal 9
Hewson Clarke (1808) 11
Maria Edgeworth (1813) 12
George Ticknor (1815) 14
Sydney Smith (1816) 16
Samuel Taylor Coleridge (1816) 16
Thomas Carlyle (1824) 17
Thomas Medwin (1824) 18
Walter Scott "Death of Lord Byron" (1824) 19
Leigh Hunt (1828) 22
Gustave Flaubert (1838) 26
Marguerite, Countess of Blessington (1834) 26
Matthew Arnold "Stanzas from the Grande Chartreuse"
    and "Memorial Verses" (1850 & 1855) 28
Samuel Rogers (1855) 29
Edward John Trelawny (1858) 31
George Eliot (1866) 34
Joaquin Miller "At Lord Byron's Tomb" (1870) 35
Oscar Wilde (1891) 37
William Graham (1898) 38

General 41
Henry, Lord Brougham "Lord Byron's Poems" (1808) 43
Leigh Hunt (1811) 44
Friedrich von Schlegel (1815) 45

William Hazlitt (1818)   46
Robert Southey "Preface" (1821)   48
William Maginn "Odoherty on Werner" (1822)   48
Samuel Taylor Coleridge (1822)   51
Thomas Lovell Beddoes (1825)   51
Thomas Carlyle (1826)   51
John Quincy Adams (1830)   51
William Hazlitt (1825)   52
John Galt (1830)   61
Johann Wolfgang von Goethe (1830)   64
William H. Prescott "English Literature of the
    Nineteenth Century" (1832)   67
Thomas Babington Macaulay "Moore's Life of
    Lord Byron" (1831)   69
Giuseppe Mazzini "Byron and Goethe" (1839)   79
Matthew Arnold (1881)   84
Algernon Charles Swinburne "Byron" (1866)   92
Robert Browning (1846)   105
William Michael Rossetti "Lord Byron" (1878)   106
William Ernest Henley "Byron" (1890)   107
George Saintsbury (1896)   109
Edward Dowden (1897)   111
Lionel Johnson "Byron" (1898)   113
G.K. Chesterton "The Optimism of Byron" (1901)   116
John Churton Collins "The Collected Works of
    Lord Byron" (1905)   120
Arthur Symons (1909)   126
Virginia Woolf (1918)   135
Katherine Fullerton Gerould "Men, Women, and the
    Byron-Complex" (1922)   136
T.S. Eliot "Byron" (1937)   137

WORKS

Childe Harold's Pilgrimage   141
Elizabeth, Duchess of Devonshire (Undated)   142
Samuel Rogers (1812)   142
Walter Scott (1812)   143
Francis Jeffrey (1812)   144
George Ellis "Review of Byron, Childe Harold" (1812)   146
Horace and James Smith "Cui bono?" (1812)   154
John Cam Hobhouse (1814 & 1816)   155
John Murray (1816)   156

Francis Jeffrey "Lord Byron's Poems" (1816)   157
George Gordon, Lord Byron (1817)   159
John Wilson (1817)   159
William Hazlitt (1818)   160
Walter Scott (1818)   161
John Wilson (1818)   164
Percy Bysshe Shelley (1818)   174
Thomas Love Peacock (1818)   175
John Addington Symonds "Lord Byron" (1880)   176
R. E. Prothero "The Poetry of Byron" (1924)   179

The Turkish Tales   183
Francis Jeffrey (1814)   184
George Ellis (1814)   194
Henry Crabb Robinson (1813)   196
Walter Scott (1813)   197
John Murray (1814)   198
Isaac Disraeli (1816)   199
William Gifford (1816)   200
Jane Austen (1818)   200

Manfred   201
John Wilson (1818)   202
Francis Jeffrey (1817)   205
Johann Wolfgang von Goethe "Byron's Manfred" (1820)   208
George Gordon, Lord Byron (1820)   210
Margaret Oliphant (1883)   210
Josiah Royce (1885)   211
John Churton Collins "The Collected Works of
    Lord Byron" (1905)   212

Beppo   214
John Murray (1818)   214
Unsigned (1818)   215
Francis Jeffrey (1818)   215
Unsigned "Letter to the Author of *Beppo*" (1818)   217

Don Juan   221
Leigh Hunt (1819)   222
Robert Southey (1820)   225
Johann Wolfgang von Goethe "Byron's *Don Juan*" (1821)   226
Samuel Taylor Coleridge (1824)   227
Caroline Norton (1837)   227

James Northcote (1830)   228
Thomas Babington Macaulay (1849)   229
John Addington Symonds "Lord Byron" (1880)   229
Algernon Charles Swinburne (1866)   230
George Bernard Shaw "Dedicatory Letter" (1903)   234
Paul Elmer More "A Note on Byron's Don Juan" (1905)   234
R.E. Prothero "The Poetry of Byron" (1924)   241

Marino Faliero   243
William Hazlitt "Lord Byron's Tragedy of
    Marino Faliero" (1821)   244
Francis Jeffrey (1821)   246
Reginald Heber (1822)   250
John Nichol (1880)   254

Cain   255
John Cam Hobhouse (1821)   255
Thomas Moore (1821)   255
Walter Scott (1821)   256
Unsigned (1821)   257
Mary Shelley (1821)   257
Percy Bysshe Shelley (1822)   258
Henry Crabb Robinson (1822)   258
Unsigned (1822)   259
Oxoniensis (H.J. Todd) (1822)   259
Leigh Hunt "A Letter on Cain to the Readers of the
    Examiner" (1822)   260
William Blake "The Ghost of Abel" (1822)   265
Reginald Heber (1822)   268
Samuel Egerton Brydges (1824)   274
Johann Wolfgang von Goethe (1824)   275

Sardanapalus   275
Francis Jeffrey (1822)   276
John Gibson Lockhart (1822)   282

Chronology   285

Index   289

Series Introduction

Bloom's Classic Critical Views is a new series presenting a selection of the most important older literary criticism on the greatest authors commonly read in high school and college classes today. Unlike the Bloom's Modern Critical Views series, which for more than 20 years has provided the best contemporary criticism on great authors, Bloom's Classic Critical Views attempts to present the authors in the context of their time and to provide criticism that has proved over the years to be the most valuable to readers and writers. Selections range from contemporary reviews in popular magazines, which demonstrate how a work was received in its own era, to profound essays by some of the strongest critics in the British and American tradition, including Henry James, G.K. Chesterton, Matthew Arnold, and many more.

Some of the critical essays and extracts presented here have appeared previously in other titles edited by Harold Bloom, such as the New Moulton's Library of Literary Criticism. Other selections appear here for the first time in any book by this publisher. All were selected under Harold Bloom's guidance.

In addition, each volume in this series contains a series of essays by a contemporary expert, who comments on the most important critical selections, putting them in context and suggesting how they might be used by a student writer to influence his or her own writing. This series is intended above all for students, to help them think more deeply and write more powerfully about great writers and their works.

Introduction by Harold Bloom

1

The ultimate contrast in English poetry is between Byron and Shakespeare. Of Byron the passional man, we know nearly everything, while of Shakespeare's inwardness we know nothing. Shelley, a superb literary critic, considered Byron's *Don Juan* to be the great poem of the age, surpassing Goethe and Wordsworth. Once I would not have agreed with Shelley, but moving toward seventy-nine and having just reread *Don Juan*, I am persuaded. Unfinished and unfinishable, Byron's masterwork ought to be his monument. It is almost as large-minded and various as its outrageous creator but will go on yielding to his legend. Byron is the eternal archetype of the celebrity, the Napoleon of the realms of rhyme. Only Shakespeare, who re-created Plutarch's Cleopatra as the matchless celebrity of the ancient world, would be capable of representing Lord Byron in a tragicomedy worthy of the still unique celebrity of the modern world, dwarfing all latecomer rock superstars.

In the two centuries since Byron died in Greece, leading a messy rebellion against the Turks (April 19, 1824, aged thirty-six), only Shakespeare has been translated and read more, first in continental Europe and then worldwide. High Romantic in his life but not in his art, which carried on from Jonathan Swift, Alexander Pope, and Laurence Sterne, the endlessly digressive Byron incarnated countless contradictions of thought and feeling. He bewildered and fascinated his contemporaries with a vitality overtly erotic, compounded of narcissism, snobbery, sadomasochism, incest, heterosexual sodomy, homosexuality, what you will. Of the two authentic English vices, humbuggery and bumbuggery, Byron scourged the first and expanded the horizons of the second.

The first matter to bear in mind concerning Byron is his royal lineage, descended on his mother's, the Gordon side, from Annabella Stuart, daughter of James I of Britain (James VI of Scotland, son of Mary, Queen of Scots). The father was "Mad

Jack" Byron, gambler and heroic womanizer, who had been guilty of incest with his sister Frances. Their daughter, Lady Augusta Leigh, the poet's half-sister, became his true beloved, thus repeating the pattern. Mad Jack died in France, poor and abandoned, when his poetical son was three. Born with a lame left foot, George Gordon, Lord Byron, became a superb swimmer and marksman and, at ten, secured the family title.

At Harrow the thirteen-year-old Lord Byron became a fierce boxer, while being inaugurated into that temple of "fagging and flogging and homoerotic initiation" (the description by John Cam Hobhouse, the poet's lifetime friend). This bisexual orientation continued at Trinity College, Cambridge, where Byron cherished a grand passion for a choirboy, John Edleston.

Living the expected debauchery of a young Lord in alternation between Cambridge and London, Byron exceeded all expectations even for Regency rakes. His invariable motive was self-dramatization, and since his lust was for lasting fame above all, he demands and rightly obtains (and rewards) appreciation. That is the enterprise of *Byron in Love: A Short Daring Life* by the admirable novelist and short story master, Edna O'Brien. Her daring is to treat Lord Byron as an Edna O'Brien protagonist, handled with gentle sympathy and a detachment that yields to his prevenient self-irony. She gives us a kind of novella, told with the rapid, fervent pace of the noble Lord narrating *Don Juan*.

2

In 1807, the nineteen-year-old Byron published *Hours of Idleness*, a lyric volume massively demolished in *The Edinburgh Review*. Though he fought back in his *English Bards, and Scotch Reviewers* (1809), a verse satire in the mode of Alexander Pope, the wound lasted. A grand tour of two years duration took him to Portugal, Spain, Albania, Greece, Constantinople, and then Athens again. The final nine months of his life—July 1823–April 1824—when he helped lead the Greeks in their war for independence against the Turks, were overdetermined by his Athens sojourn, which transmuted him from a noble versifier into a major and wildly popular poet. *Childe Harold's Pilgrimage*, Cantos I and II, published in March 1812, made him the literary and social craze of Regency London.

Rereading Cantos I and II after a half century away from them is a pleasant surprise, and helps account for their instant contemporary success. This is confessional poetry, self-obsessed, brutally nihilistic, frequently slapdash, yet always refreshingly materialistic in the mode of Lucretius's *De rerum natura*. Byron's Lucretianism later allied him to Shelley, but that difficult friendship with an intellectual and imaginative equal (the only one both poets ever enjoyed, and suffered) began during a three-month summer in Geneva, 1816, and will be considered in some depth shortly.

Edna O'Brien places Byron at fame's peak from 1812 to 1814, commencing with his inaugural speech in the House of Lords, February, 1812, a month before *Childe Harold's* publication. As an aristocratic Whig of the Holland House set, the poet aptly chose to speak against the Tory government's Framework Bill, which envisioned death by hanging for the Nottingham Luddite weavers who had destroyed the machines replacing them. I have just read what appears to be the speech, which lacks rhetorical confidence, but it made a considerable impression upon both Whigs and Tories. Like Shelley, Byron was a poet on the Left, and revolution kindled his enthusiasm, but his concern for the people is suspect. He grimly exploited the angry workers in the Lancashire coal pits he owned and expressed no guilt, since his rage for expense invariably exceeded his high revenues. Karl Marx, whose daughter translated Shelley, looked back at the self-destructive careers of both Promethean rebels and shrewdly concluded that Shelley the aristocrat always would have stood with the revolutionary Left but that Byron, had he been able to bear survival into middle age (he proclaimed the best of life to be over at twenty-three), would have sided with his hereditary nobility against the lower orders.

It needs a storyteller with the experiential skills of Edna O'Brien to intimate something of Byron's sexual, literary, and social dazzle in Whiggish London, 1812–1819. Literally scores of noblewomen, married and not, offered themselves openly or in clandestine letters to the hero of *Childe Harold*. Leslie A. Marchand's *Byron: A Biography* (three volumes, New York, 1957), properly credited by O'Brien as one of her prime sources, details these glittering years of fame, love, and Whig society, in his chapters X–XII (Volume I, pp. 327–476). Marchand is particularly vivid on Byron's erotic Waterloo, the superbly wild Lady Caroline Lamb, wife of William Lamb, and later, as Lord Melbourne, one of Queen Victoria's prime ministers (1834, 1835–1841). After one glance at Byron, Lady Caroline fled home to describe him memorably in her journal: "mad—bad—and dangerous to know," a precise self-characterization. For not quite five months, their furiously public love affair entertained and scandalized even uninhibited Whig society, until Byron, after many vacillations, escaped for solace to the amiable and vastly experienced Lady Oxford, aged forty to his twenty-four. This was socially acceptable but yielded soon to the start of his incestuous intimacy with his half-sister Lady Augusta Leigh, well described by Marchand: "amoral as a rabbit and silly as a goose."

Because of this predicament and his financial disasters, Byron understandably but crazily made his blindest mistake. He earlier had proposed marriage to the wealthy Annabella Milbanke, who now finally accepted him. They married in January 1815, by which time Augusta Leigh had given birth to Byron's daughter Medora. The marriage lasted exactly a year, ending when Annabella left him, after the birth of their daughter, Augusta Ada. Magnificent also as a letter writer, Byron permanently had limned his prospective wife's character:

She seems to have been spoiled—not as children usually are—but systematically Clarissa Harlowed into an awkward kind of correctness, with a dependence upon her own infallibility which will or may lead her into some egregious blunder.

Lovelace to her Clarissa Harlowe, Byron was Annabella's egregious blunder. Both of them deserved better than this amazing mismatch of the endlessly mobile poet and the morally staunch puritan. She undoubtedly was the most intelligent young woman he ever met and almost the poorest in judgment. Byron immortalized her as "the Princess of Parallelograms," since mathematics was her passion. Their absurd marriage Marchand categorized as "tragicomedy of the most exquisite sort" (I, 429), while O'Brien is stirred to a fine gusto:

Their arrival has the suspense and thrall of gothic fiction—a sprawling mansion, a fall of snow, servants holding lit tapers, noting that the bride looked listless and frightened and that her husband did not help her down from the carriage. And so began the most public marriage of any poet, so infamous in its time that it was lampooned in *John Bull* magazine and the subject of endless scrutiny, helped by the confession of Byron himself in his Memoirs, as Tom Moore recalled it, and by Lady Byron's numerous and increasingly incriminating testaments to her lawyers and afterwards for her own 'Histoire'. Though professing to Moore a reluctance to 'profane the chaste mysteries of the Hymen,' Byron, according to Moore, 'had Lady Byron on the sofa before dinner.'

His tenets regarding the sleeping arrangements were categoric. Enquiring if she meant to sleep with him, he claimed to have an aversion to sleeping with any woman, but that she could, if she wished, one animal being the same as the next, provided it was young. She who in her charter for a suitable husband had recoiled from insanity was to have her fill of it. Their wedding night has its literary correlation in the works of Edgar Allan Poe, a crimson curtain catching fire, a hallucinating bridegroom believing he was in hell, then pacing the long ghostly gallery with his loaded pistols. (pp. 106–107)

By the morning after, the bride had deduced the incestuous secret and soon enough endured fifteen days of cohabitation with both her husband and his sister. A later visit by Augusta extended into two months, with Byron's behavior becoming maniacal, suggesting aspects of Emily Brontë's Heathcliff, who was to be based upon him. Abandoning Byron, Annabella sued, and Regency London turned savagely upon the bisexual, incestuous, sodomistic poet it had celebrated. Legal separation between Lord and Lady Byron was formalized in April, and the poet left England, never to return, on April 24, 1816.

3

Byron's greatest poetry, from *Childe Harold's Pilgrimage*, Cantos III and IV, through *Manfred* and *Cain*, *Beppo*, and *The Vision of Judgment*, on to *Don Juan*, all has an antithetical relation to his closest friend in Italy, Percy Bysshe Shelley, perhaps the most advanced lyric poet in Western tradition, precursor of a strangely varied visionary company of literary followers: Thomas Lovell Beddoes and Robert Browning, Herman Melville and Algernon Charles Swinburne, Thomas Hardy and William Butler Yeats, Virginia Woolf and George Bernard Shaw, Wallace Stevens and Hart Crane. Byron was all things to all women, and to some men. Shelley, to Byron and those who came after, essentially was one towering image: the poet's poet (like Edmund Spenser before him), an emblem of solitary integrity, the last incarnate defense of poetry.

Friendships between great contemporary writers always are difficult and ambivalent: one thinks of Ben Jonson's dedicatory poem to Shakespeare's First Folio and of the young John Milton's tribute to the second Folio, as well as Andrew Marvell's to Milton's *Paradise Lost*. There also are the long tragedies of Melville's love for Hawthorne and Coleridge's for Wordsworth. Walt Whitman's indebtedness to Emerson was frequently denied by him, while Wallace Stevens and T.S. Eliot were hopelessly evasive about Whitman while endlessly revising him in their own major poems. Scott Fitzgerald and Ernest Hemingway are a major repetition of the Shelley-Byron mutual contamination, and similar phenomena abound in the early twenty-first century. I venture that the Byron-Shelley connection is the richest and hardest to disentangle of all imaginative rivalries between what might be termed enemy brothers, or alternatively, benignly fraternal spirits.

A good book on the subject, Charles Robinson's *Shelley and Byron: The Snake and Eagle Wreathed in Fight* (1976), is a helpful starting point in its chronicle of the mutual influences exchanged between the two poets throughout their six years of friendship from the summer of 1816 in Geneva until Shelley's death by drowning on July 8, 1822, at the age of twenty-nine, in circumstances that have never been fully clarified. In *Adonais*, his sublime elegy for John Keats, Shelley classically categorized Lord Byron as the Pilgrim of Eternity:

> ... and the mountain shepherds came,
> Their garlands sere, their major mantles rent;
> The Pilgrim of Eternity, whose fame
> Over his living head like Heaven is bent,
> An early but enduring monument,
> Came, veiling all the lightnings of his song
> In sorrow ...

As Shelley well knew, Keats and Byron disliked both each other and each other's poetry, but since Shelley by 1821 exalted the author of *Don Juan* as the greatest poet since Milton, the sorrow of the Pilgrim of Eternity is apposite. Shelley's sorrow for Keats was real enough, though Keats had kept Shelley from being too close, perhaps to avoid excessive influence. Shelley's first major poem, *Alastor, or The Spirit of Solitude* (1815) had stimulated Keats's *Endymion*, which is a critique as much as it is a visionary romance. *Alastor* (the title is Greek for an avenging daemon) itself was an agon with Wordsworth's *The Excursion*. If struggle for supremacy is to be judged by a poem's superior fecundity at engendering progeny, then Shelley won the contest. Few poems in the language have been as influential as *Alastor*. Its clear traces can be mapped not just in *Endymion* but in George Darley's *Nepenthe*, Byron's *Lament of Tasso* and *Manfred: A Dramatic Poem*, Browning's *Pauline* and *Paracelsus*, Yeats's *The Wandering of Oisin* and *The Shadowy Waters*. In Eliot's *The Waste Land* and Stevens's *The Comedian as the Letter C*, Shelley's internalized quest romance is defensively parodied but appears again positively in Hart Crane's *Voyages*. Basing himself on the *Solitary* in *The Excursion*, Shelley voyages his idealistic young poet on a mission to recover a veiled maiden who is his double, the soul within his soul or epipsyche. As he sails on to the Caucasus, he is shadowed by the Alastor or avenging daemon of his elected solitude. At last he wastes away and dies, reflecting Shelley's mistaken belief that he himself was dying of tuberculosis, which in fact he did not have. His close friend, the satirical novelist Thomas Love Peacock, recorded that he revived the vegetarian poet from this imaginary malady by feeding him a momentary but intense diet of well-peppered mutton chops.

Byron, a perpetual dieter to avoid a tendency to corpulence, empathized with Shelley's poet and gladly adopted the epipsyche myth to represent his incestuous love for his sister Augusta. *Manfred*, much admired by Goethe, follows Shelley in pragmatically believing that incest is the most poetical of circumstances, a thematic emphasis acquired by Edgar Poe from Byron and Shelley. It is a mixed pleasure to reread *Manfred* in 2009; its high gothic seems both silly and guiltily delicious. The mage Manfred wants only self-forgetfulness, but the star he conjures up is Astarte, his suicidal sister-lover, and she vanishes when he embraces her. Certainly the English public read this as Byron's own remorse, not so much for his incest with Augusta but for having to do without her in his European exile.

4

From 1817 until Shelley's death in 1822, the two Promethean poets, attacked by the Poet Laureate Robert Southey as "the Satanic School," were frequently together, first in Venice and later in Pisa. Out of his enormous debaucheries in Venice, Byron rescued a wonderful comic poem, *Beppo*, the prelude to his *Don Juan*. His own final erotic fate came to him on April 2, 1819, with the entrance into a Venetian salon of Countess Teresa Guiccioli of Ravenna, married to a ferocious husband forty years older than herself. Teresa, unique in Byron's life story, was the only woman who ever tamed him, at least partially and for three years. In only a week, Byron at thirty-two took on the role of *cavalier servente* to a noblewoman of twenty-one, but who was far more emotionally mature than the poet already composing his epic *Don Juan*.

Teresa's relative mastery of Byron seems a puzzle but clearly hers was a tenacious personality. She even secured a separation from the Pope and absorbed Byron into her family, the Gambas, who were much involved in their revolutionary schemes against the Pope and the Austrians, in which Byron participated. When Teresa and the Gambas were exiled to Pisa, Byron rather grumpily followed them but devoted most of his time there to the company of Shelley and his circle.

After Shelley's death, Byron made Genoa his final Italian abode, accompanied by Teresa and the Gambas. At thirty-five he realistically anticipated only erotic and imaginative decline and determined to end gloriously as the hero bringing Greece freedom from the Turks. Teresa was the obstacle, but the resurgent strength of Byron's will overcame hers, refusing her impossible request that she accompany him to warfare in wild Greece. In mid-July, Byron set sail with a motley crew indeed, choosing as his military aides Count Gamba and Edward John Trelawny, the Cornish adventurer and disciple of Shelley, whose 1858 *Recollections of the Last Days of Shelley and Byron* remains superbly readable, though Byron justly observed of Trelawny that even to save his life he could not tell the truth. Since Trelawny loved Shelley and came to hate Byron, readers need to be wary even as they enjoy the Cornish swaggerer's tales.

Edna O'Brien narrates Byron's Greek debacle with particular zest, conveying her own sense of release as the poet accomplishes a final transmutation from Pilgrim of Eros to Shelley's Pilgrim of Eternity. Besides Count Gamba and Trelawny, who was to abandon Byron and join the mountain warrior Odysseus, lord of Eastern Greece, Byron had his hireling army of Albanians. They were based at Missolonghi, where he assumed nominal control of Western Greece, and perhaps entertained the general delusion he yet would be crowned king. Sent by Odysseus on a mission to Byron, Trelawney arrived too late, the poet having died of malaria or rather of the ministrations of his incompetent physicians. Though the death was lingering and painful, it saved Byron's legend, since his own mercenaries and all the Greek factions were interested only in devouring both his wealth and his fame. As king of Greece, every second thought would have been his wish for a speedy death.

5

Shelley and Byron were politically and personally allied but so different intellectually and emotionally that their close friendship, with all its strains, seems a kind of miracle or literary myth. No scholar or writer of fiction has achieved a plausible account of their six-year friendship, during which they shared over two hundred and fifty days, frequently alone together, corresponded extensively, and seem to have read and discussed nearly all of each other's poetry. Only the Goethe-Schiller relationship is comparable, but those great poets led conventional existences compared to the revolutionary and erotic firebrands, Byron and Shelley, who unlike Verlaine and Rimbaud were not lovers.

Byron, except for a few allusions, carefully kept any portrait of Shelley out of his poetry. Shelley did the reverse, particularly in the remarkable conversation poem *Julian and Maddalo* (1819), where Shelley is the idealist Julian and Byron, Count Maddalo, who had weathered much of his own Prometheanism. Goethe, who admired Byron, condescendingly observed that when Byron thought, he became a child. Shelley knew better, and I am uncertain that criticism has caught up to Shelley in apprehending the brilliance, range, and power of Byron's intellect.

Julian and Maddalo is a beautiful exemplification of Shelley's middle style: urbane, conversational, somewhat understated. Partly written as an answer to *Manfred*'s quasi-Calvinistic sense of fatalism, it depicts an evening horseback ride the poets took near Venice in August 1818:

> I rode one evening with Count Maddalo
> Upon the bank of land which breaks the flow
> Of Adria towards Venice: a bare strand
> Of hillocks, heaped from ever-shifting sand,
> Matted with thistles and amphibious weeds,
> Such as from earth's embrace the salt ooze breeds,
> Is this; an uninhabited sea-side,
> Which the lone fisher, when his nets are dried,
> Abandons; and no other object breaks
> The waste, but one dwarf tree and some few stakes
> Broken and unrepaired, and the tide makes
> A narrow space of level sand thereon,
> Where 'twas our wont to ride while day went down.
> This ride was my delight. I love all waste
> And solitary places; where we taste
> The pleasures of believing what we see
> Is boundless, as we wish our souls to be.

As they ride, they debate the distinctions between Julian's apocalyptic hopes for humankind and Maddalo's savage pessimism, a dissonance repeated the next day when Julian protests:

> —it is our will
> That thus enchains us to permitted ill—
> We might be otherwise—we might be all
> We dream of happy, high, majestical.
> Where is the love, beauty, and truth we seek
> But in our mind? and if we were not weak
> Should we be less in deed than desire?'

'Ay, if we were not weak—and we aspire
How vainly to be strong!' said Maddalo;
'You talk Utopia.' . . .

As Shelley and Byron knew, this was not an argument to be won or lost by either. A few years after, both were dead. On the basis of Shelley's death poem, the unfinished *The Triumph of Life*, at the close there was little pragmatic difference between them. In the battle with life they waged, life remained conqueror.

BIOGRAPHY

GEORGE GORDON, LORD BYRON
(1788–1824)

The most notorious of the major romantic poets, George Gordon, Lord Byron, was also one of the most flamboyant personas and most fashionable dandies of his time. As the originator of the concept of the Byronic hero—a melancholy, brooding and defiant man, haunted by some secret guilt—his European readership consistently conflated the man with his writing. Byron represented a romantic myth: a member of the aristocracy, he became a deist and a liberal in politics, who championed liberty and gave his money and finally his life for the cause of Greek independence.

George Gordon Noel Byron was born, with a deformity to his right foot, in London on January 22, 1788, the son of Catherine Gordon of Gight, an impoverished Scottish heiress, and Captain John ("Mad Jack") Byron, a fortune-hunting widower with a daughter, Augusta. His father squandered his wife's inheritance, was absent at Byron's birth, and eventually eluded his creditors through his exile to France, where he died in 1791, aged thirty-six. Byron was raised by an emotionally unstable mother and a Presbyterian nurse, who imbued him with a lifelong fascination with Calvinist doctrines of innate evil and predestination. With the death in 1798 of his great uncle, the "Wicked" fifth Lord Byron, he became the sixth Baron Byron of Rochdale, heir to Newstead Abbey, the family seat in Nottinghamshire. Educated at Harrow (1801–1805), he suffered a prolonged, painful, and ultimately futile treatment of his clubfoot and formed his first passionate attachments to other boys. In the summer of 1803 he fell deeply in love with his cousin Mary Chaworth of Annesley Hall, an unrequited passion that gave rise to poems such as "Hills of Annesley" (written 1805), "The Adieu" (written 1807), "Stanzas to a Lady on Leaving England" (written 1809), and "The Dream" (written 1816). In 1804, he also began an intimate correspondence with his half-sister Augusta, who would later become his lover.

As a student at Trinity College, Cambridge (1805–1808), he fell in love with John Edleston, a choirboy at Trinity two years younger than he. During this period of his life, he began to live extravagantly, amassing debts and enjoying diversions such as boxing, fencing, and gambling more than his studies. Byron returned to Cambridge in June 1807 and formed a lifelong friendship with John Cam Hobhouse, whom he called Hobby, and joined the liberal Whig Club. In 1806, he distributed his first book of poetry, *Fugitive Pieces,* which he had printed at his own expense. A revised and expurgated version of this account of his Cambridge experiences was printed as *Poems on Various Occasions,* in an edition of one hundred copies in January 1807, later called *Hours of Idleness,* "By George Gordon, Lord Byron, A Minor," and published in June of the same year. As Byron had omitted his erotic pieces, the poems seemed mere sentimental imitations of the style of Thomas Gray, Thomas Chatterton, and Ossian and the collection received many abrasive reviews.

In February 1808, Henry Brougham's anonymous criticism of the *Hours of Idleness* appeared in the *Edinburgh Review.* Apart from justifiable criticism it also attacked the author personally and hurt Byron deeply. In a move characteristic of him, he immediately began to avenge himself through biting satire, first his "British Bards" and then "Scotch Reviewers," published as *English Bards, and Scotch Reviewers; A Satire,* in 1809. Inspired by Alexander Pope's *Dunciad* (1728/1742) and William Gifford's *Baviad* (1791) and *Maeviad* (1795), the poem uses heroic couplets to skewer most of the famous romantic poets and playwrights of Byron's lifetime: Scott, Robert Southey, William Wordsworth, and Samuel Taylor Coleridge. Byron expends his venom on critics, especially Francis Jeffrey, the editor of the *Edinburgh Review,* whom he mistakenly assumed to be the author of the scathing critique of his *Hours of Idleness.* Byron stated in the preface that he wanted to improve the writing of others by advocating neoclassical order, discipline, and clarity. He would always admire Pope and would use the heroic couplet and adopt the persona of the Augustan writer as censor and moralist in his *Hints from Horace* (written in 1811), *The Curse of Minerva* (also written in 1811), and *The Age of Bronze* (written in 1822–1823).

The satire was an immediate success with readers and critics alike. The *Gentleman's Magazine* (March 1809) praised the poem:

> The Poem before us is unquestionably the result of an impassioned yet diligent study of the best masters, grounded on a fine taste and very happy natural endowments. It unites much of the judgment of the Essay on Criticism, the playful yet poignant smile and frown of indignation and ridicule of the *Dunciad*, with the versification of the Epistle to Arbuthnot, and the acuteness of the Imitations of Horace of the same Author; at the same time that we think we have discovered a resemblance of the best epigrammatic points and brilliant turns of the Love of Fame. And with all this it is unquestionably an original work. In a word, many years have passed since the English press has given us a performance so replete with

mingled genius, good sense, and spirited animadversion" 79 *Gentleman's Magazine* (March 1809) LXXIX, 248.

When the work went into its fourth edition, Byron abandoned his anonymity and suppressed a fifth edition, as he had come to know and appreciate some of the victims of his criticism. In March 1809, he took his seat in the House of Lords and attended seven sessions of Parliament during that spring. Despite his debts, Byron intended to fulfill his dream of traveling and began his tour of the Mediterranean on July 2, 1809. With his friend Hobhouse and three servants, he sailed from England to Lisbon and went on horseback across Spain, observing the scene of Wellington's peninsular campaign and of the Spanish partisans' resistance to the French. After reaching Greece, Byron and Hobhouse went to Albania, a territory unknown to Western travelers. In Jannina, Byron bought native costumes (in one of which Thomas Phillips painted him in 1814). In Telepene, they were entertained by Ali Pasha, the tyrannical ruler of Albania and western Greece, who would become the basis of some of Byron's characters, such as Lambro, the father of Haidée in *Don Juan* (canto III).

In order to preserve the memory of his experiences, Byron began an autobiographical poem in Jannina on October 31, 1809, recording the adventures of Childe Burun, later renamed Childe Harold, and written in Spenserian stanzas. Through Missolonghi, Byron and Hobhouse traveled as far as Athens, where they arrived on Christmas night 1809, lodging at the foot of the Acropolis. Byron fell in love with the three daughters of their host, Tarsia Macri. The loss of Greece's treasures and the enslavement of the people by the Turks, however, sorrowed Byron, as he could see the ruins of the Acropolis, which Lord Elgin was shipping to England. Elgin would get his share of criticism in *Childe Harold* (canto II) and in *The Curse of Minerva* (1811). In 1810, Byron went to Cape Sounion, overlooking the island of the Cyclades, and to Marathon, where the Athenians had defeated the Persians in 490 B.C. These experiences are evoked in the stanzas on "The Isles of Greece" and on Marathon in *Don Juan* (canto III). The contrast between the former glory of ancient Greece and its contemporary impotence under Turkish rule would never give him peace.

In March 1810, Byron and Hobhouse reached Turkey, and Byron completed *Childe Harold*, canto II, while in Smyrna. After a visit to the plains of Troy, Byron swam through the Hellespont in imitation of Leander in Ovid's *Hero and Leander*. The pair spent two months in Constantinople before parting. While Hobhouse returned to England, Byron went back to Athens and settled in a Capuchin monastery below the Acropolis, where he studied Italian and modern Greek, as well as provided explanatory notes for *Childe Harold*.

Two years and twelve days after his departure, he reached England again on July 14, 1811, traveling for a time on the transport ship *Hydra*, which carried shipments of Elgin's marbles to England. Byron's statement as relayed by Trelawny "If I am a poet, the air of Greece has made me one" (Edward John Trelawny, *Recollections of the Last Days of Shelley and Byron*) expresses the fact that Byron's exposure to different cultures, peoples, and landscapes would fuel his future work. Shortly after his return, Byron was to mourn the death of his mother (who died on August 2, 1811) as well as of two former classmates and the death from consumption of John Edleston, his friend and partner from Cambridge days. "To Thyrza" is the lament of this loss, as well as "Away, Away, Ye Notes of Woe" (written 1811), "One Struggle More, and I Am Free" (written 1812), and "And Thou Art Dead, As Young and Fair" (written 1812). He also commemorated Edleston in additions to *Childe Harold* (canto II).

Byron gave his maiden speech in the House of Lords on Feburary 27, 1812, arguing in defense of the stocking weavers of Nottinghamshire, who had broken the machinery that was taking away their means of subsistence. Later, in April, he pleaded for Catholic emancipation, and in June he supported a petition for the reform of Parliament.

On March 10, 1812, John Murray II, the publisher of Walter Scott and Robert Southey, released *Childe Harold's Pilgrimage*, cantos I and II, in five hundred copies, then, after two days, three thousand copies. The book became an immediate bestseller, and Byron remarked, "I awoke one morning and found myself famous." The critics were enthusiastic: Jeffey praised "a singular freedom and boldness, both of thought and expression, and a great occasional force and felicity of diction" (*Edinburgh Review*, February 1812), and George Ellis concluded that the poem showed "some marks of carelessness, many of caprice, but many also of sterling genius" (*Quarterly Review*, March 1812). Suddenly, Byron had become the favorite of the salons and drawing rooms of Whig society. At Holland House, he met Lady Caroline Lamb, who called him "mad—bad—and dangerous to know" and who, after Byron had ended his affair with her, continued to pursue him. Being on friendly terms with Elizabeth Milbanke Lamb (Lady Caroline's mother), he proposed marriage to her niece, the intelligent twenty-year-old Anne Isabella (Annabella) Milbanke, who rejected him.

Apart from engaging in an active love life—in June 1813 he began an affair with his half sister, Augusta—Byron completed and published six highly popular verse tales, based on his travels in Greece and Turkey: *The Giaour* (June 1813), *The Bride of Abydos* (December 1813), *The Corsair* (February 1814), *Lara* (August 1814), and *The Siege of Corinth* and *Parisina* (February 1816). Reviews were mixed, but Byron's verse tales were an immediate success across Europe, giving a much desired taste of Eastern or "Orientalist" passion, eroticism, and violence. *The Bride of Abydos* (1813) was the first text in which Byron dealt with incest, a topic he would revisit in *Parisina, Manfred,* and *Cain*. On April 15, 1814, Augusta gave birth to a girl, Elizabeth Medora, who in future years would consider herself to be Byron's daughter. Byron spent much of the summer of 1814 with Augusta, while corresponding with Annabella. In a letter dated September 9, he made a tentative proposal of marriage, which Annabella promptly accepted. Byron's motives for his decision are not entirely clear; apart from monetary reasons, he seems to have hoped to find a new stability in his life and a liberation from his guilty relationship with his half sister. Byron and Annabella were married on January 2,

1815, in the parlor of her parents' home in Seaham; Byron began to be abusive during their honeymoon. At Halnaby Hall, Byron resumed work on the *Hebrew Melodies*, lyrics for airs that Jewish composer Isaac Nathan was adapting from the music of the synagogue. In April, after a tempestuous visit with Augusta, Lord and Lady Byron settled in the Duchess of Devonshire's London house, at 13 Piccadilly Terrace.

Heavy drinking and financial worries drove Byron to fits of rage and aggression, and shortly after the birth of their first child, Augusta Ada Byron (December 19, 1815), Lady Byron left London in January 1816 with the baby and Byron would never see her again. Having concluded that her husband was mentally deranged, she drew up a list of symptons that she then forwarded to two doctors. The account of Byron's violent outbursts she gave to her parents turned them against him, and they proposed a quiet separation. She also seems to have confessed to her lawyer her suspicion of incest between Byron and Augusta, adding this to the charges of adultery and violence. By the end of February, the rumors about Byron were widespread. During these weeks, he had a casual affair with Claire Clairmont, stepdaughter of William Godwin and half sister of Mary Shelley. On March 17, 1816, the terms for the legal separation were agreed on, and Byron signed the required documents on April 21.

On the same day, Byron left England for good, accompanied by his valet, Fletcher; his personal physician, John Polidori; Robert Rushton; and a Swiss servant. They reached Geneva on May 25, 1816, where Byron chanced to meet the pregnant Claire Clairmont again, who was accompanying Percy Shelley and Mary Godwin. A friendship was struck up between the poets, and they spent their time boating on Lake Leman or talking at the Villa Diodati, which Byron had rented. Mary Godwin wrote *Frankenstein; or, The Modern Prometheus*, published in 1818, as part of a writing contest. The visit to the Château de Chillon, where François Bonivard, a sixteenth-century Swiss patriot had been imprisoned, inspired Byron to compose *The Prisoner of Chillon*. In July, Byron completed canto III of *Childe Harold*, which covers his own journey from Dover to Waterloo, along the Rhine and into Switzerland. His protagonist, Harold, fades from the narrative, and the author begins to speak in his own right, expressing his sorrow at his own exile from home and analyzing Napoléon's role in European history. Murray published canto III in November and *The Prisoner of Chillon, and Other Poems* on December 5. Within a week of publication, seven thousand copies of each volume had been sold, and Francis Jeffrey again praised Byron's style. Poems written in the same month include "Darkness," which envisages the end of the world, and "Prometheus," which has defiance triumph over torture.

The Shelleys left for England in August, Byron's friend Hobhouse arrived, and Claire gave birth to Byron's and her child, Clara Allegra, in Bath on January 12, 1817. Byron fell into a depression and wrote *Manfred*, a metaphysical verse drama, which develops the themes of secret guilt, incest, and the supernatural. The Byronic hero of the play seeks forgetfulness, which he can find only in death. The publication of *Manfred* in June 1817 was greeted with mixed reviews due to its religious unorthodoxy; yet Johann Wolfgang von Goethe famously praised the play as "a wonderful phenomenon" (*London Magazine*, May 1820).

In October 1816, Byron and Hobhouse left Switzerland for Italy, going to Milan and then to Venice, where Byron felt perfectly at home, had an affair with Marianna Segati, his landlord's wife, and began to study Armenian at a monastery on the island of San Lazzaro. After visits to Ferrara, where Hobhouse and Byron looked at the cell where Torquato Tasso had been imprisoned (see "The Lament of Tasso"), and Rome, which delighted Byron, he settled at the Villa Foscarini at La Mira on the Brenta, seven miles from Venice. *Childe Harold* IV was finished and revised, containing his memories of his travels in Italy and his sojourn in Rome and reflecting on the transience of empires, on decay and death. Murray published *Childe Harold*, canto IV, on April 28, 1818; the five printings of the first edition comprised ten thousand copies and were well received.

The melancholy tone of *Childe Harold* stands in strong contrast to Byron's next work, the facetious satire *Beppo*. Back in Venice, Byron had heard about the return of a supposedly dead husband to his wife, who had meanwhile started a relationship with another man, the husband offering her the choice between himself, her lover, or a solitary life on a pension. At this time, Byron had also read John Hookham Frere's mock heroic poem *Whistlecraft* (1817) written in *ottava rima* (ababacc) and modeled on the Italian burlesque manner of Luigi Pulci, Francesco Berni, and Abate Giambattista Casti. The witty tone, the colloquialisms, and the digressions appealed to Byron, and he finished *Beppo* in October 1817. In the poem, Byron satirizes and urbanely mocks conventions by contrasting English mores with the romanticized projections of an Italian carnality and love of life. Murray published *Beppo, A Venetian Story*, without Byron's name on the title page, on February 28, 1818, with immediate success. The *Monthly Review* (March 1818) found Byron's "satire, though at times a little tinged with vulgarity, . . . usually good-humoured and often well pointed." Byron moved to the Palazzo Mocenigo overlooking the Grand Canal, where he lived with his daughter Allegra, fourteen servants, a host of animals, and a veritable harem.

In a letter to Murray dated July 10, 1818, Byron mentioned that he had written an "Ode on Venice" and "two stories—one serious & one ludicrous (a la Beppo) not yet finished—& in no hurry to be so." The "serious" poem was *Mazeppa*, a Cossack verse tale of illicit love and a wild horseback ride. The "ludicrous" work was the first canto of his comic epic, *Don Juan*. Byron was unsure whether *Don Juan* might be "too free" for the public, and the writing and publication was a long process. Cantos I and II were published on July 15, 1819; cantos III, IV, V, finished in November 1820, were not published until August 8, 1821. Cantos VI through XVI, written between June 1822 and March 1823, were published at intervals between July 15, 1823, and March 26, 1824. Canto XVII was begun in May 1823 but was never finished. A fragment of fourteen stanzas, found in his room at Missolonghi, was first published in 1903.

In spring 1819, Byron met Teresa (née Gamba), wife of the Cavaliere Guiccioli, and became her *cavaliere servente*, an accepted form of official lover for four years. The period of their relationship is presented in her *Recollections (Lord Byron jugé par les temoins de sa vie*, 1869); she became legally separated from her husband in 1820. Byron followed her to Ravenna, where they lived near Dante's tomb. Byron's connection with the Gamba family through Teresa brought the poet in touch with the revolutionary movement, so that he came under the supervision of the Austrian embassy. After Byron had returned to La Mira with Teresa, Thomas Moore paid him a visit, and Byron entrusted him with the manuscript of his *Life and Adventures* up to 1816. The manuscript was burned with Murray's assent in the drawing room of 50 Albemarle Street on May 17, 1824.

In late 1819, Byron left Venice and settled at Ravenna in the Palazzo Guiccioli, where he was received as Teresa's *cavaliere servente*. In Ravenna, he translated the first canto of Pulci's *Morgante Maggiore* (published in the *Liberal*, no. IV, July 30, 1832), then composed the five-act tragedy *Marino Faliero, Doge of Venice* (published on April 21, 1821), a play about the rebellious alliance of a doge with the populace to overthrow the state of Venice. With this drama, Byron strove to reform British drama and return it to neoclassical rules, a move not highly appreciated by readers and critics alike. He went on writing his *Memoirs*, a fifth canto of *Don Juan*, and in January 1821 began to work on the exotic historical drama *Sardanapalus*, a play about the debauched, effeminate king of Assyria and his eventual suicide.

During this time, Byron became more and more embroiled in political activities. As the *capo* of the *Americani*, a branch of the Carbonari who were fighting for the liberation of Italy from Austrian rule, he was buying and storing arms and ammunition, working together with the leading conspirators, such as Teresa's father and brother. The Carbonari movement was defeated, though, and Byron returned to his writing. Another play dealing with the relationship between the individual and the state, *The Two Foscari*, was finished in 1821, again dealing with Venetian politics. *Cain, a Mystery*, was begun as an attempt to dramatize the Old Testament. Byron's version of Lucifer's apology for himself and his accusation of God shocked the more orthodox segments of his readership. *Cain* was published in the same volume as the *Two Foscari* and *Sardanapalus* on December 19, 1821. After these grave and serious works, Byron again turned to satire with his "Vision of Judgment," an attack on Robert Southey, who had referred to Byron as a member of the "Satanic School" of poetry in his preface to his eulogy on George III, titled "Vision of Judgment." In Byron's act of revenge, the poet laureate Southey is brought before the hosts of heaven and rejected by devils and angels alike.

As Countess Teresa and her family had been expelled from Ravenna in July 1822 by the Austrian authorities, Byron also left the town for Pisa in October, where he rejoined her. In Pisa, he no longer lived among Italians but within a close circle of English friends: E.J. Trelawny, Thomas Medwin, author of the *Conversations of Lord*

Byron (1824), and Edward Elliker Williams. At Pisa, he dramatized Lee's *Kruitzner, or the German Tale*, rewriting it after a loss of the manuscript and calling it *Werner, or the Inheritance* (published on November 23, 1822). The character of Werner was later impersonated by Macready, and a successful stage production was mounted. In spring 1822, Byron's beloved daughter Allegra died at the age of six. Soon after her death, Byron wrote the last of his eight plays, *The Deformed Transformed* (published in 1824), which is based on Goethe's *Faust* and *The Three Brothers*, a novel by Joshua Pickersgill. In an attempt to become a journalist, Byron entered a literary partnership with Leigh Hunt, who had come to Pisa, and they published *The Liberal—Verse and Prose from the South*. The journal did not succeed financially, and Hunt felt let down by Byron, a disappointment he expressed in his *Correspondence of Byron and Some of His Contemporaries* (1828).

On July 8, 1822 Percy Shelley and his friend Williams were drowned in the Gulf of Spezia, and Byron and Hunt witnessed the burning of Shelley's body on the seashore near Via Reggio. Teresa's family was not allowed to remain in Pisa, so Byron moved them to Montenero near Leghorn, then to Genoa, where he continued to work on *The Liberal* with Hunt. In February 1823, Byron completed *The Island; or Christian and His Comrades* (published on June 26, 1823) based on Bligh's *Narrative of the Mutiny on the Bounty*, and Mariner's *Account of the Tonga Islands*, as well as working on *Don Juan*.

In March 1823, Byron learned that he had been elected a member of the Greek Committee, a circle of individuals active in the cause of liberating Greece. He immediately offered money and advice and was then, despite problems with his health, determined to go to Greece. Together with Pietro Gamba, Trelawny, Hamilton Browne, and six or seven servants, he sailed to Greece on July 23, 1823, and then spent the next months at Cephalonia, Argostoli, and Metaxata, trying to find out to which leader in the struggle they ought to attach themselves. When Prince Alexander Mavrocordato urged him to come to Missolonghi, Byron felt he had found the right revolutionary and arrived at Missolonghi on January 5, 1824.

Byron supplied money for troops and fortification and served as a link between Odysseus, a local leader of the insurgents, and Mavrocordato. A revolt in Morea prevented him from participating in the capture of Epacto, and a conference of the leaders never came to pass. Byron's health had now deteriorated: he fell seriously ill after a horse ride and died on April 19, 1824 at the age of thirty-six, shortly after the publication of the fifteenth and sixteenth cantos of *Don Juan*. His heart was buried in Missolonghi, while the rest of his remains were buried in Hucknell Torkard Church near Newstead, as the deans of both Westminster Abbey and St. Paul's had refused to receive his body. His death, while supporting the push for Greek freedom, increased his popularity and furthered the myth of the Byronic hero for generations of subsequent readers and admirers.

PERSONAL

Lady Caroline Lamb's description of Lord Byron—"mad, bad, and dangerous to know" (*Journal*, 1812)—expresses both the wariness toward the author of immoral tales and the fascination with the man himself. A myth in his lifetime, Byron became even more a symbol of romanticism after his early death at Missolonghi working for the cause of Greek independence. The confusion of his own identity with the characters of his poems and plays was partly intentional, partly unavoidable as the fascination with his many love affairs, the incestuous relationship with his sister, and the scandalous divorce from his wife tended to overshadow the reception of his work. The assessment of Byron's publications almost always seems to have depended on the political stance of the reader or critic and his or her view of Byron's persona and private affairs.

Hewson Clarke (1808)

The satirist Hewson Clarke (1787–1845) had been among the critics who ridiculed Byron's *Hours of Idleness*. As it was well known that Byron kept a bear during his time at Cambridge University's Trinity College, Clarke appropriates this fact to further ridicule the author.

LORD B—N TO HIS BEAR
Sad Bruin, no longer in woods thou art dancing,
With all the enjoyments that Love can afford;
No longer thy consorts around thee are prancing,
Far other thy fate—thou art slave to a Lord!

How oft when fatigued, on my sopha reposing,
Thy tricks and thy pranks rob of anguish my breast;

Have power to arouse me, to keep me from dosing,
Or what's the same thing, they can lull me to rest.

But when with the ardours of Love I am burning,
I feel for thy torments, I feel for thy care;
And weep for thy bondage, so truly discerning,
What's felt by a LORD may be felt by a BEAR!

—Hewson Clarke, *Satirist or Monthly
Meteor* 2, May 1808, p. 368.

MARIA EDGEWORTH (1813)

Maria Edgeworth (1767–1849) was an Irish novelist who lived almost her entire life on her father's estate in Ireland. Her *Letters for Literary Ladies* (1795), her first publication, argued for the education of women. She is best known though for her novels of Irish life—*Castle Rackrent* (1800), *Belinda* (1801), and *The Absentee* (1812). She also wrote a number of stories for children, including *Moral Tales* (1801). Although her works are marred somewhat by didacticism, they are notable for their realism, humor, and freshness of style. She met Byron in 1813, and Byron alluded to her in *Don Juan*, in the witty portrait of the title character's moralizing mother, whom he describes as "Miss Edgeworth's novels stepping from their covers." Maria Edgeworth's letters mention various meetings with Byron, and she collected from Lady Byron's friends a number of stories that were critical of the lord.

Madame de Staël saw a good deal of Lord Byron at Coppet and said that there is one striking characteristic resemblance between his countenance and Bonapartes—that the different parts of the physiognomy never agreed in expression. When the mouth smiled the eyes did not smile.

—Maria Edgeworth, letter to
Mrs. Ruxton, September 8, 1818

. . . Miss Montgomery a very interesting really romantic not sham romantic or affectedly romantic person—evidently a very warm hearted friend—an intimate friend of Lady Byron. Of course hates Lord Byron properly. She assured me that the account we have heard of his chief motive for marrying being revenge she believes to be true. 'There were mixed motives I grant—money—she was reputed to have a much larger fortune that she really possessed. Lord Byron was distressed for money. To be sure he could have had other fortunes but then there was vanity. Miss Milbanke was just then in London the heiress who made the best figure. When he first proposed for her he had seen her only half a dozen times in public places and large parties. Her answer was as courteous and gentle a refusal as possible—that she admired his poetry and his talents but that she really could not trust her happiness with a person of whose character she knew so little. He smothered his rage and for two years dissembled and acted as well as he could all the virtues and the part of a lover to perfection. But literally no sooner was the ceremony over than the fiend broke out. As her father handed her into the carriage he swore a terrible oath at him and not sooner was he seated in the carriage with his bride than he turned to her as they drove off and asked How she dared, how she could ever venture to marry a man whom she had refused!'

Miss Montgomery met him lately abroad. He is grown fat and quite vulgar looking she says, he has quite embruted. The ladies abroad say that he has had no success in gallantry there—nothing but what his money has purchased. Miss Montgomery saw a letter of his written just after he had received the purchase money of an estate he has sold. He wrote that he was pefectly [sic] happy for that now he had money 'and money is power and pleasure and happiness': Lord Lansdowne told us also that he appears quite gay and without any touch of remorse. It is not worth saying more of him.

—Maria Edgeworth, letter to
Mrs. Edgeworth, October 13, 1818

As Lockhart observed, how little of the truth comes out to the world in all the lives written by professed biographers. 'Moore only gives you slightly to understand that Lord Byron had in his life made somewhat too free with his constitution and therefore a slight illness overset him, But Moore knew as well as I do the truth that he for the last years of his life drank brandy to such excess that not only he never went sober to bed but it often required two stout fellows to drag him by force away from the bottle and to break bottle and glass before they could get him off—else he would have finished himself in some fit sooner even than he did. He never got up till 12 or one oclock and then he was to dose himself with soda water, and plunge into the water and go out, rowing if he could just to try to get his body and mind round again after the last nights debauch.' 'But how could he write as he did ruing the last years?' 'Why if you look at Don Juan the last cantos—much of it is sad stuff much what might be expected from a man in that state. When he was just excited enough and not too much there came some splendid lines—last rays of genius but debased and disgraced! Oh its melancholy to think of!' I was glad to hear this from Lockhart and hope he will take warning—since a man does not die 'much bolder by brandy'. The surgeon who opened Lord Byron after death declared that his liver was all gone and the brain &c he should have thought belonged to a worn out old man of 66 or 70 instead of to [a] young man of 36 or 38!

—Maria Edgeworth, letter to
Mrs. Edgeworth, January 5, 1831

George Ticknor (1815)

George Ticknor (1791–1871), a leading American scholar of his time, was a native of Boston, Massachusetts. He was professor of French and Spanish literature at Harvard University from 1817 to 1835—publishing a comprehensive history of Spanish literature in 1848—and the founder and a trustee of the Boston Public Library. During a period of several years spent travelling and studying in Europe, he visited Byron in London in 1815, just in time to record Byron's first reaction to the defeat of Napoléon at the Battle of Waterloo.

I called on Lord Byron to-day, with an introduction from Mr. Gifford. Here, again, my anticipations were mistaken. Instead of being deformed, as I had heard, he is remarkably well built, with the exception of his feet. Instead of having a thin and rather sharp and anxious face, as he has in his pictures, it is round, open, and smiling; his eyes are light, and not black; his air easy and careless, not forward and striking; and I found his manners affable and gentle, the tones of his voice low and conciliating, his conversation gay, pleasant, and interesting in an uncommon degree. I stayed with him about an hour and a half, during which the conversation wandered over many subjects. He talked, of course, a great deal about America; wanted to know what was the state of our literature, how many universities we had, whether we had any poets whom we much valued, and whether we looked upon Barlow as our Homer. He certainly feels a considerable interest in America, and says he intends to visit the United States; but I doubt whether it will not be indefinitely postponed, like his proposed visit to Persia. I answered to all this as if I had spoken to a countryman, and then turned the conversation to his own poems, and particularly to his *English Bards,* which he has so effectually suppressed that a copy is not easily to be found. He said he wrote it when he was very young and very angry; which, he added, were "the only circumstances under which a man would write such a satire." When he returned to England, he said, Lord Holland, who treated him with very great kindness, and Rogers, who was his friend, asked him to print no more of it, and therefore he had suppressed it. Since then, he said, he had become acquainted with the persons he had satirized, and whom he then knew only by their books,—was now the friend of Moore, the correspondent of Jeffrey, and intimate with the Wordsworth school, and had a hearty liking for them all,—especially as they did not refuse to know one who had so much abused them. Of all the persons mentioned in this poem, there was not one, he said, with whom he now had any quarrel, except Lord Carlisle; and, as this was a family difference, he supposed it would never be settled. On every account, therefore, he was glad it was out of print; and yet he did not express the least regret when I told him that it was circulated in America almost as extensively as his other poems. As to the poems published during his minority, he said he suppressed them because they were not worth reading, and wondered that our booksellers could find a profit in reprinting them. All this he said without affectation; in fact, just as I now repeat it. He gave great praise to Scott; said he was undoubtedly the first man of his time, and as extraordinary in everything as in poetry,—a lawyer, a fine scholar, endowed with an extraordinary memory, and blessed with the kindest feelings.

Of Gifford, he said it was impossible that a man should have a better disposition; that he was so good-natured that if he ever says a bitter thing in conversation or in a review he does it unconsciously!

Just at this time Sir James Bland Burgess, who had something to do in negotiating Jay's Treaty, came suddenly into the room, and said abruptly, "My lord, my lord, a great battle has been fought in the Low Countries, and Bonaparte is entirely defeated." "But is it true?" said Lord Byron,—"is it true?" "Yes, my lord, it is certainly true; an aide-de-camp arrived in town last night; he has been in Downing Street this morning, and I have just seen him as he was going to Lady Wellington's. He says he thinks Bonaparte is in full retreat towards Paris." After an instant's pause, Lord Byron replied, "I am d———d sorry for it"; and then, after another slight pause, he added, "I didn't know but I might live to see Lord Castlereagh's head on a pole. But I suppose I sha'n't, now." And this was the first impression produced on his impetuous nature by the news of the battle of Waterloo.

As I was going away, he carried me up stairs, and showed me his library, and collection of Romaic books, which is very rich and very curious; offered me letters for Greece; and, after making an appointment for another visit, took leave of me so cordially that I felt almost at home with him.

While I was there, Lady Byron came in. She is pretty, not beautiful,—for the prevalent expression of her countenance is that of ingenuousness. "Report speaks goldenly of her." She is a baroness in her own right, has a large fortune, is rich in intellectual endowments, is a mathematician, possesses common accomplishments in an uncommon degree, and adds to all this a sweet temper. She was dressed to go and drive, and, after stopping a few moments, went to her carriage. Lord Byron's manner to her was affectionate; he followed her to the door, and shook hands with her, as if he were not to see her for a month.

—George Ticknor, *Journal,* June 20, 1815,
Life, Letters, and Journals of George Ticknor,
ed. Anna Ticknor, 1876, vol. 1, pp. 58–60

SYDNEY SMITH (1816)

Sydney Smith (1771–1845) was an English clergyman, critic, philosopher, and humorist. Together with Francis Jeffrey and Henry Peter Brougham, he founded the *Edinburgh Review.* A cleric who became dean of St. Paul's Cathedral, he campaigned against slavery and in favor of Catholic emancipation. A witty preacher, he admired Byron's satiric abilities: "If I could envy any man for successful ill nature I should envy Lord Byron for his skill in satirical nomenclature" (letter to Elizabeth Vassal Fox, Lady Holland, June 1810).

Lord and Lady Byron are, you know, separated. He said to Rogers, that Lady Byron had parted with him, apparently in good friendship, on a visit to her father, and that he had no idea of their being about to part, when he received her decision to that effect. He stated that his own temper, naturally bad, had been rendered more irritable by the derangement of his fortune—and that Lady Byron was entirely blameless. The truth is, he is a very unprincipled fellow.

—Sydney Smith, letter to Francis,
Lord Jeffrey, March 1816

SAMUEL TAYLOR COLERIDGE (1816)

Samuel Taylor Coleridge (1772–1834) had contacted the publisher Murray, who agreed to print his poem "Christabel," in April 1816. In the same month, he first met Byron at the latter's house in Piccadilly, London, where

Coleridge recited "Kubla Khan." He later acknowledged in the preface to "Kubla Khan" that the poem, like "Christabel," had been published with the support of Byron, who had encouraged and advised him. Byron would later lament Coleridge's turn to philosophy: "I wish he would explain his explanation" (*Don Juan*, dedication).

If you had seen Lord Byron, you could scarcely disbelieve him—so beautiful a countenance I scarcely ever saw—his teeth so many stationary smiles—his eyes the open portals of the sun—things of light, and for light—and his forehead so ample, and yet so flexible, passing from marble smoothness into a hundred wreathes and lines and dimples correspondent to the feelings and sentiments he is uttering.

—Samuel Taylor Coleridge, letter, April 10, 1816

THOMAS CARLYLE (1824)

Byron's impact on the Victorians should not be underestimated. A Scottish satirical writer, essayist, and historian of Calvinist origins, Thomas Carlyle (1795–1881), expresses grief at Byron's death, which he shares with the young Alfred, Lord Tennyson. Carlyle's famous injunction in his *Sartor Resartus* (1833–1834)—"Close thy Byron; open thy Goethe" (*Sartor Resartus*, book I, chapter 9)—has to be qualified by his attempt to put Byron into the same class as the sturm und drang ("storm and stress") authors Frederich Schiller and Johann Wolfgang von Goethe, whom he calls the "Power-men." The first excerpt, from a letter to his future wife, the writer Jane Baillie Welsh, was written shortly after Byron's death.

Poor Byron! Alas poor Byron! The news of his death came down upon my heart like a mass of lead; and yet, the thought of it sends a painful twinge thro' all my being, as if I had lost a brother! O God! That so many souls of mud and clay should fill up their base existence to its utmost bound, and this, the noblest spirit in Europe, should sink before half his course was run! Late so full of fire, and generous passion, and proud purposes, and now forever dumb and cold! Poor Byron! And but a young man; still struggling amid the perplexities, and sorrows and aberrations, of a mind not arrived at maturity or settled in its proper place in life. Had he been spared to the age of three score and ten, what might he not have done, what might he not have been! But we shall hear his voice no more: I dreamed of seeing him and knowing him; but the curtain of everlasting night has hid him from our eyes. We shall go to him, he shall not return to us. Adieu my dear Jane! There is a blank in your heart, and a blank in mine, since this man passed away. Let us stand the closer by each other!

—Thomas Carlyle, letter to
Jane Welsh (May 19, 1824)

These Power-men are gone too; and, with few exceptions, save the three originals above named, their works have already followed them. The application of all this to our own literature is too obvious to require much exposition. Have we not also had our Power-men? And will not, as in Germany, to us likewise a milder, a clearer, and a truer time come around? Our Byron was in his youth but what Schiller and Goethe had been in theirs: yet the author or *Werther* wrote *Iphigenie* and *Torquato Tasso*; and he who began with the *Robbers* ended with *Wilhelm Tell*. With longer life, all things were to have been hoped for from Byron: for he loved truth in his inmost heart and would have discovered at last that his Corsairs and Harolds were not true. It was otherwise appointed. But with one man all hope does not die. If this way is the right one, we too shall find it.

—Thomas Carlyle, "The State of German
Literature," *Edinburgh Review*, October 1827

THOMAS MEDWIN (1824)

Shelley's cousin and schoolmate Captain Thomas Medwin (1788–1869), who had been a British Army officer in India, was among the people who surrounded Byron during his stay in Pisa. Shelley spent most of his time with Byron between 1821 and 1822 (until his death by drowning), and Lieutenant Edward Elliker Williams (1793–1822) and his wife and the seaman Captain Edward John Trelawny also belonged to the circle at Pisa. Medwin left important reminiscences of this period in Byron's life in his *Conversations of Lord Byron*.

(Byron:) "I have prejudices about women: I do not like to see them eat. Rousseau makes Julie *un peu gourmande;* but that is not at all according to my taste. I do not like to be interrupted when I am writing. Lady Byron did not attend to these whims of mine. The only harsh thing I ever remember saying to her was one evening shortly before our parting. I was standing before the fire, ruminating upon the embarrassment of my affairs, and other annoyances, when Lady Byron came up to me and said, 'Byron, am I in your way?'—to which I replied, 'Damnably!' I was afterwards sorry, and reproached myself for the expression: but it escaped me unconsciously—involuntarily; I hardly knew what I said. . . .

"You ask if Lady Byron were ever in love with me—I have answered that question already—No! I was the fashion when she first came out: I had the character of being a great rake, and was a great dandy—both of which young ladies like. She married me from vanity, and the hope of reforming and fixing me. She was a spoiled child, and naturally of a jealous disposition; and this was increased by the infernal machinations of those in her confidence."

—Thomas Medwin, *Conversations of Lord Byron*, 1824

WALTER SCOTT "DEATH OF LORD BYRON" (1824)

Sir Walter Scott (1771–1832) was a prolific Scottish historical novelist and poet popular throughout Europe. He had initially resented Byron's satirical portrait of him in *English Bards, and Scotch Reviewers*, but through John Murray a correspondence had started in July 1812, and Byron apologized for his attack. A friendship developed, and both expressed their high regard for each other ever after. Walter Scott had created the market for romantic narratives in verse, but Byron outrivaled him with his erotic and exotic Oriental tales, to the extent that Scott gave up the genre in favor of novel writing; *Waverley* appeared in 1814.

The errors of Lord Byron arose neither from depravity of heart—for nature had not committed the anomaly of uniting to such extraordinary talents an imperfect moral sense—nor from feelings dead to the admiration of virtue. No man had ever a kinder heart for sympathy, or a more open hand for the relief of distress; and no mind was ever more formed for the enthusiastic admiration of noble actions, providing he was convinced that the actors had proceeded on disinterested principles. Lord Byron was totally free from the curse and degradation of literature—its jealousies, we mean, and its envy. But his wonderful genius was of a nature which disdained restraint, even when restraint was most wholesome. When at school, the tasks in which he excelled were those only which he undertook voluntarily; and his situation as a young man of rank, with strong passions, and in the uncontrolled enjoyment of a considerable fortune, added to that impatience of strictures or coercion which was natural to him. As an author, he refused to plead at the bar of criticism; as a man, he would not submit to be morally amenable to the tribunal of public opinion. Remonstrances from a friend, of whose intentions and kindness he was secure, had often great weight with him; but there were few who could or dared venture on a task so difficult. Reproof he endured with impatience, and reproach hardened him in his error; so that he often resembled the gallant war-steed, who rushes forward on the steel that wounds him. In the most painful crisis of his private life, he evinced this irritability and impatience of censure in such a degree, as almost to resemble the noble victim of the bullfight, which is more maddened by the squibs, darts, and petty annoyances of the unworthy crowds beyond the lists, than by the lance of his nobler, and, so to speak, his more legitimate antagonist. In a word, much of that in which he erred, was in bravado and scorn of his censors, and was done with the motive of Dryden's despot, "to show his arbitrary power." It is needless to say, that his was a false and prejudiced view of such a contest; and that if the noble bard gained a species of triumph, by compelling the world to read poetry, though mixed with baser matter, because it was *his,* he gave, in return, an unworthy triumph to the unworthy, besides deep sorrow to those whose applause, in his cooler moments, he most valued.

It was the same with his politics, which on several occasions assumed a tone menacing and contemptuous to the constitution of his country; while in fact, Lord Byron was in his own heart sufficiently sensible, not only of his privileges as a Briton, but of the distinction attending his high birth and rank, and was peculiarly sensitive of those shades which constitute what is termed the manners of a gentleman. Indeed, notwithstanding his having employed epigrams, and all the petty war of wit, when such would have been much better abstained from, he would have been found, had a collision taken place between the aristocratic and democratic parties in the state, exerting all his energies in defence of that to which he naturally belonged. His own feeling on these subjects he has explained in the very last canto of *Don Juan;* and they are in entire harmony with the opinions which we have seen expressed in his correspondence, at a moment when matters appeared to approach a serious struggle in his native country: "If we are to fall," he expressed himself to this purpose, "let the independent aristocracy and gentry of England suffer by the sword of an arbitrary prince, who has been born and bred a gentleman, and will behead us after the manner of our ancestors; but do not let us suffer ourselves to be massacred by the ignoble swarms of ruffians, who are endeavouring to throttle their way to power." Accordingly, he expresses in the strongest terms his purpose of resisting to the last extremity the tendency to anarchy, which commercial distress had generated, and disaffection was endeavouring to turn to its own purposes. His poetry expresses similar sentiments.

It is not that I adulate the people:
Without *me* there are Demagogues enough,
And infidels, to pull down every steeple,
And set up in their stead some proper stuff.
Whether they may sow Scepticism to reap Hell,
As is the Christian dogma rather rough,
I do not know;—I wish men to be free
As much from mobs and kings—from you as me.
The consequence is, being of no party,
I shall offend all parties.

We are not, however, Byron's apologists, for *now*, alas! he needs none. His excellences will *now* be universally acknowledged, and his faults (let us hope and believe) not remembered in his epitaph. It will be recollected what a part he has sustained in British literature since the first appearance of *Childe Harold,* a space of nearly sixteen years. There has been no reposing under the shade of his laurels, no living upon the resource of past reputation; none of that *coddling* and petty precaution, which little authors call "taking care of their fame." Byron let his fame take care of itself. His foot was always in the arena, his shield hung always in the lists; and although his own gigantic renown increased the difficulty of the struggle, since he could produce nothing, however great, which exceeded the public estimate of his genius, yet he advanced to the honourable contest again and again and again, and came always off with distinction, almost always with complete triumph. As various in composition as Shakspeare himself, (this will be admitted by all who are acquainted with his *Don Juan,*) he has embraced every topic of human life, and sounded every string on the divine harp, from its slightest to its most powerful and heart-astounding tones. There is scarce a passion, or a situation, which has escaped his pen; and he might be drawn, like Garrick, between the Weeping and the Laughing Muse, although his most powerful efforts have certainly been dedicated to Melpomene. His genius seemed as prolific as various. The most prodigal use did not exhaust his powers, nay, seemed rather to increase their vigour. Neither *Childe Harold,* nor any of the most beautiful of Byron's earlier tales, contain more exquisite morsels of poetry than are to be found scattered through the cantos of *Don Juan,* amidst verses which the author appears to have thrown off with an effort as spontaneous as that of a tree resigning its leaves to the wind.—But that noble tree will never more bear fruit or blossom! It has been cut down in its strength, and the past is all that remains to us of Byron. We can scarce reconcile ourselves to the idea—scarce think that the voice is silent for ever, which, bursting so often on our ear, was often heard with rapturous admiration, sometimes with regret, but always with the deepest interest.

All that's bright must fade,
The brightest still the fleetest!

With a strong feeling of awful sorrow, we take leave of the subject. Death creeps upon our most serious, as well as upon our most idle, employments; and it is a reflection solemn and gratifying, that he found our Byron in no moment of levity, but contributing his fortune, and hazarding his life, in behalf of a people only endeared to him by their past glories, and as fellow-creatures suffering under the yoke of a heathen oppressor.

—Walter Scott, "Death of Lord Byron," 1824,
Prose Works, 1861, vol. 4, pp. 344–349

LEIGH HUNT (1828)

The English radical, critic, and poet James Henry Leigh Hunt (1784–1859) had a highly ambivalent relationship with Byron. As co-editor with his brother of *The Examiner,* a liberal newspaper, his attack of the Prince Regent had led to two years of imprisonment, during which Byron paid him a visit. Shelley, who had repeatedly saved Hunt from destitution, later suggested that Hunt join him and Byron in Italy with the intention of establishing a liberal magazine. Hunt left England for Italy in November 1821, but storm, sickness, and bad luck delayed his arrival until July 1822. The sudden death of Shelley, only a few weeks later, destroyed every future prospect for *The Liberal,* which appeared only four times. Hunt, financially dependent on Byron, was regarded as socially inferior and a burden, and Byron sailed for Greece in 1823, leaving Hunt to fend for himself. In 1828, he published his *Lord Byron and Some of His Contemporaries,* a work that shocked many, because it attempted to correct and curb the ongoing idealization of Byron.

His temper was not good. Reading one day in Montaigne the confession of that philosopher and "Seigneur," that a saddle not well fastened, or the flapping of a leather against his boot, would put him out of sorts for the day, he said it was his own case; and he seemed to think it that of every body else of any importance, if people would but confess it; otherwise they were dull or wanted vigour. For he was always mistaking the subtlety of that matter, and confounding patience with weakness, because there was a weak patience as well as a strong one. But it was not only in small things that he was "put out." I have seen the expression of his countenance on greater occasions, absolutely festered with ill-temper,—all the beauty of it corrugated and made sore,—his voice at the same time being soft, and struggling to keep itself in, as if on the very edge of endurance. On such occasions, having no address, he did not know how to let himself be extricated from his position; and if I found him in this state, I contrived to make a few remarks, as serious as possible, on indifferent subjects, and so come away. An endeavour to talk him out of it, as a weakness, he might have had reason to resent:—sympathy would probably have drawn upon you a discussion of matters too petty for your respect; and gaiety would have been treated as an assumption, necessary to be put down by sarcasms, which it would have been necessary to put down in their turn. There was no living with these eternal assumptions and inequalities. When he knew me in England, independent and able to do him service, he never ventured upon a raillery. In Italy, he soon began to treat me with it; and I was obliged, for both our sakes, to tell him I did not like it, and that he was too much in earnest. Raillery, indeed, unless it is managed with great delicacy, and borne as well by him that uses it as it is expected to be borne by its object, is unfit for grown understandings. It is a desperate substitute for animal spirits; and no more resembles them, than a jostle resembles a dance. Like boys fighting in sport, some real blow is given, and the rest is fighting in earnest. A passing, delicate raillery is another matter, and may do us both a good and a pleasure; but it requires exquisite handling. You can imagine it is Sir Richard Steele, or Garth, or any other good-natured wit, who is not in the habit of objecting. My friend Charles Lamb has rallied me, and made me love him the more. So has Mr. Shelley. But in a man of more doubtful candour or benevolence, in Addison for instance, with his natural reserve and his born *parsonism,* you would begin to suspect the motive to it; and in the case of Swift or Johnson, it no doubt much oftener produced awkward retaliations, than biographers have thought fit to record.

If Lord Byron had been a man of address, he would have been a kinder man. He never heartily forgave either you or himself for his deficiency on this point; and hence a good deal of his ill-temper, and his carelessness of your feelings. By any means, fair or foul, he was to make up for the disadvantage; and with all his exaction of conventional propriety from others, he could set it at nought in his own conduct in the most remarkable manner. He had an incontinence, I believe unique, in talking of his affairs, and showing you other people's letters. He would even make you presents of them; and I have accepted one or two that they might go no farther. But I have mentioned this before. If his five-hundred confidants, by a retinence as remarkable as

his laxity, had not kept his secrets better than he did himself, the very devil
might have been played with I know not how many people. But there was
always this saving reflection to be made, that the man who could be guilty
of such extravagances for the sake of making an impression, might be guilty
of exaggerating or inventing what astonished you; and indeed, though he
was a speaker of the truth on ordinary occasions,—that is to say, he did not
tell you he had seen a dozen horses, when he had seen only two,—yet, as he
professed not to value the truth when in the way of his advantage, (and there
was nothing he thought more to his advantage than making you stare at him,)
the persons who were liable to suffer from his incontinence, had all the right
in the world to the benefit of this consideration.

His superstition was remarkable. I do not mean in the ordinary sense,
because it was superstition, but because it was petty and old-womanish. He
believed in the ill-luck of Fridays, and was seriously disconcerted if any thing
was to be done on that frightful day of the week. Had he been a Roman, he
would have startled at crows, while he made a jest of augurs. He used to tell a
story of somebody's meeting him, while in Italy, in St. James's-street. The least
and most childish of superstitions may, it is true, find subtle corners of warrant
in the greatest minds; but as the highest pictures in Lord Byron's poetry were
imitations, so in the smallest of his personal superstitions he was maintained
by something not his own. His turn of mind was material egotism, and some
remarkable experiences, had given it a compulsory twist the other way; but
it never grew kindly or loftily in that quarter. Hence his taking refuge from
uneasy thoughts, in sarcasm, and trifling, and notoriety. What there is of a
good-natured philosophy in *Don Juan* was not foreign to his wishes; but it was
the commonplace of the age, repeated with an air of discovery by the noble
Lord, and as ready to be thrown in the teeth of those from whom he took it,
provided any body laughed at them. His soul might well have been met in St.
James's-street, for in the remotest of his poetical solitudes it was there. As to
those who attribute the superstition of men of letters to infidelity, and then
object to it for being inconsistent, because it is credulous, there is no greater
inconsistency than their own; for as it is the very essence of infidelity to doubt,
so according to the nature it inhabits, it may as well doubt whether such and
such things do not exist, as whether they do: whereas, on the other hand,
belief in particular dogmas, by the very nature of its tie, is precluded from this
uncertainty, perhaps at the expense of being more foolishly certain.

It has been thought by some, that there was madness in his composition.
He himself talked sometimes as if he feared it would come upon him. It
was difficult in his most serious moments, to separate what he spoke out of
conviction, and what he said for effect. In moments of ill-health, especially

when jaded and overwrought by the united effects of composition, and drinking, and sitting up, he might have had nervous misgivings to that effect; as more people perhaps are accustomed to have, than choose to talk about it. But I never saw any thing more mad in his conduct, than what I have just been speaking of; and there was enough in the nature of his position to account for extravagances in him, that would not have attained to that head under other circumstances. If every extravagance of which men are guilty, were to be pronounced madness, the world would be nothing but the Bedlam which some have called it; and then the greatest madness of all would be the greatest rationality; which, according to others, it is. There is no end to these desperate modes of settling and unsettling every thing at a jerk. There was great perversity and self-will in Lord Byron's composition. It arose from causes which it would do honour to the world's rationality to consider a little closer, and of which I shall speak presently. This it was, together with extravagant homage paid him, that pampered into so regal a size every inclination which he chose to give way to. But he did not take a hawk for a handsaw; nor will the world think him deficient in brain. Perhaps he may be said to have had something, in little, of the madness which was brought upon the Roman emperors in great. His real pretensions were mixed up with imaginary ones, and circumstances contributed to give the whole a power, or at least a presence in the eyes of men, which his temperament was too feeble to manage properly. But it is not in the light of a madman that the world will ever seriously consider a man whose productions delight them, and whom they place in the rank of contributors to the stock of wit. It is not as the madman witty, but as the wit, injured by circumstances considered to be rational, that Lord Byron is to be regarded. If his wit indeed would not have existed without these circumstances, then it would only show us that the perversest things have a tendency to right themselves, or produce their ultimate downfall and so far, I would as little deny that his Lordship had a spice of madness in him, as I deny that he had not every excuse for what was unpleasant in his composition; which was none of his own making. So far, also, I would admit that a great part of the world are as mad as some have declared all the rest to be; that is to say, that although they are rational enough to perform the common offices of life, and even to persuade the rest of mankind that their pursuits and passions are what they should be, they are in reality but half rational beings, contradicted in the very outset of existence, and dimly struggling through life with the perplexity sown within them.

—Leigh Hunt, *Lord Byron and Some of His Contemporaries*, 1828, pp. 82–86

GUSTAVE FLAUBERT (1838)

French translations of Byron were bestsellers in the nineteenth century, and the figure of the Byronic hero fascinated the French public especially after Byron's death in Greece. Among the French novelists, Byron exerted the greatest influence on Gustave Flaubert (1812–1880) and Victor Hugo. A letter captures young Flaubert's deep admiration: "I am learning English, I am working at it and I am assured that in two or three months I will be able to read Shakespeare and, at the end of the year, Byron, the hardest things there are to read in English" (letter from October 11, 1838). In 1835, he had written a "Portrait de lord Byron" and in his "Diary of a Madman" (*Mémoires d'un fou*, 1838) as well as *Smarh* there are many parallels with *Childe Harold*, *Cain*, and *The Giaour*. "A Trip to Hell" borrows from the first two cantos of *Childe Harold's Pilgrimage*.

⸺

Really I profoundly value only two men, Rabelais and Byron, the only two who have written in a spirit of malice toward the human race and with the intention of laughing in its face. What a tremendous position a man occupies who places himself in such a relation to the world!

—Gustave Flaubert, letter to
Ernest Chevalier, September 13, 1838

Two days ago I saw Byron's name written on one of the pillars of the dungeon where the prisoner of Chillon was confined. This sight afforded me great joy. I thought more about Byron than about the prisoner, and no ideas came to me about tyranny and slavery. All the time I thought of the pale man who one day came there, walked up and down, wrote his name on the stone, and left. One would have to be very daring or very stupid to write one's name in such a place after that.

—Gustave Flaubert, letter to
Alfred Le Poittevin, May 26, 1845

MARGUERITE, COUNTESS OF BLESSINGTON (1834)

Marguerite Gardiner, Countess of Blessington, (1789–1849) could rival Byron in the notoriety she gained for her supposedly scandalous life. Married to Lord Blessington and lover of Alfred, Count d'Orsay, she was at the center of literary life in London and a friend of Charles Dickens, Edward

Bulwer-Lytton, William Thackeray, and Benjamin Disraeli among others. While on a tour of continental Europe, she met Byron in Genoa and during six weeks of riding, dining, and conversing with the poet developed a close relationship that was to be chronicled in her *Conversations of Lord Byron* (1834). Shunned by "decent society," she may have felt a certain empathy for the poet who also had been driven out of England by disapprobation. Her detractors later claimed that she had invented most of her *Conversations of Lord Byron*, however respected biographers of Byron have defended the work. Lady Blessington wrote to her close friend Landor, upon the publication of the work, "I shall be glad to hear what you think of the *Conversation*. I could have made them better, but they would no longer be what they now are, genuine" (Quoted in J.F. Molloy, *The Most Gorgeous Lady Blessington*, vol. two, p. 20).

Byron affects a perfect indifference to the opinion of the world, yet is more influenced by it than most people,—not in his conduct, but in his dread of, and wincing under its censures. He was extremely agitated by his name being introduced in the P(ortsmouth) trial, as having assisted in making up the match, and showed a degree of irritation that proves he is as susceptible as ever to newspaper attacks, notwithstanding his boasts of the contrary. This susceptibility will always leave him at the *mercy* of all who may choose to write against him, however insignificant they may be.

I noticed Byron one day more than usually irritable, though he endeavoured to suppress all symptoms of it. After various sarcasms on the cant and hypocrisy of the times, which was always the signal that he was suffering from some attack made on him, he burst forth in violent invectives against America, and said that she now rivalled her mother country in cant, as he had that morning read an article of abuse, copied from an American newspaper, alluding to a report that he was going to reside there. We had seen the article, and hoped that it might have escaped his notice, but unfortunately he had perused it, and its effects on his temper were visible for several days after. He said that he was never sincere in his praises of the Americans, and that he only extolled their navy to pique Mr. Croker. There was something so childish in this avowal, that there was no keeping a serious face on hearing it; and Byron smiled himself, like a petulant spoiled child, who acknowledges having done something to spite a playfellow.

—Marguerite, Countess of Blessington,
Conversations of Lord Byron, 1834

MATTHEW ARNOLD
"STANZAS FROM THE GRANDE CHARTREUSE"
AND "MEMORIAL VERSES" (1850 & 1855)

A poet and a critic, Matthew Arnold (1822–1888) had a contradictory relationship to Byron. As a representative of Victorian seriousness, he could not well cherish Byron's lifestyle, yet in his "Stanzas from the Grande Chartreuse" and in his "Memorial Verses," the nostalgia of a postromantic poet for a previous age of poets shows that, despite his need to distance himself from romantic poetry, it exerted a hold over him.

What helps it now, that Byron bore,
With haughty scorn which mocked the smart,
Through Europe to the Aetolian shore
The pageant of his bleeding heart?
That thousands counted every groan,
And Europe made his woe her own?

> —Matthew Arnold, "Stanzas from the
> Grande Chartreuse," 1855, ll. 133–138

MEMORIAL VERSES
Goethe in Weimar sleeps, and Greece,
Long since, saw Byron's struggle cease.
But one such death remain'd to come;
The last poetic voice is dumb
We stand to-day by Wordsworth's tomb.

When Byron's eyes were shut in death,
We bow'd our head and held our breath.
He taught us little; but our soul
Had felt him like the thunder's roll.
With shivering heart the strife we saw
Of passion with eternal law;
And yet with reverential awe
We watch'd the fount of fiery life
Which served for that Titanic strife. . . .

Ah! since dark days still bring to light
Man's prudence and man's fiery might,
Time may restore us in his course

Goethe's sage mind and Byron's force;
But where will Europe's latter hour
Again find Wordsworth's healing power?
Others will teach us how to dare,
And against fear our breast to steel;
Others will strengthen us to bear—
But who, ah! who, will make us feel?
The cloud of mortal destiny,
Others will front it fearlessly
But who, like him, will put it by?

Keep fresh the grass upon his grave,
O Rotha, with thy living wave!
Sing him thy best! for few or none
Hears thy voice right, now he is gone.

—Matthew Arnold, "Memorial Verses," 1850

SAMUEL ROGERS (1855)

The English poet Samuel Rogers (1763–1855), who wrote in the style and poetic diction of the eighteenth century, was nonetheless highly appreciated by his contemporaries, including Byron. Rogers's most successful poem, "The Pleasures of Memory" (1792), is an abstract treatment of a serious topic. Its classical elements make the work seem old-fashioned from a romantic point of view, yet Byron praised it by claiming that, "There is not a vulgar line in the poem." In the hope of boosting sales, Byron published his *Lara* with Rogers's *Jacqueline* in 1814. The financially independent Rogers travelled widely and met Byron and Shelley at Pisa in 1821. Later living in London, he became host to many of the famous literati of his time, and many of his conversations were recorded and were later published in Alexander Dyce's *Recollections* and G.H. Powell's *Reminiscences*.

After Byron had become the *rage*, I was frequently amused at the manoeuvres of certain noble ladies to get acquainted with him by means of me: for instance, I would receive a note from Lady _____ requesting the pleasure of my company on a particular evening, with a postscript, "Pray, could you not contrive to bring Lord Byron with you?"—Once, at a great party given by Lady Jersey, Mrs. Sheridan ran up to me and said, "Do, as a favour, try if you can place Lord Byron beside me at supper."

Byron had prodigious facility of composition. He was fond of suppers; and used often to sup at my house and eat heartily (for he had then given up the hard biscuit and soda-water diet): after going home, he would throw off sixty or eighty verses, which he would send to press next morning.

He one evening took me to the green-room of Drury Lane Theatre, where I was much entertained. When the play began, I went round to the front of the house, and desired the boxkeeper to show me into Lord Byron's box. I had been there about a minute, thinking myself quite alone, when suddenly Byron and Miss Boyce (the actress) emerged from a dark corner.

In those days at least, Byron had no readiness of reply in conversation. If you happened to let fall any observation which offended him, he would say nothing at the time; but the offence would lie rankling in his mind; and perhaps a fortnight after, he would suddenly come out with some very cutting remarks upon you, giving them as his deliberate opinions, the results of his experience of your character.

Several women were in love with Byron, but none so violently as Lady Caroline Lamb. She absolutely besieged him. He showed me the first letter he received from her; in which she assured him that, if he was in any want of money, "all her jewels were at his service." They frequently had quarrels; and more than once, on coming home, I have found Lady C. walking in the garden, and waiting for me, to beg that I would reconcile them.—When she met Byron at a party, she would always, if possible, return home from it in *his* carriage, and accompanied by *him:* I recollect particularly their returning to town together from Holland House.—But such was the insanity of her passion for Byron, that sometimes, when not invited to a party where he was to be, she would wait for him in the street till it was over! One night, after a great party at Devonshire House, to which Lady Caroline had not been invited, I saw her,—yes, saw her,—talking to Byron, with half of her body thrust into the carriage which he had just entered. In spite of all this absurdity, my firm belief is that there was nothing criminal between them.

Byron at last was sick of her. When their intimacy was at an end, and while she was living in the country, she burned, very solemnly, on a sort of funeral pile, *transcripts* of all the letters which she had received from Byron, and *a copy* of a miniature (his portrait) which he had presented to her; several girls from the neighbourhood, whom she had dressed in white garments, dancing round the pile, and singing a song which she had written for the occasion, "Burn, fire, burn," &c.—She was mad; and her family allowed her to do whatever she chose.

—Samuel Rogers, *Recollection of the Table Talk of*
Samuel Rogers (collected by Alexander Dyce), 1856

EDWARD JOHN TRELAWNY (1858)

Byron's and Shelley's friend Edward John Trelawny (1792–1881) was a biographer, novelist, and adventurous seaman who served in the British Navy.
He belonged to the Pisan circle and oversaw the cremation of Shelley and
Edward Williams in 1822. At Byron's request, Trelawny also took part in the
Greek war of independence from Turkey. He recounts his role in the conflict
in, among other works, his *Recollections of the Last Days of Shelley and Byron*
(1858). Trying to be a Byronic hero in his own right, he married Tersitsa,
the sister of Odysseus, an insurgent chief, and lived in a cave. He survived
various attempts on his life and eventually returned to England where he
visited Mary Shelley and Claire Clairmont, both of whom he professed to
love. Apart from a career in politics and as a raconteur of his own life, he
wrote a fascinating account of his memories of Byron, *Records of Shelley,
Byron, and the Author* (1858), which he revised and rewrote repeatedly.

Men of books, particularly poets, are rarely men of action, their mental energy
exhausts their bodily powers. Byron has been generally considered an exception
to this rule, he certainly so considered himself: let us look at the facts.

In 1809 he first left England, rode on horseback through Spain and
Portugal, four hundred miles, crossed the Mediterranean on board a frigate,
and landed in Greece; where he passed two years in sauntering through a
portion of that small country: this, with a trip to Smyrna, Constantinople,
Malta, and Gibraltar, generally on board our men-of-war, where you have all
the ease, comfort, and most of the luxuries of your own homes—this is the
extent of the voyages and travels he was so proud of. Anything more luxurious
than sailing on those seas, and riding through those lands, and in such a
blessed climate, I know from experience is not to be found in this world.
Taking into account the result of these travels as shown in his works, he might
well boast; he often said, if he had ever written a line worth preserving it was
Greece that inspired it. After this trip he returned to England, and remained
there some years, four or five; then abandoned it for ever, passed through the
Netherlands, went up the Rhine, paused for some months in Switzerland,
crossed the Alps into Italy, and never left that peninsula until the last year of
his life. He was never in France, for when he left England, Paris was in the
hands of the Allies, and he said he could not endure to witness a country
associated in his mind with so many glorious deeds of arts and arms, bullied
by 'certain rascal officers, slaves in authority, the knaves of justice!'

To return, however, to his travels. If you look at a map you will see what a
narrow circle comprises his wanderings. Any man might go, and many have

gone without the aid of steam, over the same ground in a few months—even if he had to walk with a knapsack, where Byron rode. The pilgrim moved about like a Pasha, with a host of attendants, and all that he and they required on the journey. So far as I could learn from Fletcher, his yeoman bold—and he had been with him from the time of his first leaving England—Byron wherever he was, so far as it was practicable, pursued the same lazy, dawdling habits he continued during the time I knew him. He was seldom out of his bed before noon, when he drank a cup of very strong green tea, without sugar or milk. At two he ate a biscuit and drank soda-water. At three he mounted his horse and sauntered along the road—and generally the same road—if alone, racking his brains for fitting matter and rhymes for the coming poem, he dined at seven, as frugally as anchorites are said in story-books to have done, at nine he visited the family of Count Gamba, on his return home he sat reading or composing until two or three o'clock in the morning, and then to bed, often feverish, restless and exhausted—to dream, as he said, more than to sleep.

Something very urgent, backed by the importunity of those who had influence over him, could alone induce him to break through the routine I have described, for a day, and it was certain to be resumed on the next—he was constant in this alone.

His conversation was anything but literary, except when Shelley was near him. The character he most commonly appeared in was of the free and easy sort, such as had been in vogue when he was in London, and George IV was Regent; and his talk was seasoned with anecdotes of the great actors on and off the stage, boxers, gamblers, duellists, drunkards, etc., appropriately garnished with the slang and scandal of that day. Such things had all been in fashion, and were at that time considered accomplishments by gentlemen; and of this tribe of Mohawks the Prince Regent was the chief, and allowed to be the most perfect specimen. Byron, not knowing the tribe was extinct, still prided himself on having belonged to it; of nothing was he more indignant, than of being treated as a man of letters, instead of as a lord and a man of fashion: this prevented foreigners and literary people from getting on with him, for they invariably so offended. His long absence had not effaced the mark John Bull brands his children with; the instant he loomed above the horizon, on foot or horseback, you saw at a glance he was a Britisher. He did not understand foreigners, nor they him; and, during the time I knew him, he associated with no Italians except the family of Count Gamba. He seemed to take an especial pleasure in making a clean breast to every new comer, as if to mock their previous conceptions of him, and to give the lie to the portraits published of him. He said to me, as we were riding together alone, shortly after I knew him:

'Now, confess, you expected to find me a "Timon of Athens", or a "Timur the Tartar"; or did you think I was a mere singsong driveller of poesy, full of what I heard Braham at a rehearsal call "Entusamusy"; and are you not mystified at finding me what I am—a man of the world—never in earnest—laughing at all things mundane.'

Then he muttered, as to himself:

The world is a bundle of hay, Mankind are the asses who pull.

Any man who cultivates his intellectual faculty so highly as to seem at times inspired, would be too much above us, if, on closer inspection, we should not find it alloyed with weaknesses akin to our own. Byron soon put you at your ease on this point. Godwin, in his *Thoughts on Man,* says: 'Shakespeare, amongst all his varied characters, has not attempted to draw a perfect man'; and Pope says:

A perfect man's a thing the world ne'er saw.

At any rate I should not seek for a model amongst men of the pen; they are too thin-skinned and egotistical. In his perverse and moody humours, Byron would give vent to his Satanic vein. After a long silence, one day on horseback, he began:

'I have a conscience, although the world gives me no credit for it; I am now repenting, not of the few sins I have committed, but of the many I have not committed. There are things, too, we should not do, if they were not forbidden. My *Don Juan* was cast aside and almost forgotten, until I heard that the pharisaic synod in John Murray's back parlour had pronounced it as highly immoral, and unfit for publication. "Because thou art virtuous thinkest thou there shall be no more cakes and ale?" Now my brain is throbbing and must have vent. I opined gin was inspiration, but cant is stronger. To-day I had another letter warning me against the Snake (Shelley). He, alone, in this age of humbug, dares stem the current, as he did to-day the flooded Arno in his skiff, although I could not observe he made any progress. The attempt is better than being swept along as all the rest are, with the filthy garbage scoured from its banks.'

Taking advantage of this panegyric on Shelley, I observed, he might do him a great service at little cost, by a friendly word or two in his next work, such as he had bestowed on authors of less merit.

Assuming a knowing look, he continued:

'All trades have their mysteries; if we crack up a popular author, he repays us in the same coin, principal and interest. A friend may have repaid money lent—can't say any of mine have; but who ever heard of the interest being added thereto?'

I rejoined:

'By your own showing you are indebted to Shelley; some of his best verses are to express his admiration of your genius.'

'Ay,' he said, with a significant look, 'who reads them? If we puffed the Snake, it might not turn out a profitable investment. If he cast off the slough of his mystifying metaphysics, he would want no puffing.'

Seeing I was not satisfied he added:

'If we introduced Shelley to our readers they might draw comparisons, and they are *odorous*.'

After Shelley's death Byron, in a letter to Moore, of the 2nd of August 1822, says:

'There is another man gone, about whom the world was ill-naturedly, and ignorantly, and brutally mistaken. It will, perhaps, do him justice *now*, when he can be no better for it.'

In a letter to Murray of an earlier date, he says:

'You were all mistaken about Shelley, who was without exception, the best and least selfish man I ever knew.'

And, again, he says: 'You are all mistaken about Shelley; you do not know how mild, how tolerant, how good he was.'

What Byron says of the world, that it will, perhaps, do Shelley justice when he can be no better for it, is far more applicable to himself. If the world erred, they did so in ignorance; Shelley was a myth to them. Byron had no such plea to offer, but he was neither just nor generous, and never drew his weapon to redress any wrongs but his own.

—Edward John Trelawny, *Recollections of the Last Days of Shelley and Byron*, 1858

GEORGE ELIOT (1866)

The Victorian novelist Mary Ann (Marian) Evans (1819–1880), known by her pen name George Eliot, noted in a letter that "Byron and his poetry have become more and more repugnant to me of late years" (August 23, 1869). In her novel *Felix Holt*, the protagonist expresses a similar view.

In the act of rising, Felix pushed back his chair too suddenly against the rickety table close by him, and down went the blue-frilled work-basket, flying open, and dispersing on the floor reels, thimble, muslin work, a small sealed bottle of atta of rose, and something heavier than these—a duodecimo volume which fell close to him between the table and the fender. 'O my stars!' said Felix, 'I beg your pardon.' Esther had already started up, and with wonderful quickness had picked up half the small rolling things while Felix was lifting the basket and the book. This last had opened, and had its leaves crushed in falling; and, with the instinct of a bookish man, he saw nothing more pressing to be done than to flatten the corners of the leaves. 'Byron's Poems!' he said, in a tone of disgust, while Esther was recovering all the other articles. ' "The Dream"—he'd better have been asleep and snoring. What! do you stuff your memory with Byron, Miss Lyon?' Felix, on his side, was led at last to look straight at Esther, but it was with a strong denunciatory and pedagogic intention. Of course he saw more clearly than ever that she was a fine lady. She reddened, drew up her long neck, and said, as she retreated to her chair again—'I have a great admiration for Byron.' Mr Lyon had paused in the act of drawing his chair to the tea-table, and was looking on at this scene, wrinkling the corners of his eyes with a perplexed smile. Esther would not have wished him to know anything about the volume of Byron, but she was too proud to show any concern.

'He is a worldly and vain writer, I fear,' said Mr Lyon. He knew scarcely anything of the poet, whose books embodied the faith and ritual of many young ladies and gentlemen. 'A misanthropic debauchee,' said Felix, lifting a chair with one hand, and holding the book open in the other, 'whose notion of a hero was that he should disorder his stomach and despise mankind. His corsairs and renegades, his Alps and Manfreds, are the most paltry puppets that were ever pulled by the strings of lust and pride.' 'Hand the book to me,' said Mr Lyon. 'Let me beg of you to put it aside till after tea, father,' said Esther. 'However objectionable Mr Holt may find its pages, they would certainly be made worse by being greased with bread-and-butter.'

—George Eliot, *Felix Holt,*
The Radical, 1866, I, pp. 123–5

JOAQUIN MILLER "AT LORD BYRON'S TOMB" (1870)

Called the "Poet of the Sierras" and the "Byron of the Rockies," Cincinnatus Hiner Miller, alias Joaquin Miller (1841–1913), led a life that was even more colorful and adventurous than Byron's. Born in Liberty, Indiana, in 1837, he worked as a cook, miner, conservationist, Pony Express rider, newspaperman, teacher, and poet and, despite having stolen horses earlier in his life, also became a lawyer and judge. He lived with Indians and even tried to establish an Indian "Republic," all the while remaining an ardent admirer of Byron and his poetry. As Miller was hoping that recognition of his own poetry awaited him in London, he left for the English capital after having cards printed that read "Joaquin Miller, Byron of the Rockies." Laurel leaves from Sausalito also accompanied him for a wreath to put on Byron's tomb. After visiting the grave in England, Miller finally got a book of verse, *Pacific Poems*, printed by a vanity publisher, and he began donning such outfits as a sombrero, a bright red shirt, a blue polkadot bandanna, and high-heeled boots. Miller is an early example of Byron's influence in the United States.

AT LORD BYRON'S TOMB

O Master, here I bow before a shrine;
Before the lordliest dust that ever yet
Moved animate in human form divine.
Lo! dust indeed to dust. The mold is set
Above thee and the ancient walls are wet,
And drip all day in dank and silent gloom,
As if the cold gray stones could not forget
Thy great estate shrunk to this somber room,
But lean to weep perpetual tears above thy tomb.
Before me lie the oak-crown'd Annesley hills,
Before me lifts the ancient Annesley Hall
Above the mossy oaks. . A picture fills
With forms of other days. A maiden tall
And fair; a fiery restless boy, with all
The force of man! a steed that frets without;
A long thin sword that rusts upon the wall.
The generations pass . . . Behold! about
The ivied hall the fair-hair'd children sport and shout.
A bay wreath, wound by Ina of the West,
Hangs damp and stain'd upon the dark gray wall,
Above thy time-soil'd tomb and tatter'd crest;
A bay wreath gather'd by the seas that call
To orient Cathay, that break and fall
On shell-lined shores before Tahiti's breeze.
A slab, a crest, a wreath, and these are all
Neglected, tatter'd, torn; yet only these
The world bestows for song that rivall'd singing seas.
A bay-wreath wound by one more truly brave
Than Shastan; fair as thy eternal fame,
She sat and wove above the sunset wave,

And wound and sang thy measures and thy name.
'Twas wound by one, yet sent with one acclaim
By many, fair and warm as flowing wine,
And purely true, and tall as growing flame,
That list and lean in moonlight's mellow shine
To tropic tales of love in other tongues than thine.
I bring this idle reflex of thy task,
And my few loves, to thy forgotten tomb;
I leave them here; and here all pardon ask
Of thee, and patience ask of singers whom
Thy majesty hath silenced. I resume
My staff, and now my face is to the West;
My feet are worn; the sun is gone, a gloom
Has mantled Hucknall, and the minstrel's zest
For fame is broken here, and here he pleads for rest.

—Joaquin Miller, "At Lord Byron's Tomb,"
1870, *Poetical Works,* ed. Stuart P. Sherman,
1923, pp. 410–411

Oscar Wilde (1891)

Many purveyors of the age of decadence discovered an affinity for Byron. The Irish dramatist, dandy, and poet Oscar Wilde (1854–1900) expressed his fascination with Byron's ability to fashion his own personality in his social criticism.

With the abolition of private property, then, we shall have true, beautiful, healthy Individualism. Nobody will waste his life in accumulating things, and the symbols for things. One will live. To live is the rarest thing in the world. Most people exist, that is all. It is a question whether we have ever seen the full expression of a personality, except on the imaginative plane of art. In action, we never have. Caesar, says Mommsen, was the complete and perfect man. But how tragically insecure was Caesar! Wherever there is a man who exercises authority, there is a man who resists authority. Caesar was very perfect, but his perfection travelled by too dangerous a road. Marcus Aurelius was the perfect man, says Renan. Yes; the great emperor was a perfect man. But how intolerable were the endless claims upon him! He staggered under the burden of the empire. He was conscious how inadequate one man was to bear the weight of that Titan and too vast orb. What I mean by a perfect man is one who develops under perfect conditions; one who is not wounded, or worried, or maimed, or in danger. *Most personalities have been obliged to be rebels. Half their strength has been wasted in friction.* Byron's personality, for instance, was terribly wasted in its battle with the stupidity, and hypocrisy, and Philistinism of the English. Such battles do not always intensify strength: they often exaggerate weakness. Byron was never able to give us what he might have given us. Shelley escaped better. Like Byron, he got out of England as soon as possible. But he was not so well known. If the English had had any idea of what a great poet he really was, they would have fallen on him with tooth and nail, and made his life as unbearable to him as they possibly could. But he was not a remarkable figure in society, and consequently he escaped, to a certain degree. Still, even in Shelley the note of rebellion is sometimes too strong. The note of the perfect personality is not rebellion, but peace.

It will be a marvellous thing—the true personality of man—when we see it. It will grow naturally and simply, flower-like, or as a tree grows. It will not be at discord. It will never argue or dispute. It will not prove things. It will know everything. And yet it will not busy itself about knowledge. It will have wisdom. Its value will not be measured by material things. It will have nothing. And yet it will have everything, and whatever one takes from it, it will still have, so rich will it be. It will not be always meddling with others, or asking them to be like itself. It will love them because they will be different. And yet, while it will not meddle with others, it will help all, as a beautiful thing helps us by being what it is. The personality of man will be very wonderful. It will be as wonderful as the personality of a child.

—Oscar Wilde, from *The Soul of
Man Under Socialism* (1891)

WILLIAM GRAHAM (1898)

This excerpt records the conversations of William Graham with Jane Clermont, in which Byron and Leigh Hunt briefly figure.

It was impossible to obtain a good word for Byron from this lady [Jane Clermont], though, to do her justice, she showed no rancour, and I must admit I gradually began to feel my hero's stature dwarfing; but I was young then and impressionable, and, since, I have restored him to his old position in my affections.

"He was utterly selfish," she said; but she could not deny that he gave about a third of his money away to the poor.

"Well, he did not show much generosity to that unfortunate Leigh Hunt," she insisted; and on my replying that, after all, Leigh Hunt must have been rather a vulgar cockney bore, she riposted with, "It is, after all, natural that you should take up the cudgels for Byron, for he was a thorough Scot; his brilliancy and good looks he inherited, to a great extent, from the 'gay Gordons,' his mother's family, and his love of the bawbees and his love of dogmatic religion were both intensely Scottish. He had 'scotched, not killed the Scotsman in his blood,' as he himself said in *Don Juan,* with a vengeance. He even wanted to secure both this world and the next in some canny Scotch fashion. He would talk religion and predestination and other exploded doctrines with any old Presbyterian parson by the hour, without the remotest idea of practising any religion whatsoever; though, to do him justice, he was not in the least afraid of death. In fact, he was absolutely reckless of life."

"Well, you must admit that the final scene, the fight for Greece, was splendid?"

"I don't know that there was anything particularly splendid about it," she replied. "He was tired to death of La Guiccioli, whom he treated in a way very few women would have stood, notwithstanding the rapturous memoirs she wrote of him some years ago; and he simply invested a great deal of money in the Greek cause with the idea of being made a king, which, as Trelawny says, he undoubtedly would have been if he had lived, notwithstanding his stern republicanism.

"Byron was a great poetic genius and an extremely able man, and, in his way, a thorough man of the world, but he was utterly selfish, utterly false, and utterly spoiled and vain, while, as the French say, he was always playing to the gallery. That is my opinion, anyhow, and you may take it for what it is worth."

—William Graham, *Last Links with Byron,
Shelley, and Keats,* 1898, pp. 31–32

GENERAL

Henry, Lord Brougham
"Lord Byron's Poems" (1808)

Born in Edinburgh on September 19, 1778, Henry Brougham had a remarkable career as a political radical who fought as a lawyer and a member of the House of Commons for the abolition of slavery and brought about radical reform of the legal system. In 1802, he co-founded the *Edinburgh Review* and wrote more than eighty articles for it. He also helped to create the University of London and to provide libraries for the working class. He was made a peer in 1830 and died as Lord Brougham in Cannes on May 7, 1868. His scathing review of Byron's *Hours of Idleness* in the *Edinburgh Review* was a bitter experience for the young author. Byron was to blame Francis Jeffrey for this review and learned only years later that Henry Brougham had in fact been the source, the man who also acted on behalf of Lady Byron in her separation from her husband. The harsh review incensed Byron, prompting him to rewrite his satire *English Bards, and Scotch Reviewers* and to have it published anonymously in March 1809.

The poesy of this young lord belongs to the class which neither gods nor men are said to permit. Indeed, we do not recollect to have seen a quantity of verse with so few deviations in either direction from that exact standard. His effusions (in *Hours of Idleness)* are spread over a dead flat, and can no more get above or below the level, than if they were so much stagnant water. As an extenuation of this offence, the noble author is peculiarly forward in pleading minority. We have it in the title-page, and on the very back of the volume; it follows his name like a favourite part of his *style*. Much stress is laid upon it in the preface, and the poems are connected with this general statement of his case, by particular dates, substantiating the age at which each was written.

Now, the law upon the point of minority, we hold to be perfectly clear. It is a plea available only to the defendant; no plaintiff can offer it as a supplementary ground of action. Thus, if any suit could be brought against Lord Byron, for the purpose of compelling him to put into court a certain quantity of poetry; and if judgement were given against him; it is highly probable that an exception would be taken, were he to deliver *for poetry,* the contents of this volume. To this he might plead *minority;* but as he now makes voluntary tender of the article, he hath no right to sue, on that ground, for the price in good current praise, should the goods be unmarketable. This is our view of the law on the point, and we dare to say, so will it be ruled. Perhaps however, in reality, all that he tells us about his youth, is rather with a view to increase our wonder, than to soften our censures. He possibly means to say, 'See how a minor can write! This poem was actually composed by a young man of eighteen, and this by one of only sixteen!'—But, alas, we all remember the poetry of Cowley at ten, and Pope at twelve; and so far from hearing, with any degree of surprise, that very poor verses were written by a youth from his leaving school to his leaving college, inclusive, we really believe this to be the most common of all occurrences; that it happens in the life of nine men in ten who are educated in England; and that the tenth man writes better verse than Lord Byron. . . .

But whatever judgment may be passed on the poems of this noble minor, it seems we must take them as we find them, and be content; for they are the last we shall ever have from him. He is at best, he says, but an intruder into the groves of Parnassus; he never lived in a garret, like thorough-bred poets; and 'though he once roved a careless mountaineer in the Highlands of Scotland,' he has not of late enjoyed this advantage. Moreover, he expects no profit from his publication; and whether it succeeds or not, 'it is highly improbable, from his situation and pursuits hereafter,' that he should again condescend to become an author. Therefore, let us take what we get and be thankful. What right have we poor devils to be nice? We are well off to have got so much from a man of this Lord's station, who does not live in a garret, but 'has the sway' of Newstead Abbey. Again, we say, let us be thankful; and, with honest Sancho, bid God bless the giver, nor look the gift horse in the mouth.

—Henry, Lord Brougham, "Lord Byron's Poems,"
Edinburgh Review, January 1808, pp. 285–289

LEIGH HUNT (1811)

The English radical, critic, and poet James Henry Leigh Hunt (1784–1859) published his first major poem, "The Feast of the Poets," in March 1812 (further editions appeared in 1814, 1815, and 1832) in *The Reflector*. In the poem, he presents his satirical opinions of writers such as Southey, Coleridge, Wordsworth, and Byron and offended many of his contemporaries. In the following excerpt, Apollo is speaking to Byron.

He spoke with a warmth, but his accent was bland,
And the poet bowed down with a blush to his hand,
When Byron relieved him by taking his place,
Which he did with so kind yet unconscious a face,
So ardent a frankness, yet modest an ease,
As much as to say 'Now for me, if you please,'—
That Apollo took *his* hand, and earnestly said,
'Pray how came misanthropy into *your* head?
I suspect (it is true), that in all which you tell us
Of robbers, and rakes, and such terrible fellows,
There's something mere scorn could have never devised,
And a sorrow-wise charity roughly disguised;
But you must not be always indulging this tone;
You owe some relief to our hearts and your own;
For poets, earth's heav'n-linking spirits, were born,
What they can, to amend,—what they can't, to adorn;
And you hide the best proof of your office and right,
If you make not as I do a contrast with night,
And help to shed round you a gladness and light.
So remember; and as to the style of your song,
And to straight-forward speaking, 'twill come before long.'

—Leigh Hunt, *The Feast of the Poets*
(1811), 1814, ll. 222–242

FRIEDRICH VON SCHLEGEL (1815)

Following the translation of *Childe Harold's Pilgrimage* and the Eastern-themed tales, Byronmania also raged in Germany. The German novelist, critic, and philosopher, Friedrich von Schlegel (1772–1829), a pioneer in comparative Indo-European linguistics and comparative philology, was a contemporary of Goethe, Schiller, and Novalis and was a major figure in the early German romantic movement. In the following lecture, given at the University of Jena, he emphasizes the morbidity and tragic gloom evident in Byron's poetry.

The poetry of Byron issues neither from reminiscence nor hope, but from the depths of tragic inspiration and a peculiarly disconsolate atheistic philosophy. His verse, with all its lofty aspirations and endowments, is lost in the mazes of infidelity and despair: groping in a vast crowd of strange unearthly shapes conjured up by midnight fancy, it deifies only a morbid heroism, which it invests with the gloomy spell of varied passion. This atheistic inspiration was not altogether alien to German poetry at an earlier epoch; but a purer sphere was soon attained, the monstrosities of false tragic grandeur being banished to the extreme confines of the drama. In the higher regions of art it was speedily discovered that modern poetry cannot flow in transparent stream from the turbid eddy of froward passion; but founded on eternal hope, it must become a glorified admixture of Faith and Love, radiant as the rainbow after the storm, or the dawn of morn after the shades of night. Scott and Byron together constituting the poetry of reminiscence and the poetry of despair, may be said to form the close of a former extinct minstrelsy, rather than the commencement of a new era, of which as yet there are no manifest tokens.

—Friedrich Schlegel, *Lectures on the History of Literature Ancient and Modern*, 1815

WILLIAM HAZLITT (1818)

William Hazlitt (1778–1830) was an English writer, critic, and grammarian, who wrote humanistic essays and literary criticism, including *Characters of Shakespeare's Plays*, published in 1817. In 1798, Hazlitt was introduced to Samuel Taylor Coleridge and William Wordsworth; they would feature in his *The Spirit of the Age* (1825), a collection of portraits of his contemporaries, also including Charles Lamb, Lord Byron, Jeremy Bentham, and Sir Walter Scott. In a series of lectures delivered at the Surrey Institute in 1818, Hazlitt criticizes Byron's style as well as his politics, arguing that Byron was a political turncoat in his attitude to Napoléon. Byron reacted by writing a short essay in defense, which he ordered Murray to append to the first two cantos of Don Juan: "I tell Mr Hazlitt that I never flattered Napoleon on the throne—nor maligned him since his fall" (*The Complete Poetical Works of Lord Byron*, ed. J. McGann, vol. VI, p. 683). Murray did not publish Byron's lengthy reply, and the poet remained aggressive toward Hazlitt.

If Mr. Moore has not suffered enough personally, Lord Byron (judging from the tone of his writings) might be thought to have suffered too much to be a truly great poet. If Mr. Moore lays himself too open to all the various impulses of things, the outward shews of earth and sky, to every breath that blows, to every stray sentiment that crosses his fancy; Lord Byron shuts himself up too much in the impenetrable gloom of his own thoughts, and buries the natural light of things in 'nook monastic.' The *Giaour,* the *Corsair, Childe Harold, are* all the same person, and they are apparently all himself. The everlasting repetition of one subject, the same dark ground of fiction, with the darker colours of the poet's mind spread over it, the unceasing accumulation of horrors on horror's head, steels the mind against the sense of pain, as inevitably as the unwearied Siren sounds and luxurious monotony of Mr. Moore's poetry make it inaccessible to pleasure. Lord Byron's poetry is as morbid as Mr. Moore's is careless and dissipated. He has more depth of passion, more force and impetuosity, but the passion is always of the same unaccountable character, at once violent and sullen, fierce and gloomy. It is not the passion of a mind struggling with misfortune, or the hopelessness of its desires, but of a mind preying upon itself, and disgusted with, or indifferent to all other things. There is nothing less poetical than this sort of unaccommodating selfishness. There is nothing more repulsive than this sort of ideal absorption of all the interests of others, of the good and ills of life, in the ruling passion and moody abstraction of a single mind, as if it would make itself the centre of the universe, and there was nothing worth cherishing but its intellectual diseases. It is like a cancer, eating into the heart of poetry. But still there is power; and power rivets attention and forces admiration. 'He hath a demon:' and that is the next thing to being full of the God. His brow collects the scattered gloom: his eye flashes livid fire that withers and consumes. But still we watch the progress of the scathing bolt with interest, and mark the ruin it leaves behind with awe. Within the contracted range of his imagination, he has great unity and truth of keeping. He chooses elements and agents congenial to his mind, the dark and glittering ocean, the frail bark hurrying before the storm, pirates and men that 'house on the wild sea with wild usages.' He gives the tumultuous eagerness of action, and the fixed despair of thought. In vigour of style and force of conception, he in one sense surpasses every writer of the present day. His indignant apothegms are like oracles of misanthropy. He who wishes for 'a curse to kill with,' may find it in Lord Byron's writings. Yet he has beauty lurking underneath his strength, tenderness sometimes joined with the phrenzy of despair. A flash of golden light sometimes follows from a stroke of his pencil, like a falling meteor. The flowers that adorn his poetry bloom over charnel-houses and the grave!

—William Hazlitt, *Lectures on the English Poets,* 1818

ROBERT SOUTHEY "PREFACE" (1821)

The historian and biographer Robert Southey (1774–1843) was one of the Lake Poets, a set of conservative romantic writers that included Wordsworth and Coleridge. In 1813, Southey became England's poet laureate. Byron's attack on Southey in his *English Bards and Scotch Reviewers*, calling him a "ballad-monger," had not prevented them from meeting on friendly terms; but later Byron claimed that Southey was responsible for a scandal spread about him and Shelley. Byron dedicated *Don Juan* to the laureate, using bitingly satiric verses. Southey's introduction to Byron's *Vision of Judgment* (1821), which associates Byron with the "Satanic School" of poetry, led to a bitter controversy that was renewed even after Byron's death with the publication of Thomas Medwin's *Conversations of Lord Byron*.

What, then, should be said of those for whom the thoughtlessness and inebriety of wanton youth can no longer be pleaded, but who have written in sober manhood, and with deliberate purpose?—men of diseased hearts and depraved imaginations, who, forming a system of opinions to suit their own unhappy course of conduct, have rebelled against the holiest ordinances of human society, and, hating that revealed religion, which, with all their efforts and bravadoes, they are unable entirely to disbelieve, labor to make others as miserable as themselves, by infecting them with a moral virus that eats into the soul! The school which they have set up may properly be called the Satanic School; for though their productions breathe the spirit of Belial in their lascivious parts, and the spirit of Moloch in those loathsome images of atrocities and horror which they delight to represent, they are more especially characterized by a satanic spirit of pride and audacious impiety, which still betrays the wretched feeling of hopelessness wherewith it is allied.

—Robert Southey, "Preface" to
The Vision of Judgment, 1821

WILLIAM MAGINN
"ODOHERTY ON WERNER" (1822)

The Irish journalist and writer William Maginn (1793–1842), born in Cork, was a contributor to *Blackwood's Magazine* and, after moving to London in 1824, became for a short time the Paris correspondent to *The Representative*, a newspaper started by Byron's publisher John Murray. In 1827, Maginn helped to found the pro-Tory *Standard*, and he also wrote for the more scandalous Sunday publication, *The Age.* In cooperation with Hugh Fraser, he established *Fraser's Magazine* (1830), in which his "Homeric Ballads" appeared between 1839 and 1842. He is well known for his attack on the Cockney School of poets, and in 1819 he had written about the immorality of *Don Juan.* Despite being an arch-Tory, he treats Byron kindly, using the pen name Odoherty.

When Lord Byron first announced himself as a tragedian in regular form, there is no doubt that public curiosity was strongly, most strongly, excited. *Marino Faliero Doge of Venice* was a sad damper; yet nobody could deny that there was great and novel beauty in the conception of one character, that of the old Doge's young wife; and we all said, this is a first attempt, and Byron may hereafter write a tragedy worthy of Byron. Then came *Sardanapalus*—on the whole a heavy concern also; but still there was *Myrrha,* and there was the Vision of Nimrod and Semiramis, and there was the noble arming of the roused voluptuary; and these fine things in so far checked the frown of reprehension. *The Two Foscari* was greatly inferior; in fact, it contained a plot than which nothing could be more exquisitely absurd and unnatural—characters strained almost to the ludicrous—versification as clumsy as the grinding of the tread-mill—and *one splendid passage,*—just one. *Cain, a Mystery* was worse and worse. Byron dared to measure himself with Milton, and came off as poorly as Belial might have done from a contest with Michael. Crude metaphysics, as old as the hills, and as barren—bald, thread-bare blasphemies, and puerile ravings, formed the staple of the piece. The only tolerable touches, those of domestic love and the like, were visibly borrowed from Gesner's *Death of Abel:* and in short, one of the most audacious of all the insults that have ever been heaped upon the faith and feelings of a Christian land, was also one of the most feeble and ineffectual.

Thank God! Cain was abandoned to the Radicals—and thank God, it was too radically dull to be popular even among them.

Nevertheless, it is not to be denied, that even in Cain some occasional flashes of Lord Byron's genius were discernible; there was some deep and thrilling poetry in Cain's contemplation of the stars—enough to recall for a moment the brighter and more sustained splendours of *Manfred.*

But now at last has come forth a tragedy by the same hand (Werner), which is not only worse than any of those we have been naming, but worse, far worse, than we, even after reading and regretting them, could have believed it possible for the noble author to indite—a lame and mutilated *rifacciamento* of one of Miss Lee's Canterbury Tales, a thing, which, so far from possessing, scarcely even claims any merit beyond that of turning English prose into English blank verse—a production, in short, which is entitled to be classed with no dramatic works in our language that we are acquainted with, except, perhaps, the common paste-and-scissars *Dramas* from the Waverley novels. Ye Gods! what a descent is here for the proud soul of Harold!

We are not so absurd as to say, or to think, that a Dramatist has no right to make free with other people's fables. On the contrary, we are quite aware that that particular species of genius which is exhibited in the construction of plots, never at any period flourished in England. We all know that Shakespeare himself took his stories from Italian novels, Danish sagas, English chronicles, Plutarch's lives—from any where rather than from his own invention. But did he take *the whole* of Hamlet, or Juliet, or Richard III., or Anthony and Cleopatra, from any of these foreign sources? Did he not *invent*, in the noblest sense of the word, all the *characters* of his pieces? Who dreams that any old Italian Novelist could have formed the imagination of such a creature as Juliet? Who dreams that the Hamlet of Shakespeare, the princely enthusiast, the melancholy philosopher, that spirit refined even to pain, that most incomprehensible and unapproachable of all the creations of human genius, is the same being, in any thing but the name, with the rough, strong-hearted, bloody-handed, old Amlett of the North? Or who is there that supposes Goethe to have taken the character of *his* Faust from the old ballads and penny pamphlets about the Devil and Doctor Faustus? Or who, to come nearer home, imagines that Lord Byron himself found *his* Sardanapalus in Dionysius of Halicarnassus?

But *here* Lord Byron has *invented* nothing—absolutely, positively, undeniably, nothing. There is not one incident in his play, not even the most trivial, that is not to be found in the novel from which it is taken; occurring exactly in the same manner, brought about by exactly the same agents, and producing exactly the same effects on the plot. And then as to the characters, why, not only is every one of them to be found in the novel, but every one of them is to be found there far more fully and powerfully developed. Indeed, but for the preparation which we had received from our old familiarity with Miss Lee's own admirable work, we rather incline to think that we should have been altogether unable to comprehend the *gist* of her noble imitator, or rather copier, in several of what seem to be meant for his most elaborate delineations. The fact is, that this undeviating closeness, this humble fidelity of imitation, is a thing so perfectly new in *literature,* in any thing worthy of the name of literature, that we are sure no one, who has not read the *Canterbury Tales,* will be able to form the least conception of what it amounts to. Again, we must come back to the arras-work; and we now most solemnly assure our readers, that unless our worthy friend Mr Daniel Terry is entitled to be called a poet for *his* Rob Roy, or *his* Guy Mannering, my Lord Byron has no sort of title, none in the world, to be considered as having acted the part of a poet in the concoction and execution of *his* WERNER.

> —William Maginn, "Odoherty on Werner,"
> *Blackwood's Edinburgh Magazine,*
> December 1822, pp. 711–712

SAMUEL TAYLOR COLERIDGE (1822)

It seems, to my ear, that there is a sad want of harmony in Lord Byron's verses. Is it not unnatural to be always connecting very great intellectual power with utter depravity? Does such a combination often really exist in *rerum natura?*

> —Samuel Taylor Coleridge,
> *Table Talk,* December 29, 1822

THOMAS LOVELL BEDDOES (1825)

We ought too to look back with late repentance & remorse on our intoxicated praise, now cooling, of Lord Byron—such a man to be spoken of when the world possessed Goethe, Schiller, Shelley!

> —Thomas Lovell Beddoes, letter to
> Thomas Kelsall, March 25, 1825

THOMAS CARLYLE (1826)

Byron—good generous hapless Byron! And yet when he died he was only a *Kraftmann (Powerman* as the Germans call them). Had he lived he would have been a poet.

> —Thomas Carlyle, *Journal,* December 3,
> 1826, cited in James Anthony Froude,
> *Thomas Carlyle,* 1882, vol. 1, p. 304

JOHN QUINCY ADAMS (1830)

Byron has been extolled as the sublimest of poets. There are passages in all his poems which I have thought charming, but mixed with so much that was disgusting that I never believed his popularity would be lasting. His versification is so destitute of sustained harmony, many of his thoughts are so strained, his sentiments so unamiable, his misanthropy so gloomy, his images so grossly indelicate, his libertinism so shameless, his merriment such grinning of a ghastly smile, that I have always believed his verses would soon rank with forgotten things. But Byron was one of those writers whose lives are interwoven in all their works. The author keeps his reader forever in sight of himself. Such writers must always be vicious and miserable.

—John Quincy Adams, *Memoirs,* entry for
April 1830, 1874–77, vol. 8, p. 218

William Hazlitt (1825)

The critic, essayist, and journalist William Hazlitt (1778–1830) combined radical politics with an admiration for Napoléon. Best known for his *Characters of Shakespeare's Plays*, published in 1817, as well as *The Spirit of the Age* (1825), he was critical of Byron's politics and character, as he could not overlook Byron's aristocratic origins.

Lord Byron and Sir Walter Scott are among writers now living[1] the two, who would carry away a majority of suffrages as the greatest geniuses of the age. The former would, perhaps, obtain the preference with the fine gentlemen and ladies (squeamishness apart), the latter with the critics and the vulgar. We shall treat of them in the same connection, partly on account of their distinguished pre-eminence, and partly because they afford a complete contrast to each other. In their poetry, in their prose, in their politics, and in their tempers, no two men can be more unlike.

If Sir Walter Scott may be thought by some to have been

Born universal heir to all humanity,

it is plain Lord Byron can set up no such pretension. He is, in a striking degree, the creature of his own will. He holds no communion with his kind, but stands alone without mate or fellow—

As if a man were author of himself, And owned no other kin.

He is like a solitary peak, all access to which is cut off not more by elevation than distance. He is seated on a lofty eminence, 'cloud-capt,' or reflecting the last rays of setting suns, and in his poetical moods reminds us of the fabled Titans, retired to a ridgy steep, playing on their Pan's-pipes, and taking up ordinary men and things in their hands with haughty indifference. He raises his subject to himself, or tramples on it; he neither stoops to, nor loses himself in it. He exists not by sympathy, but by antipathy. He scorns all things, even himself. Nature must come to him to sit for her picture: he does not go to her. She must consult his time, his convenience and his humour, and wear a *sombre* or a fantastic garb, or his Lordship turns his back upon her. There is no ease, no unaffected simplicity of manner, no 'golden mean.' All is strained, or petulant in the extreme. His thoughts are sphered and crystalline; his style 'prouder than when blue Iris bends'; his spirit fiery, impatient, wayward, indefatigable. Instead of taking his impressions from without, in entire and almost unimpaired masses, he moulds them according to his own temperament, and heats the materials of his imagination in the furnace of his passions. Lord Byron's verse glows like a flame, consuming every thing in its way; Sir Walter Scott's glides like a river: clear, gentle, harmless. The poetry of the first scorches, that of the last scarcely warms. The light of the one proceeds from an internal source, ensanguined, sullen, fixed; the other reflects the hues of Heaven or the face of nature, glancing, vivid and various.

The productions of the Northern Bard have the rust and the freshness of antiquity about them; those of the Noble Poet cease to startle from their extreme ambition of novelty, both in style and matter. Sir Walter's rhymes are 'silly sooth'—

And dally with the innocence of thought, Like the old age—his Lordship's Muse spurns *the olden time,* and affects all the supercilious airs of a modern fine lady and an upstart. The object of the one writer is to restore us to truth and nature: the other chiefly thinks how he shall display his own power, or vent his spleen, or astonish the reader either by starting new subjects and trains of speculation, or by expressing old ones in a more striking and emphatic manner than they have been expressed before. He cares little what it is he says, so that he can say it differently from others. This may account for the charges of plagiarism which have been repeatedly brought against the Noble Poet. If he can borrow an image or sentiment from another, and heighten it by an epithet or an allusion of greater force and beauty than is to be found in the original passage, he thinks he shows his superiority of execution in this in a more marked manner than if the first suggestion had been his own. It is not the value of the observation itself he is solicitous about; but he wishes to shine by contrast—even nature only serves as a foil to set off his style. He therefore takes the thoughts of others (whether contemporaries or not) out of their mouths, and is content to make them his own, to set his stamp upon them, by imparting to them a more meretricious gloss, a higher relief, a greater loftiness of tone, and a characteristic inveteracy of purpose.

Even in those collateral ornaments of modern style, slovenliness, abruptness and eccentricity (as well as in terseness and significance),

Lord Byron, when he pleases, defies competition and surpasses all his contemporaries. Whatever he does, he must do in a more decided and daring manner than any one else; he lounges with extravagance, and yawns so as to alarm the reader! Self-will, passion, the love of singularity, a disdain of himself and of others (with a conscious sense that this is among the ways and means of procuring admiration) are the proper categories of his mind: he is a lordly writer, is above his own reputation, and condescends to the Muses with a scornful grace!

Lord Byron, who in his politics is a *liberal,* in his genius is haughty and aristocratic: Walter Scott, who is an aristocrat in principle, is popular in his writings, and is (as it were) equally *servile* to nature and to opinion. The genius of Sir Walter is essentially imitative, or 'denotes a foregone conclusion': that of Lord Byron is self-dependent or at least requires no aid, is governed by no law but the impulses of its own will. We confess, however much we may admire independence of feeling and erectness of spirit in general or practical questions, yet in works of genius we prefer him who bows to the authority of nature, who appeals to actual objects, to mouldering superstitions, to history, observation and tradition, before him who only consults the pragmatical and restless workings of his own breast, and gives them out as oracles to the world. We like a writer (whether poet or prose writer) who takes in (or is willing to take in) the range of half the universe in feeling, character, description, much better than we do one who obstinately and invariably shuts himself up in the Bastille of his own ruling passions. In short, we had rather be Sir Walter Scott (meaning thereby the Author of *Waverley)* than Lord Byron a hundred times over, and for the reason just given, namely, that he casts his descriptions in the mould of nature, ever-varying, never tiresome, always interesting and always instructive, instead of casting them constantly in the mould of his own individual impressions.

He gives us man as he is, or as he was, in almost every variety of situation, action and feeling. Lord Byron makes man after his own image, woman after his own heart; the one is a capricious tyrant, the other a yielding slave; he gives us the misanthrope and the voluptuary by turns; and with these two characters, burning or melting in their own fires, he makes out everlasting centos of himself. He hangs the cloud, the film of his existence over all outward things, sits in the centre of his thoughts, and enjoys dark night, bright day, the glitter and the gloom 'in cell monastic.' We see the mournful pall, the crucifix, the death's-heads, the faded chaplet of flowers, the gleaming tapers, the agonized brow of genius, the wasted form of beauty; but we are still imprisoned in a dungeon; a curtain intercepts our view; we do not breathe freely the air of nature or of our own thoughts. The other admired author draws aside the curtain, and the veil of egotism is rent; and he shows us the crowd of living men and women, the endless groups, the landscape background, the cloud and the rainbow, and enriches our imaginations and relieves one passion by another, and expands and lightens reflection, and takes away that tightness at the breast which arises from thinking or wishing to think that there is nothing in the world out of a man's self!

In this point of view, the Author of *Waverley* is one of the greatest teachers of morality that ever lived, by emancipating the mind from petty, narrow, and bigoted prejudices: Lord Byron is the greatest pamperer of those prejudices, by seeming to think there is nothing else worth encouraging but the seeds or the full luxuriant growth of dogmatism and self-conceit. In reading the *Scotch Novels,* we never think about the author, except from a feeling of curiosity respecting our unknown benefactor: in reading Lord Byron's works, he himself is never absent from our minds. The colouring of Lord Byron's style, however rich and dipped in Tyrian dyes, is nevertheless opaque, is in itself an object of delight and wonder: Sir Walter Scott's is perfectly transparent. In studying the one, you seem to gaze at the figures cut in stained glass, which exclude the view beyond, and where the pure light of Heaven is only a means of setting off the gorgeousness of art: in reading the other, you look through a noble window at the clear and varied landscape without. Or to sum up the distinction in one word, Sir Walter Scott is the most *dramatic* writer now living, and Lord Byron is the least so.

It would be difficult to imagine that the Author of *Waverley* is in the smallest degree a pedant, as it would be hard to persuade ourselves that the author of *Childe Harold* and *Don Juan* is not a coxcomb, though a provoking and sublime one. In this decided preference given to Sir Walter Scott over Lord Byron, we distinctly include the prose-works of the former; for we do not think his poetry alone by any means entitles him to that precedence. Sir Walter in his poetry, though pleasing and natural, is a comparative trifler: it is in his anonymous productions that he has shown himself for what he is.

Intensity is the great and prominent distinction of Lord Byron's writings. He seldom gets beyond force of style, nor has he produced any regular work or masterly whole. He does not prepare any plan beforehand, nor revise and retouch what he has written with polished accuracy. His only object seems to be to stimulate himself and his readers for the moment—to keep both alive, to drive away *ennui,* to substitute a feverish and irritable state of excitement for listless indolence or even calm enjoyment. For this purpose he pitches on any subject at random without much thought or delicacy.

He is only impatient to begin, and takes care to adorn and enrich it as he proceeds with 'thoughts that breathe and words that burn.' He composes (as he himself has said) whether he is in the bath, in his study, or on horseback; he writes as habitually as others talk or think; and whether we have the inspiration of the Muse or not, we always find the spirit of the man of genius breathing from his verse. He grapples with his subject, and moves, penetrates and animates it by the electric force of his own feelings. He is often monotonous, extravagant, offensive; but he is never dull or tedious, but when he writes prose.

Lord Byron does not exhibit a new view of nature, or raise insignificant objects into importance by the romantic associations with which he surrounds them, but generally (at least) takes common-place thoughts and events, and endeavours to express them in stronger and statelier language than others. His poetry stands like a Martello tower by the side of his subject. He does not, like Mr. Wordsworth, lift poetry from the ground, or create a sentiment out of nothing. He does not describe a daisy or a periwinkle, but the cedar or the cypress: not 'poor men's cottages, but princes' palaces.' His *Childe Harold* contains a lofty and impassioned review of the great events of history, of the mighty objects left as wrecks of time; but he dwells chiefly on what is familiar to the mind of every school-boy, has brought out few new traits of feeling or thought, and has done no more than justice to the reader's preconceptions by the sustained force and brilliancy of his style and imagery.

Lord Byron's earlier productions, *Lara*, the *Corsair*, etc., were wild and gloomy romances, put into rapid and shining verse. They discover the madness of poetry, together with the inspiration: sullen, moody, capricious, fierce, inexorable: gloating on beauty, thirsting for revenge: hurrying from the extremes of pleasure to pain, but with nothing permanent, nothing healthy or natural. The gaudy decorations and the morbid sentiments remind one of flowers strewed over the face of death! In his *Childe Harold* (as has been just observed) he assumes a lofty and philosophic tone, and 'reasons high of providence, fore-knowledge, will, and fate.' He takes the highest points in the history of the world, and comments on them from a more commanding eminence. He shows us the crumbling monuments of time; he invokes the great names, the mighty spirit of antiquity. The universe is changed into a stately mausoleum: in solemn measures he chaunts a hymn to fame. Lord Byron has strength and elevation enough to fill up the moulds of our classical and time-hallowed recollections, and to rekindle the earliest aspirations of the mind after greatness and true glory with a pen of fire. The names of Tasso, of Ariosto, of Dante, of Cincinnatus, of Caesar, of Scipio, lose nothing of their pomp or their lustre in his hands, and when he begins and continues a strain of panegyric on such subjects, we indeed sit down with him to a banquet of rich praise, brooding over imperishable glories,

Till Contemplation has her fill.

Lord Byron seems to cast himself indignantly from 'this bank and shoal of time,' or the frail tottering bark that bears up modern reputation, into the huge sea of ancient renown, and to revel there with untired, outspread plume. Even this in him is spleen: his contempt of his contemporaries makes him turn back to the lustrous past, or project himself forward to the dim future! Lord Byron's tragedies, *Faliero*,[2] *Sardanapalus,* etc., are not equal to his other works. They want the essence of the drama. They abound in speeches and descriptions, such as he himself might make either to himself or others, lolling on his couch of a morning, but do not carry the reader out of the poet's mind to the scenes and events recorded. They have neither action, character, nor interest, but are a sort of *gossamer* tragedies, spun out and glittering, and spreading a flimsy veil over the face of nature. Yet he spins them on. Of all that he has done in this way the *Heaven and Earth* (the same subject as Mr. Moore's Loves *of the Angels)* is the best. We prefer it even to *Manfred. Manfred* is merely himself with a fancy-drapery on. But, in the dramatic fragment published in the *Liberal,* the space between Heaven and earth, the stage on which his characters have to pass to and fro, seems to fill his Lordship's imagination; and the Deluge, which he has so finely described, may be said to have drowned all his own idle humours.

We must say we think little of our author's turn for satire. His *English Bards and Scotch Reviewers* is dogmatical and insolent, but without refinement or point. He calls people names, and tries to transfix a character with an epithet, which does not stick, because it has no other foundation than his own petulance and spite; or he endeavours to degrade by alluding to some circumstance of external situation. He says of Mr. Wordsworth's poetry, that 'it is his aversion.' That may be: but whose fault is it? This is the satire of a lord, who is accustomed to have all his whims or dislikes taken for gospel, and who cannot be at the pains to do more than signify his contempt or displeasure. If a great man meets with a rebuff which he does not like, he turns on his heel, and this passes for a repartee. The Noble Author says of a celebrated barrister and critic, that he was 'born in a garret sixteen stories high.' The insinuation is not true, or, if it were, it is low. The allusion degrades the person who makes it, not him to whom it is applied. This is also the satire of a person of birth and quality, who measures all merit by external rank, that is, by his own standard. So his Lordship, in a 'Letter to the Editor of my Grandmother's Review,' addresses him fifty times as *'my dear Robarts';* nor is there any other wit in the article. This is surely a mere assumption of superiority from his Lordship's rank, and is the sort of *quizzing* he might use to a person who came to hire himself as a valet to him at *Long's*. The waiters might laugh; the public will not. In like manner, in the controversy about Pope, he claps Mr. Bowles on the back with a coarse facetious familiarity, as if he were his chaplain whom he had invited to dine with him, or was about to present to a benefice. The reverend divine might submit to the obligation; but he has no occasion to subscribe to the jest. If it is a jest that Mr. Bowles should be a parson and Lord Byron a peer, the world knew this before; there was no need to write a pamphlet to prove it.

The *Don Juan* indeed has great power; but its power is owing to the force of the serious writing, and to the contrast between that and the flashy passages with which it is interlarded. From the sublime to the ridiculous there is but one step. You laugh and are surprised that any one should turn round and *travestie* himself: the drollery is in the utter discontinuity of ideas and feelings. He makes virtue serve as a foil to vice; *dandyism* is (for want of any other) a variety of genius. A classical intoxication is followed by the splashing of sodawater, by frothy effusions of ordinary bile. After the lightning and the hurricane, we are introduced to the interior of the cabin and the contents of the wash-hand basins. The solemn hero of tragedy plays *Scrub* in the farce. This is 'very tolerable and not to be endured.'

The noble Lord is almost the only writer who has prostituted his talents in this way. He hallows in order to desecrate, takes a pleasure in defacing the images of beauty his hands have wrought, and raises our hopes and our belief in goodness to Heaven only to dash them to the earth again, and break them in pieces the more effectually from the very height they have fallen. Our enthusiasm for genius or virtue is thus turned into a jest by the very person who has kindled it, and who thus fatally quenches the spark of both. It is not that Lord Byron is sometimes serious and sometimes trifling, sometimes profligate and sometimes moral; but when he is most serious and most moral, he is only preparing to mortify the unsuspecting reader by putting a pitiful *hoax* upon him. This is a most unaccountable anomaly. It is as if the eagle were to build its eyry in a common sewer, or the owl were seen soaring to the mid-day sun. Such a sight might make one laugh, but one would not wish or expect it to occur more than once![3]

In fact, Lord Byron is the spoiled child of fame as well as fortune. He has taken a surfeit of popularity, and is not contented to delight, unless he can shock, the public. He would force them to admire in spite of decency and common sense; he would have them read what they would read in no one but himself, or he would not give a rush for their applause. He is to be 'a chartered libertine,' from whom insults are favours, whose contempt is to be a new incentive to admiration. His Lordship is hard to please: he is equally averse to notice or neglect, enraged at censure and scorning praise. He tries the patience of the town to the very utmost, and when they show signs of weariness or disgust, threatens to *discard* them. He says he will write on, whether he is read or not. He would never write another page, if it were not to court popular applause, or to affect a superiority over it. In this respect also, Lord Byron presents a striking contrast to Sir Walter Scott. The latter takes what part of the public favour falls to his share, without grumbling (to be sure, he has no reason to complain); the former is always quarrelling with the world about his *modicum* of applause, the *spolia opima* of vanity, and ungraciously throwing the offerings of incense heaped on his shrine back in the faces of his admirers.

Again, there is no taint in the writings of the Author of *Waverley*; all is fair and natural and *above-board*; he never outrages the public mind. He introduces no anomalous character, broaches no staggering opinion. If he goes back to old prejudices and superstitions as a relief to the modern reader, while Lord Byron floats on swelling paradoxes—

Like proud seas under him;

if the one defers too much to the spirit of antiquity, the other panders to the spirit of the age, goes to the very edge of extreme and licentious speculation, and breaks his neck over it. Grossness and levity are the playthings of his pen. It is a ludicrous circumstance that he should have dedicated his *Cain* to the worthy Baronet! Did the latter ever acknowledge the obligation? We are not nice, not very nice; but we do not particularly approve those subjects that shine chiefly from their rottenness: nor do we wish to see the Muses drest out in the flounces of a false or questionable philosophy, like Portia and Nerissa in the garb of Doctors of Law. We like metaphysics as well as Lord Byron; but not to see them making flowery speeches, nor dancing a measure in the fetters of verse. We have as good as hinted, that his Lordship's poetry consists mostly of a tissue of superb common-places; even his paradoxes are *common-place*. They are familiar in the schools: they are only new and striking in his dramas and stanzas by being out of place. In a word, we think that poetry moves best within the circle of nature and received opinion: speculative theory and subtle casuistry are forbidden ground to it.

But Lord Byron often wanders into this ground wantonly, wilfully, and unwarrantably. The only apology we can conceive for the spirit of some of Lord Byron's writings, is the spirit of some of those opposed to him. They would provoke a man to write anything. 'Farthest from them is best.' The extravagance and license of the one seems a proper antidote to the bigotry and narrowness of the other. The first *Vision of Judgment* was a set-off to the second, though

> None but itself could be its parallel.

Perhaps the chief cause of most of Lord Byron's errors is, that he is that anomaly in letters and in society, a Noble Poet. It is a double privilege, almost too much for humanity. He has all the pride of birth and genius. The strength of his imagination leads him to indulge in fantastic opinions; the elevation of his rank sets censure at defiance. He becomes a pampered egotist. He has a seat in the House of Lords, a niche in the Temple of Fame. Every-day mortals, opinions, things are not good enough for him to touch or think of. A mere nobleman is, in his estimation, but 'the tenth transmitter of a foolish face': a mere man of genius is no better than a worm. His Muse is also a lady of quality. The people are not polite enough for him; the Court is not sufficiently intellectual. He hates the one and despises the other. By hating and despising others, he does not learn to be satisfied with himself. A fastidious man soon grows querulous and splenetic. If there is nobody but ourselves to come up to our idea of fancied perfection, we easily get tired of our idol.

When a man is tired of what he is, by a natural perversity he sets up for what he is not. If he is a poet, he pretends to be a metaphysician: if he is a patrician in rank and feeling, he would fain be one of the people. His ruling motive is not the love of the people, but of distinction: not of truth, but of singularity. He patronizes men of letters out of vanity, and deserts them from caprice or from the advice of friends. He embarks in an obnoxious publication to provoke censure, and leaves it to shift for itself for fear of scandal. We do not like Sir Walter's gratuitous servility: we like Lord Byron's preposterous *liberalism* little better. He may affect the principles of equality, but he resumes his privilege of peerage, upon occasion. His Lordship has made great offers of service to the Greeks—money and horses. He is at present in Cephalonia, waiting the event!

We had written thus far when news came of the death of Lord Byron, and put an end at once to a strain of somewhat peevish invective, which was intended to meet his eye, not to insult his memory. Had we known that we were writing his epitaph, we must have done it with a different feeling. As it is, we think it better and more like himself, to let what we had written stand, than to take up our leaden shafts, and try to melt them into 'tears of sensibility,' or mould them into dull praise and an affected show of candour. We were not silent during the author's life-time, either for his reproof or encouragement (such as we could give, and *he* did not disdain to accept), nor can we now turn undertakers' men to fix the glittering plate upon his coffin, or fall into the procession of popular woe. Death cancels every thing but truth, and strips a man of every thing but genius and virtue. It is a sort of natural canonization. It makes the meanest of us sacred; it installs the poet in his immortality, and lifts him to the skies. Death is the great assayer of the sterling ore of talent. At his touch the drossy particles fall off, the irritable, the personal, the gross, and mingle with the dust—the finer and more ethereal part mounts with the winged spirit to watch over our latest memory, and protect our bones from insult. We consign the least worthy qualities to oblivion, and cherish the nobler and imperishable nature with double pride and fondness.

Nothing could show the real superiority of genius in a more striking point of view than the idle contests and the public indifference about the place of Lord Byron's interment, whether in Westminster Abbey or his own family vault. A king must have a coronation—a nobleman a funeral-procession. The man is nothing without the pageant. The poet's cemetery is the human mind, in which he sows the seeds of never-ending thought—his monument is to be found in his works: Nothing can cover his high fame but Heaven; No pyramids set off his memory, But the eternal substance of his greatness. Lord Byron is dead: he also died a martyr to his zeal in the cause of freedom, for the last, best hopes of man. Let that be his excuse and his epitaph!

Notes
1. This Essay was written just before Lord Byron's death.
2 'Don Juan was my Moscow, and Faliero
   My Leipsic, and my Mont St. Jean seems Cain.' *(Don Juan,* Canto xi.)
3. This censure applies to the first Cantos of *Don Juan* much more than to the last. It has been called a *Tristram Shandy* in rhyme: it is rather a poem written about itself.

—William Hazlitt, *Lord Byron.*
The Spirit of the Age, 1825

JOHN GALT (1830)

The Scottish novelist John Galt (1779–1839) had met and befriended Byron while traveling in Europe. On his return to London, he wrote an account of his travels, and decades later he published the first full biography of Lord Byron. Galt became an important figure as the secretary to the Canada Company, yet his novels deal mainly with his Scottish origin.

I am not disposed to think with many of those who rank the genius of Byron almost as supreme, that he has shown less skill in the construction of his plots, and the development of his tales, than might have been expected from one so splendidly endowed; for it has ever appeared to me that he has accomplished in them every thing he proposed to attain, and that in this consists one of his great merits. His mind, fervid and impassioned, was in all his compositions, except *Don Juan,* eagerly fixed on the catastrophe. He ever held the goal full in view, and drove to it in the most immediate manner. By this straightforward simplicity all the interest which intricacy excites was of necessity disregarded. He is therefore not treated justly when it is supposed that he might have done better had he shown more art: the wonder is that he should have produced such magnificent effects with so little. He could not have made the satiated and meditative Harold so darkling and excursive, had he treated him as the hero of a scholastic epic. The might of the poet in such creations lay in the riches of his diction, and in the felicity with which he described feelings in relation to the aspect of scenes and the reminiscences with which the scenes themselves were associated.

If in language and plan he be so excellent, it may be asked why should he not be honoured with that pre-eminent niche in the temple which so many in the world have by suffrage assigned to him? Simply because with all the life and beauty of his style, the vigour and truth of his descriptions, the boldness of his conceptions, and the reach of his vision in the dark abysses of passion, Lord Byron was but imperfectly acquainted with human nature. He looked but on the outside of man. No characteristic action distinguishes one of his heroes from another, nor is there much dissimilarity in their sentiments; they have no individuality; they stalk and pass in mist and gloom, grim, ghastly, and portentous, mysterious shadows, entities of the twilight, weird things like the sceptred effigies of the unborn issue of Banquo.

Combined with vast power, Lord Byron possessed, beyond all question, the greatest degree of originality of any poet of this age. In this rare quality he has no parallel in any age. All other poets and inventive authors are measured in their excellence by the accuracy with which they fit sentiments appropriate not only to the characters they create, but to the situations in which they place them: the works of Lord Byron display the opposite to this and with the most extraordinary splendour. He endows his creations with his own qualities; he finds in the situations in which he places them only opportunities to express what he has himself felt or suffered; and yet he mixes so much probability in the circumstances, that they are always eloquently proper. He does every thing, as it were, the reverse of other poets; in the air and sea, which have been in all times the emblems of change and the similitudes of inconstancy, he has discovered the very principles of permanency. The ocean in his view, not by its vastness, its unfathomable depths, and its limitless extent, becomes an image of deity, but by its unchangeable character!

The variety of his productions present a prodigious display of power. In his short career he has entitled himself to be ranked in the first class of the British poets for quantity alone. By *Childe Harold*, and his other poems of the same mood, he has extended the scope of feeling, made us acquainted with new trains of association, awakened sympathies which few suspected themselves of possessing; and he has laid open darker recesses in the bosom than were previously supposed to exist. The deep and dreadful caverns of remorse had long been explored; but he was the first to visit the bottomless pit of satiety.

The delineation of that Promethean fortitude which defied conscience, as he has shown it in *Manfred*, is his greatest achievement. The terrific fables of Marlowe, and of Goethe, in their respective versions of the legend of Faustus, had disclosed the utmost writhings which remorse, in the fiercest of its torments, can express; but what are those Laocoon agonies to the sublime serenity of *Manfred*. In the power, the originality, and the genius combined, of that unexampled performance, Lord Byron has placed himself on an equality with Milton. The Satan of the *Paradise Lost* is animated by motives, and dignified by an eternal enterprise. He hath purposes of infinite prospect to perform, and an immeasurable ambition to satisfy. Manfred hath neither purpose, nor ambition, nor any desire that seeks gratification. He hath done a deed which severs him from hope, as everlastingly as the apostacy with the angels has done Satan. He acknowledges no contrition to bespeak commiseration, he complains of no wrong to justify revenge, for he feels none; he despises sympathy, and almost glories in his perdition. He is like the spirit of one who, after crimes, having committed self-slaughter, stands calm in the bucket as he is lowered down the hatchway of hell.

The creation of such a character is in the sublimest degree of originality; to give it appropriate thoughts and feelings required powers worthy of the conception; and to make it susceptible of being contemplated as within the scope and range of human sympathy, places Byron above all his contemporaries and antecedents. Milton has described in Satan the greatest of human passions, supernatural attributes, directed to immortal intents, and stung with inextinguishable revenge; but Satan is only a dilatation of man. Manfred is loftier, and worse than Satan; he has conquered punishment, having within himself a greater than hell can inflict. There is a fearful mystery in this conception; it is only by solemnly questioning the spirits that lurk within the dark metaphors in which Manfred expresses himself, that the hideous secrets of the character can be conjectured.

But although in intellectual power, and in creative originality, Byron is entitled to stand on the highest peak of the mountain, his verse is often so harsh, and his language so obscure, that in the power of delighting he is only a poet of the second class. He had all the talent and the means requisite to imbody his conceptions in a manner worthy of their might and majesty; his treasury was rich in every thing rare and beautiful for illustration, but he possessed not the instinct requisite to guide him in the selection of the things necessary to the inspiration of delight;—he could give his statue life and beauty, and warmth, and motion, and eloquence, but not a tuneful voice.

Some curious metaphysicians, in their subtle criticism, have said that *Don Juan* was but the bright side of *Childe Harold,* and that all its most brilliant imagery was similar to that of which the dark and the shadows were delineated in his other works. It may be so. And, without question, a great similarity runs through every thing that has come from the poet's pen; but it is a family resemblance, the progeny are all like one another; but where are those who are like them? I know of no author in prose or rhyme, in the English language, with whom Byron can be compared. Imitators of his manner there will be often and many, but he will ever remain one of the few whom the world acknowledges are alike supreme, and yet unlike each other—epochal characters, who mark extraordinary periods in history.

Raphael is the only man of pre-eminence whose career can be compared with that of Byron, at an age when the genius of most men is but in the dawning, they had both attained their meridian of glory, and they both died so early, that it may be said they were lent to the world only to show the height to which the mind may ascend when time shall be allowed to accomplish the full cultivation of such extraordinary endowments.

—John Galt, *The Life of Lord Byron,*
1830, chapter 49

Johann Wolfgang von Goethe (1830)

Although Byron knew little German, he was eager to acquaint himself— albeit in translation—with the works of Goethe (1749–1832). Byron was drawn particularly to *Faust (Part One)*, to which his drama *Manfred* is clearly indebted, as Goethe recognized in his positive review. Byron further dedicated his drama *Sardanapalus* to "the Illustrious Goethe," his "liege-lord," and in the preface to his posthumously published work, *The Deformed Transformed,* acknowledged its connections to Goethe's *Faust.* Goethe was no less taken with the genius of Byron, to which he paid enthusiastic tribute in some detail in his conversations with Eckermann in the 1820s. In the second part of his *Faust,* Euphorion, the son born to Faust and Helen of Troy who soars high but plunges—Icaruslike—to his death, assumes the characteristics of Byron.

Goethe continued to talk of Lord Byron. "With that disposition," said he, "which always leads him into the illimitable, the restraint he imposed upon himself by the observance of the three unities becomes him. If he had but known how to endure moral restraint also! That he could not was his ruin; it may be said he was destroyed by his own unbridled temperament.

"But he was too much in the dark about himself. He lived impetuously for the day, and neither knew nor thought what he was doing. Permitting everything to himself, and excusing nothing in others, he necessarily put himself in a bad position, and made the world his foe. At the very beginning, he offended the most distinguished literary men by his *English Bards and Scotch Reviewers.* To be permitted only to live after this, he was obliged to go back a step. In his succeeding works, he continued in the path of opposition and fault-finding. Church and State were not left unassailed. This reckless conduct drove him from England, and would in time have driven him from Europe also. Everywhere it was too narrow for him, with the most perfect personal freedom he felt confined; the world seemed a prison. His Grecian expedition was the result of no voluntary resolution; his misunderstanding with the world drove him to it.

"Not only did the renunciation of what was hereditary and patriotic cause the personal destruction of this distinguished man; but his revolutionary turn, and the constant mental agitation with which it was combined, did not allow his talent a fair development. Moreover, his perpetual negation and fault-finding is injurious even to his excellent works. For not only does the discontent of the poet infect the reader, but the end of all opposition is negation; and negation is nothing. If I call *bad* bad, what do I gain? But if I call *good* bad, I do a great deal of mischief. He who will work aright must never rail, must not trouble himself at all about what is ill done, but only do well himself. The great point is, not to pull down, but to build up; in this humanity finds pure joy.

"Lord Byron," continued Goethe, "is to be regarded as a man, as an Englishman, and as a great talent. His good qualities belong chiefly to the man, his bad to the Englishman and the peer, his talent is incommensurable.

"All Englishmen are, as such, without reflection, properly so called; distractions and party spirit will not permit them to perfect themselves in quiet. But they are great as practical men.

"Thus, Lord Byron could never attain reflection on himself, and on this account his maxims in general are not successful, as is shown by his creed, 'much money, no authority,' for much money always paralyses authority.

"But where he will create, he always succeeds; with him inspiration supplies the place of reflection. He was obliged to go on poetizing; and then everything that came from the man, especially from his heart, was excellent. He produced his best things as women do pretty children, without thinking about it or knowing how it was done.

"He is a great talent, a born talent, and I never saw the true poetical power greater in any man. In the apprehension of external objects, and a clear penetration into past situations, he is quite as great as Shakespeare. But, as a pure individuality, Shakespeare is his superior. This was felt by Byron; and on this account he does not say much of Shakespeare, although he knows whole passages by heart. He would willingly have denied him altogether; for Shakespeare's cheerfulness is in his way, and he feels that he is no match for it. Pope he does not deny, for he had no cause to fear him: on the contrary, he mentions him, and shows him respect when he can; for he knows well enough that Pope is a mere foil to himself."

Goethe seemed inexhaustible on the subject of Byron. After a few digressions, he proceeded thus:

"His high rank as an English peer was very injurious to Byron; for every talent is oppressed by the outer world—how much more, then, when there is such high birth and so great a fortune? A middle rank is much more favourable to talent, so we find all great artists and poets in the middle classes. Byron's predilection for the unbounded could not have been nearly so dangerous with more humble birth and smaller means. As it was, he was able to put every fancy into practice, and this involved him in innumerable scrapes. Besides, how could one of such high rank be inspired with awe and respect by any rank whatever? He spoke out whatever he felt, and this brought him into ceaseless conflict with the world.

"It is surprising to remark," continued Goethe, "how large a portion of the life of a rich Englishman of rank is passed in duels and elopements. Lord Byron himself says, that his father carried off three ladies. And let any man be a steady son after that.

"Properly speaking, he lived perpetually in a state of nature, and with his mode of existence the necessity for self-defence floated daily before his eyes. Hence his constant pistolshooting. Every moment he expected to be called out.

"He could not live alone. Hence, with all his oddities, he was very indulgent to his associates. He one evening read his fine poem on the death of Sir John Moore, and his noble friends did not know what to make of it. This did not move him, but he put it away again. As a poet, he really showed himself a lamb. Another would have commended them to the devil."

—Johann Wolfgang von Goethe, quoted in
Johann Peter Eckermann, *Conversations with Goethe*, 1830, tr. John Oxenford

WILLIAM H. PRESCOTT "ENGLISH LITERATURE OF THE NINETEENTH CENTURY" (1832)

The American historian William Hickling Prescott (1796–1859) is best known for his *History of the Conquest of Mexico* (1843). While a student at Harvard, he lost sight in his left eye and later his vision in the other eye was impaired also. This triggered his decision to become a man of letters, and he launched his career with an essay on Byron that appeared in the prestigious *North American Review* in 1821. Over the next two decades, he published many articles in the journal, and they were later collected in *Biographical and Critical Miscellanies* (1845) and *Critical and Historical Essays* (1850).

Byron was a paradox in everything. He was at once a cold-blooded satirist and a man of sentiment; an aristocrat and a radical; a Platonist and an Epicurean; the most sublime and the most sensual of mortals; 'half dust, half deity,' to borrow his own phrase; but the most barefaced paradox, was his ostentatious defence in prose of Pope's poetical system, which, in his poetry, he had been all his life endeavoring to subvert. The key to Byron's eccentricities is to be found in his total want of principle, and his uncontrollable passions. To the last is to be referred, moreover, much of what is grand and striking in his poetry. Many were led to charge him with affectation. The history of his life, however, which may be called passion put into action, shows how uniformly he sacrificed to his passions all his worldly interests and better hopes. His poetry gains somewhat in effect by our conviction of this, for sincerity is essential to the full success of the poet as of the orator; and, in this point of view, the exhibition of actual vice is less detrimental to his interest than the affectation of it.

Much stress has been laid on the mischievous tendency of Byron's philosophy. But, in truth, there is little in his writings to deserve that name. He had no principles to build on, and seems to have been incapable of forming any settled system, or even a systematic attack on any thing. He levelled his shafts pretty indiscriminately at whatever men prize most in this life, or look forward to with hope in the next. This sort of random aim was little better than shooting in the dark. The following sarcastic lines show the miscellaneous range of his hostilities.

> I do believe,
> *Though I have found them not,* that there may be
> Words which are things,—hopes which will not deceive,
> And virtues which are merciful, nor weave
> Snares for the failing; I would also deem,
> O'er other's griefs that some sincerely grieve;
> That two, or one, are almost what they seem,—
> That goodness is no name, and happiness no dream.

Byron's poetry is much more to be dreaded, for the morbid appetite for stimulants which it has a tendency to nourish, especially in young minds, as well as for the light-hearted raillery with which it touches the most serious topics, and the seductive coloring which it too often throws over the grossest pleasures of the senses. He must have sat to himself for his portrait of Rousseau.

> Here the self-torturing sophist, wild Rousseau,
> The apostle of affliction, he who threw
> Enchantment over passion, and from woe
> Wrung overwhelming eloquence, first drew
> The breath which made him wretched; yet he knew
> How to make madness beautiful, and cast
> O'er erring deeds and thoughts, a heavenly hue
> Of words, like sunbeams, dazzling as they past
> The eyes, which o'er them shed tears feelingly and fast.

Byron's poetry is eminently characteristic of the present age. It is essentially undramatic, and altogether repugnant to the social spirit of the age of Shakspeare. It is no less so to the placid tenor and perspicuity of Queen Anne's. It is purely egotistical, devoted in some form or other to self-analysis, the most melancholy, in its influence on the soul, of all occupations. It deals largely in abstruse speculations on moral or metaphysical theorems. It is written entirely for the closet, and pre-supposes a more deeply thinking and deeply read community, than has existed in any preceding period. His attempts in the drama have signally failed, and it may be doubted even, whether he could ever have established his present reputation in other walks, in any other than the present age, so mutually well adapted to each other were his own character and that of the times.

Some persons at this day, especially those wedded to the discipline of the preceding school of poetry, contest Byron's pretensions to high rank in his art. These critics are too much annoyed by his defects, by his hyperbolical passion, by the shadowy mists which hang over many of his fine thoughts, by the startling abruptions, and even dislocations of his periods, in short, by his perpetual lapses, in every way, from what they have been taught to venerate as classical decorum.

It is remarkable, that Mr. Gifford, whose poetical character was formed on the models of the last age, should have been among the first to detect the existence of the celestial spark in the young poet's breast, and confidently to predict his future triumphs; a prediction abundantly verified by the event, for there certainly has been no poet in our time, who, notwithstanding some discrepancy of judgment, has produced so general and deep a sensation. There is, probably, no poet in the language indeed, who has touched with a bolder hand the various chords of passion, who has shown more of the sadness of remorse, the bitterness of hatred, the deep tenderness of love, or any other expression of an agonized and overexcited sensibility; no one who has shed such enchanting colors over the shadowy past, or sketched with more delicate hand the features of the various races with whom he has mingled, or incorporated his own soul, as it were, with such grand and beautiful forms of nature. He is, indeed, emphatically the poet of passion. We must not omit his extraordinary mastery of our language, which he has made an instrument of greater compass, on the whole, than any writer since the time of Milton; not for the utterance of a monotonous melody, which depends chiefly on the accurate measurement of feet and syllables, and belongs rather to the eye than the ear, but that various harmony, which, adapting the expression, as far as possible, to the various movements of the spirit, can proceed only from thoughts that 'voluntary move harmonious numbers.'

—William H. Prescott, "English Literature of the
Nineteenth Century," *North American Review*,
July 1832, pp. 176–178

Thomas Babington Macaulay
"Moore's Life of Lord Byron" (1831)

Thomas Babington Macaulay, the first Baron Macaulay (1800–1859), was a British poet and historian and a Whig politician who was one of the two Members of Parliament for Edinburgh. He wrote a voluminous *History of*

England, which became a bestseller, and many essays, reviews, and letters. Politically, he worked for the abolition of slavery and, while serving on the Supreme Council of India, he was instrumental in creating the foundations of bilingual colonial India as well as establishing a criminal law system.

During the twenty years which followed the death of Cowper, the revolution in English poetry was fully consummated. None of the writers of this period, not even Sir Walter Scott, contributed so much to the consummation as Lord Byron. Yet Lord Byron contributed to it unwillingly, and with constant self-reproach and shame. All his tastes and inclinations led him to take part with the school of poetry which was going out against the school which was coming in. Of Pope himself he spoke with extravagant admiration. He did not venture directly to say that the little man of Twickenham was a greater poet than Shakspeare or Milton; but he hinted pretty clearly that he thought so. Of his contemporaries, scarcely any had so much of his admiration as Mr. Gifford, who, considered as a poet, was merely Pope, without Pope's wit and fancy, and whose satires are decidedly inferior in vigour and poignancy to the very imperfect juvenile performance of Lord Byron himself. He now and then praised Mr. Wordsworth and Mr. Coleridge, but ungraciously and without cordiality. When he attacked them, he brought his whole soul to the work. Of the most elaborate of Mr. Wordsworth's poems he could find nothing to say, but that it was "clumsy, and frowsy, and his aversion." *Peter Bell* excited his spleen to such a degree that he evoked the shades of Pope and Dryden, and demanded of them whether it were possible that such trash could evade contempt? In his heart he thought his own *Pilgrimage of Harold* inferior to his Imitation of Horace's *Art of Poetry,* a feeble echo of Pope and Johnson. This insipid performance he repeatedly designed to publish, and was withheld only by the solicitations of his friends. He has distinctly declared his approbation of the unities, the most absurd laws by which genius was ever held in servitude. In one of his works, we think in his letter to Mr. Bowles, he compares the poetry of the eighteenth century to the Parthenon, and that of the nineteenth to a Turkish mosque, and boasts that, though he had assisted his contemporaries in building their grotesque and barbarous edifice, he had never joined them in defacing the remains of a chaster and more graceful architecture. In another letter he compares the change which had recently passed on English poetry to the decay of Latin poetry after the Augustan age. In the time of Pope, he tells his friend, it was all Horace with us. It is all Claudian now.

For the great old masters of the art he had no very enthusiastic veneration. In his letter to Mr. Bowles he uses expressions which clearly indicate that he preferred Pope's *Iliad* to the original. Mr. Moore confesses that his friend was no very fervent admirer of Shakspeare. Of all the poets of the first class, Lord Byron seems to have admired Dante and Milton most. Yet in the fourth canto of *Childe Harold,* he places Tasso, a writer not merely inferior to them, but of quite a different order of mind, on at least a footing of equality with them. Mr. Hunt is, we suspect, quite correct in saying that Lord Byron could see little or no merit in Spenser.

But Byron the critic and Byron the poet were two very different men. The effects of the noble writer's theory may indeed often be traced in his practice. But his disposition led him to accommodate himself to the literary taste of the age in which he lived; and his talents would have enabled him to accommodate himself to the taste of any age. Though he said much of his contempt for mankind, and though he boasted that amidst the inconstancy of fortune and of fame he was all-sufficient to himself, his literary career indicated nothing of that lonely and unsocial pride which he affected. We cannot conceive him, like Milton or Wordsworth, defying the criticism of his contemporaries, retorting their scorn, and labouring on a poem in the full assurance that it would be unpopular, and in the full assurance that it would be immortal. He has said, by the mouth of one of his heroes, in speaking of political greatness, that "he must serve who fain would sway;" and this he assigns as a reason for not entering into political life. He did not consider that the sway which he had exercised in literature had been purchased by servitude, by the sacrifice of his own taste to the taste of the public.

He was the creature of his age; and whenever he had lived he would have been the creature of his age. Under Charles the First Byron would have been more quaint than Donne. Under Charles the Second the rants of Byron's rhyming plays would have pitted it, boxed it, and galleried it, with those of any Bays or Bilboa. Under George the First the monotonous smoothness of Byron's versification and the terseness of his expression would have made Pope himself envious.

As it was, he was the man of the last thirteen years of the eighteenth century, and of the first twenty-three years of the nineteenth century. He belonged half to the old, and half to the new school of poetry. His personal taste led him to the former; his thirst of praise to the latter; his talents were equally suited to both. His fame was a common ground on which the zealots of both sides, Gifford, for example, and Shelley, might meet. He was the representative, not of either literary party, but of both at once, and of their conflict, and of the victory by which that conflict was terminated. His poetry fills and measures the whole of the vast interval through which our literature has moved since the time of Johnson. It touches the *Essay on Man* at the one extremity, and the *Excursion* at the other.

There are several parallel instances in literary history. Voltaire, for example, was the connecting link between the France of Lewis the Fourteenth and the France of Lewis the Sixteenth, between Racine and Boileau on the one side, and Condorcet and Beaumarchais on the other. He, like Lord Byron, put himself at the head of an intellectual revolution, dreading it all the time, murmuring at it, sneering at it, yet choosing rather to move before his age in any direction than to be left behind and forgotten. Dryden was the connecting link between the literature of the age of James the First, and the literature of the age of Anne. Oromasdes and Arimanes fought for him. Arimanes carried him off. But his heart was to the last with Oromasdes. Lord Byron was, in the same manner, the mediator between two generations, between two hostile poetical sects. Though always sneering at Mr. Wordsworth, he was yet, though perhaps unconsciously, the interpreter between Mr. Wordsworth and the multitude. In the *Lyrical Ballads* and the *Excursion* Mr. Wordsworth appeared as the high priest of a worship, of which nature was the idol. No poems have ever indicated a more exquisite perception of the beauty of the outer world, or a more passionate love and reverence for that beauty. Yet they were not popular; and it is not likely that they ever will be popular as the poetry of Sir Walter Scott is popular. The feeling which pervaded them was too deep for general sympathy. Their style was often too mysterious for general comprehension. They made a few esoteric disciples, and many scoffers. Lord Byron founded what may be called an exoteric Lake school; and all the readers of verse in England, we might say in Europe, hastened to sit at his feet. What Mr. Wordsworth had said like a recluse, Lord Byron said like a man of the world, with less profound feeling, but with more perspicuity, energy, and conciseness. We would refer our readers to the last two cantos of *Childe Harold* and to *Manfred,* in proof of these observations.

Lord Byron, like Mr. Wordsworth, had nothing dramatic in his genius. He was indeed the reverse of a great dramatist, the very antithesis to a great dramatist. All his characters, Harold looking on the sky, from which his country and the sun are disappearing together, the Giaour, standing apart in the gloom of the side aisle, and casting a haggard scowl from under his long hood at the crucifix and the censer, Conrad leaning on his sword by the watch-tower, Lara smiling on the dancers, Alp gazing steadily on the fatal cloud as it passes before the moon, Manfred wandering among the precipices of Berne, Azzo on the judgment-seat, Ugo at the bar, Lambro frowning on the siesta of his daughter and Juan, Cain presenting his unacceptable offering, are essentially the same. The varieties are varieties merely of age, situation, and outward show. If ever Lord Byron attempted to exhibit men of a different kind, he always made them either insipid or unnatural. Selim is nothing.

Bonnivart is nothing. Don Juan, in the first and best cantos, is a feeble copy of the Page in the *Marriage of Figaro.* Johnson, the man whom Juan meets in the slave-market, is a most striking failure. How differently would Sir Walter Scott have drawn a bluff, fearless Englishman, in such a situation! The portrait would have seemed to walk out of the canvass.

Sardanapalus is more coarsely drawn than any dramatic personage that we can remember. His heroism and his effeminacy, his contempt of death and his dread of a weighty helmet, his kingly resolution to be seen in the foremost ranks, and the anxiety with which he calls for a looking-glass, that he may be seen to advantage, are contrasted, it is true, with all the point of Juvenal. Indeed the hint of the character seems to have been taken from what Juvenal says of Otho:

> Speculum civilis sarcina belli. Nimirum summi ducis est occidere Galbam, Et curare cutem summi constantia civis, Bedriaci in campo spolium affectare Palati, Et pressum in faciem digitis extendere panem.

These are excellent lines in a satire. But it is not the business of the dramatist to exhibit characters in this sharp antithetical way. It is not thus that Shakspeare makes Prince Hal rise from the rake of Eastcheap into the hero of Shrewsbury, and sink again into the rake of Eastcheap. It is not thus that Shakspeare has exhibited the union of effeminacy and valour in Antony. A dramatist cannot commit a greater error than that of following those pointed descriptions of character in which satirists and historians indulge so much. It is by rejecting what is natural that satirists and historians produce these striking characters. Their great object generally is to ascribe to every man as many contradictory qualities as possible: and this is an object easily attained. By judicious selection and judicious exaggeration, the intellect and the disposition of any human being might be described as being made up of nothing but startling contrasts. If the dramatist attempts to create a being answering to one of these descriptions, he fails, because he reverses an imperfect analytical process. He produces, not a man, but a personified epigram. Very eminent writers have fallen into this snare. Ben Jonson has given us a Hermogenes, taken from the lively lines of Horace; but the inconsistency which is so amusing in the satire appears unnatural and disgusts us in the play. Sir Walter Scott has committed a far more glaring error of the same kind in the novel of Peveril. Admiring, as every judicious reader must admire, the keen and vigorous lines in which Dryden satirised the Duke of Buckingham, Sir Walter attempted to make a Duke of Buckingham to suit them, a real living Zimri; and he made, not a man, but the most grotesque of all monsters. A writer who should attempt to introduce into a play or a novel such a Wharton as the Wharton of Pope, or a Lord Hervey answering to Sporus, would fail in the same manner.

But to return to Lord Byron; his women, like his men, are all of one breed. Haidee is a half-savage and girlish Julia; Julia is a civilised and matronly Haidée. Leila is a wedded Zuleika, Zuleika a virgin Leila. Gulnare and Medora appear to have been intentionally opposed to each other. Yet the difference is a difference of situation only. A slight change of circumstances would, it should seem, have sent Gulnare to the lute of Medora, and armed Medora with the dagger of Gulnare.

It is hardly too much to say, that Lord Byron could exhibit only one man and only one woman, a man proud, moody, cynical, with defiance on his brow, and misery in his heart, a scorner of his kind, implacable in revenge, yet capable of deep and strong affection: a woman all softness and gentleness, loving to caress and to be caressed, but capable of being transformed by passion into a tigress.

Even these two characters, his only two characters, he could not exhibit dramatically. He exhibited them in the manner, not of Shakspeare, but of Clarendon. He analysed them; he made them analyse themselves; but he did not make them show themselves. We are told, for example, in many lines of great force and spirit, that the speech of Lara was bitterly sarcastic, that he talked little of his travels, that if he was much questioned about them, his answers became short, and his brow gloomy. But we have none of Lara's sarcastic speeches or short answers. It is not thus that the great masters of human nature have portrayed human beings. Homer never tells us that Nestor loved to relate long stories about his youth. Shakspeare never tells us that in the mind of Iago every thing that is beautiful and endearing was associated with some filthy and debasing idea.

It is curious to observe the tendency which the dialogue of Lord Byron always has to lose its character of a dialogue, and to become soliloquy. The scenes between Manfred and the Chamois-hunter, between Manfred and the Witch of the Alps, between Manfred and the Abbot, are instances of this tendency. Manfred, after a few unimportant speeches, has all the talk to himself. The other interlocutors are nothing more than good listeners. They drop an occasional question or ejaculation which sets Manfred off again on the inexhaustible topic of his personal feelings. If we examine the fine passages in Lord Byron's dramas, the description of Rome, for example, in *Manfred,* the description of a Venetian revel in *Marino Faliero,* the concluding invective which the old doge pronounces against Venice, we shall find that there is nothing dramatic in these speeches, that they derive none of their effect from the character or situation of the speaker, and that they would have been as fine, or finer, if they had been published as fragments of blank verse by Lord Byron. There is scarcely a speech in Shakspeare of which the same could be said. No skilful reader of the plays of Shakspeare can endure to see what are called the fine things taken out, under the name of "Beauties" or of "Elegant Extracts," or to hear any single passage, "To be or not to be," for example, quoted as a sample of the great poet. "To be or not to be" has merit undoubtedly as a composition. It would have merit if put into the mouth of a chorus. But its merit as a composition vanishes when compared with its merit as belonging to *Hamlet*. It is not too much to say that the great plays of Shakspeare would lose less by being deprived of all the passages which are commonly called the fine passages, than those passages lose by being read separately from the play. This is perhaps the highest praise which can be given to a dramatist.

On the other hand, it may be doubted whether there is, in all Lord Byron's plays, a single remarkable passage which owes any portion of its interest or effect to its connection with the characters or the action. He has written only one scene, as far as we can recollect, which is dramatic even in manner, the scene between Lucifer and Cain. The conference is animated, and each of the interlocutors has a fair share of it. But this scene, when examined, will be found to be a confirmation of our remarks. It is a dialogue only in form. It is a soliloquy in essence. It is in reality a debate carried on within one single unquiet and sceptical mind. The questions and the answers, the objections and the solutions, all belong to the same character.

A writer who showed so little dramatic skill in works professedly dramatic was not likely to write narrative with dramatic effect. Nothing could indeed be more rude and careless than the structure of his narrative poems. He seems to have thought, with the hero of the *Rehearsal,* that the plot was good for nothing but to bring in fine things. His two longest works, *Childe Harold* and *Don Juan,* have no plan whatever. Either of them might have been extended to any length, or cut short at any point. The state in which the *Giaour* appears illustrates the manner in which all Byron's poems were constructed. They are all, like the *Giaour,* collections of fragments; and, though there may be no empty spaces marked by asterisks, it is still easy to perceive, by the clumsiness of the joining, where the parts for the sake of which the whole was composed end and begin.

It was in description and meditation that Byron excelled. "Description," as he said in *Don Juan,* "was his forte." His manner is indeed peculiar, and is almost unequalled; rapid, sketchy, full of vigour; the selection happy; the strokes few and bold. In spite of the reverence which we feel for the genius of Mr. Wordsworth we cannot but think that the minuteness of his descriptions often diminishes their effect. He has accustomed himself to gaze on nature with the eye of a lover, to dwell on every feature, and to mark every change of aspect. Those beauties which strike the most negligent observer, and those which only a close attention discovers, are equally familiar to him and are equally prominent in his poetry. The proverb of old Hesiod, that half is often more than the whole, is eminently applicable to description. The policy of the Dutch who cut down most of the precious trees in the Spice Islands, in order to raise the value of what remained, was a policy which poets would do well to imitate. It was a policy which no poet understood better than Lord Byron. Whatever his faults might be, he was never, while his mind retained its vigour, accused of prolixity.

His descriptions, great as was their intrinsic merit, derived their principal interest from the feeling which always mingled with them. He was himself the beginning, the middle, and the end, of all his own poetry, the hero of every tale, the chief object in every landscape. Harold, Lara, Manfred, and a crowd of other characters, were universally considered merely as loose incognitos of Byron; and there is every reason to believe that he meant them to be so considered. The wonders of the outer world, the Tagus, with the mighty fleets of England riding on its bosom, the towers of Cintra everhanging the shaggy forest of cork-trees and willows, the glaring marble of Pentelicus, the banks of the Rhine, the glaciers of Clarens, the sweet Lake of Leman, the dell of Egeria with its summer-birds and rustling lizards, the shapeless ruins of Rome overgrown with ivy and wall-flowers, the stars, the sea, the mountains, all were mere accessaries, the background to one dark and melancholy figure.

Never had any writer so vast a command of the whole eloquence of scorn, misanthropy and despair. That Marah was never dry. No art could sweeten, no draughts could exhaust, its perennial waters of bitterness. Never was there such variety in monotony as that of Byron. From maniac laughter to piercing lamentation, there was not a single note of human anguish of which he was not master. Year after year, and month after month, he continued to repeat that to be wretched is the destiny of all; that to be eminently wretched is the destiny of the eminent; that all the desires by which we are cursed lead alike to misery, if they are not gratified, to the misery of disappointment, if they are gratified, to the misery of satiety. His heroes are men who have arrived by different roads at the same goal of despair, who are sick of life, who are at war with society, who are supported in their anguish only by an unconquerable pride resembling that of Prometheus on the rock or of Satan in the burning marl, who can master their agonies by the force of their will, and who, to the last, defy the whole power of earth and heaven. He always described himself as a man of the same kind with his favourite creations, as a man whose heart had been withered, whose capacity for happiness was gone and could not be restored, but whose invincible spirit dared the worst that could befall him here or hereafter.

How much of this morbid feeling sprang from an original disease of the mind, how much from real misfortune, how much from the nervousness of dissipation, how much was fanciful, how much was merely affected, it is impossible for us, and would probably have been impossible for the most intimate friends of Lord Byron, to decide. Whether there ever existed, or can ever exist, a person answering to the description which he gave of himself may be doubted; but that he was not such a person is beyond all doubt. It is ridiculous to imagine that a man whose mind was really imbued with scorn of his fellow-creatures would have published three or four books every year in order to tell them so; or that a man who could say with truth that he neither sought sympathy nor needed it would have admitted all Europe to hear his farewell to his wife, and his blessings on his child. In the second canto of *Childe Harold,* he tells us that he is insensible to fame and obloquy:

"Ill may such contest now the spirit move, Which heeds nor keen reproof nor partial praise." Yet we know on the best evidence that, a day or two before he published these lines, he was greatly, indeed childishly, elated by the compliments paid to his maiden speech in the House of Lords.

We are far, however, from thinking that his sadness was altogether feigned. He was naturally a man of great sensibility; he had been ill educated; his feelings had been early exposed to sharp trials; he had been crossed in his boyish love; he had been mortified by the failure of his first literary efforts; he was straitened in pecuniary circumstances; he was unfortunate in his domestic relations; the public treated him with cruel injustice: his health and spirits suffered from his dissipated habits of life; he was, on the whole, an unhappy man. He early discovered that, by parading his unhappiness before the multitude, he produced an immense sensation. The world gave him every encouragement to talk about his mental sufferings. The interest which his first confessions excited induced him to affect much that he did not feel; and the affectation probably reacted on his feelings. How far the character in which he exhibited himself was genuine, and how far theatrical, it would probably have puzzled himself to say.

There can be no doubt that this remarkable man owed the vast influence which he exercised over his contemporaries at least as much to his gloomy egotism as to the real power of his poetry. We never could very clearly understand how it is that egotism, so unpopular in conversation, should be so popular in writing; or how it is that men who affect in their compositions qualities and feelings which they have not, impose so much more easily on their contemporaries than on posterity. The interest which the loves of Petrarch excited in his own time, and the pitying fondness with which half Europe looked upon Rousseau, are well known. To readers of our age, the love of Petrarch seems to have been love of that kind which breaks no hearts, and the sufferings of Rousseau to have deserved laughter rather than pity, to have been partly counterfeited, and partly the consequences of his own perverseness and vanity.

What our grandchildren may think of the character of Lord Byron, as exhibited in his poetry, we will not pretend to guess. It is certain, that the interest which he excited during his life is without a parallel in literary history. The feeling with which young readers of poetry regarded him can be conceived only by those who have experienced it. To people who are unacquainted with real calamity, "nothing is so dainty sweet as lovely melancholy." This faint image of sorrow has in all ages been considered by young gentlemen as an agreeable excitement. Old gentlemen and middle-aged gentlemen have so many real causes of sadness that they are rarely inclined "to be as sad as night only for wantonness." Indeed they want the power almost as much as the inclination. We know very few persons engaged in active life who, even if they were to procure stools to be melancholy upon, and were to sit down with all the premeditation of Master Stephen, would be able to enjoy much of what somebody calls the "ecstasy of woe."

Among that large class of young persons whose reading is almost entirely confined to works of imagination, the popularity of Lord Byron was unbounded. They bought pictures of him; they treasured up the smallest relics of him; they learned his poems by heart, and did their best to write like him, and to look like him. Many of them practised at the glass in the hope of catching the curl of the upper lip, and the scowl of the brow, which appear in some of his portraits. A few discarded their neckcloths in imitation of their great leader. For some years the Minerva press sent forth no novel without a mysterious, unhappy, Lara-like peer. The number of hopeful undergraduates and medical students who became things of dark imaginings, on whom the freshness of the heart ceased to fall like dew, whose passions had consumed themselves to dust, and to whom the relief of tears was denied, passes all calculation. This was not the worst. There was created in the minds of many of these enthusiasts a pernicious and absurd association between intellectual power and moral depravity. From the poetry of Lord Byron they drew a system of ethics, compounded of misanthropy and voluptuousness, a system in which the two great commandments were, to hate your neighbour, and to love your neighbour's wife.

This affectation has passed away; and a few more years will destroy whatever yet remains of that magical potency which once belonged to the name of Byron. To us he is still a man, young, noble, and unhappy. To our children he will be merely a writer; and their impartial judgment will appoint his place among writers, without regard to his rank or to his private history. That his poetry will undergo a severe sifting, that much of what has been admired by his contemporaries will be rejected as worthless, we have little doubt. But we have as little doubt, that, after the closest scrutiny, there will still remain much that can only perish with the English language.

—Thomas Babington Macaulay, "Moore's Life
of Lord Byron," 1831, *Critical, Historical, and
Miscellaneous Essays,* 1860, vol. 2, pp. 352–356

GIUSEPPE MAZZINI "BYRON AND GOETHE" (1839)

Giuseppe Mazzini (1805–1872) was an Italian patriot, philosopher, and politician. He fought for the unification of Italy and its liberation from foreign powers, promoted republicanism, and spent many years in exile in Switzerland and England. In his essay on Byron and Goethe, he famously characterizes the former as a subjective individualist, the latter as an objective one.

Byron and Goethe summed up. Was it a defect in them? No; it was the law of the times, and yet society at the present day, twenty years after they have ceased to sing, assumes to condemn them for having been born too soon. Happy indeed are the poets whom God raises up at the commencement of an era, under the rays of the rising sun. A series of generations will lovingly repeat their verses, and attribute to them the new life which they did but foresee in the germ.

Byron and Goethe summed up. This is at once the philosophical explanation of their works, and the secret of their popularity. The spirit of an entire epoch of the European world became incarnate in them ere its decease, even as—in the political sphere—the spirit of Greece and Rome became incarnate before death in Caesar and Alexander. They were the poetic expression of that principle, of which England was the economic, France the political, and Germany the philosophic expression: the last formula, effort, and result of a society founded on the principle of Individuality. That epoch, the mission of which had been, first through the labours of Greek philosophy, and afterwards through Christianity, to rehabilitate, emancipate, and develop individual man—appears to have concentrated in them, in Fichte, in Adam Smith, and in the French school *des droits de l'homme,* its whole energy and power, in order fully to represent and express all that it had achieved for mankind. It was much; but it was not the whole; and therefore it was doomed to pass away. The epoch of individuality was deemed near the goal; when lo! immense horizons were revealed; vast unknown lands in whose untrodden forests the principle of individuality was an insufficient guide. By the long and painful labours of that epoch, the human unknown quantity had been disengaged from the various quantities of different nature by which it had been surrounded; but only to be left weak, isolated, and recoiling in terror from the solitude in which it stood. The political schools of the epoch had proclaimed the sole basis of civil organisation to be the right to liberty and equality (liberty for all), but they had encountered social anarchy by the way. The Philosophy of the Epoch had asserted the Sovereignty of the human *Ego,* and had ended in the mere adoration of *fact,* in *Hegelian* immobility. The Economy of the epoch imagined it had organised *free* competition, while it had but organised the oppression of the weak by the strong; of labour by capital; of poverty by wealth. The Poetry of the epoch had represented individuality in its every phase; had translated in sentiment what science had theoretically demonstrated; and it had encountered the void. But as society at last discovered that the destinies of the race were not contained in a mere problem of liberty, but rather in the harmonisation of liberty with association;—so did poetry discover that the life it had hitherto drawn from individuality alone was doomed to perish for want of aliment; and that its future existence depended on enlarging and transforming its sphere. Both society and poetry uttered a cry of despair: the death-agony of a form of society produced the agitation we have seen constantly increasing in Europe since 1815: the death-agony of a form of poetry evoked Byron and Goethe. I believe this point of view to be the only one that can lead us to a useful and impartial appreciation of these two great spirits.

There are two forms of Individuality; the expressions of its internal and external, or—as the Germans would say—of its subjective and objective life. Byron was the poet of the first, Goethe of the last. In Byron the *Ego* is revealed in all its pride of power, freedom, and desire, in the uncontrolled plenitude of all its faculties; inhaling existence at every pore, eager to seize "the life of life." The world around him neither rules nor tempers him. The Byronian Ego aspires to rule *it;* but solely for dominion's sake, to exercise upon it the Titanic force of his will. Accurately speaking, he cannot be said to derive from it either colour, tone, or image; for it is *he* who colours; he who sings; he whose image is everywhere reflected and reproduced. His poetry emanates from his own soul; to be thence diffused upon things external; he holds his state in the centre of the Universe, and from thence projects the light radiating from the depths of his own mind; as scorching and intense as the concentrated solar ray. Hence that terrible unity which only the superficial reader could mistake for monotony.

Byron appears at the close of one epoch, and before the dawn of the other; in the midst of a community based upon an aristocracy which has outlived the vigour of its prime; surrounded by a Europe containing nothing grand, unless it be Napoleon on one side and Pitt on the other, genius degraded to minister to egotism; intellect bound to the service of the past. No seer exists to foretell the future: belief is extinct; there is only its pretence: prayer is no more; there is only a movement of the lips at a fixed day or hour, for the sake of the family, or what is called *the people:* love is no more; desire has taken its place; the holy warfare of ideas is abandoned; the conflict is that of interests. The worship of great thoughts has passed away. That which *is,* raises the tattered banner of some corpse-like traditions; that which *would be,* hoists only the standard of physical wants, of material appetites: around him are ruins, beyond him the desert; the horizon is a blank. A long cry of suffering and indignation bursts from the heart of Byron: he is answered by anathemas. He departs; he hurries through Europe in search of an ideal to adore; he traverses it distracted, palpitating, like Mazeppa on the wild horse; borne onwards by a fierce desire; the wolves of envy and calumny follow in pursuit. He visits Greece; he visits Italy; if anywhere a lingering spark of the sacred fire, a ray of divine poetry, is preserved, it must be *there.* Nothing. A glorious past, a degraded present; none of life's poetry; no movement, save that of the sufferer turning on his couch to relieve his pain. Byron, from the solitude of his exile, turns his eyes again towards England; he sings. What does he sing? What springs from the mysterious and unique conception which rules, one would say in spite of himself, over all that escapes him in his sleepless vigil? The funeral hymn, the death-song, the epitaph of the aristocratic idea; we discovered it, we Continentalists; not his own countrymen. He takes his types from amongst those privileged by strength, beauty, and individual power. They are grand, poetical, heroic, but solitary; they hold no communion with the world around them, unless it be to rule over it; they defy alike the good and evil principle; they "will bend to neither." In life and in death "they stand upon *their* strength;" they resist every power, for their own is all their own; it was purchased by

Superior science—penance—daring—
And length of watching—strength of mind—and skill
In knowledge of our fathers.

Each of them is the personification, slightly modified, of a single type, a single idea—the *individual;* free, but nothing more than free; such as the epoch now closing has made him;—Faust, but without the compact which submits him to the enemy; for the heroes of Byron make no such compact. Cain kneels not to Arimanes; and Manfred, about to die, exclaims—

> The mind, which is immortal, makes itself
> Requital for its good and evil thoughts—
> Is its own origin of ill, and end—
> And its own place and time, its innate sense,
> When stripped of this mortality, derives
> No colour from the fleeting things without,
> But is absorbed in sufferance or in joy;
> Born from the knowledge of its own desert.

They have no kindred: they live from their own life only: they repulse humanity, and regard the crowd with disdain. Each of them says: *I have faith in myself*; never, *I have faith in ourselves*. They all aspire to power or to happiness. The one and the other alike escape them; for they bear within them, untold, unacknowledged even to themselves, the presentiment of a life that mere liberty can never give them. Free they are; iron souls in iron frames, they climb the alps of the physical world as well as the alps of thought; still is their visage stamped with a gloomy and ineffaceable sadness; still is their soul—whether, as in Cain and Manfred, it plunge into the abyss of the infinite, "intoxicated with eternity," or scour the vast plain and boundless ocean with the Corsair and Giaour—haunted by a secret and sleepless dread. It seems as if they were doomed to drag the broken links of the chain they have burst asunder, rivetted to their feet. Not only in the petty society against which they rebel does their soul feel fettered and restrained; but even in the world of the spirit. Neither is it to the enmity of society that they succumb; but under the assaults of this nameless anguish; under the corroding action of potent faculties "inferior still to their desires and their conceptions;" under the deception that comes from within. What can they do with the liberty so painfully won? On whom, on what, expend the exuberant vitality within them? *They are alone;* this is the secret of their wretchedness and impotence. They "thirst for good"—Cain has said it for them all—but cannot achieve it; for they have no mission, no belief, no comprehension even of the world around them. They have never realised the conception of *Humanity* in the multitudes that have preceded, surround, and will follow after them; never thought on their own place between the past and future; on the continuity of labour that unites all the generations into one Whole; on the common end and aim, only to be realised by the common effort; on the spiritual post-sepulchral life even on earth of the individual, through the thoughts he transmits to his fellows; and, it may be—when he lives devoted and dies in faith—through the guardian agency he is allowed to exercise over the loved ones left on earth.

Gifted with a liberty they know not how to use; with a power and energy they know not how to apply; with a life whose purpose and aim they comprehend not;—they drag through their useless and convulsed existence. Byron destroys them one after the other, as if he were the executioner of a sentence decreed in heaven. They fall unwept, like a withered leaf into the stream of time.

> Nor earth nor sky shall yield a single tear,
> Nor cloud shall gather more, nor leaf shall fall,
> Nor gale breathe forth one sigh for thee, for all.

They die, as they have lived, alone; and a popular malediction hovers round their solitary tombs. This, for those who can read with the soul's eyes, is what Byron sings; or rather what Humanity sings through him. The emptiness of the life and death of solitary individuality has never been so powerfully and efficaciously summed up as in the pages of Byron. The crowd do not comprehend him: they listen; fascinated for an instant; then repent, and avenge their momentary transport by calumniating and insulting the poet. His intuition of the death of a form of society they call wounded self-love; his sorrow for *all* is misinterpreted as cowardly egotism. They credit not the traces of profound suffering revealed by his lineaments; they credit not the presentiment of a new life which from time to time escapes his trembling lips; they believe not in the despairing embrace in which he grasps the material universe—stars, lakes, alps, and sea—and identifies himself with it, and through it with God, of whom—to him at least—it is a symbol. They do, however, take careful count of some unhappy moments, in which, wearied out by the emptiness of life, he has raised—with remorse I am sure—the cup of ignoble pleasures to his lips, believing he might find forgetfulness there. How many times have not his accusers drained this cup, without redeeming the sin by a single virtue; without—I will not say bearing—but without having even the capacity of appreciating the burden which weighed on Byron! And did he not himself dash into fragments the ignoble cup, so soon as he beheld something worthy the devotion of his life?

—Giuseppe Mazzini, "Byron and Goethe," 1839,
Essays, ed. William Clarke, 1887, pp. 86–93

MATTHEW ARNOLD (1881)

The English poet and cultural critic Matthew Arnold (1822–1888), who worked as an inspector of schools and later became professor of poetry at Oxford University, is known for quintessential Victorian poems such as "Dover Beach" and "The Scholar Gypsy." He has been regarded as a Victorian "sage," who instructed his readers on contemporary social and ethical issues. His attitude about Byron was ambivalent, and his evaluation of the quality of Byron's poetry weighs his literary importance against his technical poetic merits.

In spite of his prodigious vogue, Byron has never yet, perhaps, had the serious admiration which he deserves. Society read him and talked about him, as it reads and talks about *Endymion* today; and with the same sort of result. It looked in Byron's glass as it looks in Lord Beaconsfield's, and sees, or fancies that it sees, its own face there; and then it goes its way, and straightway forgets what manner of man it saw. Even of his passionate admirers, how many never got beyond the theatrical Byron, from whom they caught the fashion of deranging their hair, or of knotting their neck-handkerchief, or of leaving their shirt-collar unbuttoned; how few profoundly felt his vital influence, the influence of his splendid and imperishable excellence of sincerity and strength!

His own aristocratic class, whose cynical make-believe drove him to fury; the great middle-class, on whose impregnable Philistinism he shattered himself to pieces,—how little have either of these felt Byron's vital influence! As the inevitable break-up of the old order comes, as the English middle-class slowly awakens from its intellectual sleep of two centuries, as our actual present world, to which this sleep has condemned us, shows itself more clearly,—our world of an aristocracy materialised and null, a middle-class purblind and hideous, a lower class crude and brutal,—we shall turn our eyes again, and to more purpose, upon this passionate and dauntless soldier of a forlorn hope, who, ignorant of the future and unconsoled by its promises, nevertheless waged against the conservation of the old impossible world so fiery battle; waged it till he fell,—waged it with such splendid and imperishable excellence of sincerity and strength.

Wordsworth's value is of another kind. Wordsworth has an insight into permanent sources of joy and consolation for mankind which Byron has not; his poetry gives us more which we may rest upon than Byron's,—more which we can rest upon now, and which men may rest upon always. I place Wordsworth's poetry, therefore, above Byron's on the whole, although in some points he was greatly Byron's inferior, and although Byron's poetry will always, probably, find more readers than Wordsworth's, and will give pleasure more easily. But these two, Wordsworth and Byron, stand, it seems to me, first and pre-eminent in actual performance, a glorious pair, among the English poets of this century. Keats had probably, indeed, a more consummate poetic gift than either of them; but he died having produced too little and being as yet too immature to rival them. I for my part can never even think of equaling with them any other of their contemporaries;—either Coleridge, poet and philosopher wrecked in a mist of opium; or Shelley, beautiful and ineffectual angel, beating in the void his luminous wings in vain. Wordsworth and Byron stand out by themselves. When the year 1900 is turned, and our nation comes to recount her poetic glories in the century which has just then ended, the first names with her will be these.

—Matthew Arnold, preface to his
edition of *Byron's Poems*, 1881

When at last I held in my hand the volume of poems which I had chosen from Wordsworth, and began to turn over its pages, there arose in me almost immediately the desire to see beside it, as a companion volume, a like collection of the best poetry of Byron. Alone amongst our poets of the earlier part of this century, Byron and Wordsworth not only furnish material enough for a volume of this kind, but also, as it seems to me, they both of them gain considerably by being thus exhibited. There are poems of Coleridge and of Keats equal, if not superior, to anything of Byron or Wordsworth; but a dozen pages or two will contain them, and the remaining poetry is of a quality much inferior. Scott never, I think, rises as a poet to the level of Byron and Wordsworth at all. On the other hand, he never falls below his own usual level very far; and by a volume of selections from him, therefore, his effectiveness is not increased. As to Shelley there will be more question; and indeed Mr. Stopford Brooke, whose accomplishments, eloquence, and love of poetry we must all recognise and admire, has actually given us Shelley in such a volume. But for my own part I cannot think that Shelley's poetry, except by snatches and fragments, has the value of the good work of Wordsworth and Byron; or that it is possible for even Mr. Stopford Brooke to make up a volume of selections from him which, for real substance, power, and worth, can at all take rank with a like volume from Byron or Wordsworth.

Shelley knew quite well the difference between the achievement of such a poet as Byron and his own. He praises Byron too unreservedly, but he sincerely felt, and he was right in feeling, that Byron was a greater poetical power than himself. As a man, Shelley is at a number of points immeasurably Byron's superior; he is a beautiful and enchanting spirit, whose vision, when we call it up, has far more loveliness, more charm for our soul, than the vision of Byron. But all the personal charm of Shelley cannot hinder us from at last discovering in his poetry the incurable want, in general, of a sound subject-matter, and the incurable fault, in consequence, of unsubstantiality. Those who extol him as the poet of clouds, the poet of sunsets, are only saying that he did not, in fact, lay hold upon the poet's right subject-matter; and in honest truth, with all his charm of soul and spirit, and with all his gift of musical diction and movement, he never, or hardly ever, did. Except, as I have said, for a few short things and single stanzas, his original poetry is less satisfactory than his translations, for in these the subject-matter was found for him. Nay, I doubt whether his delightful Essays and Letters, which deserve to be far more read than they are now, will not resist the wear and tear of time better, and finally come to stand higher, than his poetry.

There remain to be considered Byron and Wordsworth. That Wordsworth affords good material for a volume of selections, and that he gains by having his poetry thus presented, is an old belief of mine which led me lately to make up a volume of poems chosen out of Wordsworth, and to bring it before the public. By its kind reception of the volume, the public seems to show itself a partaker in my belief. Now Byron also supplies plenty of material for a like volume, and he too gains, I think, by being so presented. Mr. Swinburne urges, indeed, that 'Byron, who rarely wrote anything either worthless or faultless, can only be judged or appreciated in the mass; the greatest of his works was his whole work taken together.' It is quite true that Byron rarely wrote anything either worthless or faultless; it is quite true also that in the appreciation of Byron's power a sense of the amount and variety of his work, defective though much of his work is, enters justly into our estimate. But although there may be little in Byron's poetry which can be pronounced either worthless or faultless, there are portions of it which are far higher in worth and far more free from fault than others. And although, again, the abundance and variety of his production is undoubtedly a proof of his power, yet I question whether by reading everything which he gives us we are so likely to acquire an admiring sense even of his variety and abundance, as by reading what he gives us at his happier moments. Varied and abundant he amply proves himself even by this taken alone. Receive him absolutely without omission or compression, follow his whole outpouring stanza by stanza and line by line from the very commencement to the very end, and he is capable of being tiresome.

Byron has told us himself that the Giaour 'is but a string of passages.' He has made full confession of his own negligence. 'No one,' says he, 'has done more through negligence to corrupt the language.' This accusation brought by himself against his poems is not just; but when he goes on to say of them, that 'their faults, whatever they may be, are those of negligence and not of labour,' he says what is perfectly true. 'Lara,' he declares, 'I wrote while undressing after coming home from balls and masquerades, in the year of revelry, 1814. The Bride was written in four, the Corsair in ten days." He calls this 'a humiliating confession, as it proves my own want of judgment in publishing, and the public's in reading, things which cannot have stamina for permanence.' Again he does his poems injustice; the producer of such poems could not but publish them, the public could not but read them. Nor could Byron have produced his work in any other fashion; his poetic work could not have first grown and matured in his own mind, and then come forth as an organic whole; Byron had not enough of the artist in him for this, nor enough of self-command. He wrote, as he truly tells us, to relieve himself, and he went on writing because he found the relief become indispensable. But it was inevitable that works so produced should be, in general, 'a string of passages,' poured out, as he describes them, with rapidity and excitement, and with new passages constantly suggesting themselves, and added while his work was going through the press. It is evident that we have here neither deliberate scientific construction, nor yet the instinctive artistic creation of poetic wholes; and that to take passages from work produced as Byron's was is a very different thing from taking passages out of the Oedipus or the Tempest, and deprives the poetry far less of its advantage.

Nay, it gives advantage to the poetry, instead of depriving it of any. Byron, I said, has not a great artist's profound and patient skill in combining an action or in developing a character,—a skill which we must watch and follow if we are to do justice to it. But he has a wonderful power of vividly conceiving a single incident, a single situation; of throwing himself upon it, grasping it as if it were real and he saw and felt it, and of making us see and feel it too. The Giaour is, as he truly called it, 'a string of passages,' not a work moving by a deep internal law of development to a necessary end; and our total impression from it cannot but receive from this, its inherent defect, a certain dimness and indistinctness. But the incidents of the journey and death of Hassan, in that poem, are conceived and presented with a vividness not to be surpassed; and our impression from them is correspondingly clear and powerful. In Lara, again, there is no adequate development either of the character of the chief personage or of the action of the poem; our total impression from the work is a confused one. Yet such an incident as the disposal of the slain Ezzelin's body passes before our eyes as if we actually saw it. And in the same way as these bursts of incident, bursts of sentiment also, living and vigorous, often occur in the midst of poems which must be admitted to be but weakly-conceived and loosely-combined wholes. Byron cannot but be a gainer by having attention concentrated upon what is vivid, powerful, effective in his work, and withdrawn from what is not so.

Byron, I say, cannot but be a gainer by this, just as Wordsworth is a gainer by a like proceeding. I esteem Wordsworth's poetry so highly, and the world, in my opinion, has done it such scant justice, that I could not rest satisfied until I had fulfilled, on Wordsworth's behalf, a long-cherished desire;—had disengaged, to the best of my power, his good work from the inferior work joined with it, and had placed before the public the body of his good work by itself. To the poetry of Byron the world has ardently paid homage; full justice from his contemporaries, perhaps even more than justice, his torrent of poetry received. His poetry was admired, adored, 'with all its imperfections on its head,'—in spite of negligence, in spite of diffuseness, in spite of repetitions, in spite of whatever faults it possessed. His name is still great and brilliant. Nevertheless the hour of irresistible vogue has passed away for him; even for Byron it could not but pass away. The time has come for him, as it comes for all poets, when he must take his real and permanent place, no longer depending upon the vogue of his own day and upon the enthusiasm of his contemporaries. Whatever we may think of him, we shall not be subjugated by him as they were; for, as he cannot be for us what he was for them, we cannot admire him so hotly and indiscriminately as they. His faults of negligence, of diffuse-ness, of repetition, his faults of whatever kind, we shall abundantly feel and unsparingly criticise; the mere interval of time between us and him makes disillusion of this kind inevitable. But how then will Byron stand, if we relieve him too, so far as we can, of the encumbrance of his inferior and weakest work, and if we bring before us his best and strongest work in one body together? That is the question which I, who can even remember the latter years of Byron's vogue, and have myself felt the expiring wave of that mighty influence, but who certainly also regard him, and have long regarded him, without illusion, cannot but ask myself, cannot but seek to answer. . . .

Byron found our nation, after its long and victorious struggle with revolutionary France, fixed in a system of established facts and dominant ideas which revolted him. The mental bondage of the most powerful part of our nation, of its strong middle-class, to a narrow and false system of this kind, is what we call British Philistinism. That bondage is unbroken to this hour, but in Byron's time it was even far more deep and dark than it is now.

Byron was an aristocrat, and it is not difficult for an aristocrat to look on the prejudices and habits of the British Philistine with scepticism and disdain. Plenty of young men of his own class Byron met at Almack's or at Lady Jersey's, who regarded the established facts and reigning beliefs of the England of that day with as little reverence as he did. But these men, disbelievers in British Philistinism in private, entered English public life, the most conventional in the world, and at once they saluted with respect the habits and ideas of British Philistinism as if they were a part of the order of creation, and as if in public no sane man would think of warring against them. With Byron it was different. What he called the cant of the great middle part of the English nation, what we call its Philistinism, revolted him; but the cant of his own class, deferring to this Philistinism and profiting by it, while they disbelieved in it, revolted him even more. 'Come what may,' are his own words, 'I will never flatter the million's canting in any shape.' His class in general, on the other hand, shrugged their shoulders at this cant, laughed at it, pandered to it, and ruled by it. The falsehood, cynicism, insolence, misgovernment, oppression, with their consequent unfailing crop of human misery, which were produced by this state of things, roused Byron to irreconcilable revolt and battle. They made him indignant, they infuriated him; they were so strong, so defiant, so maleficent,—and yet he felt that they were doomed. 'You have seen every trampler down in turn,' he comforts himself with saying, 'from Buonaparte to the simplest individuals.' The old order, as after 1815 it stood victorious, with its ignorance and misery below, its cant, selfishness, and cynicism above, was at home and abroad equally hateful to him. 'I have simplified my politics,' he writes, 'into an utter detestation of all existing governments.' And again: 'Give me a republic. The king-times are fast finishing; there will be blood shed like water and tears like mist, but the peoples will conquer in the end. I shall not live to see it, but I foresee it.'

Byron himself gave the preference, he tells us, to politicians and doers, far above writers and singers. But the politics of his own day and of his own class,—even of the Liberals of his own class,—were impossible for him. Nature had not formed him for a Liberal peer, proper to move the Address in the House of Lords, to pay compliments to the energy and self-reliance of British middle-class Liberalism, and to adapt his politics to suit it. Unfitted for such politics, he threw himself upon poetry as his organ; and in poetry his topics were not Queen Mab, and the Witch of Atlas, and the Sensitive Plant—they were the upholders of the old order, George the Third and Lord Castlereagh and the Duke of Wellington and Southey, and they were the canters and tramplers of the great world, and they were his enemies and himself.

Such was Byron's personality, by which 'he is different from all the rest of English poets, and in the main greater.' But he posed all his life, says M. Scherer. Let us distinguish. There is the Byron who posed, there is the Byron with his affectations and silliness, the Byron whose weakness Lady Blessington, with a woman's acuteness, so admirably seized: 'His great defect is flippancy and a total want of self-possession.' But when this theatrical and easily criticised personage betook himself to poetry, and when he had fairly warmed to his work, then he became another man; then the theatrical personage passed away; then a higher power took possession of him and filled him; then at last came forth into light that true and puissant personality, with its direct strokes, its ever-welling force, its satire, its energy, and its agony. This is the real Byron; whoever stops at the theatrical preludings does not know him. And this real Byron may well be superior to the stricken Leopardi, he may well be declared 'different from all the rest of English poets, and in the main greater,' in so far as it is true of him, as M. Taine well says, that 'all other souls, in comparison with his, seem inert'; in so far as it is true of him that with superb, exhaustless energy, he maintained, as Professor Nichol well says, 'the struggle that keeps alive, if it does not save, the soul'; in so far, finally, as he deserves (and he does deserve) the noble praise of him which I have already quoted from Mr. Swinburne; the praise for 'the splendid and imperishable excellence which covers all his offences and outweighs all his defects: the excellence of sincerity and strength.'

True, as a man, Byron could not manage himself, could not guide his ways aright, but was all astray. True, he has no light, cannot lead us from the past to the future; 'the moment he reflects, he is a child.' The way out of the false state of things which enraged him he did not see,—the slow and laborious way upward; he had not the patience, knowledge, self-discipline, virtue, requisite for seeing it. True, also, as a poet, he has no fine and exact sense for word and structure and rhythm; he has not the artist's nature and gifts. Yet a personality of Byron's force counts for so much in life, and a rhetorician of Byron's force counts for so much in literature! But it would be most unjust to label Byron, as M. Scherer is disposed to label him, as a rhetorician only. Along with his astounding power and passion he had a strong and deep sense for what is beautiful in nature, and for what is beautiful in human action and suffering. When he warms to his work, when he is inspired, Nature herself seems to take the pen from him as she took it from Wordsworth, and to write for him as she wrote for Wordsworth, though in a different fashion, with her own penetrating simplicity. Goethe has well observed of Byron, that when he is at his happiest his representation of things is as easy and real as if he were improvising. It is so; and his verse then exhibits quite another and a higher quality from the rhetorical quality,—admirable as this also in its own kind of merit is,—of such verse as

Minions of splendour shrinking from distress,

and of so much more verse of Byron's of that stamp. Nature, I say, takes the pen for him; and then, assured master of a true poetic style though he is not, any more than Wordsworth, yet as from Wordsworth at his best there will come such verse as

Will no one tell me what she sings?

so from Byron, too, at his best, there will come such verse as

He heard it, but he heeded not; his eyes
Were with his heart, and that was far away.

Of verse of this high quality, Byron has much; of verse of a quality lower than this, of a quality rather rhetorical than truly poetic, yet still of extraordinary power and merit, he has still more. To separate, from the mass of poetry which Byron poured forth, all this higher portion, so superior to the mass, and still so considerable in quantity, and to present it in one body by itself, is to do a service, I believe, to Byron's reputation, and to the poetic glory of our country.

Such a service I have in the present volume attempted to perform. To Byron, after all the tributes which have been paid to him, here is yet one tribute more—

Among thy mightier offerings here are mine!

not a tribute of boundless homage certainly, but sincere; a tribute which consists not in covering the poet with eloquent eulogy of our own, but in letting him, at his best and greatest, speak for himself. Surely the critic who does most for his author is the critic who gains readers for his author himself, not for any lucubrations on his author;—gains more readers for him, and enables those readers to read him with more admiration.

And in spite of his prodigious vogue, Byron has never yet, perhaps, had the serious admiration which he deserves. Society read him and talked about him, as it reads and talks about Endymion to-day; and with the same sort of result. It looked in Byron's glass as it looks in Lord Beaconsfield's, and sees, or fancies that it sees, its own face there; and then it goes its way, and straightway forgets what manner of man it saw. Even of his passionate admirers, how many never got beyond the theatrical Byron, from whom they caught the fashion of deranging their hair, or of knotting their neck-handkerchief, or .of leaving their shirt-collar unbuttoned; how few profoundly felt his vital influence, the influence of his splendid and imperishable excellence of sincerity and strength!

His own aristocratic class, whose cynical make-believe drove him to fury; the great middle-class, on whose impregnable Philistinism he shattered himself to pieces,—how little have either of these felt Byron's vital influence! As the inevitable break-up of the old order comes, as the English middle-class slowly awakens from its intellectual sleep of two centuries, as our actual present world, to which this sleep has condemned us, shows itself more clearly,—our world of an aristocracy materialised and null, a middle-class purblind and hideous, a lower class crude and brutal,—we shall turn our eyes again, and to more purpose, upon this passionate and dauntless soldier of a forlorn hope, who, ignorant of the future and unconsoled by its promises, nevertheless waged against the conservation of the old impossible world so fiery battle; waged it till he fell,—waged it with such splendid and imperishable excellence of sincerity and strength.

Wordsworth's value is of another kind. Wordsworth has an insight into permanent sources of joy and consolation for mankind which Byron has not; his poetry gives us more which we may rest upon than Byron's,—more which we can rest upon now, and which men may rest upon always. I place Wordsworth's poetry, therefore, above Byron's on the whole, although in some points he was greatly Byron's inferior, and although Byron's poetry will always, probably, find more readers than Wordsworth's, and will give pleasure more easily. But these two, Wordsworth and Byron, stand, it seems to me, first and pre-eminent in actual performance, a glorious pair, among the English poets of this century. Keats had probably, indeed, a more consummate poetic gift than either of them; but he died having produced too little and being as yet too immature to rival them. I for my part can never even think of equalling with them any other of their contemporaries;—either Coleridge, poet and philosopher wrecked in a mist of opium; or Shelley, beautiful and ineffectual angel, beating in the void his luminous wings in vain. Wordsworth and Byron stand out by themselves. When the year 1900 is turned, and our nation comes to recount her poetic glories in the century which has then just ended, the first names with her will be these.

—Matthew Arnold, from "Byron," 1881,
Essays in Criticism: Second Series, 1888

ALGERNON CHARLES SWINBURNE "BYRON" (1866)

A founding member of the Pre-Raphaelite Brotherhood, Algernon Charles Swinburne (1837–1909) was also part of the aristocracy like Byron and

Shelley. An *enfant terrible* with red hair and a penchant for flogging since his school days at Eton, his decadent poetry as well as his dissolute lifestyle caused numerous scandals. Shocking his Victorian readers with sexually explicit poetry (*Poems and Ballads*, 1866), he relished his own infamy, even propagating outrageous rumors about himself and the obscenity or blasphemy of his poetry. As in the case of Byron, controversy about Swinburne's persona and lifestyle tended to overshadow serious critical engagement of his work.

The most delicate and thoughtful of English critics (Matthew Arnold) has charged the present generation of Englishmen with forgetfulness of Byron. It is not a light charge: and it is not ungrounded. Men born when this century was getting into its forties were baptized into another church than his with the rites of another creed. Upon their ears, first after the cadences of elder poets, fell the faultless and fervent melodies of Tennyson. To them, chief among the past heroes of the younger century, three men appeared as predominant in poetry; Coleridge, Keats, and Shelley. Behind these were effaced, on either hand, the two great opposing figures of Byron and Wordsworth. No man under twenty can just now be expected to appreciate these. The time was when all boys and girls who paddled in rhyme and dabbled in sentiment were wont to adore the presence or the memory of Byron with foolish faces of praise. It is of little moment to him or to us that they have long since ceased to cackle and begun to hiss. They have become used to better verse and carefuller workmen; and must be forgiven if after such training they cannot at once appreciate the splendid and imperishable excellence which covers all his offences and outweighs all his defects: the excellence of sincerity and strength. Without these no poet can live; but few have ever had so much of them as Byron. His sincerity indeed is difficult to discover and define; but it does in effect lie at the root of all his good works: deformed by pretension and defaced by assumption, masked by folly and veiled by affectation; but perceptible after all, and priceless.

It is no part of my present office to rewrite the history of a life in which every date and event that could be given would now seem trite and stale to all possible readers. If, after so many promises and hints, something at once new and true shall at length be unearthed or extricated, which may affect for the better or the worse our judgment of the man, it will be possible and necessary to rewrite it. Meantime this among other chances 'lies on the lap of the gods'; and especially on the lap of a goddess who still treads our earth. Until she speaks, we cannot guess what she may have to say; and can only pass by with reverent or with sceptical reticence.[1]

This much however we may safely assert: that no man's work was ever more influenced by his character; and that no man's character was ever more influenced by his circumstances. Rather from things without than from things within him did the spirit of Byron assume colour and shape. His noblest verse leapt on a sudden into life after the heaviest evils had fallen upon him which even he ever underwent. From the beginning indeed he had much to fight against; and three impediments hung about him at starting, the least of which would have weighed down a less strong man: youth, and genius, and an ancient name.[2] In spite of all three he made his way; and suffered for it. At the first chance given or taken, every obscure and obscene thing that lurks for pay or prey among the fouler shallows and thickets of literature flew against him; every hound and every hireling lavished upon him the loathsome tribute of their abuse; all nameless creatures that nibble and prowl, upon whom the serpent's curse has fallen, to go upon his belly and eat dust all the days of his life, assailed him with their foulest venom and their keenest fangs. And the promise given of old to their kind was now at least fulfilled: they did bruise his heel. But the heads of such creatures are so small that it is hard to bruise them in return; it would first be necessary to discern them.

That Byron was able to disregard and to outlive the bark and the bite of such curs as these is small praise enough: the man who cannot do as much is destructible, and therefore contemptible. He did far more than this; he withstood the weight of circumstances to the end; not always without complaint, but always without misgiving. His glorious courage, his excellent contempt for things contemptible, and hatred of hateful men, are enough of themselves to embalm and endear his memory in the eyes of all who are worthy to pass judgment upon him. And these qualities gave much of their own value to verse not otherwise or not always praiseworthy. Even at its best, the serious poetry of Byron is often so rough and loose, so weak in the screws and joints which hold together the framework of verse, that it is not easy to praise it enough without seeming to condone or to extenuate such faults as should not be overlooked or forgiven. No poet is so badly represented by a book of selections. It must show something of his weakness; it cannot show all of his strength. Often, after a noble overture, the last note struck is either dissonant or ineffectual. His magnificent masterpiece, which must endure for ever among the precious relics of the world, will not bear dissection or extraction. The merit of *Don Juan* does not lie in any part, but in the whole. There is in that great poem an especial and exquisite balance and sustenance of alternate tones which cannot be expressed or explained by the utmost ingenuity of selection. Haidee is supplanted by Dudu, the shipwreck by the siege, the Russian court by the English household; and this perpetual change, this tidal variety of experience and emotion, gives to the poem something of the breadth and freshness of the sea. Much of the poet's earlier work is or seems unconsciously dishonest; this, if not always or wholly unaffected, is as honest as the sunlight, as frank as the sea-wind. Here, and here alone, the student of his work may recognise and enjoy the ebb and flow of actual life. Here the pulse of vital blood may be felt in tangible flesh. Here for the first time the style of Byron is beyond all praise or blame: a style at once swift and supple, light and strong, various and radiant. Between *Childe Harold* and *Don Juan* the same difference exists which a swimmer feels between lake-water and sea-water: the one is fluent, yielding, invariable; the other has in it a life and pulse, a sting and a swell, which touch and excite the nerves like fire or like music. Across the stanzas of Don *Juan* we swim forward as over 'the broad backs of the sea'; they break and glitter, hiss and laugh, murmur and move, like waves that sound or that subside. There is in them a delicious resistance, an elastic motion, which salt water has and fresh water has not. There is about them a wide wholesome air, full of vivid light and constant wind, which is only felt at sea. Life undulates and death palpitates in the splendid verse which resumes the evidence of a brave and clear-sighted man concerning life and death. Here, as at sea, there is enough and too much of fluctuation and intermission; the ripple flags and falls in loose and lazy lines: the foam flies wide of any mark, and the breakers collapse here and there in sudden ruin and violent failure. But the violence and weakness of the sea are preferable to the smooth sound and equable security of a lake: its buoyant and progressive impulse sustains and propels those who would sink through weariness in the flat and placid shallows. There are others whom it sickens, and others whom it chills; these will do well to steer inshore.

It is natural in writing of Byron to slide into remembrances of what is likest to his verse. His work and Shelley's, beyond that of all our other poets, recall or suggest the wide and high things of nature; the large likeness of the elements; the immeasurable liberty and the stormy strength of waters and winds. They are strongest when they touch upon these; and it is worth remark how few are the poets of whom this can be said. Here, as elsewhere, Shakespeare is supreme when it pleased him; but it pleased him rarely. No poetry of shipwreck and the sea has ever equalled the great scene of *Pericles;* no such note of music was ever struck out of the clash and contention of tempestuous elements. In Milton the sublimity is chiefly of sound; the majesty of melodies unsurpassed from all time wellnigh excludes and supplants all other motives of material beauty. In the minds of mediaeval poets there was no width or depth to receive and contain such emotion. In Spenser, despite his fertile and fluent ingenuity, his subtle and sleepy graces, the effeminacy of colour no less than the monotony of metre makes it hopeless to look for any trace of that passionate sense of power and delight in great outer things of which we speak here. Among later men, Coleridge and Keats used nature mainly as a stimulant or a sedative; Wordsworth as a vegetable fit to shred into his pot and pare down like the outer leaves of a lettuce for didactic and culinary purposes.[2] All these doubtless in their own fashion loved her, for her beauties, for her uses, for her effects; hardly one for herself.

Turn now to Byron or to Shelley. These two at least were not content to play with her skirts and paddle in her shallows. Their passion is perfect, a fierce and blind desire which exalts and impels their verse into the high places of emotion and expression. They feed upon nature with a holy hunger, follow her with a divine lust as of gods chasing the daughters of men. Wind and fire, the cadences of thunder and the clamours of the sea, gave to them no less of sensual pleasure than of spiritual sustenance. These things they desired as others desire music or wine or the beauty of women. This outward and indifferent nature of things, cruel in the eyes of all but her lovers, and even in theirs not loving, became as pliant to their grasp and embrace as any Clymene or Leucothea to Apollo's. To them the large motions and the remote beauties of space were tangible and familiar as flowers. Of this poetry, where description melts into passion and contemplation takes fire from delight, the highest sample is Shelley's 'Ode to the West Wind'. An imperfect mastery of his materials keeps the best things of Byron some few degrees below an equal rank. One native and incurable defect grew up and strengthened side by side with his noblest qualities: a feeble and faulty sense of metre. No poet of equal or inferior rank ever had so bad an ear. His smoother cadences are often vulgar and facile; his fresher notes are often incomplete and inharmonious. His verse stumbles and jingles, stammers and halts, where there is most need for a swift and even pace of musical sound. The rough sonorous changes of the songs in *The Deformed Transformed* rise far higher in harmony and strike far deeper into the memory than the lax easy lines in which he at first indulged; but they slip too readily into notes as rude and weak as the rhymeless tuneless verse in which they are so loosely set, as in a cheap and casual frame. The magnificent lyric measures of *Heaven and Earth* are defaced by the coarse obtrusion of short lines with jagged edges: no small offence in a writer of verse. Otherwise these choral scenes are almost as blameless as they are brilliant. The poet who above others took delight in the sense of sounding storms and shaken waters could not but exult over the vision of deluge with all his strength and breadth of wing. Tempest and rebellion and the magnificence of anguish were as the natural food and fire to kindle and sustain his indomitable and sleepless spirit. The godless martyrdom of rebels; the passion that cannot redeem; the

Thebaid whose first hermit was Cain, the Calvary whose first martyr was Satan; these, time after time, allured and inspired him. Here for once this inner and fiery passion of thought found outer clothing and expression in the ruin of a world. Both without and within, the subject was made for him, and lay ready shapen for the strong impressure of his hand. His love of wide and tempestuous waters fills his work throughout as with the broad breath of a sea-wind. Even the weakest of his poems, a thing still-born and shapeless, is redeemed and revived by one glorious verse:—

When the Poles crashed, and water was the world.

This passion and power in dealing with the higher things of nature, with her large issues and remote sources, has been bestowed upon Victor Hugo alone among our contemporaries. He also can pass beyond the idyllic details of landscape, and put out from shore into the wide waste places of the sea. And this of course is the loftiest form of such poetry as deals with outward nature and depends upon the forms of things. In Byron the power given by this passion is the more conspicuous through his want of dramatic capacity. Except in the lighter and briefer scenes of *Don Juan,* he was never able to bring two speakers face to face and supply them with the right words. In structure as in metre his elaborate tragedies are wholly con-demnable; filled as they are in spirit with the overflow of his fiery energy. *Cain* and *Manfred* are properly monologues decorated and set off by some slight appendage of ornament or explanation. In the later and loftier poem there is no difference perceptible, except in strength and knowledge, between Lucifer and Cain. Thus incompetent to handle the mysteries and varieties of character, Byron turns always with a fresh delight and a fresh confidence thither where he feels himself safe and strong. No part of his nature was more profound and sincere than the vigorous love of such inanimate things as were in tune with his own spirit and senses. His professions of contempt were too loud to express it; scorn is brief or silent; anger alone finds vent in violent iteration and clamorous appeal. He had too much of fury and not enough of contempt; he foams at things and creatures not worth a glance or a blow. But when once clear of men and confronted with elements, he casts the shell of pretence and drops the veil of habit; then, as in the last and highest passage of a poem which has suffered more from praise than any other from dispraise, his scorn of men caught in the nets of nature and necessity has no alloy of untruth; his spirit is mingled with the sea's, and overlooks with a superb delight the ruins and the prayers of men.

This loftiest passage in *Childe Harold* has been so often mouthed and mauled by vulgar admiration that it now can scarcely be relished. Like a royal robe worn out, or a royal wine grown sour, it seems the worse for having been so good. But in fact, allowing for one or two slips and blots, we must after all replace it among the choice and high possessions of poetry. After the first there is hardly a weak line; many have a wonderful vigour and melody; and the deep and glad disdain of the sea for men and the works of men passes into the verse in music and fills it with a weighty and sonorous harmony grave and sweet as the measured voice of heavy remote waves. No other passage in the fourth canto will bear to be torn out from the text; and this one suffers by extraction. The other three cantos are more loosely built and less compact of fabric; but in the first two there is little to remember or to praise. Much of the poem is written throughout in falsetto; there is a savour in many places as of something false and histrionic. This singular and deep defect, which defaces so much of Byron's work, seems also to have deformed his personal character, to have given a twist to his enmities and left a taint upon his friendships. He was really somewhat sombre and sad at heart, and it pleased him to seem sadder than he was. He was impressible and susceptible of pleasure, able to command and enjoy it; and of this also it pleased him to make the most in public. But in fact he was neither a Harold nor a Juan; he was better than these in his own way, and assumed their parts and others with a hypocrisy but half insincere. The fault was probably in great part unconscious, and transparent as a child's acting. To the keen eye and cool judgment of Stendhal it was at once perceptible. Byron's letter to him in defence of Scott was doubtless not insincere; yet it is evident that the writer felt himself to be playing a graceful part to advantage. This fretful and petulant appetite for applause, the proper apanage of small poets and lowly aspirants, had in Byron's case to wrestle with the just pride of place and dignity of genius; no man ever had more of these; yet they did not always support him; he fell even into follies and vulgarities unworthy of a meaner name than his. In effect, when his errors were gravest, he erred through humility and not through pride. Pride would have sustained him far above the remarks and reviews of his day, the praise or dispraise of his hour. As it was, he was vulnerable even by creeping things; and at times their small stings left a poison behind which turned his blood. The contagion of their touch infected him; and he strove under its influence to hiss and wound as they. Here and there in his letters and reflections, in the loose records of his talk and light fragments of his work, the traces of infection are flagrant.

But these defects were only as scars on the skin, superficial and removable; they are past and done with; while all of him that was true and good remains, as it will to all time. Justice cannot be done to it here or now. It is enough if after careful selection as little injustice be done as possible. His few sonnets, unlike Shelley's, are all good; the best is that on Bonnivard, one of his noblest and completest poems. The versified narratives which in their day were so admirable and famous have yielded hardly a stray sheaf to the gleaner. They have enough of vigour and elasticity to keep life in them yet; but once chipped or broken their fabric would crumble and collapse. The finest among them is certainly either *The Giaour* or *The Siege of Corinth;* the weakest is probably either *Parisina* or *The Bride of Abydos.* But in none of these is there even a glimpse of Byron's higher and rarer faculty. All that can be said for them is that they gave tokens of a talent singularly fertile, rapid and vivid; a certain power of action and motion which redeems them from the complete stagnation of dead verses; a command over words and rhymes never of the best and never of the worst. In *The Giaour,* indeed, there is something of a fiery sincerity which in its successors appears diluted and debased. [4]

The change began in Byron when he first found out his comic power, and rose at once beyond sight or shot of any rival. His early satires are wholly devoid of humour, wit, or grace; the verse of *Beppo,* bright and soft and fluent, is full at once of all. The sweet light music of its few and low notes was perfect as a prelude to the higher harmonies of laughter and tears, of scorn and passion, which as yet lay silent in the future. It is mere folly to seek in English or Italian verse a precedent or a parallel. The scheme of metre is Byron's alone; no weaker hand than his could ever bend that bow, or ever will. Even the Italian poets, working in a language more flexible and ductile than ours, could never turn their native metre to such uses, could never handle their national weapon with such grace and strength. The *terza rima* remains their own, after all our efforts to adapt it; it bears here only forced flowers and crude fruits;[5] but the *ottava rima* Byron has fairly conquered and wrested from them. Before the appearance of *Beppo* no one could foresee what a master's hand might make of the instrument; and no one could predict its further use and its dormant powers before the advent of *Don Juan.* In the *Vision of Judgment* it appears finally perfected; the metre fits the sense as with close and pliant armour, the perfect panoply of Achilles. A poem so short and hasty, based on a matter so worthy of brief contempt and long oblivion as the funeral and the fate of George III, bears about it at first sight no great sign or likelihood of life. But this poem which we have by us stands alone, not in Byron's work only, but in the work of the world. Satire in earlier times had changed her rags for robes; Juvenal had clothed with fire, and Dryden with majesty, that wandering and bastard Muse. Byron gave her wings to fly with, above the reach even of these. Others have had as much of passion and as much of humour; Dryden had perhaps as much of both combined. But here and not elsewhere a third quality is apparent: the sense of a high and clear imagination. The grave and great burlesque of King George and St. Peter is relieved and sustained by the figures of Michael and Satan. These two, confronted and corresponding as noon and night, lift and light up the background of satire, blood-red or black according to the point of view. Above all, the balance of thought and passion is admirable; human indignation and divine irony are alike understood and expressed: the pure and fiery anger of men at sight of wrongdoing, the tacit inscrutable derision of heaven. Upon this light and lofty poem a commentary might be written longer than the text and less worth reading; but here it shall not be. Those who read it with the due delight, not too gravely and not too lightly, will understand more than can now be set down; those who read it otherwise will not understand anything. Even these can hardly fail to admire the vigour and variety of scorn, the beauty and the bitterness of verse, which raise it beyond comparison with any other satire. There is enough and too much of violence and injustice in the lines on Southey; but it must be remembered that he was the first to strike, and with an unfair weapon. A poet by profession, he had assaulted with feeble fury another poet, not on the fair and open charge of bad verses, but under the impertinent and irrelevant plea that his work was an affliction or an offence to religion and morality—the most susceptible, as the most intangible, among the creatures of metaphor. A man less irritable and less powerful than Byron might be forgiven for any reprisals; and the excellence of his verses justifies their injustice. But that Southey, who could win and retain for life the love and the praise of Landor, was capable of conscious baseness or falsity, Byron himself in sober moments should hardly have believed. Between official adoration and not less official horror—between George deified and Byron denounced—the Laureate's position was grotesque enough. It was almost a good office to pelt him with the names of hireling and apostate; these charges he could reject and refute. The facts were surely sufficient: that, as to religion, his 'present Deity' was the paltriest maniac among kings and Caesars; as to morality, his feelings or his faith obliged him to decry as pernicious the greatest work of his opponent.

Side by side with the growth of his comic and satiric power, the graver genius of Byron increased and flourished. As the tree grew higher it grew shapelier; the branches it put forth on all sides were fairer of leaf and fuller of fruit than its earlier offshoots had promised. But from these hardly a stray bud or twig can be plucked off by way of sample. No detached morsel of *Don Juan,* no dismembered fragment of *Cain,* will serve to show or to suggest the excellence of either. These poems are coherent and complete as trees or flowers; they cannot be split up and parcelled out like a mosaic of artificial jewellery, which might be taken to pieces by the same artisan who put it together. It must then be remembered that any mere selection from the verse of Byron, however much of care and of goodwill be spent upon the task, must perforce either exclude or impair his very greatest work. Cancel or select a leaf from these poems, and you will injure the whole framework equally in either case.

It is not without reluctance that I have given any extracts from *Don Juan;* it is not without a full sense of the damage done to these extracts by the very act of extraction. But I could only have left them untouched with a reluctance even greater; and this plea, if it can, must excuse me. As fragments they are exquisite and noble, like the broken hand or severed foot of a Greek statue; but here as much is lost as there. Taken with their context, they regain as much of beauty and of force as the sculptured foot or hand when, reunited to the perfect body, they resume their place and office among its vital and various limbs. This gift of life and variety is the supreme quality of Byron's chief poem; a quality which cannot be expressed by any system of extracts. Little can here be given beyond a sample or two of tragic and serious work. The buoyant beauty of surrounding verse, the 'innumerable laughter' and the profound murmur of its many measures, the fervent flow of stanzas now like the ripples and now like the gulfs of the sea, can no more be shown by process of selection than any shallow salt pool left in the sand for sunbeams to drain dry can show the depth and length of the receding tide.

It would be waste of words and time here to enlarge at all upon the excellence of the pure comedy of *Don Juan.* From the first canto to the sixteenth; from the defence of Julia, which is worthy of Congreve or Moliere, to the study of Adeline, which is worthy of Laclos or Balzac; the elastic energy of humour never falters or flags. English criticism, with a mournful murmur of unanimous virtue, did at the time, and may yet if it please, appeal against the satire which strikes home and approve the satire that flies abroad. It was said, and perhaps is still said, that the poem falls off and runs low towards the end. Those who can discover where a change for the worse begins might at least indicate the landmark, imperceptible to duller eyes, which divides the good from the bad. Others meantime will retain their belief that this cry was only raised because in these latter cantos a certain due amount of satire fell upon the false and corrupt parts of English character, its mealy-mouthed vices and its unsound virtues. Had the scene been shifted to Italy or France, we might have heard little of the poet's failing power and perverse injustice.

It is just worth a word of notice that Byron, like Fielding before him, has caught up a well-known name and prefixed it to his work, without any attempt or desire to retain the likeness or follow the tradition attached to it. With him Don Juan is simply a man somewhat handsomer and luckier than others of his age. This hero is not even a reduced copy of the great and terrible figure with which he has nothing in common but a name. The Titan of embodied evil, the likeness of sin made flesh, which grew up in the grave and bitter imagination of a Spanish poet, steeped in the dyes and heated by the flames of hell, appears even in the hands of Molière diminished, and fallen as it were from Satan to Belial; but still splendid with intellect and courage that tower above the meaner minds and weaker wills of women and of men; still inflexible to human appeal and indomitable by divine anger. To crush him, heaven is compelled to use thunder and hell-fire; and by these, though stricken, he is not subdued. The sombre background of a funereal religion is not yet effaced; but it tasked the whole strength of Moliere, gigantic as that strength was, to grapple with the shadow of this giant, to transfigure upon a new stage the tragic and enormous incarnation of supreme sin. As it is, even when playing with his debtors or his peasants, the hero of Molière retains always some feature of his first likeness, some shadow of his early shape. But further than France the terrible legend has never moved. Rigid criticism would therefore say that the title of Byron's masterpiece was properly a misnomer: which is no great matter after all, since the new Juan can never be confounded with the old.

Of Byron's smaller poems there is less to say, and less space to say it. Their splendid merits and their visible defects call neither for praise nor blame. Their place and his, in the literature of England, are fixed points: no critical astronomy of the future can lower or can raise them: they have their own station for all time among the greater and the lesser stars. As a poet, Byron was surpassed, beyond all question and all comparison, by three men at least of his own time; and matched, if not now and then overmatched, by one or two others. The verse of Wordsworth, at its highest, went higher than his; the verse of Landor flowed clearer. But his own ground, where none but he could set foot, was lofty enough, fertile and various. Nothing in Byron is so worthy of wonder and admiration as the scope and range of his power. New fields and ways of work, had he lived, might have given room for exercise and matter for triumph to 'that most fiery spirit'.[6] As it is, his work was done at Missolonghi; all of his work for which the fates could spare him time. A little space was allowed him to show at least a heroic purpose, and attest a high design; then, with all things unfinished before him and behind, he fell asleep after many troubles and triumphs. Few can ever have gone wearier to the grave; none with less fear. He had done enough to earn his rest. Forgetful now and set free for ever from all faults and foes, he passed through the doorway of no ignoble death out of reach of time, out of sight of love, out of hearing of hatred, beyond the blame of England and the praise of Greece. In the full strength of spirit and of body his destiny overtook him, and made an end of all his labours. He had seen and borne and achieved more than most men on record. 'He was a great man, good at many things, and now he has attained this also, to be at rest.'

Notes

1. It will be evident that these lines were written before the appearance of the book in which Madame de Boissy thought fit to let the world know that she had nothing to tell worth its hearing with regard to the man whose love had made her famous, but was not the less willing to put forth that nothing in two leaden volumes of verbiage. The worst consequence of this miscarriage was not the collapse of such faint hopes or surmises as we might yet have cherished of some benefit to be received in the way of biography, some new and kindly light to be thrown on the life and character of Byron; it was the opportunity given to a filthy female moralist and novelist who was not slow to avail herself of such an occasion 'to expound her beastly mind to all'. Evidently the laurels of Mrs. Behn had long kept her successor from sleeping; it was not enough to have copied the authoress of *Oroonoko* in the selection of a sable and a servile hero; her American imitator was bent on following her down fouler ways than this. But I feel that an apology is due to the virtuous memory of the chaste Aphra; she was indeed the first 'nigger novelist', and she was likewise a vendor and purveyor of obscene fiction; but here the parallel ends; for I am not aware that she ever applied her unquestionable abilities in that unlovely line of business to the defamation at second hand of the illustrious and defenceless dead.

2. That his youth and his rank were flung in his face with vulgar insolence on the publication of his first little book it can hardly be necessary to remind any reader of Byron; but possibly even these offences might have been condoned in a scribbler whose work had given no offensive promise of greatness yet to be. In the verses on Lochnagar at least an ominous threat or presage of something new and splendid must have been but too perceptible to the discerning eye of criticism.

3. I remember some critical cackling over this phrase when it first appeared as over a senseless insult offered to the name and genius of a great poet. Insult is no habit of mine; and the term here used implies no more than he that runs may read in the text of Wordsworth; in whom, after the somewhat early subsidence of that 'simple, sensuous, and passionate' delight in nature of which in two of his most famous poems he has for ever embalmed his recollection, the place of this rapturous instinct of submission and absorption, which other poets have seen who never have ceased to feel in sight of natural glory and beauty, was taken by a meditative

and moralizing spirit too apt to express itself in the tone of a preacher to whom all the divine life of things outside man is but as raw material for philosophic or theological cookery. How far this method of contemplating and interpreting the splendours and terrors of nature differs from that of his greatest contemporaries it is surely neither irrelevant nor impertinent to point out once more. Wide apart as lay their lines of work, it is true alike of Shelley and of Keats that for them it was not fated, nor could it ever have been possible, to outlive The hour Of splendour in the grass, of glory in the flower; nor could Byron, while retaining as did Wordsworth the freshness and the force of his genius, have outlived his more fiery delight in the triumphant life of sea and cloud and storm.

4. Remembering the success of these stories, we may believe that Byron's contempt for the critical fashions of a time which extolled his worst work was not wholly affected or assumed; and understand how the instincts of opposition and reaction drove him back into that open idolatry of Pope and his school which he expressed loudly and foolishly enough. Probably at heart he did really prefer Pope to all men. His critical faculty, if I may steal one phrase from a treasury that may well spare me the loan, was 'zero, or even a frightful *minus* quantity'; his judgment never worth the expense of a thought or a word. Besides, he had striven to emulate or at least to copy the exquisite manner of Pope in his satires, and must have seen how great and impassable a gulf lay between the master and his pupil. This would naturally lead him to over-estimate what he could not attain: the delicate merit, the keen perfection, the equable balance offeree and finish, of sense and style, which raised his favourite so high among writers, if they left him somewhat low among poets; and having himself so bad an ear for metre, he may even have imagined that Pope's verse was musical.

5. I do not of course forget that our own time has produced two noble poems in this foreign and alien metre; but neither *Casa Guidi Windows* nor 'The Defence of Guenevere' will suffice to establish its general excellence or fitness. The poets have done so well because they could do no less; but there may be at once good material and good workmanship without good implements. Neither of them has done more to give footing in England to the metre of their poems than did Byron himself by his 'Prophecy of Dante'. They have done better than this; but this they have not done.

6. The, noble verses of Shelley are fitter to be spoken over Byron than over any first or last Napoleon. To no other man could they be so well applied: for the world indeed took more of warmth from the fire of his spirit while alive than from any other then kindled:—

What! alive and so bold, O Earth?
Art thou not over-bold?
What! leapest thou forth as of old
In the light of thy morning mirth,
The last of the flock of the starry fold?
Thou wert warming thy fingers old
O'er the embers covered and cold
Of that most fiery spirit, when it fled:
What, Mother, do you laugh now he is dead?

—Algernon Charles Swinburne, "Byron,"
1866, *Essays and Studies,* 1875

ROBERT BROWNING (1846)

Because of a possible unwillingness to admit to any "anxiety of influence,"
Robert Browning (1812–1889) rarely acknowledged his appreciation of
Byron; yet there are certain parallels between the two, such as the use
of the dramatic monologue. The husband of the poet Elizabeth Barrett
Browning (here addressed as "Ba"), Browning is known for poems such as
"My Last Duchess" and "Porphyria's Lover" and the blank-verse poem *The
Ring and the Book,* in which he combines a Victorian "modernism" with
romantic elements.

Ba, Lord Byron is altogether in my affection again . . . I have read on to the
end, and am quite sure of the great qualities which the last ten or fifteen
years had partially obscured. Only a little longer life and all would have
been gloriously right again. I read this book of Moore's too long ago: but I
always retained my first feeling for Byron in many respects . . . the interest
in the places he had visited, in relics of him. I would at any time have gone
to Finchley to see a curl of his hair or one of his gloves, I am sure—while
Heaven knows that I could not get up enthusiasm enough to cross the
room if at the other end of it all Wordsworth, Coleridge and Southey
were condensed into the little China bottle yonder, after the Rosicrucian
fashion . . . they seem to 'have their reward' and want nobody's love or faith.
Just one of those trenchant opinions which I found fault with Byron for
uttering,—as 'proving nothing'! But telling a weakness to Ba is not telling it
to 'the world,' as poor authors phrase it!

—Robert Browning, letter to Elizabeth
Barrett Browning, August 22, 1846

WILLIAM MICHAEL ROSSETTI
"LORD BYRON" (1878)

Brother of the painter Dante Gabriel Rossetti, William Michael Rossetti (1829–1919) was an English writer and critic. He was one of the seven founding members of the Pre-Raphaelite Brotherhood in 1848 and became the movement's unofficial organizer and bibliographer. Although Rossetti worked as a civil servant, he also published criticism and biographies (for example about John William Polidori, Byron's physician, and about Dante Gabriel) and edited the poems of his sister, Christina Rossetti.

His poetry has two main constituents—passion and wit. Were we compelled rigidly to assess the value of these two constituents, according to the positive merit of their respective products, we should probably have to say that the wit was the finer power of the two. The great superiority of *Don Juan* (and, as a minor sample, the *Vision of Judgment*) to all his other work consists ultimately in this—that here the passion and the wit are perpetually interpenetrating and enhancing one another, and are both perfectly limpid and unforced. There is no overloading or attitudinizing in the passion: in the wit, no conventional standard of substance or of form. It is not, however, necessary to settle with any nicety the rival claims of passion and of wit as the informing powers of Byron's work; nor even does the mind acquiesce in either or both of these excellent qualities as the final characteristics. The great thing in Byron is GENIUS—that quality so perilous to define, so evanescent in its aroma, so impossible to mistake. If ever a man breathed whom we recognize (athwart much poor and useless work, when strictly tested) as emphatically the Genius, that man was Byron: and, if ever genius made poetry its mouthpiece, covering with its transcendent utterances a multitude of sins whether against art or against the full stature of perfect manhood, Byron's is that poetry. It is therefore as imperishable as genius itself. Its forms have much of the transitory, much even of the spurious: they have already been "found out" to a great extent, and, after suffering a term of more than merited depreciation by reaction, are righting themselves in rather a battered and blowzed condition. But these are the forms: the essence is the genius, and that knows no vicissitude, and acknowledges no fleeting jurisdiction.

—William Michael Rossetti,
"Lord Byron," *Lives of Famous Poets,*
1878, p. 307

William Ernest Henley "Byron" (1890)

The Victorian writer W.E. Henley (1849–1903) had become a poet during a long stay in the hospital, where his left leg was amputated because of tubercular bone infection at the age of sixteen. He was a friend of James McNeill Whistler and Auguste Rodin and worked with Robert Louis Stevenson on four plays, among them *Deacon Brodie* (1879). Henley was labeled the "arch anti-decadent" and published poems such as "Invictus" and "England, My England," which inspired the British troops in World War I. He published an edition of Byron's works, the first volume of which appeared in 1897.

Two obvious reasons why Byron has long been a prophet more honoured abroad than at home are his life and his work. He is the most romantic figure in the literature of the century, and his romance is of that splendid and daring cast which the people of Britain—'an aristocracy materialised and null, a middle class purblind and hideous, a lower class crude and brutal'—prefers to regard with suspicion and disfavour. He is the type of them that prove in defiance of precept that the safest path is not always midway, and that the golden rule is sometimes unspeakably worthless: who set what seems a horrible example, create an apparently shameful precedent, and yet contrive to approve themselves an honour to their country and the race. To be a good Briton a man must trade profitably, marry respectably, live cleanly, avoid excess, revere the established order, and wear his heart in his breeches pocket or anywhere but on his sleeve. Byron did none of these things, though he was a public character, and ought for the example's sake to have done them all, and done them ostentatiously. He lived hard, and drank hard, and played hard. He was flippant in speech and eccentric in attire. He thought little of the sanctity of the conjugal tie, and said so; and he married but to divide from his wife—who was an incarnation of the national virtue of respectability—under circumstances too mysterious not to be discreditable. He was hooted into exile, and so far from reforming he did even worse than he had done before. After bewildering Venice with his wickedness and consorting with atheists like Shelley and conspirators like young Gamba, he went away on a sort of wild-goose chase to Greece, and died there with every circumstance of publicity. Also his work was every whit as abominable in the eyes of his countrymen as his life. It is said that the theory and practice of British art are subject to the influence of the British schoolgirl, and that he is unworthy the name of artist whose achievement is of a kind to call a blush to the cheek of youth. Byron was contemptuous of youth, and did not hesitate to write—in *Beppo* and in *Cain*, in *Manfred* and *Don Juan* and the *Vision*—exactly as he pleased. In three words, he made himself offensively conspicuous, and from being infinitely popular became utterly contemptible. Too long had people listened to the scream of this eagle in wonder and in perturbation, and the moment he disappeared they grew ashamed of their emotion and angry with its cause, and began to hearken to other and more melodious voices—to Shelley and Keats, to Wordsworth and Coleridge and the 'faultless and fervent melodies of Tennyson.' In course of time Byron was forgotten, or only remembered with disdain; and when Thackeray, the representative Briton, the artist Philistine, the foe of all that is excessive or abnormal or rebellious, took it upon himself to flout the author of *Don Juan* openly and to lift up his heavy hand against the fops and fanatics who had affected the master's humours, he did so amid general applause. Meanwhile, however, the genius and the personality of Byron had come to be vital influences all the world over, and his voice had been recognised as the most human and the least insular raised on English ground since Shakespeare's. In Russia he had created Pushkin and Lermontoff; in Germany he had awakened Heine, inspired Schumann, and been saluted as an equal by the poet of *Faust* himself; in Spain he had had a share in moulding the noisy and unequal talent of Espronceda; in Italy he had helped to develop and to shape the melancholy and daring genius of Leopardi; and in France he had been one of the presiding forces of a great aesthetic revolution. To the men of 1830 he was a special and peculiar hero. Hugo turned in his wake to Spain and Italy and the East for inspiration. Musset, as Mr. Swinburne has said—too bitterly and strongly said—became in a fashion a Kaled to his Lara, 'his female page or attendant dwarf.' He was in some sort the grandsire of the Buridan and the Antony of Dumas. Berlioz went to him for the material for his *Harold en Italie,* his *Corsaire* overture, and his *Episode.* Delacroix painted the *Barque de Don Juan* from him, with the *Massacre de Scio,* the *Marino Faliero,* the *Combat du Giaour et du Pacha,* and many a notable picture more. Is it at all surprising that M. Taine should have found heart to say that alone among modern poets Byron 'atteint a la cime'? or that Mazzini should have reproached us with our unaccountable neglect of him and with our scandalous forgetfulness of the immense work done by him in giving a 'European *role* to English literature' and in awakening all over the Continent so much 'appreciation and sympathy for England'?

—William Ernest Henley, "Byron,"
Views and Reviews, 1890

GEORGE SAINTSBURY (1896)

The English writer and critic George Saintsbury (1845–1933) had become professor of rhetoric and English literature at the University of Edinburgh in 1895. He held the position until 1915, and, apart from publications on French literature, he also wrote on Dryden and Scott, as well as various histories: *History of Elizabethan Literature* (1887), *History of Nineteenth Century Literature* (1896), and *A Short History of English Literature* (1898). Despite being a literary scholar, Saintsbury is remembered today mainly for his *Notes on a Cellar-Book* (1920), a celebration of wine.

Although opinions about Byron differ very much, there is one point about him which does not admit of difference of opinion. No English poet, perhaps no English writer except Scott (or rather "The Author of *Waverley*"), has ever equalled him in popularity at home; and no English writer, with Richardson and Scott again as seconds, and those not very close ones, has equalled him in contemporary popularity abroad. The vogue of Byron in England, though overpowering for the moment, was even at its height resisted by some good judges and more strait-laced moralists; and it ebbed, if not as rapidly as it flowed, with a much more enduring movement. But abroad he simply took possession of the Continent of Europe and kept it. He was one of the dominant influences and determining causes of the French Romantic movement; in Germany, though the failure of literary talent and activity of the first order in that country early in this century made his school less important, he had great power over Heine, its one towering genius; and he was almost the sole master of young Russia, young Italy, young Spain, in poetry. Nor, though his active and direct influence has of course been exhausted by time, can his reputation on the Continent be said to have ever waned.

These various facts, besides being certain in themselves, are also very valuable as guiding the inquirer in regions which are more of opinion. The rapidity of Byron's success everywhere, the extent of it abroad (where few English writers before him had had any at all), and the decline at home, are all easily connected with certain peculiarities of his work. That work is almost as fluent and facile as Scott's, to which, as has been said, it owes immense debts of scheme and manner; and it is quite as faulty. Indeed Scott, with all his indifference to a strictly academic correctness, never permitted himself the bad rhymes, the bad grammar, the slipshod phrase in which Byron unblushingly indulges. But Byron is much more monotonous than Scott, and it was this very monotony, assisted by an appearance of intensity, which for the time gave him power. The appeal of Byron consists very mainly, though no doubt not wholly, in two things: the lavish use of the foreign and then unfamiliar scenery, vocabulary, and manners of the Levant, and the installation, as principal character, of a personage who was speedily recognised as a sort of fancy portrait, a sketch in cap and yataghan, of Byron himself as he would like to be thought. This Byronic hero has an ostentatious indifference to moral laws, for the most part a mysterious past which inspires him with deep melancholy, great personal beauty, strength, and bravery, and he is an all-conquering lover. He is not quite so original as he seemed, for he is in effect very little more than the older Romantic villain-hero of Mrs. Radcliffe, the Germans, and Monk Lewis, costumed much more effectively, placed in scheme and companionship more picturesquely, and managed with infinitely greater genius. But it is a common experience in literary history that a type more or less familiar already, and presented with striking additions, is likely to be more popular than something absolutely new. And accordingly Byron's bastard and second-hand Romanticism, though it owed a great deal to the terrorists and a great deal more to Scott, for the moment altogether eclipsed the pure and original Romanticism of his elders Coleridge and Wordsworth, of his juniors Shelley and Keats.

But although the more extreme admirers of Byron would no doubt dissent strongly from even this judgment, it would probably be subscribed, with some reservations and guards, by not a few good critics from whom I am compelled to part company as to other parts of Byron's poetical claim. It is on the question how much of true poetry lies behind and independent of the scenery and properties of Byronism, that the great debate arises. Was the author of the poems from *Childe Harold* to *Don Juan* really gifted with the poetical "sincerity and strength" which have been awarded him by a critic of leanings so little Byronic in the ordinary sense of Matthew Arnold? Is he a poetic star of the first magnitude, a poetic force of the first power, at all? There may seem to be rashness, there may even seem to be puerile insolence and absurdity, in denying or even doubting this in the face of such a European concert as has been described and admitted above. Yet the critical conscience admits of no transaction; and after all, as it was doubted by a great thinker whether nations might not go mad like individuals, I do not know why it should be regarded as impossible that continents should go mad like nations.

At any rate the qualities of Byron are very much of a piece, and, even by the contention of his warmest reasonable admirers, not much varied or very subtle, not necessitating much analysis or disquisition. They can be fairly pronounced upon in a judgment of few words. Byron, then, seems to me a poet distinctly of the second class, and not even of the best kind of second, inasmuch as his greatness is chiefly derived from a sort of parody, a sort of imitation, of the qualities of the first. His verse is to the greatest poetry what melodrama is to tragedy, what plaster is to marble, what pinchbeck is to gold. He is not indeed an impostor; for his sense of the beauty of nature and of the unsatisfactoriness of life is real, and his power of conveying this sense to others is real also. He has great, though uncertain, and never very *fine,* command of poetic sound, and a considerable though less command of poetic vision. But in all this there is a singular touch of illusion, of what his contemporaries had learnt from Scott to call gramarye. The often cited parallel of the false and true Florimels in Spenser applies here also. The really great poets do not injure each other in the very least by comparison, different as they are. Milton does not "kill" Wordsworth; Spenser does not injure Shelley; there is no danger in reading Keats immediately after Coleridge. But read Byron in close juxtaposition with any of these, or with not a few others, and the effect, to any good poetic taste, must surely be disastrous; to my own, whether good or bad, it is perfectly fatal. The light is not that which never was on land or sea; it is that which is habitually just in front of the stage: the roses are rouged, the cries of passion even sometimes (not always) ring false. I have read Byron again and again; I have sometimes, by reading Byron only and putting a strong constraint upon myself, got nearly into the mood to enjoy him. But let eye or ear once catch sight or sound of real poetry, and the enchantment vanishes.

—George Saintsbury, *A History of Nineteenth Century Literature,* 1896, pp. 78–81

EDWARD DOWDEN (1897)

Edward Dowden (1843–1913) was an Irish critic and poet who is noted for his critical work on Shakespeare. He lectured at Dublin, Oxford, and Cambridge and also published books on Shelley (*Life of Shelley,* 1886) and Robert Southey.

To acquire a right feeling for Byron and his poetry is a discipline in equity. It is easy to yield to a sense of his power, to the force and sweep of his genius; it is easy to be repelled by his superficial insincerity, his license, his cynicism, his poverty of thought, his looseness of construction, his carelessness in execution. To know aright the evil and the good is difficult. It is difficult to feel justly towards this dethroned idol (presently, perhaps, to be re-enthroned), an idol in whose composition iron and clay are mingled with fine gold.

But what interests us in Byron and in Byron's work is precisely this mingling of noble and ignoble, of gold and a base alloy. We do not thank any one for extracting the gold and presenting it alone. We can get swifter and clearer lyric poetry from Shelley, a truer and finer feeling for nature from Wordsworth, more exquisite satiric art from Pope, dramatic power incomparably wider and deeper from Shakespeare. Seen in elegant extracts, Byron is impoverished, or rather Byron ceases to be Byron. Matthew Arnold's volume of selections from Byron, compiled with such excellent intentions, proves at least that his poetry is not of the kind that can be pinned in a specimen case, like preserved butterflies. Line upon line, here a little and there a little, is the way in which such work as his should *not* be read. We must take him or leave him as he is,—the immortal spoilt by his age, great and petty, weak and strong, exalted and debased. A glorious wave that curls upon the sea-beach, though it leave sea-wrack and refuse on the sands, is more stimulating, more health-giving, than a pitcher of such salt water in one's dressing-room, even if it be free from every floating weed.

In its mingled elements Byron's poetry represents at once the mind and character of the writer and the temper of his age. He was an aristocrat, and at the same time he was revolutionary. He had the pride of ancestry, but nothing of the hereditary dignity, the fine traditions of civility, the trained mastery of men and events, which belong to the best types of his class. The Revolution and the Reaction helped to spoil him as an English nobleman. In a time of disorder and disintegration he fell into the coarse ways of the *jeunesse doree* of the period of the Regency. The taint of vulgar aristocracy helped to spoil him as a Republican. He had a strong feeling for the Revolutionary movement as a destructive force; he sympathized with its negative tendencies; he enjoyed the sense of emancipation from the old restraints; he loved to demonstrate the boundless freedom of the individual, in his passions, his self-will, his audacities of belief or unbelief, his scorn for things commonly regarded with veneration or esteem. But he cared little for the principles or tendencies of the Revolution which are positive, constructive, social; he had neither the power of thought nor the patience which are needed by one who would build up; it was enough for him if he could deliver a reeling blow at despotisms, half-realized creeds, lifeless conventions, and dull respectabilities, or could mock at them in their state of infirmity. He had lost faith in what was old, and had not gained a new faith. He could do little more than plead for an emancipation of egoism, and into his egoism ran that sentiment of the infinite, that limitless desire, which Rousseau's passionate heart, his ardent feeling for nature, and those boundless horizons opened by the Revolution had made a common possession of the time. He asserted with emphasis the prerogative of man to do what he likes, where he likes, when he likes, how he likes; and the privilege of woman to lay her passion at the feet of such a proud insurgent. He idealized in his poetry all revolters against the social order, a Cain, a Corsair, a Manfred, all who seek for isolation, for solitude, or find the end of their being in abandonment to personal passion in disregard of social duty. His mockery was a dissolvent of accepted conventions and traditional manners and morals. He took part in popular movements of political emancipation less in the spirit of faith and hope than because his imagination had been captivated by the new force of the people, because it pleased him to deploy his own energy, and because he hated and despised the spent forces, or what seemed to be such, on the side of conservation. To the last he was haunted by the ghosts of traditional beliefs, which had ceased to live within him as vital powers. He was a democrat among aristocrats and an aristocrat among democrats; a sceptic among believers and a believer among sceptics. And yet his line of advance was not a *via media,* nor was it determined by a spirit of moderation or critical balance. He never attempted to effect a conciliation between the powers that clashed or jarred within him. A certain intellectual good sense indeed he had, but this was liable to be overpowered by the turbulent rush of his temper; and when a reasonable mood re-emerged, good sense would take the form of ironical laughter at himself and at the world. To his quick sense of humor more than to anything else he owed the sanity which controls or modifies his perturbations of mind. With a keen perception of human folly, he could mock absurdity, affectation, extravagance in other men; it was his merit that he could turn the light of laughter upon himself, and chasten his own follies by ridicule.

—Edward Dowden, *The French Revolution and English Literature,* 1897, pp. 261–265

LIONEL JOHNSON "BYRON" (1898)

The British poet and critic Lionel Pigot Johnson (1867–1902) spent his scholarly life in London, struggling with his repressed homosexuality and alcoholism. As the cousin of Alfred Lord Douglas, he repudiated his former friend Oscar Wilde, calling him in a sonnet "The Destroyer of a Soul." Johnson converted to Roman Catholicism in 1891. He was a member of the Rhymer's Club, and many of his poems reflect his interest in the Irish literary renaissance. He died of a stroke at the age of thirty-five. His most influential poem is "The Dark Angel."

Byron the poet? Emphatically, he was *not* a poet; not if Shakespeare and Milton are poets. He was a magnificent satirist; the *Vision of Judgment, Don Juan,* and *Beppo* are very glories of wit, indignation, rhetoric; accomplished to the uttermost, marvellous and immortal; filled with scathing laughter, rich with a prodigal profusion of audacious fancy and riot of rhyme. Here the man is himself, eloquent and vehement of speech, alive and afire. No coarseness, cruelty, insolence, can blind us to the enduring excellence of these writings, to their virility and strength. *This* Byron is deathless. But the Byron of love lyrics, and tragedies, and romantic tales, is a poet of infinite tediousness in execrable verse; in the severely courteous French phrase, he "does not permit himself to be read." And he is not read; no one now reads *Lara,* or *Parisina,* or *The Corsair,* or *The Giaour,* or *The Bride of Abydos,* or *The Siege of Corinth,* or *The Island,* or the weary, weary plays. They are dead, and past resurrection; their passion is as poor and tawdry a thing as that of *Frankenstein* or *The Mysteries of Udolpho;* their garish theatricality is laughable, and we can scarce believe that these things of nought were once preferred to the noble simplicities and rough, true music of Scott. Among the poems of farewell, regret, despair, is there one, except, may be, "When we two parted," that can be read with more than a mild and languid pleasure? In all the moralisings, and meanderings, and maunderings of *Childe Harold,* is there anything better than a few bursts of sounding rhetoric and impressive declamation, superbly and masterfully trivial? Dullness is the word, dullness unspeakable. Outside his own royal province of satire, he created nothing of power, nothing but frantic efforts to be powerful; and he turned the lovely speech of English poetry into a hideous noise. Coleridge, master of music, says of him, "It seems, to my ear, that there is a sad want of harmony in Lord Byron's verses"; and again, "How lamentably the *art* of versification is neglected by most of the poets of the present day! By Lord Byron, as it strikes me, in particular." In our times, Mr. Swinburne, to whom none will deny a mastery of his craft, has poured upon Byron's inharmonies the contempt, not of parody—that were impossible—but of faithful imitation. . . .

But Byron was accepted abroad—he enfranchised English literature, he was the genius of English poetry incarnate before the eyes of Europe, he moved the aged Goethe and the youthful Hugo. Why? Surely for a simple reason: Byron is very easy to understand, he deals rhetorically with elemental emotions, and he enjoyed the fame of being "at war with society"—an aristocrat in exile, a champion of the peoples. Now, rhetoric and oratory and eloquence make a wide appeal; they are seldom subtle, but they address themselves with pungent and poignant vigour to the simple feelings of men. "Give me liberty or give me death!"—that is the kind of thing; a sonorous and impassioned commonplace, flung out upon the air to thrill the hearts of thousands. Byron's best verse has this quality: he possessed the imagination of the orator, the faculty of finding large and bold phrases. Stanza upon stanza of *Childe Harold* reads like the finest things in Irish or American oratory—grandiose and sweeping. "Roll on, thou deep and dark-blue ocean, roll!" You can see the outstretched arm, hear the resonant voice, of Byron the declaimer; and the effect upon ears unversed in the niceties and delicacies of English poetry was prodigious. The blaring magniloquence of Lucan has certain attractions not possessed by the majestic, melancholy, subtle Virgilian lines; and Byron was much of a Lucan. "The Isles of Greece" and "Ode to Napoleon" and "Lines on Completing My Thirty-sixth Year"—emphatic, strenuous, impressive—have the true oratorical note and ring:

> The sword, the banner, and the field,
> Glory and Greece, around me see!
> The Spartan, borne upon his shield,
> Was not more free.

There is a trumpet call in that; but for greatness of beauty we turn from it to the last chorus of Shelley's *Hellas,* and hear a music of the morning stars. Byron could shout magnificently, laugh splendidly, thunder tumultuously; but he could not sing. There was something in him of Achilles, nothing whatever of Apollo. Think only of these mighty masters of passion—Aeschylus, Lucretius, Dante, Milton, Hugo; what sweetness proceeding from what strength! They are filled with a lyrical loveliness, the very magic of music, the beauty almost unbearable. By the side of these Byron is but a brazen noise. His *saeva indignatio* becomes a mere petulance of arrogance when we think of Dante; one line of Milton rebukes his haste of speech. He took Europe by storm; but a far more impassioned figure is that of Wordsworth, with his whole being, body and soul, shaken by the "divine madness" of inspiration, by converse with eternity, by commune with "the most ancient heavens." *There* was the true passion, not in Byron, hurriedly throwing off a few hundred lines of romantic rant after coming home from some silly dissipation. He has no trace of the poet consecrate, such as marks many a nameless balladist. Who would not rather have written *Helen of Kirkconnel,* so fierce and loving, desolate and defiant, a cry imperishable and perfect, than all the famed rigmarole of rhetoric called *Childe Harold?* In that long and elaborate work there are precisely two lines of pure poetry, the lines on the Dying Gladiator:

> He heard it, but he heeded not: his eyes
> Were with his heart, and that was far away.

That, and perhaps a score of other lines in Byron, have an enduring freshness and fragrance of thought and word. For the rest, he was pleased in poetry, as in life, to "cut a dash," with the result that both his verse and himself are sorrily discredited; things, as George Borrow has it, of "mouthings and coxcombry." Landor, in stately Latin, once exhorted him to amend his morals and his style. He did neither, and his style remained even more detestable than his morals. When Tennyson heard of Byron's death, he went out upon the seashore and wrote upon the sand the words, "Byron is dead!" Seas of oblivion have swept over Byron, and washed away his fame, as the sea washed away those words. It may be that his most celebrated passage will be remembered only by the scornful ridicule of Browning. The poets whom he insulted or patronised—Wordsworth and Coleridge, and Shelley and Keats—have long since taken their starry stations in altitudes beyond sight of him, and Byron, "The Claimant" of English poetry, has been found out. He retains but one glory—his gift of wit and satire, his superb recklessness of mocking phrase and rhyme. There, all that was potent and sincere in him became triumphant, and the writer of Don Juan is a deathless delight. But the "poet of passion" is dead. Peacock killed him long ago in Nightmare Abbey. His wailings and howlings wring no man's heart, stir no man's pulses; we no longer believe in the Byron of dazzling devilry and burning poetry, volcanic and voluptuous. In place of him we contemplate an ill-mannered and cross-grained fellow, charlatan and genius, whose voluminous writings are mostly dull and mostly ill-written—gone for ever, that Byron of the fatal fascination, the passionate and patrician glory, whose freaks and whimsies threw Europe into fits, whose poems revealed to the universe the fact that Shakespeare's England had at last produced a poet.

—Lionel Johnson, "Byron,"
Academy, May 7, 1898, pp. 489–490

G.K. Chesterton
"The Optimism of Byron" (1901)

Gilbert Keith Chesterton (1874–1936) wrote approximately eighty books, several hundred poems, two hundred short stories, four thousand essays, and several plays. His prolific and diverse output included journalism, philosophy, poetry, and detective fiction among other writings. His best-known creation is the priest-detective Father Brown, who appeared in short stories, while *The Man Who Was Thursday* remains his best-known novel. Interested in the occult and specifically ouija boards in his youth, he became an orthodox Christian later. His collection of short biographies,

Twelve Types (*Varied Types*), gives his thoughts on authors such as Charlotte Brontë, William Morris, and Byron. His interpretation of Byron attempts to show that, despite the melancholy surface of many of his works, he was a humorous author: "His affected pessimism was only the blackboard on which he wrote with white chalk."

———

Everything is against our appreciating the spirit and the age of Byron. The age that has just passed from us is always like a dream when we wake in the morning, a thing incredible and centuries away. And the world of Byron seems a sad and faded world, a weird and inhuman world, where men were romantic in whiskers, ladies lived, apparently, in bowers, and the very word has the sound of a piece of stage scenery. Roses and nightingales recur in their poetry with the monotonous elegance of a wall-paper pattern. The whole is like a revel of dead men, a revel with splendid vesture and half-witted faces. But the more shrewdly and earnestly we study the histories of men, the less ready shall we be to make use of the word "artificial." Nothing in the world has ever been artificial. Many customs, many dresses, many works of art are branded with artificiality because they exhibit vanity and self-consciousness: as if vanity were not a deep and elemental thing, like love and hate and the fear of death. Vanity may be found in darkling deserts, in the hermit and in the wild beasts that crawl around him. It may be good or evil, but assuredly it is not artificial: vanity is a voice out of the abyss.

The remarkable fact is, however, and it bears strongly on the present position of Byron, that when a thing is unfamiliar to us, when it is remote and the product of some other age or spirit, we think it not savage or terrible, but merely artificial. There are many instances of this: a fair one is the case of tropical plants and birds. When we see some of the monstrous and flamboyant blossoms that enrich the equatorial woods, we do not feel that they are conflagrations of nature; silent explosions of her frightful energy. We simply find it hard to believe that they are not wax flowers grown under a glass case. When we see some of the tropic birds, with their tiny bodies attached to gigantic beaks, we do not feel that they are freaks of the fierce humour of Creation. We almost believe that they are toys out of a child's playbox, artificially carved and artificially coloured. So it is with the great convulsion of Nature which was known as Byronism. The volcano is not an extinct volcano now; it is the dead stick of a rocket. It is the remains not of a natural but of an artificial fire.

But Byron and Byronism were something immeasurably greater than anything that is represented by such a view as this: their real value and meaning are indeed little understood. The first of the mistakes about Byron lies in the fact that he is treated as a pessimist. True, he treated himself as such, but a critic can hardly have even a slight knowledge of Byron without knowing that he had the smallest amount of knowledge of himself that ever fell to the lot of an intelligent man. The real character of what is known as Byron's pessimism is better worth study than any real pessimism could ever be.

It is the standing peculiarity of this curious world of ours that almost everything in it has been extolled enthusiastically and invariably extolled to the disadvantage of everything else. One after another almost every one of the phenomena of the universe has been declared to be alone capable of making life worth living. Books, love, business, religion, alcohol, abstract truth, private emotion, money, simplicity, mysticism, hard work, a life close to nature, a life close to Belgrave Square are every one of them passionately maintained by somebody to be so good that they redeem the evil of an otherwise indefensible world. Thus, while the world is almost always condemned in summary, it is always justified, and indeed extolled, in detail after detail.

Existence has been praised and absolved by a chorus of pessimists. The work of giving thanks to Heaven is, as it were, divided ingeniously among them. Schopenhauer is told off as a kind of librarian in the House of God, to sing the praises of the austere pleasures of the mind. Carlyle, as steward, undertakes the working department and eulogises a life of labour in the fields. Omar Khayyam is established in the cellar, and swears that it is the only room in the house. Even the blackest of pessimistic artists enjoys his art. At the precise moment that he has written some shameless and terrible indictment of Creation, his one pang of joy in the achievement joins the universal chorus of gratitude, with the scent of the wild flower and the song of the bird.

Now Byron had a sensational popularity, and that popularity was, as far as words and explanations go, founded upon his pessimism. He was adored by an overwhelming majority, almost every individual of which despised the majority of mankind. But when we come to regard the matter a little more deeply we tend in some degree to cease to believe in this popularity of the pessimist. The popularity of pure and unadulterated pessimism is an oddity; it is almost a contradiction in terms. Men would no more receive the news of the failure of existence or of the harmonious hostility of the stars with ardour or popular rejoicing than they would light bonfires for the arrival of cholera or dance a breakdown when they were condemned to be hanged. When the pessimist is popular it must always be not because he shows all things to be bad, but because he shows some things to be good.

Men can only join in a chorus of praise, even if it is the praise of denunciation. The man who is popular must be optimistic about something, even if he is only optimistic about pessimism. And this was emphatically the case with Byron and the Byronists. Their real popularity was founded not upon the fact that they blamed everything, but upon the fact that they praised something. They heaped curses upon man, but they used man merely as a foil. The things they wished to praise by comparison were the energies of Nature. Man was to them what talk and fashion were to Carlyle, what philosophical and religious quarrels were to Omar, what the whole race after practical happiness was to Schopenhauer, the thing which must be censured in order that somebody else may be exalted. It was merely a recognition of the fact that one cannot write in white chalk except on a blackboard.

Surely it is ridiculous to maintain seriously that Byron's love of the desolate and inhuman in nature was the mark of vital scepticism and depression. When a young man can elect deliberately to walk alone in winter by the side of the shattering sea, when he takes pleasure in storms and stricken peaks, and the lawless melancholy of the older earth, we may deduce with the certainty of logic that he is very young and very happy. There is a certain darkness which we see in wine when seen in shadow; we see it again in the night that has just buried a gorgeous sunset. The wine seems black, and yet at the same time powerfully and almost impossibly red; the sky seems black, and yet at the same time to be only too dense a blend of purple and green. Such was the darkness which lay around the Byronic school. Darkness with them was only too dense a purple. They would prefer the sullen hostility of the earth because amid all the cold and darkness their own hearts were flaming like their own firesides.

Matters are very different with the more modern school of doubt and lamentation. The last movement of pessimism is perhaps expressed in Mr. Aubrey Beardsley's allegorical designs. Here we have to deal with a pessimism which tends naturally not towards the oldest elements of the cosmos, but towards the last and most fantastic fripperies of artificial life. Byronism tended towards the desert; the new pessimism towards the restaurant. Byronism was a revolt against artificiality; the new pessimism is a revolt in its favour.

The Byronic young man had an affectation of sincerity; the decadent, going a step deeper into the avenues of the unreal, has positively an affectation of affectation. And it is by their fopperies and their frivolities that we know that their sinister philosophy is sincere; in their lights and garlands and ribbons we read their indwelling despair. It was so, indeed, with Byron himself; his really bitter moments were his frivolous moments. He went on year after year calling down fire upon mankind, summoning the deluge and the destructive sea and all the ultimate energies of nature to sweep away the cities of the spawn of man. But through all this his subconscious mind was not that of a despairer; on the contrary, there is something of a kind of lawless faith in thus parleying with such immense and immemorial brutalities. It was not until the time in which he wrote *Don Juan* that he really lost this inward warmth and geniality, and a sudden shout of hilarious laughter announced to the world that Lord Byron had really become a pessimist.

One of the best tests in the world of what a poet really means is his metre. He may be a hypocrite in his metaphysics, but he cannot be a hypocrite in his prosody. And all the time that Byron's language is of horror and emptiness, his metre is a bounding pas de quatre. He may arraign existence on the most deadly charges, he may condemn it with the most desolating verdict, but he cannot alter the fact that on some walk in a spring morning when all the limbs are swinging and all the blood alive in the body, the lips may be caught repeating:

Oh, there's not a joy the world can give like that it takes away,
When the glow of early youth declines in beauty's dull decay;
'Tis not upon the cheek of youth the blush that fades so fast,
But the tender bloom of heart is gone ere youth itself be past.

That automatic recitation is the answer to the whole pessimism of Byron. The truth is that Byron was one of a class who may be called the unconscious optimists, who are very often, indeed, the most uncompromising conscious pessimists, because the exuberance of their nature demands for an adversary a dragon as big as the world. But the whole of his essential and unconscious being was spirited and confident, and that unconscious being, long disguised and buried under emotional artifices, suddenly sprang into prominence in the face of a cold, hard, political necessity. In Greece he heard the cry of reality, and at the time that he was dying, he began to live. He heard suddenly the call of that buried and subconscious happiness which is in all of us, and which may emerge suddenly at the sight of the grass of a meadow or the spears of the enemy.

—G.K. Chesterton, "The Optimism of Byron,"
1901, *Varied Types*, 1908, pp. 29–39

JOHN CHURTON COLLINS "THE COLLECTED WORKS OF LORD BYRON" (1905)

The English literary critic John Churton Collins (1848–1908) taught English literature at the University of Birmingham. His essay "The Collected

Works of Lord Byron" was published in the *Quarterly Review* in April 1905 in reaction to R.D. Prothero's edition of Byron's *Letters and Journals* and E.H. Coleridge's edition of the *Poetical Works*. In the following excerpt, he attempts to explain Byron's greatness with reference to *Don Juan* but also stresses the insincerity of much of his work.

Few critical problems would be more difficult to solve than to determine Byron's relative position among poets. Of no man of genius can it be so truly said that he is of those whom Chapman admirably described as having Strange gifts from Nature, but no soul Infused quite through to make them of a piece. His inspired power, his essential sincerity as a poet, lay partly in the intensity with which he felt and expressed the passions and realized all that in circumstance and situation appealed to them, and partly in what Matthew Arnold has so happily designated his Titanism. The moment he quits these spheres he becomes a rhetorician, but a rhetorician so eloquent and moving, so brilliant and impressive, that the note of falsetto is not at first sight discernible. We see his power, in quintessence, in such passages as the journey and death of Hassan; Alp's journey along the beach; the death of Selim; the stanzas on Waterloo; the falls of Velino; the thunderstorm; the apostrophe to Rome; the dying gladiator; the last two stanzas of the shipwreck, and innumerable other passages in which these and similar notes are struck. But his serious poetry has not only no unity, it has not even permeating enthusiasm. Ecstasy exhausted and in collapse, mere talent succeeds to genius, the interstices between each effort of inspired energy being filled up by more or less successfully disguised falsetto.

In the other sphere, the sphere of satire and comedy, his masterpiece— and here his power is sustained—is *The Vision of Judgment*; while in *Don Juan* we have, what we have nowhere else, the true, full man in absolute and naked simplicity, a comprehensive illustration of his amazing versatility and dexterity, of his genius for comedy and satire—perhaps his most remarkable characteristic—as well as of all those qualities of sincerity which inform and vitalize his serious poetry.

Byron's insincerity—in other words, his rhetoric and falsetto—is most discernible in those parts of his poetry which are in execution most brilliant, and which are generally singled out for special commendation by his admirers. First would come his descriptions of nature and his affectation of being Nature's devoted worshipper. It may fairly be questioned whether Byron was ever profoundly moved by Nature, or whether he ever regarded her in any other light than a theme for rhetorical display. In his earlier poems all his descriptions are perfectly commonplace and of the order of Shenstone's, who seems, judging from the *Hours of Idleness*, to have been a favourite with him. In the first two cantos of *Childe Harold* his descriptions are mere rhetoric. The Morean sunset in the third canto of The Corsair is little more than a brilliant declamation. At last, in the third canto of *Childe Harold*, the note changes; but it changes because, to employ his own expression, Shelley "had dosed him with Wordsworth." From this moment Nature became a favourite, for he saw from Wordsworth what capital could be made out of such a theme; and "description" being, as he himself boasted, "his forte," delineations of Nature fill thenceforward a very wide space in his poetry. Of their power and beauty there can be no question, but there can be as little question of the purely rhetorical quality of much of this part of his work. Not, however, of all of it, for affectation passes at once into inspired sincerity the moment he deals with such phases of Nature as respond to his own moods. He "loved her," he tells us, "best in wrath"; and in her wrath and her awe-compelling forms of sublimity and grandeur she took possession of him and made him her prophet. There is no note of falsetto, or, if there appears to be such a note, it is only in clumsiness of expression, when his themes are the falls of Velino, or the thunderstorm in the Alps, or the elemental wastes of mountain or of ocean, or the ravages of death and time.

His falsetto becomes at once apparent when, in wholesale plagiarisms from Wordsworth, he adopts Wordsworth's metaphysical philosophy; because it is quite evident that, so far from believing in it, he did not even comprehend it. He saw how happily it lent itself to effective rhetoric, but he did not see how incongruous was the essential materialism of his own conception of life and nature with conceptions as essentially transcendental. When he writes—

> I live not in myself, but I become
> Portion of that around me . .
> And thus I am absorbed, and this is life.
> Are not the mountains, waves, and skies a part
> Of me and of my soul, as I of them?
> Not a beam, nor air, nor leaf is lost
> But hath a part of being, and a sense
> Of that which is of all Creator and defence

—we instinctively feel that it is what the Greeks so happily called paren-thyrsos. . . .

To pass to his masterpieces; *Childe Harold* and *Don Juan*, regarded comprehensively, are perhaps the two most brilliant achievements in the poetry of the world, and they are achievements which have nothing in common. Each moves in a sphere of its own, as each exhibits powers differing not in degree merely, but in kind. *Childe Harold* is a superb triumph partly of pure rhetoric and partly of rhetoric touched with inspired enthusiasm. In Don Juan we are in another world and under the spell of another genius. The sentimentalist has passed into the cynic, the moralist into the mocker. We are no longer in the temples and palaces of poetry, but in its profane places and meaner habitations. The theme now is not Nature in her glory, but humanity in its squalor; not the world as God made it, but as the devil rules it. For the series of splendid pageants, for the raptures and sublimities of its predecessor, has been substituted, in broad, free fresco, the tragic farce into which man's lusts and lawlessness, madness and follies, have perverted life. It was into this mock-heroic that Byron, disengaging himself from all that vanity had induced him to affect, and from all that his cleverness and command of rhetoric had enabled him to assume, poured out his powers in sheer and absolute sincerity—the Titanism which was of the very essence of his genius, the scorn and mockery, the wit, the persiflage, the irony, "the sense of tears in human things," the brutal appetites, the more refined affections of which he was still, in some of his moods, susceptible.

Don Juan is admirable alike in conception, in range, in expression. To give unity to a work which blends all that amuses and entertains us in Lazarillo de Tormes, Gil Bias, the Novelle Amorose, and Horace Walpole's Letters, much of what impresses and charms us in the *Odyssey* and the *Aeneid*, which has all the cynicism of La Rochefoucauld and Swift, all the callous levity of the worst school of our comedy, and yet subdues us with a pathos which has now the note of Ecclesiastes and now the note of Catullus—this indeed required a master-hand. The unity of the poem is the unity impressed on it by truth, by truth to nature and truth to life, for Byron in writing it did but hold up the mirror to himself and his own experiences.

"What an antithetical mind!" (he himself wrote after reading certain letters of Burns)—"tenderness, roughness, delicacy, coarseness, sentiment, sensuality, soaring and grovelling, dirt and deity, all mixed up in that one compound of inspired clay."

Such, in fact, was Byron himself, and such is this poem, the glory and the shame of our poetry. But if much is to be forgiven to one who loves greatly, something may be forgiven to one who hates rightly. The justification of *Don Juan* is its ruthless exposure of some of the most despicable characteristics of the English people: the ubiquity of hypocrisy, the ubiquity of cant; immorality masking as morality, and ceremony as religion, for the vilest purposes, the one to make capital out of the frailties and lapses of those who are at least sincere, the other as a means for dignifying almost every form which moral cowardice and moral vanity can assume.

In its execution *Don Juan* deserves all the praise which Byron's most extravagant admirers have heaped on it. Never was our language so completely clay in the moulder's hands. Whatever he has to express seems to embody itself spontaneously in the complicated form of verse which he has chosen. With a skill and ease which, in our literature at least, are unrivalled, he has blended every extreme in nature and life, in style and tone, without producing the effect either of incongruity or even of impropriety. *Don Juan* has little enough in common with the *Odyssey*, and yet in some respects it recalls it. In both poems the similitude which at once suggests itself is the element so closely associated with the action of both—the sea. A freshness, a breeziness, a pungency as of the brine-laden air of beach or cliff seems to pervade it. Over the spacious expanse of its narrative, teeming with life and in ever-changing play, now in storm and now in calm, roll and break, wave after wave in endless succession, the incomparable stanzas on whose lilt and rush we are swept along.

The importance of Byron in English poetry is not to be estimated by ordinary critical tests; it is not by its quality that his work is to be judged. The application of perfectly legitimate criteria to his poetry would justify us in questioning whether he could be held to stand high even among the "Dii minores" of his art; it would certainly result in assigning him a place very much below Wordsworth and Shelley, and even below Keats. Of many, nay, of most of the qualities essential in a poet of a high order, there is no indication in anything he has left us. Of spiritual insight he has nothing; of morality and the becoming, except in their coarser aspects, he has no sense. If the beautiful appealed to him, it appealed to him only in its material expression and sentimentally as it affected the passions. Of no poet could it be said with so much truth—and how much does that truth imply!—that he had not "music in his soul." Turn where we will in his work, there is no repose, no harmony; all is without balance, without measure, and, if we accept *Don Juan* and *The Vision of Judgment*, without unity. At his worst he sinks below Peter Pindar; at his best his accent is never that of the great masters. A certain ingrained coarseness, both in taste and feeling, which became more emphasized as his powers matured, not only made him insensible of much which appeals to the poet as distinguished from the rhetorician, but is accountable for the jarring notes, the lapses into grossness, and the banalities which so often surprise and distress us in his poetry.

As an artist, his defects are equally conspicuous. In architectonic he is as deficient as Tennyson. *Childe Harold*, as well as all his minor narratives, simply resolve themselves into a series of pageants or episodes. Some, notably the *Giaour*, are little more than congeries of brilliant scraps. No eminent English poet, with the exception of Browning, had so bad an ear. His cacophanies are often horrible; his blank-verse is generally indistinguishable from prose; and his rhythm in rhymed verse is without delicacy, and full of discords. Every solecism in grammar, every violation of syntax and of propriety of expression, might be illustrated from his diction and style. Nor is this all. His claim to originality can only be conceded with much modification in its important aspects, and with very much more modification in the less important.

These are large deductions to make; and yet Goethe placed Byron next to Shakespeare among the English poets; and in fame and popularity, by the consentient testimony of every nation in Europe, next to Shakespeare among Shakespeare's countrymen, he still stands. Such a verdict it is much more easy to understand than to justify. To his countrymen Byron's flaws and limitations will always be more perceptible and important than they will be to the people of the Continent; while, in all that appeals to humanity at large, his work will come more nearly home on the other side of the Channel than that of any other English poet except Shakespeare; and necessarily so. Byron's poetry originally was not so much an appeal to England as to Europe. His themes, his characters, his inspiration, his politics, his morals, were all derived from the Continent or from the East. England was little more than the incarnation of everything against which he reacted, at first with contempt and then in fury. The trumpet-voice of the world of the Revolution and of the revolt against the principles of the Holy Alliance, it was on the Continent that he found most response. And there indeed he can never cease to be popular. The laureate of its scenery, the rhapsodist of its traditions, the student and painter of almost every phase of its many-sided life, the poet of the passions which burn with fiercer fire in the South than in the colder regions of the North, he neither has nor is likely to have, with the single exception of Shakespeare, an English rival across the Channel.

The greatness of Byron lies in the immense body and mass of the work which he has informed and infused with life, in his almost unparalleled versatility, in the power and range of his influential achievement. Youth and mature age alike feel his spell, for of the passions he is the Orpheus, of reflection the Mephistopheles. There is not an emotion, there is scarcely a mood, to which he does not appeal, and to which he has not given expression. Of almost every side of life, of almost every phase of human activity, he has left us studies more or less brilliant and impressive. He had, in extraordinary measure, nearly every gift, intellectually speaking, which man can possess, from mere cleverness to rapt genius; and there was hardly any species of composition which he did not more or less successfully attempt. In his inspired moments what Longinus sublimely observes of Demosthenes may with the strictest propriety be applied to his eloquence, "One could sooner face with unflinching eyes the descending thunderbolt than stand undazzled as his bursts of passion, in swift-succeeding flash on flash, are fulmined forth."

As Goethe and Wordsworth were the Olympians, so he was the Titan of the stormy and chaotic age in which he lived; and his most authentic poetry is typical of his temper and attitude. He has impressed on our literature the stamp of a most fascinating and commanding personality, and on the literature of every nation in Europe he has exercised an influence to which no other British writer except Shakespeare has even approximated. Among his disciples and imitators in Germany are to be numbered Wilhelm Miiller, Heine, Von Platen, Adalbert Chamisso, Karl Lebrecht, Immermann and Christian Grabbe. How deeply he has impressed himself on the genius of France is sufficiently testified by the poetry of Lamartine, Victor Hugo, Casimir de la Vigne, and Alfred de Musset. The most brilliant of the modern poets of Spain, Espronceda, is little more than his echo. In the Netherlands he has found imitators in Willem Bilderdijk, Isaac de Costa, Jakobus Van Lennep, and Nicolaes Beets. On the poetry of Russia he has exercised wide and deep influence, as we need go no further than Poucshkin and Lermontoff to see.[3] Such is the intrinsic power and attraction of a great part of his poetry that he will always be a favourite—if not in the first rank of their favourites—with his countrymen; and, although no purely critical estimate would place him on a level with at least five, if not more, of our poets, yet it must be admitted that, next to Shakespeare, he would probably be most missed.

Note

3. See Otto Weddigen's excellent monograph, Lord Byron's *Einfluss auf die Europäischen Litteraturen der Neuzeit*.

—John Churton Collins, from "The Collected Works of Lord Byron," *Studies in Poetry and Criticism*, 1905, pp. 107–123

ARTHUR SYMONS (1909)

Arthur William Symons (1865–1945), a poet, editor, critic, member of the Rhymers' Club, and author of *The Symbolist Movement in Literature* (1899), wrote on Byron in his book *The Romantic Movement in English Poetry*, published in 1909.

The life of Byron was a masque in action, to which his poetry is but the moralising accompaniment of words. 'One whose dust was once all fire' (words which Byron used of Rousseau, and which may still more truthfully be used of himself), Byron still lives for us with such incomparable vividness because he was a man first and a poet afterwards. He became a poet for that reason, and that reason explains the imperfection of his poetry. Most of his life he was a personality looking out for its own formula, and his experiments upon that search were of precisely the kind to thrill the world. What poet ever had so splendid a legend in his lifetime? His whole life was lived in the eyes of men, and Byron had enough of the actor in him to delight in that version of 'all the world's a stage.' His beauty and his deformity, his 'tenderness, roughness, delicacy, coarseness, sentiment, sensuality, soaring and grovelling, dirt and deity, all mixed up in that one compound of inspired clay' (it is his own summary of Burns), worked together with circumstances to move every heart to admiration and pity. He was a poet, and he did what others only wrote; he seemed to write what others dared not think. . . .

'My qualities,' he tells us of his school-days at Harrow, 'were much more oratorical than poetical, and Dr. Drury, my grand patron, had a great notion that I should turn out an orator, from my fluency, my turbulence, my voice, my copiousness of declamation, and my action.' The criticism justified itself; Byron's qualities in verse are indeed 'much more oratorical than poetical'; and, in all his earlier work, theory accentuated this natural tendency so fatally that we have to scrape off a great deal of false glitter if we are to find the good metal which is often enough to be found, even in the metrical romances, with their pseudo-romance, founded on direct observation, their pseudo passion, doing injustice to a really passionate nature, their impossible heroes, not without certain touches of just self-portraiture, their impossible heroines, betraying after all a certain first-hand acquaintance with the 'dreadful heart of woman.' In narrative verse Byron finally made for himself a form of his own which exactly suited him, but in lyrical verse he never learnt to do much that he could not already do in the *Hours of Idleness*. His 'last lines' are firmer in measure, graver in substance, but they are written on exactly the same principle as the 'Well! thou art happy' of 1808. There is the same strained simplicity of feeling, in which a really moved directness comes through the traditional rhetoric of the form. Every stanza says something, and it says exactly what he means it to say, without any of the exquisite evasions of a more purely poetic style; without, too, any of the qualifying interruptions of a more subtle temperament. Byron's mind was without subtlety; whatever he felt he felt without reservation, or the least thinking about feeling: hence his immediate hold upon the average man or woman, who does not need to come to his verse, as the verse of most other poets must be approached, with a mind already prepared for that communion. There is force, clearness, but no atmosphere; everything is seen detached, a little bare, very distinct, in a strong light: without shadows.

In studying Byron one is always face to face with the question: Can intention, in art, ever excuse performance? Can (one is tempted to say) the sum of a number of noughts arrive at an appreciable figure? Wordsworth wearies us by commonplace of thought and feeling, by nervelessness of rhythm, by a deliberate triviality; Coleridge offers us metaphysics for poetry; Browning offers us busy thinking about life for meditation; there is not a scene in Shakespeare which is perfect as a scene of Sophocles is perfect; but with Byron the failure is not exceptional, it is constant; it is like the speech of a man whose tongue is too large for his mouth. There are indeed individual good lines in Byron, a great number of quite splendid lines, though none indeed of the very finest order of poetry; but there is not a single poem, not a single passage of the length of 'Kubla Khan,' perhaps not a single stanza, which can be compared as poetry with a poem or passage or stanza of Keats or Shelley, such as any one will find by merely turning over the pages of those poets for five minutes at random. What is not there is precisely the magic which seems to make poetry its finer self, the perfume of the flower, that by which the flower is remembered, after its petals have dropped or withered. Even Browning abandons himself at times to the dream which floats, musically or in soft colour, through the senses of his mind. But Byron, when he meditates, meditates with fixed attention; if he dreams, he dreams with open eyes, to which the darkness is aglow with tumultuous action; he is at the mercy of none of those wandering sounds, delicate spirits of the air, which come entreating their liberty from the indefinite, in the releasing bondage of song. He has certain things to say, he has certain impulses to embody; he has, first, a certain type of character, then a view of the world which is more obviously the prose than the poetic view of the world, but certainly a wide view, to express; and it remains for him, in this rejection or lack of all the lesser graces, to be either Michael Angelo or Benjamin Haydon.

Or, at least, so it would seem; and yet, so it does not seem to be. Byron is not Michael Angelo, not merely because his conceptions were not as great as Michael Angelo's, but because he had not the same power of achieving his conceptions, because he had not the same technical skill. When Michael

Angelo left great naked vestiges of the rock still clinging about the emerging bodies of his later sculpture, it was not because he could not finish them with the same ivory smoothness as the 'Pieta' in St. Peter's; it was because he had found out all the art of man's visible body, and had apprehended that deeper breathing of the spirit of life, which is in the body, yet which is not the body; and was caught in the agony of the last conflict with the last mystery. To leave an appealing or terrifying or lamentable incompleteness, where before there had been the clear joy of what is finished and finite: there, precisely, was the triumph of his technique. But Byron is not Haydon, because he is not a small man struggling to be a great man, painting large merely because he cannot paint small, and creating chaos on the canvas out of ambition rather than irresistible impulse. He is fundamentally sincere, which is the root of greatness; he has a firm hold on himself and on the world; he speaks to humanity in its own voice, heightened to a pitch which carries across Europe. No poet had ever seemed to speak to men so directly, and it was through this directness of his vision of the world, and of his speech about it, that he became a poet, that he made a new thing of poetry.

Look, for instance, at his epithets and at his statements, and you will find, whenever he is at his best, an unparalleled justness of expression, a perfect hitting of the mark, which will sometimes seem rather the vigour of prose than the more celestial energy of poetry, but not always. When, in *The Vision of Judgment,* George III is brought pompously to the gate of Heaven and is seen to be nothing but

> An old man
> With an old soul, and both extremely blind;

when, in *Childe Harold,* Napoleon is seen

> With a deaf heart that never seemed to be
> A listener to itself;

when

> France gets drunk with blood to vomit crime;

when Cromwell

> Hewed the throne down to a block;

when history is defined as 'the Devil's scripture,' Rome as 'the Niob of nations,' ivy as 'the garland of eternity'; when Castlereagh's speeches are summed up:

Nor even a sprightly blunder's spark can blaze
From that Ixion grindstone's ceaseless toil,
That turns and turns to give the world a notion
Of endless torment and perpetual motion;

there is at least, in all these vivid and unforgettable phrases, a heat of truth
which has kindled speech into a really imaginative fervour. Seen in the form
which perhaps more immediately impressed the world, as being liker to the
world's notion of poetry—

Admire—exult—despise—laugh—weep—for here
There is such matter for all feeling: Man!

it is sheer rhetoric, and, for all its measure of personal sincerity, becomes false
through over-emphasis. The closer Byron's writing seems to come to prose
the nearer it really comes to poetry, because it comes nearer to humanity
and to the world, his subject-matter, which appears to take him for its voice,
rather than to be chosen by him with any conscious selection.

Byron loved the world for its own sake and for good and evil. His
quality of humanity was genius to him, and stood to him in the place of
imagination. Whatever is best in his work is full of this kind of raw or
naked humanity. It is the solid part of his rhetoric, and is what holds us still
in the apparently somewhat theatrical addresses to the Dying Gladiator
and the like. Speaking straight, in *Don Juan* and *The Vision of Judgment*,
it creates almost a new kind of poetry, the poetry of the world, written
rebelliously, but on its own level, by a man to whom the world was the one
reality. Only Byron, and not Shelley, could lead the revolt against custom
and convention, against the insular spirit of England, because to Byron
custom and convention and the insular spirit were so much more actual
things. . . .

Byron was at once the victim and the master of the world. Two enemies,
always in fierce grapple with one another, yet neither of them ever thrown,
Byron and the world seem to touch at all points, and to maintain a kind
of equilibrium by the equality of their strength. To Byron life itself was
imaginative, not the mere raw stuff out of which imagination could shape
something quite different, something far more beautiful, but itself, its
common hours, the places he passed on the way, a kind of poem in action.
All his verse is an attempt to make his own poetry out of fragments of this
great poem of life, as it came to him on his heedful way through the midst
of it. . . .

Byron has power without wisdom, power which is sanity, and human at heart, but without that vision which is wisdom. His passion is without joy, the resurrection, or that sorrow deeper than any known unhappiness, which is the death by which we attain life. He has never known what it is to be at peace, with himself or with outward things. There is a certain haste in his temper, which does not allow him to wait patiently upon any of the spiritual guests who only come unbidden, and to those who await them. His mind is always full of busy little activities, with which a more disinterested thinker would not be concerned. Himself the centre, he sees the world revolving about him, seemingly as conscious of him as he of it. It is not only that he never forgets himself, but he never forgets that he is a lord, and that one of his feet is not perfect.

In his letters, with their brilliant common sense, their wit, their clear and defiant intellect, their intolerant sincerity, as in his poems, it is not what we call the poet who speaks, it is what we call the natural man. Byron is the supreme incarnation of the natural man. . . .

And . . . not so very long before it was too late, he discovered how he was meant to write in verse, 'with common words in their common places,' as Jeffrey defined it; and then, for the first time, his verse became as good as his prose, and a stanza of his rhyme could be matched as mere writing against a paragraph from one of his letters. Neither Keats nor Shelley, not even Wordsworth, much less Coleridge, was content with our language as we have it; all, on theory or against theory, used inversions, and wrote otherwise than they would speak; it was Byron, with his boisterous contempt for rules, his headlong way of getting to the journey's end, who discovered that poetry, which is speech as well as song, and speech not least when it is most song, can be written not only with the words we use in talking, but in exactly the same order and construction. And, besides realising this truth for other people who were to come later and make a different use of the discovery, he realised for himself that he could make poetry entirely conversational, thus getting closer to that world which was 'too much with him.' Who in English poetry before Byron has ever talked in verse? Taking a hint from Frere, who had nothing to say, and did but show how things might be said, Byron gave up oratory and came nearer than he had yet come to poetry by merely talking. 'I have broken down the poetry as nearly as I could to common language,' he says in a letter. referring to *Sardanapalus;* but in such attempts to be "as simple and severe as Alfieri," the lamentable attempts of the dramas, there is only too thorough a 'breaking down' of poetry to a level which is not even that of good prose. In *Beppo,* in *The Vision of Judgment,* and in *Don Juan,* words, style, language, subject, are at one; the colloquial manner is used for what is really talk, extraordinarily brilliant talk, and at the same time, as Goethe saw, a 'classically elegant comic style'; the natural man is at last wholly himself, all of himself, himself not even exaggerated for effect.

Never, in English verse, has a man been seen who was so much a man and so much an Englishman. It is not man in the elemental sense, so much as the man of the world, whom we find reflected, in a magnificent way, in this poet for whom (like the novelists, and unlike all other poets) society exists as well as human nature. No man of the world would feel ashamed of himself for writing poetry like *Don Juan,* if he could write it; and not only because the poet himself seems conscious of all there is ridiculous in the mere fact of writing in rhyme, when everything can be so well said in prose. It is the poetry of middle age (premature with Byron, 'ennuyé at nineteen,' as he assures us), and it condenses all the temporary wisdom, old enough to be a little sour and not old enough to have recovered sweetness, of perhaps the least profitable period of life. It is sad and cynical with experience, and is at the stage between storm and peace; it doubts everything, as everything must be doubted before it can be understood rightly and rightly apprehended; it regrets youth, which lies behind it, and hates the thought of age, which lies before it, with a kind of passionate self-pity; it has knowledge rather than wisdom, and is a little mirror of the world, turned away from the sky, so that only the earth is visible in it. Shakespeare has put all the world's motley into his picture; but is not the world, to Shakespeare, that 'insubstantial pageant' which is always about to fade, and which fades into nothingness whenever Hamlet gets alone with his soul, or Macbeth with his conscience, or even Othello with his honour? Byron's thought, which embraced Europe as another man's thought might have embraced the village from which he had risen, was too conscious of politics, nations, events, Napoleon, George III, and other trifles in eternity, to be quite free to overlook the edge of the globe, and bring back news, or at least a significant silence, from that ultimate inspection. He taught poetry to be vividly interested in all earthly things, and for their own sake; and if any one had reminded him with Calderon that 'Life's a dream, and dreams themselves are a dream,' he would have replied that, at all events, the dream is a real thing, and the only reality, to the dreamer, and that he was not yet through with his sleep. . . .

The melancholy of Childe Harold, of Byron himself, which has been so often associated with the deeper and more thoughtful melancholy of René, of Obermann, is that discontent with the world which comes from too great love of the world, and not properly an intellectual dissatisfaction at all. It gave birth to a whole literature of pessimism, in which what had been in

Byron an acute personal ache became an imagined travailing of the whole world in a vast disgust at its own existence. Where Byron, as he admitted, 'deviated into the gloomy vanity of "drawing from self,"' less energetic and more contemplative writers spoke for humanity, as they conceived it, and found everything grey with their own old age of soul, which had never been young. It was only Byron who could say, after a visit to the opera, on which he comments with the most cheerful malice: 'How I do delight in observing life as it really is!' And it is just here that he distinguishes himself from his followers, in his right to say, as he said:

But I have lived, and have not lived in vain.

Byron is a moralist, and a moralist of great simplicity. He had

That just habitual scorn, which could contemn
Men and their thoughts,

at the same time that he was conscious of his own most human weaknesses; and, in a fragment not included in *Don Juan,* he cries, very sincerely:

I would to heaven that I were so much clay,
As I am blood, bone, marrow, passion, feeling.

He speaks his impressive epitaph over human greatness and the wrecks of great cities, because it is the natural impulse of the natural man; and his moralisings, always so personal, are generally what would seem to most people the obvious thought under the circumstances. When he is most moved, by some indignation, which in verse and prose always made him write best, he seems to resign himself to what was noblest in him: the passion for liberty (a passion strong enough to die for, as he proved), the passion against injustice, the passion of the will to live and the will to know, fretting against the limits of death and ignorance. It was then that 'thoughts which should call down thunder' came to him, calling down thunder indeed, on the wrongs and hypocrisies of his time and country, as a moralist more intellectually disinterested, further aloof from the consequences of his words, could not have done. Byron had no philosophy; he saw no remedy or alternative for any evil, least of all in his own mind, itself more tossed than the world without him. He had flaming doubts, stormy denials; he had the idealism of revolt, and fought instead of dreaming. His idolatry of good is shown by his remorseful consciousness of evil, morbid, as it has seemed to those who have not realised that every form of spiritual energy has something of the divine in it, and is on its way to become divine. *Cain* is a long, restless, proud, and helpless questioning of the powers of good and evil, by one who can say:

> I will have nought to do with happiness
> Which humbles me and mine,

with a pride equal to Lucifer's; and can say also, in all the humility of admitted defeat:

> Were I quiet earth,
> That were no evil.

'Obstinate questionings,' resolving themselves into nothing except that pride and that humility of despair, form the whole drama in which Byron has come nearest to abstracting thinking, in his 'gay metaphysical style,' as he called it. 'Think and endure' is Lucifer's last counsel to Cain. 'Why art thou wretched?' he has already asked him; and been answered: 'Why do I exist?' Cain's arraignment of God, which has nothing startling to us, who have read Nietzsche, raised all England in a kind of panic; religion itself seemed to be tottering. But Byron went no further in that direction; his greater strength lay elsewhere. Dropping heroics, he concludes, at the time that he is writing *Don Juan,* that man 'has always been and always will be an unlucky rascal,' with a tragic acquiescence in that summary settlement of the enigma, laughingly. Humour was given us that we might disguise from ourselves the consciousness of our common misery. Humour turned by thought into irony, which is humour thinking about itself, is the world's substitute for philosophy, perhaps the only weapon that can be turned against it with success. Byron used the world's irony to condemn the world. He had conquered its attention by the vast clamour of his revolt; he had lulled it asleep by an apparent acceptance of its terms; now, like a treacherous friend, treacherous with the sublime treachery of the intellect, he drove the nail into its sleeping forehead. And so we see Byron ending, after all the 'daring, dash, and grandiosity' (to use Goethe's words, as they are rendered by Matthew Arnold) of his earlier work, a tired and melancholy jester, still fierce at heart. Byron gives us, in an overwhelming way, the desire of life, the enjoyment of life, and the sense of life's deceit, as it vanishes from between our hands, and slips from under our feet, and is a voice and no more. In his own way he preaches 'vanity of vanities,' and not less cogently because he has been drunk with life, like Solomon himself, and has not yet lost the sense of what is intoxicating in it. He has given up the declamation of despair, as after all an effect, however sincere, of rhetoric; his jesting is more sorrowful than his outcries, for it shows him to have surrendered.

> We live and die,
> But which is best, you know no more than I.

All his wisdom (experience, love of nature, passion, tenderness, pride, the thirst for knowledge) comes to that in the end, not even a negation.

—Arthur Symons, *The Romantic Movement in English Poetry*, 1909, pp. 239–240, 244–249, 253–256, 260–263

VIRGINIA WOOLF (1918)

Adeline Virginia Woolf (1882–1941) was an English novelist and essayist, who is regarded as one of the foremost modernists and feminist writers. Between the world wars, she became a significant figure in London literary society and a member of the Bloomsbury Group. Her best-known works include the novels *Mrs. Dalloway* (1925), *To the Lighthouse* (1927), and *Orlando* (1928), which employ stream-of-consciousness techniques in their narration. Her essay "A Room of One's Own" (1929) is famous for its dictum, "a woman must have money and a room of her own if she is to write fiction." In her diary, Woolf reflects on her reading of Byron, expressing admiration.

Anyhow, I was very glad to go on with my Byron. He has at least the male virtues. In fact, I'm amused to find how easily I can imagine the effect he had upon women—especially upon rather stupid or uneducated women, unable to stand up to him. So many, too, would wish to reclaim him.... I'm much impressed by the extreme badness of B.'s poetry—such of it as Moore quotes with almost speechless admiration. Why did they think this Album stuff the finest fire of poetry? It reads hardly better than L.E.L. or Ella Wheeler Wilcox. And they dissuaded him from doing what he knew he could do, which was to write satire. He came home from the East with satires (parodies of Horace) in his bag and *Childe Harold*. He was persuaded that *Childe Harold* was the best poem every written. But he never as a young man believed in his poetry; a proof, in such a confident dogmatic person, that he hadn't the gift. The Wordsworths and the Keatses believe in that as much as they believe in anything....

At any rate Byron had superb force; his letters prove it. He had in many ways a very fine nature too; though as no one laughed him out of his affectations he became more like Horace Cole than one could wish. He could only be laughed at by a woman, and they worshipped instead. I haven't yet come to Lady Byron, but I suppose, instead of laughing, she merely disapproved. And so he became Byronic.

—Virginia Woolf, from *A Writer's Diary*, August 7, 1918

Katherine Fullerton Gerould "Men, Women, and the Byron-Complex" (1922)

In the nonacademic world of letters no one, apparently, either knows or cares whether Byron was a great poet. After a hundred years, the sole question that impassions people is: 'Just how much of a cad was he?'

Ninety-eight years ago, in April, Lord Byron died at Missolonghi. *Astarte* has, within the year, been publicly reissued; two volumes of new Byron letters have been put forth by John Murray within a few months. It is natural that the files of the recent British reviews should be full of him. Natural, indeed, that ever since 1905 (when Lord Lovelace first made his extraordinary gesture of publication), any index of periodical literature should have been studded with Byron's name. Yet out of all the welter of articles and essays resultant upon *Astarte* and the new Letters, one curious fact emerges, dominant, obtrusive. As it was through all the nineteenth century, so now in the twentieth.

None of the recent critics (unless it be Lord Ernle) cares a hang about Byron's poetry, or his prose. Mr. Percy Lubbock says frankly—too frankly, if that be his real opinion,—that everyone will read the Hobhouse collection of letters with only one purpose: to see if anything new can be gathered about the Byron-Augusta scandal. There *is* nothing new about Byron and Augusta in the Hobhouse collection, and therefore it is worth nothing. We would give it all for a slim volume of Keats's letters. Thus Mr. Lubbock. Mr. Maurice Hewlett, reviewing the volumes in the *London Mercury,* never hints at whether or not they sustain Byron's reputation as one of the great English letter-writers. He uses his three pages to vilify Byron the man, as far as his vocabulary will allow. After a hundred years, one ought to be able to consider a man's poetry on its merit. But in the nonacademic world of letters no one, apparently, either knows or cares whether Byron was a great poet. No one except Lord Ernle either knows or cares, as we have said, whether he was a better or a worse letter-writer than we had thought. After a hundred years, the sole question that impassions people is: 'Just how much of a cad was he?' One looks in vain for another instance quite like this. Lord Byron was not a king, not a great warrior or a great statesman; he was not the leader of a cause, the founder of a party, the winner or loser of a battlefield. His one adventure into public affairs—the espousing of the Greek cause—came late, and amounted to little. He was never, to any group of enthusiasts, a symbol; his name was never the equivalent of a theory or an ideal. He 'stood for' nothing, and therefore gathered no loyalties about him like a borrowed garment.

His poetry and his personality were all that he had to make him significant. Scandal about Shelley has never been wanting; and we have recently acquired a scandal (God save the mark!) about Wordsworth. Yet people go on estimating the *Lyrical Ballads* and *Prometheus Unbound* much as they did before. Critics, however, persist still in abandoning criticism when they speak of Byron. You search their pages for any hint that he wrote *Lara*, *The Bride of Abydos*, or *The Giaour*; and when they mention *Don Juan*, their sole interest seems to lie in being able to name the woman he was living with when he produced a particular canto. The sequence of his works serves as a mere corroborative footnote to the *chronique scandaleuse* of his life.

Scandals a hundred years old usually lack spice for anyone save the antiquary. But, though no one since Matthew Arnold, except Paul Elmer More, has bothered much about Byron's poetry, they are bothering still about Lord Byron and his amours. One would think he was a sufficiently great poet to be spoken of as such. Or Mr. Lubbock or Mr. Hewlett—since they were supposed to be reviewing the Murray volumes—might have thrown in a word or two about Byron's letters, which, as letters, are among the best we have. But no: Byron still arouses an emotion purely personal. People persist in taking him as if he were the defendant in a criminal suit. They are as passionately partisan as if he had not, for years, been dust beneath the stones of Hucknall Torkard church.

—Katherine Fullerton Gerould, "Men, Women,
and the Byron-Complex," *The Atlantic Monthly*,
September 1922, vol. 130, no. 3, pp. 289–295

T.S. ELIOT "BYRON" (1937)

The American poet, dramatist, and critic Thomas Stearns Eliot (1888–1965) became a proponent of modernism with his early poetry (such as "The Love Song of J. Alfred Prufrock" and *The Waste Land*), but after his conversion to Anglicanism, he turned into an increasingly conservative writer. Known for his dismissive essays about Shakespeare's *Hamlet* and other literary classics, as well as for his promotion of the seventeenth-century metaphysical poets, Eliot gives Byron short shrift, claiming that he did not contribute anything to the development of the English poetic language.

Of Byron one can say, as of no other English poet of his eminence, that he added nothing to the language, that he discovered nothing in the sounds, and developed nothing in the meaning, of individual words. I cannot think of any other poet of his distinction who might so easily have been an accomplished foreigner writing in English. The ordinary person talks English, but only a few people in every generation can write it; and upon this undeliberate collaboration between a great many people talking a living language and a very few people writing it, the continuance and maintenance of a language depends. Just as an artisan who can talk English beautifully while about his work or in a public bar, may compose a letter painfully written in a dead language bearing some resemblance to a newspaper leader, and decorated with words like "maelstrom" and "pandemonium": so does Byron write a dead or dying language.

—T.S. Eliot, "Byron," 1937, from
On Poetry and Poets, 1943

WORKS

CHILDE HAROLD'S PILGRIMAGE

On March 10, 1812, John Murray published *Childe Harold's Pilgrimage*, cantos I and II. The five hundred quarto copies, priced at 30 shillings each, sold out in a few days, leading to Byron's observation, "I awoke one morning and found myself famous" (quoted by Moore). Further editions sold equally well, and in less than six months, sales had reached 4,500 copies. Even Francis Jeffrey, Byron's old antagonist from the *Edinburgh Review*, praised the work, and Byron apologized for his attack on Jeffrey in *English Bards, and Scotch Reviewers*.

    Childe Harold's Pilgrimage, cantos I and II, can be read as Byron's poetic journal of his Mediterranean tour in 1809–11. His colorful descriptions of Spain and Portugal and the exoticism of Albania and Greece are sprinkled with scenes of violence, such as a Spanish bullfight and feuding Albanians. The international popularity of the work's eventual four cantos derived partly from its appeal as a travelogue but more from its articulation of young Harold's *Weltschmerz* (world weariness), caused by the chaos of the aftermath of the French Revolution and the Napoleonic Wars. The work is a quest poem, subtitled *A Romaunt*, and Harold is like the knights in medieval romances who go in search of an elusive goal: certainty and self-assertion. Archaisms such as the use of the Spenserian stanza are intermingled with satire, narrative digression, and moral commentary. Sites associated with the Napoleonic campaign, such as Cintra, Talavera, and Albuera, elicit comments on the follies of war (canto I); the ruins of Greece evoke thoughts on the evils of tyranny and on the transience of powerful civilizations (canto II). Contemporary readers persistently equated the protagonist, Harold, with the author, and similarly restless, melancholy, and alienated Byronic heroes would appear in Byron's future works, such as the *Giaour, Conrad, Manfred,* and *Cain*.

ELIZABETH, DUCHESS OF DEVONSHIRE (UNDATED)

Elizabeth Cavendish, Duchess of Devonshire (formerly Elizabeth Christiana Hervey, later Lady Elizabeth Foster, 1759–1824), is best known as the friend of Georgiana, Duchess of Devonshire. She lived with Georgiana and her husband William, the fifth Duke of Devonshire, for twenty-five years and married the duke after his wife's death. The extract is taken from an undated letter to her son Augustus Foster.

The subject of conversation, of curiosity, of enthusiasm almost, one might say, of the moment, is not Spain or Portugal, Warriors or Patriots, but Lord Byron! You probably read the *Edinburgh Review*'s criticism of his "Minor Poems", published in 1808, not merely severe, but flippant. They prophesied and entreated never to hear more as a Poet of this young Lord. On this, stung to the quick, he published, without a name, his *English Bards and Scotch Reviewers*. The prodigious success of this made him publish a second edition with his name and additional lines and notes, and going abroad, said that on his return he would answer to any who called on him. He returned sorry for the severity of some of his lines, and with a new poem, Childe Harold, which he published. This poem is on every table, and himself courted, visited, flattered, and praised whenever he appears. He has a pale, sickly, but a handsome countenance, a bad figure, animated and amusing conversation, and, in short, he is really the only topic almost of every conversation—the men jealous of him, the women of each other.

—Elizabeth, Dutchess of Devonshire,
quoted in Vere Foster, *The Two Duchesses*,
1889, pp. 375–376

SAMUEL ROGERS (1812)

A friend of Scott, Wordsworth, and Byron, Samuel Rogers (1763–1855), the son of a wealthy banker, enjoyed a considerable reputation as a poet and man of letters. As host to many famous writers and intellectuals in London, he was appreciated as a good friend who had reconciled Thomas Moore with Byron and helped authors in trouble. He was also praised in his circle for his conversational powers. The following extract from his *Table-Talk* was published posthumously in 1856.

Byron sent me *Childe Harold* in the printed sheets before it was published; and I read it to my sister. "This", I said, "in spite of all its beauty, will never please the public: they will dislike the querulous repining tone that pervades it, and the dissolute character of the hero." But I quickly found that I was mistaken. The genius which the poem exhibited, the youth, the rank of the author, his romantic wanderings in Greece,—these combined to make the world stark mad about *Childe Harold* and Byron. I knew two old maids in Buckinghamshire who used to cry over the passage about Harold's "laughing dames" that "long had fed his youthful appetite", &c.

—Samuel Rogers, *Recollections of the Table-Talk of Samuel Rogers*, ed. A. Dyce. 3rd ed., 1856, p. 233

WALTER SCOTT (1812)

The Scottish historical novelist Walter Scott (1771–1832) had resented Byron's attack on him in *English Bards, and Scotch Reviewers*, but a correspondence was struck up between them in July 1812 through John Murray. Byron apologized for his offensiveness in the early satire, a friendship soon developed, and they began to express high opinions of each other as men and authors. The excerpt is taken from a letter written to Joanna Baillie shortly after the publication of *Childe Harold's Pilgrimage*, cantos I and II, in April 1812 and gives Scott's first impressions.

Have you seen the pilgrimage of Childe Harold, by Lord Byron: it is, I think, a very clever poem, but gives no good symptom of the writer's heart or morals. His hero notwithstanding the affected antiquity of the style in some parts is a modern man of fashion and fortune worn out and satiated with the pursuits of dissipation, and although there is a caution against it in the preface, you cannot for your soul avoid concluding that the author, as he gives an account of his own travels, is also doing so in his own character. Now really this is too bad. Vice ought to be a little more modest and it must require impudence at least equal to the noble lord's other powers to claim sympathy gravely for the ennui arising from his being tired of his wassailers and his paramours. There is a monstrous deal of conceit in it too for it is informing the inferior part of the world that their little old-fashioned scruples and limitations are not worthy of his regards while his fortune and possessions are such as have put all sorts of gratification too much in his power to afford him any pleasure. Yet with all this conceit and assurance, there is much poetical merit in the book, and I wish you would read it.

—Walter Scott, *The Letters of Sir Walter Scott*, ed. H.J.C Grierson, Davidson Cook, W.M. Parker and others 1932–37, vol. III, pp. 98–99

Francis Jeffrey (1812)

Francis Jeffrey, Lord Jeffrey (1773–1850) was a Scottish judge and literary critic, the founder and editor of the *Edinburgh Review* from 1803 to 1829. Jeffrey's review of *Childe Harold's Pilgrimage,* cantos I and II, appeared in the *Edinburgh Review* two months after the publication of the poem.

The most surprising thing about the present work, indeed, is, that it should please and interest so much as it does, with so few of the ordinary ingredients of interest or poetical delight. There is no story or adventure—and, indeed, no incident of any kind; the whole poem—to give a very short account of it—consisting of a series of reflections made in travelling through a part of Spain and Portugal, and in sailing up the Mediterranean to the shores of Greece. These reflections, too, and the descriptions out of which they arise, are presented without any regular order or connexion—being sometimes strung upon the slender thread of Childe Harold's Pilgrimage, and sometimes held together by the still slighter tie of the author's local situation at the time of writing. As there are no incidents, there cannot well be any characters;—and accordingly, with the exception of a few national sketches, which form part of the landscape of his pilgrimage, that of the hero himself is the only delineation of the kind that is offered to the reader of this volume;—and this hero, we must say, appears to us as oddly chosen as he is imperfectly employed. Childe Harold is a sated epicure—sickened with the very fulness of prosperity—oppressed with ennui, and stung with occasional remorse;—his heart hardened by sensual indulgence, and his opinion of mankind degraded by his acquaintance with the baser part of them. In this state he wanders over the fairest and most interesting parts of Europe, in the vain hope of stimulating his palsied sensibility by novelty; or at least of occasionally forgetting his mental anguish in the toils and perils of his journey. Like Milton's fiend, however, he "sees undelighted all delight, and passes on through the great wilderness of the world with a heart shut to all human sympathy,—sullenly despising the stir both of its business and its pleasures—but hating and despising himself most of all, for beholding it with so little emotion.

Lord Byron takes the trouble to caution his readers against supposing that he meant to shadow out his own character under the dark impulsive traits of that which we have just exhibited; a caution which was surely unnecessary—though it is impossible not to observe, that the mind of the noble author has been so far tinged by his strong conception of this Satanic personage, that the sentiments and reflections which he delivers in his own name, have all received a shade of the same gloomy and misanthropic colouring which invests those of his imaginary hero. The general strain of those sentiments, too, is such as we should have thought very little likely to attract popularity, in the present temper of this country. They are not only complexionally dark and disdainful, but run directly counter to very many of our national passions, and most favoured propensities. Lord Byron speaks with the most unbounded contempt of the Portuguese—with despondence of Spain—and in a very slighting and sarcastic manner of wars, and victories, and military heroes in general. Neither are his religious opinions more orthodox, we apprehend, than his politics; for he not only speaks without any respect of priests, and creeds, and dogmas of all descriptions, but doubts very freely of the immortality of the soul, and other points as fundamental.

Such are some of the disadvantages under which this poem lays claim to the public favour; and it will be readily understood that we think it has no ordinary merit, when we say, that we have little doubt that it will find favour, in spite of these disadvantages. Its chief excellence is a singular freedom and boldness, both of thought and expression, and, great occasional force and felicity of diction, which is the more pleasing that it does not appear to be the result either of long labour or humble imitation. There is, indeed, a tone of self-willed independence and originality about the whole composition—a certain plain manliness and strength of manner, which is infinitely refreshing after the sickly affectations of so many modern writers; and reconciles us not only to the asperity into which it sometimes degenerates, but even in some degree to the unamiableness upon which it constantly borders. We do not know, indeed, whether there is not something piquant in the very novelty and singularity of that cast of misanthropy and universal scorn, which we have noticed as among the repulsive features of the composition. It excites a kind of curiosity, at least, to see how objects, which have been usually presented under so different an aspect, appear through so dark a medium; and undoubtedly gives great effect to the flashes of emotion and suppressed sensibility that occasionally burst through the gloom. The best parts of the poem, accordingly, are those which embody those stern and disdainful reflexions, to which the author seems to recur with unfeigned cordiality and eagerness—and through which we can sometimes discern the strugglings of a gentler feeling, to which he is afraid to abandon himself. There is much strength, in short, and some impetuous feeling in this poem—but very little softness; some pity for mankind—but very little affection; and no enthusiasm in the cause of any living men, or admiration of their talents or virtues. The author's inspiration does not appear to have brought him any beatific visions, nor to have peopled his fancy, with any forms of loveliness; and though his lays are often both loud and lofty, they neither "lap us in Elysium," nor give us any idea that it was in Elysium that they were framed.

The descriptions are often exceedingly good; and the diction, though unequal and frequently faulty, has on the whole a freedom, copiousness and vigour, which we are not sure that we could match in any cotemporary poet. Scott alone, we think, possesses a style equally strong and natural; but Scott's is more made up of imitations, and indeed is frequently a mere cento of other writers—while Lord Byron's has often a nervous simplicity and manly freshness which reminds us of Dryden, and an occasional force and compression, in some of the smaller pieces especially, which afford no unfavourable resemblance of Crabbe.

The versification is in the stanza of Spencer; and none of all the imitators of that venerable bard have availed themselves more extensively of the great range of tones and manners in which his example entitles them to indulge. Lord Byron has accordingly given us descriptions in all their extremes;—sometimes compressing into one stanza the whole characteristic features of a country, and sometimes expanding into twenty the details of a familiar transaction;—condescending, for pages together, to expatiate in minute and ludicrous representations—and mingling long apostrophes, execrations, and the expression of personal emotion, with the miscellaneous picture which it is his main business to trace on the imagination of his readers. Not satisfied even with this license of variety, he has passed at will, and entirely, from the style of Spencer, to that of his own age,—and intermingled various lyrical pieces with the solemn stanza of his general measure.

—Francis Jeffrey, *Edinburgh Review* 19,
February 1812, issued May 1812,
XIX, pp. 466–477, 468

George Ellis "Review of Byron, Childe Harold" (1812)

The English historian, critic, and editor George Ellis (1753–1815) was one of the founders of the counter-revolutionary periodical the *Anti-Jacobin*, a friend of Scott and George Canning, and a frequent contributor to the *Quarterly*. His review of *Childe Harold's Pilgrimage*, cantos I and II, appeared in the same month as Jeffrey's assessment.

We do not know whether Lord Byron ever had it in contemplation to write an epic poem; but we conceive that the subject, which he selected, is perfectly suited to such a purpose; that the foundation which he has laid is sufficiently solid, and his materials sufficiently ample for the most magnificent superstructure; but we doubt whether his plan be well conceived, and we are by no means disposed to applaud, in every instance, the selection of his ornaments.

Of the plan indeed we are unable to speak with perfect confidence, because it has not been at all developed in the two cantos which are now given to the public; but it appears to us that the "Childe Harold," whom we suppose, in consequence of the author's positive assurance, to be a mere creature of the imagination, is so far from effecting the object for which he is introduced, and "giving some connection to the piece," that he only tends to embarrass and obscure it. We are told, however, that "friends, on whose opinions Lord Byron sets a high value," have suggested to him that he might be "suspected" of having sketched in his hero a portrait of real life; a suspicion for which, he says, "in some very trivial particulars there—might be grounds; but in the main points I hope none whatever." Now if he was so anxious to repel a suspicion which had occurred to friends, on whom he set a high value; if he was conscious that the imaginary traveller, whom, from an unwillingness to appear as the hero of his own tale, he had substituted for himself, was so unamiable; we are at a loss to guess at his motives for choosing such a representative. If, for the completion of some design which has not yet appeared, but which is to be effected in the sequel of the poem, it was necessary to unite, in the person of the pilgrim, the eager curiosity of youth with the fastidiousness of a sated libertine, why revert to the rude and simple ages of chivalry in search of a character which can only exist in an age of vicious refinement? Again, if this apparent absurdity was unavoidable; if the "Childe," and "the little page," and the "staunch yeoman," whom the Childe addresses in his farewell to his native land, could not be spared, why is this, group of antiques sent on a journey through Portugal and Spain, during the interval between the convention of Cintra and the battle of Talavera?

It may perhaps be said that this anachronism, being convenient, is in some measure pardonable; and that the other inconsistencies which we have pointed out do not, after all, detract much from the general effect of the poem. But we answer that such inconsistencies appear to us to be perfectly needless; that they may be easily removed; and that they are by no means innocent if they have led Lord Byron (as we suspect) to adopt that motley mixture of obsolete and modern phraseology by which the ease and elegance of his verses are often injured, and to degrade the character of his work by the insertion of some passages which will probably give offence to a considerable portion of his readers.

The metre adopted throughout this "Romaunt" is the stanza of Spencer; and we admit that, for every ancient word employed by the modern poet, the authority of Spencer may be pleaded. But we think that to intersperse such words as ee, nice, feere, ne, losel, eld, &c. amidst the richest decorations of modern language, is to patch embroidery with rags. Even if these words had not been replaced by any substitutes, and if they were always correctly inserted, their uncouth appearance would be displeasing; but Lord Byron is not always correct in his use of them. For instance, when he says, (Canto I. st. 67.)

> Devices quaint, and Frolics ever new,
> Tread on each other's kibes,

—it must be supposed that he did not mean to personify devices and frolics for the purpose of afflicting them with chilblains. When, again, in describing All Pacha, he censures (C. II. st. 62.)—

> those ne'er forgotten acts of *ruth*
> Beseeming all men ill, but most the man
> In years, that mark him with a tyger's tooth, &c.

it is plain that the noble lord must have considered "ruth" as synonymous, not with pity, but with cruelty. In a third instance where we are told that "Childe Harold had a mother," the equivocal meaning of the first word has evidently a ludicrous effect, which could not have escaped the attention of our author whilst writing in the language of his own day. On such errors as these, however, which obviously originate, not in any want of genius, but in accidental heedlessness, we do not mean to lay any stress; we complain only of the habitual negligence, of the frequent laxity of expression—of the feeble or dissonant rhymes which almost always disfigure a too close imitation of the language of our early poets, and of which we think that the work before us offers too many examples.

Spencer, it must be observed, is always consistent. He lived at a time when pedantry was the prevailing fault, not of the sedentary and studious, but of the flighty and illiterate; when daily attempts were made to introduce into our vocabulary the mangled elements of the more sonorous languages of Greece and Rome; and when this anomalous jargon was hailed, by many of his contemporaries, as a model of melody and refinement. Anxious to preserve the purity and simplicity of his native tongue, the "well of English undefiled," he appealed from the vitiated taste of the court to the good sense of the nation at large: he thought that significant words were not degraded by passing through the lips of the vulgar; his principal aim was to be generally intelligible: he formed his style on the homely models which had been bequeathed to him by preceding writers, and trusted to his own genius for the supply of the necessary embellishments. The extent of that genius is displayed in the extraordinary variety and elegance of the decorations, thus composed from the most common materials. Spencer was in England, as La Fontaine in France, the creators of that style which our neighbours have so aptly denominated "le genre naif." The flowers which he scatters over his subject are, indeed, all of native growth: and they have a life and fragrance which is not always found in those more gaudy exotics, imported by succeeding poets, with which our language has been enriched and perhaps overloaded. Hence, though it is easy to catch his manner in short and partial imitations, it is almost impossible to preserve, throughout a long poem, his peculiar exuberance united with his characteristic simplicity. Lord Byron has shewn himself, in some passages, a tolerably successful copyist; but we like him much better in those where he forgets or disdains to copy; and where, without sacrificing the sweetness and variety of pause by which Spencer's stanza is advantageously distinguished from the heroic couplet, he employs a pomp of diction suited to the splendour of the objects which he describes. We rejoice when, dismissing from his memory the wretched scraps of a musty glossary, he exhibits to its, in natural and appropriate language, the rich scenery and golden sunshine of countries which are the

> Boast of the aged, lesson of the young;
> Which sages venerate, and bards adore,
> As Pallas and the Muse unveil their awful lore.

But we have not yet exhausted our complaints against the wayward hero of the poem, whose character, we think, is most capriciously and uselessly degraded. The moral code of chivalry was not, we admit, quite pure and spotless; but its laxity in some points was redeemed by the noble spirit of gallantry which it inspired; a gallantry which courted personal danger in the defence of the sovereign, because he is the fountain of honour; of women because they are often lovely and always helpless; and of the priesthood because they are at once disarmed and sanctified by their profession. Now Childe Harold, if not absolutely craven and recreant, is at least a mortal enemy to all martial exertions, a scoffer at the fair sex, and apparently disposed to consider, all religions as different modes of superstition.

The reflections which occur to him, when he surveys the preparations for the conflicts between the French and the allied armies, are that these hosts

> Are met (as if at home they could not die)
> To feed the crow on Talavera's plain.—

There shall they rot; ambition's honours' fools!
"Yes, honour decks the turf that wraps their clay!"
Vain sophistry! in these behold the tools,
The broken tools that tyrants cast away, &c.
Enough of battle's minions!—let them play
Their game of lives, and barter breath for fame;
Fame, that will scarce reanimate their clay,
Though thousands fill to deck some single name.
In sooth, 'twere sad to thwart their noble aim,
Who strike, blest hirelings! for their country's good,
And die, that living might have proved her shame.
　　　　　—St. 41, 42, 44.—

　　he would not delight
(Born beneath some remote inglorious star)
In themes of bloody fray, or gallant fight,
But loath'd the bravo's trade, and laughed at martial wight."
　　　　　—C. ii. St. 39.

Now surely, it was not worth while to conjure a *Childe Harold* out of some old tapestry, and to bring him into the field of Talavera, for the purpose of indulging in such meditations as these. It is undoubtedly true that the cannon and the musketry must often anticipate the stroke of time; and carry off, in the vigour of life, many who might have been reserved at home to a long protracted decay. It is moreover true that the buried will rot; that the unburied may become food for crows, and consequently, that the man who has bartered life for fame has no chance, when once killed, of coming to life again. But these truths, we apprehend, are so generally admitted that it is needless to inculcate them. It is certainly untrue that fame is of little value. It is something to be honoured by those whom we love. It is something to the soldier when he returns to the arms of a mother, a wife, or a sister, to see in their eyes the tears of exultation mixing with those of affection, and of pious gratitude to heaven for his safety. These joys of a triumph, it may be said, are mere illusions; but for the sake of such illusions is life chiefly worth having. When we read the preceding sarcasms on the "bravo's trade," we are induced to ask, not without some anxiety and alarm, whether such are indeed the opinions which a British peer entertains of a British army.

　　The second feature in Childe Harold's character, which was introduced, we presume, for the purpose of giving to it an air of originality, renders it, if not quite unnatural, at least very unpoetical. Of this indeed the author seems to have been aware; but instead of correcting what was harsh and exaggerated in his sketch of the woman hater, he has only had recourse to the expedient of introducing, under various pretexts, those delineations of female beauty which a young poet may be naturally supposed to pen with much complacency. This we think ill judged. The victim of violent and unrequited passion, whether crushed into the sullenness of apathy, or irritated into habitual moroseness, may become, in the hands of an able poet, very generally and deeply interesting; the human heart is certainly disposed to beat in unison with the struggles of strong and concentrated feeling; but the boyish libertine whose imagination is chilled by his sated apetites, whose frightful gloom is only the result of disappointed selfishness; and "whose kiss had been pollution," cannot surely be expected to excite any tender sympathy, and can only be viewed with unmixed disgust. Some softening of such a character would become necessary even if it were distinguished by peculiar acuteness of remark, or by dazzling flashes of wit. But there is not much wit in designating women as "wanton things," or as "lovely harmless things," or in describing English women as "Remoter females famed for sickening prate;" nor is there much acuteness in the observation that

—Pomp and power alone are woman's care,
And where these are, light Eros finds a fere;
Maidens, like moths, are ever caught by glare,
And Mammon wins his way where seraphs might despair.

We utterly dislike the polyglot line compounded of Greek, Saxon, and modern English; and do not much admire the confusion of images in the others; but we wish to abstain from minute criticism, and are only anxious to remonstrate against those blemishes which, in our opinion, detract from the general beauty of the poem.

Having already given our reasons for thinking that the perversity of character attributed to the hero of the piece is far too highly coloured, it is needless to comment on that settled despair,

That will not look beyond the tomb,
But cannot hope for rest before.—(p. 52.)

This is the consummation of human misery; and if it had been the author's principal object, in delineating this fictitious personage, to hold him up to his young readers as a dreadful example of early profligacy, such a finishing to the picture might be vindicated as consistent and useful. In that case, however, it would have been doubly essential to divest the "Childe" of his chivalrous title and attributes; and the attention of the poet and of the reader being engrossed by one dismal object, it would have become necessary, to sacrifice a large portion of that elegance and animation by which the present work is confessedly distinguished. . . .

It will now be proper to take a slight survey of the remaining contents of this volume.

On the subject of the notes, which are always lively and amusing, and sometimes convey much curious information, we should have had no comments to make, if Lord Byron had not occasionally amused himself with provoking controversy, and, in one instance at least, without any very legitimate reason.

He was, indeed, bound to state the grounds on which lie had thought it necessary, in his poem, to designate Lord Elgin as "the last, the worst dull spoiler" of Athens; as a man whom Scotland must blush to own; as a "modern Pict,"—"cold as the crags upon his native coast, his mind as barren and his heart as hard;"—but we doubt whether the plea adduced by the poet would be admitted in any sober and impartial court of justice, as a complete excuse for so much invective. This allegation in the note amounts to this:—that whilst the Consul of France has been endeavouring to obtain from the Turkish government their permission to seize and send to Paris the most valuable remnants of antiquity which still remained at Athens, our ambassador at Constantinople had contrived, by means of a more active agent, to get possession of the said antiquities, and to ship them to England; and that the same agent, in executing his commission, has "wantonly and uselessly defaced a whole range of basso-relievos in one compartment of the temple" which he was suffered to pillage. Supposing this statement to be correct, the Athenians have, undoubtedly, good reason to complain; and if Lord Byron, indignantly keeling his share in the degradation of the national character consequent upon such acts of outrage, had contented himself with producing his charge; with proving that the immediate instrument of the mischief had acted under the authority of a British ambassador, and with arguing against such an abuse of the influence derived from this high situation; we should have thought his spirit and his eloquence well employed. But it surely is not quite fair to begin by executing a supposed delinquent, and then to put him upon his defence. We can forgive, in a young and ardent traveller, the bitter expression of disappointed curiosity; but Lord Byron, as a traveller and a scholar, may, perhaps, derive some advantage from the spirit of depredation of which he so feelingly complains. He has printed in his Appendix an extract from Meletius, containing a transcript of the Hellenic inscription, &c. on the marbles found at Orchomemius; now we are informed that the marble containing this inscription is at present in England; and that, by a reference to the original, Lord Byron may easily satisfy himself that the copy given by Meletius in his Geography is full of inaccuracies.

In the note inserted at p. 143, Lord Byron has certainly replied, with great liberality and decorum, to a set of critics, who, in their censures of his earlier works, had not set him the example of extreme urbanity; but the instance of unprovoked pugnacity to which we allude is exhibited in pp. 146 and 147, where he denies to Mr. Thornton any "claims to public confidence from a fourteen years' residence at Pera;" assuring its that "this can give him no more insight into the real state of Greece and her inhabitants than as many years spent at Wapping into that of the western Highlanders." But, in the first place, if Lord Byron be right, Mr. Thornton cannot be wholly wrong; for, on comparing their respective opinions, it will be found that, in all essential points, they very nearly coincide. Secondly, as Constantinople and its immediate vicinity may furnish about one hundred thousand specimens of Greeks of different ranks and conditions, whilst Wapping cannot be supposed to offer very numerous samples of western Highlanders, we cannot consider the noble lord's illustration as very apposite. Thirdly, as Lord Byron admits, (pp. 159, 160,) that the best account of Turkish manners is Mr. "Thornton's English," it is not very probable that so accurate an observer of character, in instances where the means of observation were comparatively rare, should have been totally blind to the manners of a people with whom, during fourteen years, he must have been in habits of daily intercourse. Whilst we feel ourselves indebted to Lord Byron for the light which he has thrown on the character and manners of the Albanians, we are sorry that, in criticizing an intelligent and, apparently, accurate writer, he should condescend, more than once, to employ a tone of sarcasm which nearly borders on coarseness and vulgarity.

The notes are followed by a series of small lyric pieces, fourteen in number, some of which (and particularly the last) we should have been glad to transcribe, but that we are conscious of having already exhausted, and, perhaps, abused, the privilege of quotation.

Of the Appendix, which consists of various specimens of the Romaic, we need only say, that we consider it as a valuable supplement to this entertaining "Pilgrimage." National songs, and popular works of amusement, throw no small light on the manners of a people; they are materials which most travellers have within their reach, but which they almost always disdain to collect. Lord Byron has shewn a better taste; and it is to be hoped that his example will, in future, be generally followed.

It is now time to take leave—we hope not a long leave—of Childe Harold's migrations; but we are unwilling to conclude our article without repeating our thanks to the author for the amusement which he has afforded us. The applause which he has received has been very general, and, in our opinion, well deserved. We think that the poem exhibits some marks of carelessness, many of caprice, but many also of sterling genius. On the latter we have forborne to expatiate, because we apprehend that our readers are quite as well qualified as ourselves to estimate the merits of pleasing versification, of lively conception, and of accurate expression. Of those errors of carelessness from which few poems are, in the first instance, wholly exempt, we have not attempted to form a catalogue, because they can scarcely fail to be discovered by the author, and may be silently corrected in a future edition. But it was our duty attentively to search for, and honestly to point out the faults arising from caprice, or from a disregard of general opinion; because it is a too common, though a very mischievous prejudice, to suppose that genius and eccentricity are usual and natural companions; and that, to discourage extravagance is to check the growth of excellence. Lord Byron has shewn that his confidence in his own powers is not to be subdued by illiberal and unmerited censure; and we are sure that it will not be diminished by our animadversions: we are not sure that we should have better consulted his future fame, or our own character for candour, if we had expressed our sense of his talents in terms of more unqualified panegyric.

—George Ellis, "Review of Byron, *Childe Harold,*"
Quarterly Review 7, March 1812, issued
May 1812, VII, pp. 180–200

HORACE AND JAMES SMITH "CUI BONO?" (1812)

The brothers Horace (1779–1849) and James Smith (1775–1839) produced an anonymous volume of parodies, *Rejected Addresses,* in 1812. Byron admired their parody of *Childe Harold's Pilgrimage,* cantos I and II, and quoted these two stanzas addressing the crowds flocking to the Drury Lane Theatre in a conversation with Lady Blessington. Byron's use of the Spenserian stanza and diction is mocked by the authors.

Ye reckless dupes, who hither wend your way,
To gaze on dupes who meet an equal doom,
Pursuing pastimes glittering to betray,
Like falling stars in life's eternal gloom,
What seek ye here? Joy's evanescent bloom?
Woe's me! the brightest wreaths she ever gave

Are but as flowers that decorate a tomb,
Man's heart, the mournful urn o'er which they wave,
Is sacred to despair, its pedestal the grave.

Has life so little store of real woes,
That here ye wend to taste fictitious grief?
Or is it that from truth such anguish flows
Ye court the lying drama for relief?
Long shall ye find the pang, the respite brief,
Or if one tolerable page appears
In folly's volume, 'tis the actor's leaf,
Who dries his own by drawing other's tears,
And raising present mirth, makes glad his future years.

—Horace and James Smith, "Cui bono?,"
in *Rejected Addresses*, 1812

JOHN CAM HOBHOUSE (1814 & 1816)

The politician John Cam Hobhouse (1786–1869) was a leading advocate of political reform and an outspoken critic of the Peterloo Massacre, the 1819 skirmish when cavalry charged a large group of Manchester demonstrators assembled to demand parliamentary reform. Since their days at Cambridge's Trinity College, Hobhouse had been a close friend of Byron and had accompanied him on his travels. Two years after the publication of *Childe Harold*, cantos I and II, Hobhouse commented on it in his diary on March 23, 1814.

This evening, after dinner, I read aloud *The Rape of the Lock*, and the "Elegy on the Death of an Unfortunate Lady", also *The Characters of Women*. Nothing will do after Pope. I am convinced that even my friend's poetry would have been thought monstrous and affected in an age still ringing with melody and sense of that great writer. Indeed, the great success of *Childe Harold* is due chiefly to Byron's having dared to give utterance to certain feelings which every one must have encouraged in the melancholy and therefore morbid hours of his existence, and also by the intimate knowledge which he has shown of the turns taken by the passion of women.

Two and a half years later, he saw canto III in manuscript form. The following extract is from his diary entry of September 1, 1816.

Byron has given me another canto of *Childe Harold* to read. It is very fine in parts, but I don't know whether I like it so much as his first cantos. There is an air of mystery and metaphysics about it.

> —John Cam Hobhouse (Lord Broughton),
> *Recollections of a Long Life*, ed. Lady Dorchester,
> 1910–11, vol. I, p. 99–100, vol. II, p. 11

JOHN MURRAY (1816)

Son of the eponymous founder of the publishing house, John Murray (1778–1843) became the most important and influential publisher in Great Britain. His home in London, Mayfair, was the center of a literary circle, and he published Walter Scott, Washington Irving, Jane Austen, and many of Byron's major works. Byron was his close friend, and on March 10, 1812, Murray published *Childe Harold,* which sold out in five days. On May 17, 1824 Murray participated in the notorious burning of Byron's two volumes of memoirs that Byron had given him for later publication. The following letter from September 12, 1816, tells Byron of Gifford's reaction to canto III.

I have rarely addressed you with more pleasure than upon the present occasion. I was thrilled with delight yesterday by the announcement of Mr. Shelley with the MS. of "Childe Harold." I had no sooner got the quiet possession of it than, trembling with auspicious hope about it, I carried it direct to Mr. Gifford. He has been exceedingly ill with jaundice, and unable to write or do anything. He was much pleased by my attention. I called upon him to-day. He said he was unable to leave off last night, and that he had sat up until he had finished every line of the canto. It had actually agitated him into a fever, and he was much worse when I called. He had persisted this morning in finishing the volume, and he pronounced himself infinitely more delighted than when he first wrote to me. He says that what you have heretofore published is nothing to this effort. He says also, besides its being the most original and interesting, it is the most finished of your writings; and he has undertaken to correct the press for you.

Never, since my intimacy with Mr. Gifford, did I see him so heartily pleased, or give one-fiftieth part of the praise, with one-thousandth part of the warmth. He speaks in ecstasy of the Dream—the whole volume beams with genius. I am sure he loves you in his heart; and when he called upon me some time ago, and I told him that you were gone, he instantly exclaimed

in a full room, "Well! he has not left his equal behind him—that I will say!"
Perhaps you will enclose a line for him.

—John Murray, from Samuel Smiles, ed.,
A Publisher and His Friends, 1891, I, pp. 365–366

Francis Jeffrey "Lord Byron's Poems" (1816)

The co-founder and editor of the *Edinburgh Review,* Francis Jeffrey (1773–
1850) wrote a review of *Childe Harold's Pilgrimage,* canto III, in 1817 that reconciled Byron even further with him: "I am perfectly pleased with Jeffrey's
also [he had stated his appreciation of Scott's review], which I wish you to
tell him," he wrote in a letter of March 10, 1817, to Thomas Moore: "I wish
you would also add, what you know, that I was not, and indeed, am not
even now, the misanthropical and gloomy gentleman he takes me for, but
a facetious companion, well to do with those with whom I am intimate,
and as loquacious and laughing, as if I were a much cleverer fellow. I suppose now I shall never be able to shake off my sables in public imagination." (Thomas Moore, *Life of Lord Byron. With His Letters and Journals,* IV,
pp. 72–74).

The most considerable of these ["the Noble author's most recent publications"],
is the Third Canto of *Childe Harold*, a work which has the disadvantage of all
continuations in admitting of little absolute novelty in the plan of the work,
or the cast of its character, and must, besides, remind all Lord Byron's readers
of the extraordinary effect produced by the sudden blazing forth of his genius
upon their first introduction to that title. In spite of all this, however, we are
persuaded that this Third Part of the poem will not be pronounced inferior
to either of the former; and, we think, will probably be ranked above them
by those who have been most delighted with the whole. The great success of
this singular production, indeed, has always appeared to us an extraordinary
proof of its merits; for, with all its genius, it does not belong to a sort of poetry
that rises easily to popularity.—It has no story or action—very little variety of
character—and a great deal of reasoning and reflection of no very attractive
tenor. It is substantially a contemplative and ethical work, diversified with
fine description, and adorned or overshaded by one emphatic person, who is
sometimes the author, and sometimes the object of the reflections on which
the interest is chiefly rested. It required, no doubt, great force of writing, and
a decided tone of originality to recommend a performance of this sort so

powerfully as this has been recommended to public notice and admiration—
and those high characteristics belong perhaps still more eminently to the part
that is now before us, than to any of the former. There is the same stern and
lofty disdain of mankind, and their ordinary pursuits and enjoyments, with
the same bright gaze on nature, and the same magic power of giving interest
and effect to her delineations—but mixed up, we think, with deeper and
more matured reflections, and a more intense sensibility to all that is grand
or lovely in the external world.—Harold, in short, is somewhat older since he
last appeared upon the scene—and while the vigour of his intellect has been
confirmed, and his confidence in his own opinions increased, his mind has
also become more sensitive; and his misanthropy, thus softened over by habits
of calmer contemplation, appears less active and impatient, even although
more deeply rooted than before. Undoubtedly the finest parts of the poem
before us, are those which thus embody the weight of his moral sentiments,
or disclose the lofty sympathy which binds the despiser of Man to the glorious
aspects of Nature. It is in these, we think, that the great attractions of the work
consist, and the strength of the author's genius is seen. The narrative and
description are of far inferior interest. With reference to the sentiments and
opinions, however, which thus give its distinguishing character to the piece,
we must say, that it seems no longer possible to ascribe them to the ideal
person whose name it bears, or to any other than the author himself.—Lord
Byron, we think, has formerly complained of those who identified him with
his hero, or supposed that Harold was but the expositor of his own feelings
and opinions;—and in noticing the former portions of the work, we thought it
unbecoming to give any countenance to such a supposition.—In this last part,
however, it is really impracticable to distinguish them.—Not only do the author
and his hero travel and reflect together—but, in truth, we scarcely ever have
any notice to which of them the sentiments so energetically expressed are to
be ascribed; and in those which are unequivocally given as those of the Noble
author himself, there is the very same tone of misanthropy, sadness and scorn,
which we were formerly willing to regard as a part of the assumed costume of
the Childe. We are far from supposing, indeed, that Lord Byron would disavow
any of these sentiments; and though there are some which we must ever think
it most unfortunate to entertain, and others which it appears improper to
have published, the greater part are admirable, and cannot be perused without
emotion even by those to whom they may appear erroneous.

—Francis Jeffrey, "Lord Byron's Poems,"
Edinburgh Review 27, December 1816,
issued February 1817, XXVII, pp. 292–293

GEORGE GORDON, LORD BYRON (1817)

Byron regarded the third canto of *Childe Harold* as his favorite, as he states in a letter to Thomas Moore dated January 28, 1817.

I rejoice to hear of your forthcoming in February, though I tremble for the magnificence which you attribute to the new Childe Harold. I am glad you like it: it is a fine indistinct piece of poetical desolation, and my favourite. *I was half mad* during the time of its composition, between metaphysics, mountains, lakes, love unextinguishable, thoughts unutterable, and the nightmare of my own delinquencies. I should, many a good day, have blown my brains out, but for the recollection that it would have given pleasure to my mother-in-law; and even then, if I could have been certain to haunt her, and fling the shattered scalp of my sinciput and occiput in her frightful face—but I won't dwell on these trifling family matters.

—George Gordon, Lord Byron, quoted in
Thomas Moore, *Letters and Journals of Lord Byron
with Notices on His Life,* 1831, vol. II, p. 51

JOHN WILSON (1817)

The Scottish writer John Wilson (1785–1854) is most frequently identified with the pseudonym Christopher North of *Blackwood's Edinburgh Magazine*. In his review of *Manfred* for the periodical, he comments on *Childe Harold* and puts it into the context of the sublime.

In the third canto of *Childe Harold*, accordingly, he has delivered up his soul to the impulses of Nature, and we have seen how that high communion has elevated and sublimed it. He instantly penetrated into her hearts, as he had before into the hearts of Man; and, in a few months of solitary wandering among the Alps, his soul became as deeply imbued with her glory and magnificence, as if, from youth, he had dedicated himself to no other power, and had for ever devoutly worshipped at her altar. He leapt at once into the first rank of descriptive poets. He came into competition with Wordsworth upon his own ground, and with his own weapons; and, in the first encounter, he vanquished and overthrew him. His description of the stormy night among the Alps—of the blending—the mingling—the fusion of his own soul, with the raging elements around him,—is alone worth all the dull metaphysics of *The Excursion,* and shows that he might enlarge the limits of human consciousness regarding the operations of matter upon mind, as widely as he has enlarged them regarding the operations of mind upon itself.

—John Wilson, *Blackwood's*
Edinburgh Magazine 1, 1817, p. 289

WILLIAM HAZLITT (1818)

The critic, essayist, and journalist William Hazlitt (1778–1830) combined radical politics with an admiration for Napoléon. When it came to Byron, he could not overlook the poet's aristocratic origins and entitlement, a bias that added to his critical assessment of Byron's politics and character. This review of *Childe Harold's Pilgrimage*, canto IV, first published in the *Yellow Dwarf* (1818), was reprinted in the author's *Complete Works*.

In general, the idle wants, the naughty airs, the ill humours and *ennui*, the contempt for others, and disgust at themselves, common to exalted birth and station, are suffered to corrupt and stagnate in the blood that inherits them;— they are a disease in the flesh, an obstinate tumour in the mind, a cloud upon the brow, a venom that vents itself in hateful looks and peevish words to those about them; but in this poem and this author they have acquired 'an understanding and a tongue',—a sublimed by imagination, systematized by sophistry—mount the stepts of the Capitol, fulmine over Greece, and are poured in torrents o abuse on the world. It is well if the world like it—we are tired of the monotony of his Lordship's griefs, of which we can perceive neither beginning nor end. 'They are begot of nothing, born of nothing.' He is in despair, because he has nothing to complain of—miserable, because he is in want of nothing. 'He has tasted of all earth's bliss, both living and loving', and therefore he describes himself as suffering the tortures of the damned. He is in love with misery, because he has possessed every enjoyment; and because he has had his will in every thing, is inconsolable because he cannot have impossibilities. His Lordship, in fact, makes out his own hard case to be, that he has attained all those objects that the rest of the world admire; that he has met with none of those disasters which embitter their lives; and he calls upon us to sympathise with his griefs and his despair.

This will never do. It is more intolerable than even Mr Wordsworth's arbitrary egotism and pampered self-sufficiency. *He* creates a factitious interest out of nothing: Lord Byron would destroy our interest in all that is. Mr Wordsworth, to salve his own self-love, makes the merest toy of his own mind,—the most insignificant object he can meet with,—of as much importance as the universe: Lord Byron would persuade us that the universe itself is not worth his or our notice; and yet he would expect us to be occupied with him.

———— The man whose eye
Is ever on himself doth look on one,
The least of Nature's works, one who might move
The wise man to that scorn which wisdom holds
Unlawful ever.

These lines, written by one of these two poets, might be addressed to both of them with equal propriety.

Lord Byron, in this the fourth and last Canto of *Childe Harold's Pilgrimage*, seems to have worn out the glowing fervor of his genius to a *calx*, and to have exhausted the intense enthusiasm of his favourite topics of invective. There is little about himself, historically speaking—there is no plot, no story, no interest excited, no catastrophe. The general reflections are connected together merely by the accidental occurrence of different objects—the Venus of Medici, or the statue of Pompey,—the Capitol at Rome, or the ridge of Sighs at Venice,—Shakespear, and Mrs Radcliffe,—Bonaparte, and his Lordship in person,—are brought together as in a phantasmagoria, and with as little attention to keeping or perspective, as in Hogarth's famous print for reversing the laws of vision. The judgments pronounced are often more dogmatical than profound, and with all their extravagance of expression, common-place. His Lordship does not understand the Apollo Belvidere or the Venus de Medicis, any more than Bonaparte. He cants about the one and against the other, and in doing the last, cuts his own throat.

—William Hazlitt, *The Complete Works of William Hazlitt*, ed. P.P. Howe, 1930–34, xix, pp. 35–43, 35–36

WALTER SCOTT (1818)

Scott also reviewed *Childe Harold's Pilgrimage*, canto IV, in an unsigned review in the *Quarterly*. Byron commented on this review in a letter of November 24, 1818, to John Murray: "You ask me of the two reviews—I will tell you. Scott's is the review of one poet on another—his friend; and Wilson's the review of a poet, too, on another—his idol; for he likes me better than he chooses to avow to the public, with all his eulogy. I speak judging only from the article, for I don't know him personally." (*The Works of Lord Byron. Letters and Journals*, ed. R.E. Prothero, 1898–1901, IV, pp. 274–275).

From the copious specimens which we have given, the reader will be enabled to judge how well the last part of this great poem has sustained Lord Byron's high reputation. Yet we think it possible to trace a marked difference, though none in the tone of thought and expression, betwixt this canto and the first three. There is less of passion, more of deep thought and sentiment, at once collected and general. The stream which in its earlier course bounds over cataracts and rages through narrow and rocky defiles, deepens, expands, and becomes less turbid as it rolls on, losing the aspect of terror and gaining that of sublimity. Eight years have passed between the appearance of the first volume and the present which concludes the work, a lapse of time which, joined with other circumstances, may have contributed somewhat to moderate the tone of Childe Harold's quarrel with the world, and, if not to reconcile him to his lot, to give him, at least, the firmness which endures it without loud complaint.—To return, however, to the proposition with which we opened our criticism, certain it is, that whether as Harold or as Lord Byron no author has ever fixed upon himself personally so intense a share of the public attention. His descriptions of present and existing scenes however striking and beautiful, his recurrence to past actions however important and however powerfully described, become interesting chiefly from the tincture which they receive from the mind of the author. The grot of Egeria, the ruins of the Palatine, are but a theme for his musings, always deep and powerful though sometimes gloomy even to sullenness. This cast of solemnity may not perhaps be justly attributed to the native disposition of the author, which is reported to be as lively as, judging from this single poem at least, we might pronounce it to be grave. But our ideas of happiness are chiefly caught by reflection from the minds of others, and hence it may be observed that those enjoy the most uniform train of good spirits who are thinking much of others and little of themselves. The contemplation of our minds, however salutary for the purposes of self-examination and humiliation, must always be a solemn task, since the best will find enough for remorse, the wisest for regret, the most fortunate for sorrow. And to this influence more than to any natural disposition to melancholy, to the pain which necessarily follows this anatomizing of his own thoughts and feelings which is so decidedly and peculiarly the characteristic of the Pilgrimage, we are disposed in a great measure to ascribe that sombre tint which pervades the poem. The poetry which treats of the actions and sentiments of others may be grave or gay according to the light in which the author chuses to view his subject, but he who shall mine long and deeply for materials in his own bosom will encounter abysses at the depth of which he must necessarily tremble. This moral truth appears to us to afford, in a great measure, a key to the peculiar tone of Lord Byron. How then, will the reader ask, is our proposition to be reconciled to that which preceded it? If the necessary result of an inquiry into our own thoughts be the conviction that all is vanity and vexation of spirit, why should we object to a style of writing, whatever its consequences may be, which involves in it truths as certain as they are melancholy? If the study of our own enjoyments leads us to doubt the reality of all except the indisputable pleasures of sense, and inclines us therefore towards the Epicurean system,—it is nature, it may be said, and not the poet which urges us upon the fatal conclusion. But this is not so. Nature, when she created man a social being, gave him the capacity of drawing that happiness from his relations with the rest of his race, which he is doomed to seek in vain in his own bosom. These relations cannot be the source of happiness to us if we despise or hate the kind with whom it is their office to unite us more closely. If the earth be a den of fools and knaves, from whom the man of genius differs by the more mercurial and exalted character of his intellect, it is natural that he should look down with pitiless scorn on creatures so inferior. But if, as we believe, each man, in his own degree, possesses a portion of the ethereal flame, however smothered by unfavourable circumstances, it is or should be enough to secure the most mean from the scorn of genius as well as from the oppression of power, and such being the case, the relations which we hold with society through all their gradations are channels through which the better affections of the loftiest may, without degradation, extend themselves to the lowest. Farther, it is not only our social connections which are assigned us in order to qualify that contempt of mankind, which too deeply indulged tends only to intense selfishness; we have other and higher motives for enduring the lot of humanity—sorrow, and pain, and trouble— with patience of our own griefs and commiseration for those of others. The wisest and the best of all ages have agreed that our present life is a state of trial not of enjoyment, and that we now suffer sorrow that we may hereafter be partakers of happiness. If this be true, and it has seldom been long, or at least ultimately, doubted by those who have turned their attention to so serious an investigation, other and worthier motives of action and endurance must necessarily occur to the mind than philosophy can teach or human pride supply. It is not our intention to do more than merely indicate so ample a topic for consideration. But we cannot forbear to add that the vanishing of Lord Byron's Pilgrim strongly reminded us of the close of another work, the delight of our childhood. Childe Harold, a prominent character in the first volume of the Pilgrimage, fades gradually from the scene like the spectre associate who performed the first stages of his journey with a knight-errant, bearing all the appearance of a living man, but who lessened to the sight by degrees, and became at length totally invisible when they approached the cavern where his mortal remains were deposited.

—Walter Scott, *Quarterly Review,*
April 1818, issued September 1818,
XIX, pp. 215–232, 227–231

JOHN WILSON (1818)

This Scottish writer and critic for *Edinburgh Blackwood's Magazine*, who was appointed chairman of moral philosophy at the University of Edinburgh in 1820, reviewed *Childe Harold*, canto IV, for the *Edinburgh Review* but also for *Blackwood's* in 1818. Byron repudiated Wilson's comparison of him and Rousseau in his "Detached Thoughts" in 1821: "I can't see any point of resemblance: he wrote prose, I verse: he was of the people, I of the Aristocracy: he was a philosopher, I am none." (*The Works of Lord Byron. Letters and Journals,* ed. R.E. Prothero, 1898–1901, V, p. 408f)

There are two writers, in modern literature, whose extraordinary power over the minds of men, it may truly be said, has existed less in their works than in themselves,—Rousseau and Lord Byron. They have other points of resemblance. Both are distinguished by the most ardent and vivid delineations of intense conception, and by an intense sensibility of passion, rather than of affection. Both, too, by this double power, have held a dominion over the sympathy of their readers, far beyond the range of those ordinary feelings which are usually excited by the mere efforts of genius. The impression of this interest still accompanies the perusal of their writings: But there is another interest of more lasting, and far stronger power, which the one has possessed, and the other now possesses,—which lies in the continual embodying of the individual character,—it might almost be said, of the very person of the writer. When we speak or think of Rousseau or Byron, we are not conscious of speaking or thinking of an author. We have a vague but empassioned remembrance of men of surpassing genius, eloquence and power,—of prodigious capacity both of misery and happiness. We feel as if we had transiently met such beings in real life, or had known them in the dim and dark communion of a dream. Each of their works presents, in succession, a fresh idea of themselves; and, while the productions of other great men stand out from them, like something they have created, theirs, on the contrary, are images, pictures, busts of their living selves,—clothed, no doubt, at different times in different drapery, and prominent from a different background,—but uniformly impressed with the same form, and mien, and lineaments, and not to be mistaken for the representations of any other of the children of men.

But this view of the subject, though universally felt to be a true one, requires perhaps a little explanation. The personal character of which we have spoken, it should be understood, is not, altogether, that on which the seal of life has been set,—and to which, therefore, moral approval or condemnation is necessarily annexed, as to the language or conduct of actual existence. It is the character, so to speak, which is prior to conduct, and yet open to good and to ill,—the constitution of the being, in body and in soul. Each of those illustrious writers has, in this light, filled his works with expressions of his own character,—has unveiled to the world the secrets of his own being,—the mysteries of the framing of man. They have gone down into those depths which every man may sound for himself, though not for another; and they have made disclosures to the world of what they beheld and knew there— disclosures that have commanded and enforced a profound and universal sympathy, by proving that all mankind, the troubled and the untroubled, the lofty and the low, the strongest and the frailest, are linked together by the bonds of a common but inscrutable nature.

Thus, each of these wayward and richly-gifted spirits has made himself the object of profound interest to the world,—and that too, during periods of society when ample food was everywhere spread abroad for the meditations and passions of men. What love and desire,—what longing and passionate expectation hung upon the voice of Rousseau, the idol of his day!—That spell is broken. We now can regard his works in themselves, in great measure free from all the delusions and illusions that, like the glories of a bright and vapoury atmosphere, were for ever rising up and encircling the image of their wonderful creator. Still is the impression of his works vivid and strong. The charm which cannot pass away is there,—life breathing in dead words,—the pulses of passion,—the thrilling of the frame,—the sweet pleasure stealing from senses touched with ecstasy into sounds which the tongue frames, and the lips utter with delight. All these still are there,—the fresh beauty, the undimmed lustre—the immortal bloom and verdure and fragrance of life. These, light and vision-like as they seem, endure as in marble. But that which made the spirits of men, from one end of Europe to the other, turn to the name of Rousseau,—that idolizing enthusiasm which we can now hardly conceive, was the illusion of one generation, and has not survived to another. And what was the spell of that illusion? Was it merely that bewitching strain of dreaming melancholy which lent to moral declamation the tenderness of romance? Or that fiery impress of burning sensibility which threw over abstract and subtle disquisitions all the colours of a lover's tale? These undoubtedly—but not these alone. It was that continual impersonation of himself in his writings, by which he was for ever kept brightly present before the eyes of men. There was in him a strange and unsated desire of depicturing himself, throughout all the changes of his being. His wild temper only found ease in tracing out, in laying bare to the universal gaze, the very groundwork, the most secret paths, the darkest coverts of one of the most wayward and unimaginable minds ever framed by nature. From the moment that his first literary success had wedded him to the public, this was his history,—and such his strange, contradictory, divided life. Shy, and shunning the faces of men in his daily walks, yet searching and rending up the inmost recesses of his heart for the inspection of that race which he feared or hated. As a man, turning from the light, as from something unsupportably loathsome, and plunging into the thickest shades. Yet, in that other existence which he held from imagination, living only in the presence of men,—in the full broad glare of the world's eye,—and eagerly, impetuously, passionately, unsparingly seizing on all his own most hidden thoughts—his loneliest moods—his most sacred feelings—which had been cherished for the seclusion in which they sprung—for their own still deep peace—and for their breathings of unbeheld communions,—seizing upon all these, and flinging them out into the open air, that they might feed the curiosity of that eager, idle, frivolous world from which he had fled in misanthropical disgust—that he might array an exhibition to their greedy gaze,—and that he, the morbid and melancholy lover of solitude, might act a conspicuous and applauded part on the crowded theatre of public fame.

It might, on a hasty consideration, seem to us, that such undisguised revelation of feelings and passions, which the becoming pride of human nature, jealous of its own dignity, would, in general, desire to hold in unviolated silence, could produce in the public mind only pity, sorrow, or repugnance. But, in the case of men of real genius, like Rousseau or Byron, it is otherwise. Each of us must have been aware in himself of a singular illusion, by which these disclosures, when read with that tender or high interest which attaches to poetry, seem to have something of the nature of private and confidential communications. They are not felt, while we read, as declarations published to the world,—but almost as secrets whispered to chosen ears. Who is there that feels, for a moment, that the voice which reaches the inmost recesses of his heart is speaking to the careless multitudes around him? Or, if we do so remember, the words seem to pass by others like air, and to find their way to the hearts for whom they were intended,—kindred and sympathizing spirits, who discern and own that secret language, of which the privacy is not violated, though spoken in hearing of the uninitiated,—because it is not understood. There is an unobserved beauty that smiles on us alone; and the more beautiful to us, because we feel as if chosen out from a crowd of lovers. Something analogous to this is felt in the grandest scenes of Nature and of Art. Let a hundred persons look from a hilltop over some transcendent landscape. Each will select from the wide-spread glory at his feet, for his more special love and delight, some different glimpse of sunshine,—or solemn grove,—or embowered spire,—or brown-mouldering ruin,—or castellated cloud. During their contemplation, the soul of each man is amidst its own creations, and in the heart of his own solitude;—nor is the depth of that solitude broken, though it lies open to the sunshine, and before the eyes of unnumbered spectators. It is the same in great and impressive scenes of art,—for example, in a theatre. The tenderest tones of acted tragedy reach our hearts with a feeling as if that inmost soul which they disclose revealed itself to us alone. The audience of a theatre forms a sublime unity to the actor; but each person sees and feels with the same incommunicated intensity, as if all passed only before his own gifted sight. The publicity which is before our eyes is not acknowledged by our minds; and each heart feels itself to be the sole agitated witness of the pageant of misery.

But there are other reasons why we read with complacency writings which, by the most public declaration of most secret feelings, ought, it might seem, to shock and revolt our sympathy. A great poet may address the whole world in the language of intensest passion, concerning objects of which, rather than speak, face to face, with any one human being on earth, he would perish in his misery. For it is in solitude that he utters what is to be wafted by all the winds of heaven. There are, during his inspiration, present with him only the shadows of men. He is not daunted, or perplexed, or disturbed, or repelled by real living breathing features. He can updraw just as much as he chuses of the curtain that hangs between his own solitude and the world of life. He thus pours his soul out, partly to himself alone,—partly to the ideal abstractions, and impersonated images that float round him at his own conjuration,—and partly to human beings like himself, moving in the dark distance of the every-day world. He confesses himself, not before men, but before the Spirit of Humanity. And he thus fearlessly lays open his heart,—assured that nature never prompted unto genius that which will not triumphantly force its wide way into the human heart. We can thus easily imagine the poet whom, in real life, the countenances and voices of his fellow-men might silence into shame, or fastidiousness, or timidity, or aversion or disdain,—yet kindling in his solitude into irrepressible passion and enthusiasm towards human nature and all its transitory concerns,—anxiously moulding himself into the object of men's most engrossing and vehement love or aversion,—identifying his own existence with all their strongest and profoundest passions,—claiming kindred with them, not in their Virtues alone, but in their darkest vices and most fatal errors;—yet, in the midst of all this, proudly guarding his own prevailing character, so that it shall not merge in the waves of a common nature, but stand "in shape and gesture proudly eminent," contemplated with still-increasing interest by the millions that, in spite of themselves, feel and acknowledge its strange and unaccountable ascendency.

The reasons then are obvious, why a writer of very vivid sensibilities may, by empassioned self-delineation, hold a wondrous power over the entranced minds of his readers. But this power is in his living hands; and, like the wand of the magician, it loses its virtue on its master's death. We feel chiefly the influence of such a writer, while he lives—our contemporary—going with us a fellow-voyager on the stream of life, and from time to time flashing towards us the emanations of his spirit. Our love—our expectation follow the courses of his mind, and, if his life repel us not, the courses of his life. It was the strange madness of Rousseau to pour the blaze of his reputation over the scandals of his life. But this was later in his career; and his name for a long time in Europe was that of an hermit-sage,—a martyr of liberty and virtue,—a persecuted good man loving a race unworthy of him, and suffering alike from their injustice and from the excess of his own spirit. He made a character for himself;—and whatever he had made it, it might have been believed. It was an assumed ideal impersonation of a character of literary and philosophical romance. At last, indeed, he broke up his own spell. But if he could have left the delusion behind him, he could not have left the power;—for the power hangs round the living man: it does not rest upon the grave.

When death removes such a writer from our sight, the magical influence of which we have spoken gradually fades away; and a new generation, free from all personal feelings towards the idol of a former age, may perhaps be wearied with that perpetual self-reference which to them seems merely the querulousness or the folly of unhappy or diseased egoism. It is even probable, that they may perversely withhold a portion of just admiration and delight from him who was once the undisputed sovereign of the soul, and that they may show their surprise at the subjection of their predecessors beneath the tyrannical despotism of genius, by scorning themselves to bow before its power, or acknowledge its legitimacy. It is at least certain, that by the darkness of death such luminaries, if not eclipsed, are shorn of their beams. So much, even in their works of most general interest, derives its beauty and fascination from a vivid feeling, in the reader's mind, of its being a portraiture of one with whom he has formed a kind of strange, wild and disturbed friendship, that they who come after, and have never felt the sorcery of the living man, instead of being kindled up by such pictures into impassioned wonder and delight, may gaze on them with no stronger emotion than curiosity, and even turn from them with indifference. Such must be more or less the fate of all works of genius, however splendid and powerful, of which the chief interest is not in universal truth, so much as in the intensity of individual feeling, and the impersonation of individual character.

It would, indeed, be in most violent contradiction to all we have formerly written of Lord Byron, were we to say that he stands in this predicament. Yet, there is a certain applicability of our observations even to him as well as to Rousseau, with whom, perhaps too fancifully, we have now associated his nature and his name. Posterity may make fewer allowances for much in himself and his writings, than his contemporaries are willing to do; nor will they, with the same passionate and impetuous zeal, follow the wild voice that too often leads into a haunted wilderness of doubt and darkness. To them, as to us, there will always be something majestic in his misery—something sublime in his despair. But they will not, like us, be withheld from sterner and severer feelings, and from the more frequent visitings of moral condemnation, by that awful commiseration and sympathy which a great poet breathes at will into all hearts, from his living agonies,—nor, by that restless, and watchful, and longing anxiety, to see again and again the princely sufferer rising up with fresh confessions of a still more magnificent sorrow,—nor, by that succession of affecting appeals to the frailties and troubles of our own hearts, which now keeps him vividly, and brightly, in our remembrance, wherever his soul, tempest-like, may have driven him over earth and sea,—nor, above all, by the cheering and lofty hope now felt by them who wish to see genius the inseparable companion of virtue,—that he whose inspiration holds us, always in wonder, and so often in delight, may come ere long to breathe a serener atmosphere of thought,—and, after all his wanderings, and all his woes,—with subsided passions, and invigorated intellect, calmly rest at last in the collected majesty of his power.

We are not now writing a formal critique on the genius of Byron, but rather expressing our notions of the relation in which he stands with the lovers of poetry. There is felt to be between him and the public mind, a stronger personal bond than ever linked its movements to any other living poet. And we think that this bond will in future be still more closely rivetted. During the composition of the first cantos of *Childe Harold*, he had but a confused idea of the character he wished to delineate,—nor did he perhaps very distinctly comprehend the scope and tendencies of his own genius. Two conceptions, distinct from each other, seem therein to be often blended,—one, of ideal human beings, made up of certain troubled powers and passions,—and one, of himself ranging the world of Nature and Man in wonder and delight and agitation, in his capacity of a poet. These conceptions, which frequently jostled and interfered with each other, he has since more distinctly unfolded in separate poems. His troubled imaginary beings,—possessing much of himself, and far more not of himself, he has made into Giaours, Conrads, Laras and Alps,—and his conception of himself has been expanded into Childe Harold, as we now behold him on that splendid pilgrimage. It is not enough to say that the veil is at last thrown off. It is a nobler creature who is before us. The ill-sustained misanthropy, and disdain of the two first Cantos, more faintly glimmer throughout the third, and may be said to disappear wholly from the fourth, which reflects the high and disturbed visions of earthly glory, as a dark swollen tide images the splendours of the sky in portentous colouring, and broken magnificence.

We have admitted, that much of himself is depicted in all his heroes; but when we seem to see the poet shadowed out in all those states of disordered being which such heroes exhibit, we are far from believing that his own mind has gone through those states of disorder, in its own experience of life. We merely conceive of it as having felt within itself the capacity of such disorders, and therefore exhibiting itself before us in possibility. This is not general—it is rare with great poets. Neither Homer, nor Shakspeare, nor Milton, ever so show themselves in the characters which they portray. Their poetical personages have no reference to themselves; but are distinct, independent creatures of their minds, produced in the full freedom of intellectual power. In Byron, there does not seem this freedom of power. There is little appropriation of character to events. Character is first, and all in all. It is dictated—compelled by some force in his own mind necessitating him,—and the events obey. These poems, therefore, with all their beauty and vigour, are not, like Scott's poems, full and complete narrations of some one definite story, containing within itself a picture of human life. They are merely bold, confused, and turbulent exemplifications of certain sweeping energies and irresistible passions. They are fragments of a poet's dark dream of life. The very personages, vividly as they are pictured, are yet felt to be fictitious; and derive their chief power over us from their supposed mysterious connexion with the poet himself, and, it may be added, with each other. The law of his mind is, to embody his own peculiar feelings in the forms of other men. In all his heroes we accordingly recognise—though with infinite modifications, the same great characteristics,—a high and audacious conception of the power of the mind,—an intense sensibility of passion,—an almost boundless capacity of tumultuous emotion,—a haunting admiration of the grandeur of disordered power,—and, above all, a soul-felt, blood-felt delight in beauty,—a beauty which, in his wild creations, is often scared away from the agitated surface of life by stormier passions, but which, like a bird of calm, is for ever returning, on its soft, silvery wings, before the black swell has finally subsided into sunshine and peace. . . .

The Pilgrimage of Childe Harold has now been brought to its close; and of his character there remains nothing more to be laid open to our view. It is impossible to reflect on the years which have elapsed since this mysterious stranger was first introduced to our acquaintance, without feeling that our own spirits have undergone in that time many mighty changes—sorrowful in some it may be, in others happy changes. Neither can we be surprised, knowing as we well do who Childe Harold is, that he also has been changed. He represented himself, from the beginning, as a ruin; and when we first gazed upon him, we saw indeed in abundance the black traces of recent violence and convulsion. The edifice has not been rebuilt; but its hues have been sobered by the passing wings of time, and the calm slow ivy has had leisure to wreathe the soft green of its melancholy among the fragments of the decay. In so far, the Pilgrim has become wiser. He seems to think more of others and with a greater spirit of humanity. There was something tremendous, and almost fiendish, in the air with which he surveyed the first scenes of his wanderings; and no proof of the strength of genius was ever exhibited so strong and unquestionable, as the sudden and entire possession of the minds of Englishmen by such a being as he then appeared to be. He looked upon a bull-fight, and a field of battle, with no variety of emotion. Brutes and men were, in his eyes, the same blind, stupid victims of the savage lust of power. He seemed to shut his eyes to every thing of that citizenship and patriotism which ennobles the spirit of the soldier, and to delight in scattering the dust and ashes of his derision over all the most sacred resting-places of the soul of man.

Even then, we must allow, the original spirit of the Englishman and the poet broke triumphantly, at times, through the chilling mist in which it had been spontaneously enveloped. In Greece, above all, the contemplation of Athens, Salamis, Marathon, Thermopylae and Plataea, subdued the prejudices of him who had gazed unmoved upon the recent glories of Trafalgar and Talavera. The nobility of manhood appeared to delight this moody visitant; and he accorded, without reluctance, to the shades of long-departed heroes that reverent homage, which, in the strange mixture of envy and scorn wherewith the contemplative so often regard active men, he had refused to the living, or to the newly dead.

At all times, however, the sympathy and respect of Childe Harold—when these have been excited by any circumstances external to himself—have been given almost exclusively to the intellectual, and refused to the moral greatness of his species. There is certainly less of this in his last Canto. Yet we think that the ruins of Rome might have excited within him not a few glorious recollections, quite apart from those vague lamentations and worshippings of imperial power, which occupy so great a part of the conclusion of his Pilgrimage. The stern purity and simplicity of domestic manners—the devotion of male and female bosoms—the very names of Lucretia, Valeria, and the mother of the Gracchi, have a charm about them at least as enduring as any others, and a thousand times more delightful than all the iron memories of conquerors and consuls.—But the mind must have something to admire—some breathing-place of veneration—some idol, whether of demon or of divinity, before which it is its pride to bow. Byron has chosen too often to be the undoubting adorer of Power. The idea of tyrannic and unquestioned sway seems to be the secret delight of his spirit. He would pretend, indeed, to be a republican,—but his heroes are all stamped with the leaden signet of despotism; and we sometimes see the most cold, secluded, immitigable tyrant of the whole, lurking beneath the "scallop-shell and sandal-shoon" of the Pilgrim himself.

In every mien and gesture of this dark being, we discover the traces of one that has known the delights, and sympathized with the possessors of intellectual power; but too seldom any vestiges of a mind that delights in the luxuries of quiet virtue, or that could repose itself in the serenity of home. The very possession of purity would sometimes almost seem to degrade, in his eyes, the intellectual greatness with which it has been sometimes allied. He speaks of Pompey with less reverence than Caesar; and, in spite of many passing visitings of anger and of scorn, it is easy to see that, of all cotemporary beings, there is ONE only with whom he is willing to acknowledge mental sympathy—one only whom he looks upon with real reverence—one only whose fortunes touch the inmost sanctuaries of his proud soul—and that this one is no other than that powerful, unintelligible, unrivalled spirit, who, had he possessed either private virtue or public moderation, might still have been in a situation to despise the offerings of even such a worshipper as Harold.

But there would be no end of descanting on the character of the Pilgrim, nor of the moral reflections which it awakens. Of the Poet himself, the completion of this wonderful performance inspires us with lofty and magnificent hopes. It is most assuredly in his power to build up a work that shall endure among the most august fabrics of the genius of England. Indeed, the impression which the collective poetry of our own age makes upon our minds is, that it contains great promise of the future; and that, splendid as many of its achievements have been, some of our living poets seem destined still higher to exalt the imaginative character of their countrymen. When we look back and compare the languid, faint, cold delineations of the very justest and finest subjects of inspiration, in the poetry of the first half of the last century, with the warm, life-flushed and life-breathing pictures of our own, we feel that a great accession has been made to the literature of our day,—an accession not only of delight, but of power. We cannot resist the persuasion, that if literature, in any great degree, impresses and nourishes the character of a people,—then this literature of ours, pregnant it is with living impressions,—gathered from Nature in all her varieties of awfulness and beauty,—gathered too from those high and dread Passions of men, which our ordinary life scarcely shows, and indeed could scarcely bear, but which, nevertheless, have belonged, and do belong, to our human life,—and held up in the powerful representations of the poets to our consciousness at times, when the deadening pressure of the days that are going by might bereave us of all genial hope and all dignified pride,—we say it is impossible for us to resist the belief that such pregnant, glowing, powerful poetry, must carry influences into the heart of this generation, even like those which are breathed from the heart of Nature herself—or like those which lofty passions leave behind them in bosoms which they have once possessed. The same spirit of poetical passion which so uniformly marks the works of all our living poets, must exist very widely among those who do not aspire to the name of genius; it must be very widely diffused throughout the age, and, as we think, must very materially influence the reality of life. Yet highly as we estimate the merits of our modern poetry, it is certain, that the age has not yet produced any one great epic or tragic performance. Vivid and just delineations of passion there are in abundance,—but of moments of passions—fragments of representation. The giant grasp of thought, which conceives, and brings into full and perfect life, full and perfect passion—passion pervading alike action and character, through a majestic series of events, and at the same time cast in the mould of grand imagination,—this seems not to be of our age. In the delineation of external nature, which, in a poet's soul, requires rather moral beauty than intellectual strength, this age has excelled. But it has produced no poem gloriously illustrative of the agencies, existences, and events, of the complex life of man. It has no Lear—no Macbeth—no Othello. Some such glory as this Byron may yet live to bring over his own generation. His being has in it all the elements of the highest poetry. And that being he enjoys in all the strength of its prime. We might almost say, that he needs but to exercise his will to construct a great poem. There is, however, much for him to alter in what may be called, his Theory of Imagination respecting Human Life. Some idols of his own setting-up he has himself overthrown. There are yet some others, partly of gold, and partly of clay, which should be dashed against the floor of the actuary. We have already spoken of his personal character, as it shines forth in his poetry. This personal character exists in the nature of his imagination, and may therefore be modified—purified—dignified by his own will. His imagination does, to his own eyes, invest him with an unreal character. Purposes, passions, loves, deeds, events, may seem great and paramount in imagination, which have yet no power to constrain to action; and those which perhaps may govern our actions, vanish altogether from our imagination. There is a region—a world—a sphere of being in imagination, which, to our real life, is no more than the world of a dream; yet, long as we are held in it by the transport of our delusion, we live, not in delight only, but in the conscious exaltation of our nature. It is in this world that the spirit of Byron must work a reformation for itself. He knows, far better than we can tell him, what have been the most hallowed objects of love and of passion to the souls of great poets in the most splendid eras of poetry,—and he also knows well, that those objects, if worshipped by him with becoming and steadfast reverence, will repay the worship which they receive, by the more fervent and divine inspiration which they kindle.

—John Wilson, *Edinburgh Review*, dated June
1818, issued September 1818, XXX, pp. 87–120

Percy Bysshe Shelley (1818)

In his preface to *The Revolt of Islam* (1818), Percy Bysshe Shelley (1792–1822) had already given his diagnosis of the causes, such as the French Revolution, of melancholy and misanthropy in contemporary literature. His admiration of Byron was complicated by his disillusionment at Byron's love affairs in Italy. When Thomas Love Peacock criticized the misanthropy and gloom in *Childe Harold's Pilgrimage*, canto IV, Shelley expressed his agreement in a letter of December 17 or 18, 1818, posted from Naples.

I entirely agree with what you say about *Childe Harold*. The spirit in which it is written is, if insane, the most wicked and mischievous insanity that ever was given forth. It is a kind of obstinate and self-willed folly, in which he hardens himself. I remonstrated with him in vain on the tone of mind from which such a view of things alone arises. For its real root is very different from its apparent one. Nothing can be less sublime than the true source of these expressions of contempt and desperation. The fact is that first, the Italian women with whom he associates are perhaps the most contemptible of all who exist under the moon—the most ignorant, the most disgusting, the most bigoted; countesses smell so strongly of garlic, that an ordinary Englishman cannot approach them. Well, L.B. is familiar with the lowest sort of these women, the people his gondolieri pick up in the streets. He associates with wretches who seem almost to have lost the gait and physiognomy of man, and who do not scruple to avow practices which are not only not named, but I believe seldom even conceived in England. He says he dissapproves [sic], but he endures. He is heartily and deeply discontented with himself; and contemplating in the distorted mirror of his own thoughts the nature and the destiny of man, what can he behold but objects of contempt and despair? But that he is a great poet, I think the address to Ocean proves. And he has a certain degree of candour while you talk to him, but unfortunately it does not outlast your departure. No, I do not doubt, and for his sake I ought to hope, that his present career must end soon in some violent circumstance.

—Percy Bysshe Shelley, *The Letters of Percy Bysshe Shelley*, ed. F.L. Jones, 1964, II, pp. 57–58

THOMAS LOVE PEACOCK (1818)

A close friend of Shelley, Thomas Love Peacock (1785–1866) was an English satirist and author. In his novel *Nightmare Abbey* (1818), Peacock portrays the author of *Childe Harold's Pilgrimage* as Mr. Cypress and has him echo stanzas 124 and 126 of canto IV. Most of Cypress's conversation in chapter XI is made up of phrases borrowed from the fourth canto of Byron's work, the section in which Peacock locates the misanthropy he despised.

MR CYPRESS
Sir, I have quarrelled with my wife; and a man who has quarrelled with his wife is absolved from all duty to his country. I have written an ode to tell the people as much, and they may take it as they list.

SCYTHROP
Do you suppose, if Brutus had quarrelled with his wife, he would have given it as a reason to Cassius for having nothing to do with his enterprise? Or would Cassius have been satisfied with such an excuse?

MR FLOSKY

Brutus was a senator; so is our dear friend: but the cases are
different. Brutus had some hope of political good: Mr Cypress has
none. How should he, after what we have seen in France?

SCYTHROP

A Frenchman is born in harness, ready saddled, bitted, and bridled,
for any tyrant to ride. He will fawn under his rider one moment, and
throw him and kick him to death the next; but another adventurer
springs on his back, and by dint of whip and spur on he goes as before.
We may, without much vanity, hope better of ourselves.

MR CYPRESS

I have no hope for myself or for others. Our life is a false nature;
it is not in the harmony of things; it is an all-blasting upas,
whose root is earth, and whose leaves are the skies which rain their
poison-dews upon mankind. We wither from our youth; we gasp with
unslaked thirst for unattainable good; lured from the first to the
last by phantoms—love, fame, ambition, avarice—all idle, and all
ill—one meteor of many names, that vanishes in the smoke of death.[8]

—Thomas Love Peacock, *Nightmare Abbey*, XL

JOHN ADDINGTON SYMONDS "LORD BYRON" (1880)

John Addington Symonds (1840–1893) was an English poet and cultural
historian who advocated male love in writings such as *Soldier Love and
Related Matter.* His autobiography self-consciously deals with his own
homosexuality. Symonds wrote a critical introduction to a collection of
poetry, *The English Poets,* in 1880.

The first thing that strikes a student of Byron's collected works is the quantity
of poetry produced by him in a short lifetime. The second is the variety of
forms attempted—the scope and range of intellectual power displayed. The
third is the inequality of the performance, due apparently in certain cases
to baste of composition, in others to imperfect sympathy with the subjects
treated, or again to some contemptuous compliance with a fashion which the
author only tolerated.

Byron's character is stamped upon his work in a remarkable degree; and
his character was powerfully biassed by external circumstance. The critic
cannot therefore neglect his biography. . . .

His genius received its first true awakening upon his travels. Greece made him a poet, and he returned to England with two Cantos of *Childe Harold* ready for publication. It is difficult to speak in measured terms of a poem which has suffered more from eulogy and popularity than any other poem of equal excellence from depreciation or neglect. The celebrated passages of *Childe Harold*, quoted, extracted, learned by heart at school, and incorporated into guide-books, have become a bye-word and a weariness to the present generation. We do not know how to render justice to the sonorous rhetoric and the often magnificent poetry of a masterpiece that has been subjected to processes so vulgarising. Some deductions, on sounder critical grounds, must also be made from the first enthusiasm that welcomed *Childe Harold*. The poem is written in a declamatory style, which savours of an age when Campbell's Pleasures of Hope was thought to soar above the level of prize poetry. The Pilgrim is a rococo creation, to whom Byron failed to communicate the breath of life. When this fictitious hero disappears from the scene, the stanzas invariably improve. Therefore the third and fourth Cantos, written in the plenitude of Byron's power, where *Childe Harold* has been all but forgotten, might pass for a separate composition. With the person of the Pilgrim, the affectation of Spenserian language, sparely but awkwardly employed in the first Canto, is dropped. The vein of meditation is richer, deeper, more dignified in utterance. The personal emotion of the poet, saddened and elevated by his cruel experience of life, finds vent in larger harmonies and more impassioned bursts of eloquence. His sympathy with the oppressed, and his sense of the world's past greatness, attain the altitude of lyrical inspiration in the apostrophe to Rome; while his enjoyment of nature in her grander aspects, and the consolation he received from her amid the solitudes of sea and lake and mountain, are expressed with sublimity in the passages upon the Ocean and the Jura thunderstorm.

After the publication of the first two Cantos, Byron woke in London and "found himself famous." What was far worse for him than fame, fashion claimed the new poet for her own. Though still isolated from true friends and family connections, he became the darling of society, poured forth for its amusement those Oriental tales, of which *The Giaour* alone retains sufficient vitality or perfume of true poetry to make its perusal at the present day desirable. Byron did not excel in the art of telling a simple story, unvaried by digressions, unassisted by contrasts of pathos and humour. One of his latest compositions in the narrative style, *The Island* is a total failure. The best of his earlier tales, *The Prisoner of Chillon* and *Mazeppa* were produced after the period of his fashionable fame, when, in the quietude of exile, he wrote with sobered feelings for himself. They owe, moreover, their greater purity of outline and sincerity of feeling to the form of monologue adopted. For the moment Byron becomes Bonnivard and Mazeppa, speaking through their lips of sufferings with which he felt the liveliest sympathy.

The life he led in London between 1812 and 1816, confirmed Byron's affectations and increased his tendency to cynicism. But while warping his character and enslaving his genius to trumpery standards of taste, it supplied him with much of the material which was to be wrought up into *Don Juan*. We have therefore no reason to deplore the fact that he lived through it. On the other hand we may perhaps be thankful that his uncongenial union with Lady Byron came to an abrupt conclusion at the beginning of 1816. His temper needed to be deepened by pain; nor was it till the blow of Lady Byron's separation struck him, that the gravest chords of his genius uttered a note. From that time forward, in the ennobled Cantos of *Childe Harold*, no less than in occasional lyrics, the sorrow which drove him into exile and flung him for repose and consolation upon Nature, formed one of the principal topics of his purest poetry. The public who raved about *Lara* and *The Corsair*, must have felt that there was yet a greater Byron to arise, when they read the *Domestic Pieces*, so indiscreetly committed by friends to the pages of the London newspapers. Even though we may condemn, on principles of taste, the self-revelation which from this time forward became one of Byron's habits, though we may fail to appreciate the professed scorn of the world which he mingled with a free recourse to its confidence and sympathy upon delicate matters of his private life, there is no disputing the energy communicated to his genius by these trials.

The formation of Shelley's friendship at this epoch must be reckoned one of the most fortunate and decisive events of Byron's life. The immediate result of their intercourse at Geneva was evident in the poems composed during 1816 and 1817; in the loftier inspiration of *Childe Harold*, in the lyrical gravity of Prometheus, and in the maturer reflections of Manfred. The reading of Goethe's *Faust* was not without its share of influence, manifest in the general conception of both *Manfred* and *The Deformed Transformed*. Yet neither of these plays can be said to have been modelled upon Faust. Byron's genius could not work upon the same lines as Goethe's; nor can dramas, hurriedly conceived and rapidly executed, without a distinct philosophical intention, be compared with the slowly elaborated masterpiece of a lifetime, which condenses and anticipates the profoundest thoughts of the nineteenth century. In *Manfred* the type of character which had previously been sketched by Byron in his romantic poems, receives more concentrated expression. Manfred is the incarnation of a defiant, guilty, self-reliant personality, preserved from despair by its disdainful pride, linked to the common joys and sorrows of humanity by the slender but still vital thread of a passion which is also an unforgotten and unforgivable crime. The egotism which is the source and secret of his vaunted strength, foredooms Manfred to destruction; yet at the close of his course, he does not flinch. Such self-sustained stubbornness was Byron's ideal. But he infected the type with something melodramatic, which lowered it below the defiance of the Greek Prometheus, and he prepared no reconciliation of opposing motives in his dramatic scheme. Tested by common experience, the character he created in Manfred was soon found wanting in the essential elements of reality.

—John Addington Symonds, "Lord Byron," in
The English Poets, ed. Thomas Humphry Ward,
1880, IV, pp. 244–255, 246–247

R.E. PROTHERO "THE POETRY OF BYRON" (1924)

Rowland Edmund Prothero, the first Baron Ernle, (1851–1937) was a British scholar, author, and politician. A fellow of All Souls' College, Oxford, and a Member of Parliament representing Oxford, he published widely on farming, in addition to producing *Letters and Journals of Lord Byron* (1898–1901). His *Centenary Reflections on Childe Harold's Pilgrimage and Don Juan* was published in 1924.

The period of Byron's most undisputed ascendancy in England comprised the four years from 1812 to 1816. They yielded little which compares in merit with the poetry of the exile. Apart from its biographical value, 'Hours of Idleness: By George Gordon, Lord Byron, a Minor', is, as a whole, neither better nor worse than the Album poetry of the Della Cruscans, with which the title and the contents, especially the literary mormonism of the odes to various ladies, inevitably provoke comparison. As satire, 'English Bards and Scotch Reviewers' is inferior to 'The Age of Bronze', and cannot be mentioned in the same breath with 'Don Juan' or 'The Vision of Judgment'. The last two Cantos of 'Childe Harold' are incomparably finer than the first two instalments. With the exception of one or two passages from 'The Giaour', the Turkish Tales, though they hold high rank among metrical narratives, offer little to the discriminating anthologist. The lines beginning 'And thou art dead, as young and fair', and 'the Destruction of Sennacherib' from the 'Hebrew Melodies', would probably find a place in any selection. The main interest of the early poetry lies, it may therefore be said, less in its merit than in the reasons for its immense popularity. Yet it is obviously impossible to recapture, at this distance of time, the 'first rapture' of contemporaries. In 1812, in the midst of a life-and-death struggle with France, it was not a victorious admiral or general whom society crowded to see, and petted and spoiled. It was a youthful poet who, himself a non-combatant, had ventured to speak of soldiers fallen at Talavera or Albuera as 'Ambition's honoured fools', and to express his loathing for the 'bravo's trade of war'.

In the fashionable world Byron's youth, rank, and personal beauty favoured 'Childe Harold's' triumph. Politics also, which, four years later, contributed largely to his ruin, aided his sudden rise to fame. The French Revolution had split the Whigs in two. It drove the main body into the Tory camp: it inspired Fox and his friends to head the movement which culminated in the Reform Bill of 1832. At this moment, nothing seemed more permanent than the New Whigs 'not getting into place'. Their leaders solaced their exclusion from office with an Epicurean aestheticism and the patronage of letters. Byron, by his genius, his passion for freedom, his detestation of war, promised to be an invaluable recruit to their cause. He might prove a more powerful spokesman than their drawing-room minstrel, Tommy Moore. He was, moreover, one of themselves. During the London season of 1812, scores of political ladies, including the most exclusive leaders of fashion, talked Byron and 'Childe Harold' at crowded tea-tables, routs, or assemblies. But the spell was cast over too wide a field to be explained by personal or party influences. Nor can the secret wholly lie in the special attraction which pictures, painted on the spot, of famous cities and historic lands must have had for a generation debarred from travel by ubiquitous war. A more permanent distinction lies in the originality of the design. 'Childe Harold' is not adapted or imitated from anything that had gone before in English literature. It has neither ancestors nor progeny. It is the first travel-poem in the English language, and, except for the few and feeble copies which Mr Chew unearths, it is also the last. Even with all these advantages, the poem, and the equally popular Eastern Tales, could not have gained so instantaneous and prodigious a success, unless Byron had touched chords to which the country was ready to respond.

In the turmoil of wars and revolutions, men sickened of the conventional insipidities of classic verse. They themselves were living romance. If poetry was to quicken their pulses and heat their imaginations, it must have in it something of the excitement and turbulence of the times in which they lived. Few and chosen were they who could draw themselves apart from the rushing torrent of life, and muse on the hills above Tintern Abbey or even sail on a voyage with the Ancient Mariner. Scott's metrical romances, with their fire of patriotism, their love of wild nature, their enthusiasm for historical tradition, their incomparable power of story-telling, met, as their eager welcome shows, a public need. But their scenes were laid in the remote past and the note of passion was not struck. Byron appealed to the same popular taste, with the added force of applying to contemporary life the form and passion of romantic poetry.

Staled by familiarity, the first two Cantos of 'Childe Harold' to-day seem nothing but a series of youthful *impressions de voyage*—spirited sketches, tinged with romantic melancholy, of travel in foreign countries. To Byron's own contemporaries the poem meant much more. Its freshness hid from them defects which are obvious to fastidious eyes. Accustomed only to the classical treatment of external objects, they found novelty and originality in descriptions of the feelings which those objects aroused in the imagination of the poet. For them, the poem throbbed with something of the vitality, the energy, the intensity of passion which characterised their own surroundings. It opened a new world to the imagination, widened the field, and varied the resources of poetry to correspond with their own expanding horizons. It imported the touch of cosmopolitanism and the continental flavour which their own reaction from insularity was beginning to demand. It carried them to scenes which were painted by a man with his eyes on the spot, who derived his local colour, not from the library, but from his own first-hand observation. It showed them the country in which the battles of England were being fought; it restored to life the hallowed land of Hellas; it contrasted the glories of its liberty with the degradation of its slavery; it opened the gates of the mysterious East which fascinated all adventurous spirits of the age, and among them Bonaparte and Chateaubriand. It preached, with eager enthusiasm, the literary crusade to succour the Christian races in their struggle for freedom from the yoke of Islam; and the strong note of passion rings true, for it was the cause in which Byron died.

Except in one point, the strength of the appeal, which 'Childe Harold' made to Byron's contemporaries, need not be developed further. Assuming for the moment that the hero of the poem is a portrait of himself, the Childe's attitude of brooding dissatisfied melancholy seems a pose. In a young man who, though he never had the tranquil depths of nature on which the joy of life depends, was brim-full of its gaiety, and neither friendless nor unaimable, it appears to be an affectation and an insincerity. It did not so strike his own generation. They found in it the poetic expression of a feeling which was so characteristic of the age as to be genuinely representative. What is now regarded as a blemish was, at the time, one of the secrets of the poem's success. It is significant that Goethe's Werther, Chateaubriand's Rene, Senancour's Obermann, all adopt the same attitude as 'Childe Harold.' Melancholy, said

Victor Hugo, is a note of the romantic movement. The identity of tone is not due to imitation. It is created by the romantic and revolutionary atmosphere of France, Germany, and England. Under the name of *ennui*, Horace Walpole described the same feeling, seventy years earlier:

> 'Oh! my dear Sir' (so he writes to John Chute, Aug. 20, 1743), 'don't you find that nine parts in ten of the world are of no use but to make you wish yourself with that tenth part? I am so far from growing used to mankind by living amongst them, that my natural ferocity and wildness does but every day grow worse. They tire me, they fatigue me: I don't know what to do with them; I fling open the windows and fancy I want air: . . . I literally seem to have murdered a man whose name was Ennui, for his ghost is ever before me.'

The feeling is an expression of the rising revolt against the order and repression, the complacent optimism, the starvation of many needs and moods of the imagination, which characterised the 18th century. It spread far and wide; it struck its roots deep. It assumed various forms, and the refuges in which men sought ways of escape were diverse. On the artistic and literary side, it underlay the Romantic movement. As it descended from the *salon* to the streets, and deepened from dissatisfaction with society into fierce hostility to its exising order, it became the parent of revolution. When Byron, therefore, embodied this prevailing mood in the character of his hero, he expressed a feeling with which, in one or other of its multitudinous forms, all men of more than average sensibility were, like himself, saturated.

The analytic self-reflective vein is now familiar in modern verse. But a generation, which for many years had known nothing but impersonal poetry, found in 'Childe Harold', as well as the poetic embodiment of a prevalent feeling, the fresh attraction of a veiled revelation of the poet's personality. Byron himself disavowed the self-portraiture. There is no reason to doubt his sincerity. He was probably unaware, at that stage of his career, of what he was doing. The Childe's railings at humanity, his splenetic misanthropy, his craving for solitude, appear, as has been said, to be artificial. But they were characteristic of the times in which Byron had grown to manhood. They were the air breathed by an age of revolt, to which 'whatever is' seemed 'wrong'. They were part of the poet's own nature; they were also representative. Byron may, therefore, have intended to give them dramatic shape in the person of an imaginary hero, not realising that, in so doing, he was but repeating the portrait of himself which he had painted in 'Hours of Idleness'.

Weary of love, of life, devoured with spleen,
I rest a perfect Timon, not nineteen.

—R.E. Prothero, "The Poetry of Byron," in
Quarterly Review, CCXLI, 1924, pp. 250–253

THE TURKISH TALES

Following his travels in Albania, Greece, and Turkey, Byron published a series of Eastern-themed poems between 1813 and 1816. *The Giaour* (June 1813) went through eight editions by the end of the year, while Byron continued to add new sections to the poem, imparting a highly fragmentary character to it. In the tale, the Turkish lord Hassan punishes the infidelity of his wife, Leila, by drowning her in a sack (the usual punishment and one that Byron had prevented at Piraeus in 1810). In revenge, the lover, called the Giaour (meaning non-Muslim) kills Hassan.

The Bride of Abydos (December 1813) sold equally well (six thousand copies in one month). In this tale, Byron, who was having an affair with his half sister, Augusta, dealt with the theme of incest for the first time: Zuleika, daughter of the Pasha Giaffir is loved by Selim, her supposed half brother (which he is not), the leader of a band of pirates. When they are seen together in the harem, Selim is shot, and Zuleika dies of a broken heart. Illicit love, violence, and brutal death are the key ingredients of this group of Byron's writings.

His third poem in the series, *The Corsair,* was published in February 1816 and was written in heroic couplets. The sales of this poem were unprecedented: ten thousand copies on the day of publication. Again, the poem features a mysterious and lonely hero defying society, a mixture of Byronic hero and gothic villain. While trying to rescue women of the harem, he is captured. Gulnare saves him from impalement by killing the pasha. After their flight to the pirates' lair, they discover that Conrad's beloved Medora has died of a broken heart, and they subsequently disappear. *Lara,* published in August 1814, was the sequel to *The Corsair* and features Conrad's return to the feudal castle of his origins, accompanied by Gulnare. *The Siege of Corinth* and *Parisina* were published in February 1816.

The reception of these poems was in many ways contradictory. While the public reaction was enthusiastic, critics often faulted the fragmentary structure of *The Giaour*; while many lauded the depiction of characters typically unfamiliar to English readers, the characters were sometimes viewed as less than credible or not fully realized. Apart from any moral criticism, the tales were sometimes regarded as too vague and melodramatic.

Francis Jeffrey (1814)

Jeffrey had favorably reviewed *The Giaour* in the July 1813 issue of the *Edinburgh Review*, commenting on its fragmentary structure, the quality of the verse, and the character of the hero. His review of *The Corsair* and *The Bride of Abydos* is a more sustained attempt at analyzing the nature of Byron's poetry. Jeffrey espouses a cyclical theory of taste, and his positive view of romantic primitivism should be contrasted with Thomas Love Peacock's negative account in *The Four Ages of Poetry* (1820).

Lord Byron has clear titles to applause, in the spirit and beauty of his fiction and versification, and the splendour of many of his descriptions: But it is to his pictures of the stronger passions, that he is indebted for the fulness of his fame. He has delineated, with unequalled force and fidelity, the workings of those deep and powerful emotions which alternately enchant and agonize the minds that are exposed to their inroads; and represented, with a terrible energy, those struggles and sufferings and exaltations, by which the spirit is at once torn and Transported, and traits of divine inspiration, or demoniacal possession, thrown across the tamer features of humanity. It is by this spell, 1814 chiefly, we think, that he has fixed the admiration of the public; and while other poets delight by their vivacity, or enchant by their sweetness, he alone has been able to *command* the sympathy, even of reluctant readers, by the natural magic of his moral sublimity, and the terrors and attractions of those overpowering feelings, the depths and the heights of which he seems to have so successfully explored. All the considerable poets of the present age have, indeed, possessed this gift in a greater or lesser degree: but there is no man, since the time of Shakespeare himself, in whom it has been made manifest with greater fulness and splendour, than in the noble author before us: and there are various considerations that lead us to believe, that it is chiefly by its means that he has attained the supremacy with which he seems now to be invested.

It must have occurred, we think, to every one who has attended to the general history of poetry, and to its actual condition among ourselves, that it is destined to complete a certain cycle, or great revolution, with respect at least to some of its essential qualities; and that we are now coming round to a taste and tone of composition, more nearly akin to that which distinguished the beginning of its progress, than any that has prevailed in the course of it.

In the rude ages, when such compositions originate, men's passions are violent, and their sensibility dull. Their poetry deals therefore in strong emotions, and displays the agency of powerful passions; both because these are the objects with which they arc most familiar in real life, and because nothing of a weaker cast could make any impression on the rugged natures for whose entertainment they are devised.

As civilization advances, men begin to be ashamed of the undisguised vehemence of their primitive emotions; and learn to subdue, or at least to conceal, the fierceness of their natural passions. The first triumph of regulated society, is to be able *to* protect its members from actual violence; and the first trait of refinement in manners, is to exclude the coarseness and offence of unrestrained and selfish emotions. The complacency however with which these achievements are contemplated, naturally leads to too great an admiration of the principle from which they proceed. All manifestation of strong feeling is soon proscribed as coarse and vulgar; and first a cold and ceremonious politeness, and afterwards a more gay and heartless dissipation, represses, and in part eradicates the warmer affections and generous passions of our nature, along with its more dangerous and turbulent emotions. It is needless to trace the effects of this revolution in manners and opinions of society upon that branch of literature, which necessarily reflects all its variations. It is enough to say, in general, that, in consequence of this change, poetry becomes first pompous and lately—then affectedly refined and ingenious—and finally gay, witty, discursive and familiar.

There is yet another stage, however, in the history of man and his inventions. When the pleasures of security are no longer new, and the dangers of excessive or intemperate vehemence cease to be thought of in the upper ranks of society, it is natural that the utility of the precautions which had been taken against them should be brought into question, and their severity in a great measure relaxed. There is in the human breast a certain avidity for strong sensation, which cannot he long repressed even by the fear of serious disaster. The consciousness of having subdued and disarmed the natural violence of mankind, is sufficiently lively to gratify this propensity, so long as the triumph is recent, and the hazards still visible from which it has effected our deliverance. In like manner, while it is a new thing, and somewhat of a distinction, to be able to laugh gracefully at all things, the successful derision of affection and enthusiasm is found to do pretty nearly as well as their possession; and hearts comfortably hardened by dissipation, feel little want of gratifications which they have almost lost the capacity of receiving. When these, however, come to be but vulgar accomplishments—when generations have passed away, during which all persons of education have employed themselves in doing the same frivolous things, with the same despair either of interest or glory, it can scarcely fail to happen, that the more powerful spirits will awaken to a sense of their own degradation and unhappiness;—a disdain and impatience of the petty pretensions and joyless elegancies of fashion will gradually arise: and strong and natural sensations will again be sought, without dread of their coarseness, in every scene which promises to supply them. This is the stage of society in which fanaticism has its second birth, and political enthusiasm its first true development—when plans of visionary reform, and schemes of boundless ambition are conceived, and almost realized by the energy with which they are pursued—the era of revolutions and projects—of vast performances, and infinite expectations.

Poetry, of course, reflects and partakes in this great transformation. It becomes more enthusiastic, authoritative and impassioned; and feeling the necessity of dealing in more powerful emotions than suited the tranquil and frivolous age which preceded, naturally goes back to those themes and characters which animated the energetic lays of its first rude inventors. The feats of chivalry, and the loves of romance,[1] are revived with more than their primitive wildness and ardour. For the sake of the natural feeling they contain, the incidents and diction of the old vulgar ballads are once more imitated and surpassed; and poetry does not disdain, in pursuit of her new idol of strong emotion, to descend to the very lowest conditions of society, and to stir up the most revolting dregs of utter wretchedness and depravity.

This is the age to which we are now arrived:—and if we have rightly seized the principle by which we think its peculiarities are to be accounted for, it will not be difficult to show, that the poet who has devoted himself most exclusively, and most successfully, to the delineation of the stronger and deeper passions, is likely to be its reigning favourite. Neither do we think that we can have essentially mistaken that principle:—at least it is a fact, independent of all theory, not only that all the successful poets of the last twenty years have dealt much more in powerful sensations, than those of the century that went before; but that, in order to attain this object, they have employed themselves upon subjects which would have been rejected as vulgar and offensive by the fastidious delicacy of that age of fine writing. Instead of ingenious essays, elegant pieces of gallantry, and witty satires all stuck over with classical allusions, we have, in our popular poetry, the dreams of convicts, and the agonies of Gypsey women,—and the exploits of buccaneers, freebooters, and savages—and pictures to shudder at, of remorse, revenge, and insanity—and the triumph of generous feelings in scenes of anguish and terror—and the heroism of low-born affection and the tragedies of vulgar atrocity. All these various subjects have been found interesting, and have succeeded, in different degrees, in spite of accompaniments which would have disgusted an age more recently escaped from barbarity. And as they agree in nothing but in being the vehicles of strong and natural emotions, and have generally pleased, nearly in proportion to the quantity of that emotion they conveyed, it is difficult not to conclude, that they have pleased only for the sake of that quality—a growing appetite for which may be regarded as the true characteristic of this age of the world.

In selecting subjects and characters for this purpose, it was not only natural, but in a great measure necessary, to go back to the only ages when strong passions were indulged, or at least displayed without controul, by persons in the better ranks of society, in the same way as, in order to get perfect models of muscular force and beauty, we still find that we must go back to the works of those days when men went almost naked, and were raised to the rank of heroes for feats of bodily strength and activity. The savages and barbarians that are still to be found in the world, are, no doubt, very exact likenesses of those whom civilization has driven out of it; and they may be used accordingly for most of the purposes for which their antient prototypes are found serviceable. In poetry, however, it happens again, as in sculpture, that it is safer, at least for a moderate genius, rather to work upon the relics we have of antiquity, than upon what is most nearly akin to it among our own contemporaries; both because there is a certain charm and fascination in what is antient and long remembered, and because those particular modifications of energetic forms and characters, which have already been made the subject of successful art, can be more securely and confidently managed in imitation, than the undefined vastness of a natural condition, however analogous to that from which they were selected.—Mr Southey, accordingly, who has gone in search of strong passions among the savages of America, and the gods and enchanters of India, has had far less success than Mr Scott, who has borrowed his energies from the more familiar scenes of European chivalry, and built his fairy castles with materials already tried and consecrated in the fabric of our old romances. The noble author before us has been obliged, like them, to go out of his own age and country in quest of the same indispensable ingredients; and his lot has fallen among the Turks and Arabs of the Mediterranean:—ruffians and desperadoes, certainly not much more amiable in themselves than the worst subjects of the others,—but capable of great redemption in the hands of a poet of genius, by being placed within the enchanted circle of antient Greece, and preserving among them so many vestiges of Roman pride and magnificence. There is still one general remark, however, to be made, before coming immediately to the merit of the pieces before us.

Although the necessity of finding beings capable of strong passions, thus occasions the revival, in a late stage of civilization, of the characters and adventures which animated the poetry of rude ages, it must not be thought that they are made to act and feel, on this resurrection, exactly as they did in their first natural presentation. They were then produced, not as exotics or creatures of the imagination, but merely as better specimens of the ordinary nature with which their authors were familiar; and the astonishing situations and appalling exploits in which they were engaged, were but a selection from the actual occurrences of the times. Neither the heroes themselves, nor their first celebrators, would have perceived any sublimity in the character itself or the tone of feeling, which such scenes and such exploits indicate to the more reflecting readers of a distant generation; and would still less have thought of analyzing the workings of those emotions, or moralizing on the incidents to which they gave birth. In this primitive poetry, accordingly, we have rather the result than the delineation of strong passions—the events which they produce, rather than the energy that produces them. The character of the agent is unavoidably disclosed indeed in short and impressive glimpses—but it is never made the direct subject of exhibition; and the attention of the reader is always directed to what he does—not to what he feels. A more refined, reflecting, and sensitive generation, indeed, in reading these very legends, supposes what *must* have been felt, both before and after the actions that are so minutely recorded; and thus lends to them, from the stores of its own sensibility, a dignity and an interest which they did not possess in the minds of their own rude composers. When the same scenes and characters, however, are ultimately called back to feed the craving of a race disgusted with heartless occupations, for natural passions and overpowering emotions, it would go near to defeat the very object of their revival, if these passions were still left to indicate themselves only by the giant vestiges of outrageous deeds, or acts of daring and desperation. The passion itself must now be pourtrayed—and all its fearful workings displayed in detail before us. The minds of the great agents must be unmasked for us—and all the anatomy of their throbbing bosoms laid open to our gaze. We must be made to understand what they feel and enjoy and endure;—and all the course and progress of their *possession,* and the crossing and mingling of their opposite affections, must be rendered sensible to our touch; till, without regard to their external circumstances, we can enter into all the motions of their hearts, and read, and shudder as we read, the secret characters which stamp the capacity of unlimited suffering on a nature which we feel to be our own.

It is chiefly by these portraitures of the interior of human nature that the poetry of the present day is distinguished from all that preceded it—and the difference is perhaps most conspicuous when the persons and subjects are borrowed from the poetry of an earlier age. Not only is all this anatomy of the feelings superadded to the primitive legend of exploits, but in many cases feelings are imputed to the agents, of which persons in their condition were certainly incapable, and which no description could have made intelligible to their contemporaries—while, in others, the want of feeling, probably a little exaggerated beyond nature also, is dwelt upon, and made to produce great effect as a trait of singular atrocity, though far too familiar to have excited any sensation either in the readers or spectators of the times to which the adventures naturally belong. Our modern poets, in short, have borrowed little more than the situations and unrestrained passions of the state of society from which they have taken their characters—and have added all the sensibility and delicacy from the stores of their own experience. They have lent their knights and squires of the fifteenth century the deep reflection and considerate delicacy of the nineteenth,—and combined the desperate and reckless valour of a Buccaneer or Corsair of any age, with the refined gallantry and sentimental generosity of an English gentleman of the present day. The combination we believe to be radically incongruous; but it was almost indispensable to the poetical effect that was in contemplation. The point was, to unite all the fine and strong feelings to which cultivation and reflection alone can give birth, with those manners and that condition of society, in which passions are uncontrouled, and their natural indications manifested without reserve. It was necessary, therefore, to unite two things that never did exist together in any period of society; and the union, though it may startle sober thinkers a little, is perhaps within the legitimate prerogatives of poetry. The most outrageous, and the least successful attempt of this sort we remember, is that of Mr Southey, who represents a wild Welch chieftain, who goes a buccaneering to America in the twelfth century, with all the softness, decorum, and pretty behaviour of Sir Charles Grandison. But the incongruity itself is universal—from Campbell, who invests a Pennsylvanian farmer with the wisdom and mildness of Socrates, and the dignified manners of an old Croix de St Louis—to Scott, who makes an old, bloodyminded and mercenary ruffian talk like a sentimental hero and poet, in his latter days—or the author before us, who has adorned a merciless corsair on a rock in the Mediterranean, with every virtue under heaven—except common honesty.

Of that noble author, and the peculiarity of his manner, we have not much more to say, before proceeding to give an account of the pieces now before us. His object obviously is, to produce a great effect, partly by the novelty of his situations, but chiefly by the force and energy of his sentiments and expressions; and the themes which he has selected, though perhaps too much resembling each other, are unquestionably well adapted for this purpose. There is something grand and imposing in the unbroken stateliness, courage, and heroic bigotry of a Turk of the higher order; and a certain voluptuous and barbaric pomp about his establishment, that addresses itself very forcibly to the imagination. His climate too, and most of its productions, are magnificent—and glow with a raised and exotic splendour; but the ruins of Grecian art, and of Grecian liberty and glory with which he is surrounded, form by far the finest of his accompaniments. There is nothing, we admit, half so trite in poetry as commonplaces of classical enthusiasm; but it is for this very reason that we admire the force of genius by which Lord Byron has contrived to be original, natural, and pathetic, upon a subject so unpromising, and apparently so long exhausted. How he has managed it, we do not yet exactly understand; though it is partly, we have no doubt, by placing us in the midst of the scene as it actually exists, and superadding the charm of enchanting landscape to that of interesting recollections. Lord Byron, we think, is the only modern poet who has set before our eyes a visible picture of the present aspect of scenes so famous in story; and, instead of feeding us with the unsubstantial food of historical associations, has spread around us the blue waters and dazzling skies—the ruined temples and dusky olives—the desolated cities, and turbaned population, of modern Attica. We scarcely knew before that Greece was still a beautiful country.

He has also made a fine use of the gentleness and submission of the females of these regions, as contrasted with the lordly pride and martial ferocity of the men: and though we suspect he has lent them more *soul* than of right belongs to them, as well as more delicacy and reflection; yet there is something so true to female nature in general, in his representations of this sort, and so much of the Oriental softness and acquiescence in his particular delineations, that it is scarcely possible to refuse the picture the praise of being characteristic and harmonious, as well as eminently sweet and beautiful in itself.

The other merits of his composition are such as his previous publications had already made familiar to the public,—an unparalleled rapidity of narrative, and condensation of thoughts and images—a style always vigorous and original, though sometimes quaint and affected, and more frequently strained, harsh, and abrupt—a diction and versification invariably spirited, and almost always harmonious and emphatic: Nothing diluted in short, or diffused into weakness, but full of life, and nerve, and activity—expanding only in the eloquent expression of strong and favourite affections, and everywhere else concise, energetic, and impetuous—hurrying on with a disdain of little ornaments and accuracies, and not always very solicitous about being comprehended by readers of inferior capacity.

The more considerable of the two poems now before us, entitled *The Corsair*, exhibits all those qualities, perhaps, in a more striking light than any of the author's other publications. It is written in the regular heroic couplet, with a spirit, freedom, and variety of tone, of which, notwithstanding the example of Dryden, we scarcely believed that measure susceptible. In all the descriptive and serious pieces of Dryden, and in all his writings, indeed, except his Political Satires and his immortal Ode, there are innumerable flat, dull, and prosaic passages;—lines without force, spirit, or energy, and in fact without any other merit than that of accurate versification, and easy and natural diction. Nothing can be more exquisite than the couplets of Pope, for the expression of pointed remark, wit, sarcasm, or epigram; but there is nothing in Pope of impetuous passion or enthusiastic vehemence; and his acknowledged mastery in this species of versification had almost brought it to be considered as appropriate to such subjects,—when Goldsmith, and after him Rogers and Campbell, came to show that it was also capable of strains of the deepest tenderness and sweetest simplicity. Still, however, all these were compositions of a measured and uniform structure—and it was yet to be proved that this, the most ponderous and stately verse in our language, could be accommodated to the variations of a tale of passion and of pity, and to all the breaks, starts and transitions of an adventurous and dramatic narration. This experiment Lord Byron has made, with equal boldness and success— and has satisfied us, at least, that the oldest and most respectable measure that is known among us, is at least as flexible as any other—and capable, in the hands of a master, of vibrations as strong and rapid as those of a lighter structure. We shall not be positive that the charm may not be partly at least in the subject—but we certainly never read so many ten-syllabled couplets together before, with so little feeling of heaviness or monotony. . . .

Our readers are now in a condition to judge for themselves of the merits of this singular production—nor are we tempted to interfere with any remarks of our own. The obvious and radical objection, of all the incidents being borrowed from situations that are scarcely *conceivable* by the greater part of his readers, has been already considered in the remarks which we made at the beginning: a more reasonable objection, we think is, that the character of the hero is needlessly loaded in the description with crimes and vices of which his conduct affords no indication. He is spoken of as an abandoned and unfeeling ruffian—and he uniformly comports himself as a perfect pattern of tenderness and humanity. Nay, he even carries his generosity a good deal farther than, we believe, the most moral of his readers would think necessary—for our own part, at least, we do not hesitate to profess that we should have very little scruple about taking the *life* of any worthy gentleman over night, who had put every thing in order for impaling us in the morning.

The Corsair has detained us so long, that we must make short work with *The Bride of Abydos*—which *is* a piece indeed of a slighter structure, and more easily despatched. This is a Turkish tale, like *The Giaour,* written in yet more irregular verse, and abounding more in soft and tender scenes, and less in terrors and horrors than any of Lord Byron's other publications. It contains many passages of great interest and beauty—and as many specimens of rich and splendid description as could be selected out of any work of the same extent. The story is wild and tragical—but neither complicated nor horrible. . . .

After these long extracts, we can afford to say but little of Lord Byron's poetical peculiarities. We still wish he would present us with personages with whom we could more entirely sympathize. At present, he will let us admire nothing but adventurous courage in men, and devoted gentleness in women. There is no intellectual dignity or accomplishment about any of his characters; and no very enlightened or equitable principles of morality. We have made the best apology we could for this tribe of heroes, in the remarks we have ventured upon at the beginning; and are aware of the difficulty of exhibiting strong passions in respectable persons. But it belongs to a genius like his, to overcome such difficulties; and he will never be thoroughly nor universally pleasing, till he learns to bespeak our interest for beings a little more like those whom we have been accustomed to love and admire.

We must say a word or two, also, upon the faults of his style and diction—some of which seem to be growing into manner and habit with him. He has a sort of emphatic obscurity, for instance, every now and then, that is always distressing, and sometimes absurd. Speaking of the wild ditty sung by the pirates, for example, he says,

> Such were the sounds that thrilled the rocks among,
> And *unto ears as rugged seemed a song.*

And a little after,

> —————— she that day had past
> In watching all *that hope proclaimed a mast.*

And again, in the latter poem, with a still more lamentable failure of the intended effect—

> A cup, too, on the board was set,
> That *did not seem to hold sherbet.*

His construction too is often ungrammatical or imperfect—as when giving directions to alter the guard of his sword, he says,

Last time, it more fatigued my arm than foes.

To *fatigue* foes with a sabre, is at all events a very strange mode of annoyance. In a subsequent passage, it is said,

He sate him down in silence, and his look
Resumed the calmness which before forsook.

Forsook what?—The verb is unquestionably active, and not neuter. The whole passage indeed is clumsy in diction, and, we would almost say, vulgar in expression. For example,

The feast was ushered in; but sumptuous fare,
He shunned as if some poison mingled there.
For one so long condemned to toil and fast,
Methinks he strangely spares the rich repast.
"What ails thee, Dervise?—eat—dost thou suppose
This feast a Christian's? or my friends thy foes?

The following triplet is heavy, and almost unintelligible—it would be agreeably lightened by striking out the middle line.

But he has said it—and the jealous well,
Those tyrants teazing, tempting to rebel,
Deserve the fate their fretting lips foretell.

There are various imitations of living authors—who would, no doubt, have been proud to have had the noble author acknowledge his obligations—and there is no one certainly who can better afford to acknowledge them. All that we object to however, is, that he sometimes imitates what had better be let alone—as the quaint jingle of Crabbe in such a line as this—

Or fallen too low, to fear a farther fall.

And the dangerous simplicity and daring pathos of Campbell, in such as this—

Another—and another—and another.

These are small matters, we allow; and if every one thought as little of them as we do, we doubt whether we should have condescended to take any notice of them. But many who have a good deal to say in awarding poetical glory, consider them as of no light importance; and therefore it becomes us, as

professed critics, to admonish the noble author of their existence.—We hope
he is not in earnest in meditating even a temporary divorce from his Muse—
and would humbly suggest to him to do away the reproach of the age, by
producing a tragic drama of the old English school of poetry and pathos. He
has all the air, we think, of being the knight for whom the accomplishment of
that great adventure is reserved.

Note

1. The Greek and Roman classics afford no resource in this emergency; partly
   because by far the greater part of them belong to a period of society as
   artificial, and as averse to the undisguised exhibition of natural passions, as
   that which preceded this revulsion; and partly because, at all events, the study
   of them is associated with the coldest and dullest period of modern literature,
   and their mythology and other jargon incorporated with the compositions
   that come now to be looked upon with the greatest derision and disdain.

> —Francis Jeffrey, from his unsigned review of
> *The Corsair* and *The Bride of Abydos, Edinburgh
> Review,* April 1814, issued July 1814,
> XXIII, 198–229

GEORGE ELLIS (1814)

The critic George Ellis endorses Jeffrey's view of Byron's heroes but does
not accept his theory of a poetic cycle, much less the modern preoccupa-
tion with feelings.

It is contended that poetry is destined to complete a certain cycle or great
revolution, accompanying and dependant on a correspondent cycle of the
feelings as well as of the manners of society. That, originating in times of
turbulence and anarchy, it was at first coarse and vehement;—then pompous
and stately;—then affectedly refined and ingenious—and finally gay, witty,
discursive, and familiar. That at this stage of refinement, however, mankind
become disgusted with the heartless frivolity of their gratifications, and
acquire a longing for strong emotions, so that poetry, following the current
of popular opinion, is compelled to seek for subjects in the manners of ruder
ages, to revive the feats of chivalry, and the loves of romance; or to wander, in
search of unbridled passion, amongst nations yet imperfectly civilized. Lastly,
that this is the period at which we are now arrived: that a growing appetite
for turbulent emotion is the peculiar characteristic of the age; that we are no
longer satisfied with viewing the mere effects of strong passion, but require

the passion itself to be dissected before our eyes; and that Lord Byron, having surpassed all his contemporaries in this species of moral anatomy, has, of course, attained the pinnacle of popular favour.

Now we venture to contend that the poetical cycle here described is purely imaginary; and that if any indications of it were, indeed, discoverable in the history of our own poetry, it would not be fair to deduce, from them, a correspondent cycle of the national 'appetite' for any sort of emotions. Language and manners are, from age to age, either progressively improved, or at least changed, and the trace of such changes may be found in the works of contemporary poets; but the passions of mankind are always the same, and always capable of being called out by a proper degree of excitement. If centuries have passed away since the birth of Shakespeare, does it follow that an *appetite* for those emotions, which he alone was able to rouse, lay dormant during the interval, and has only revived within the last twenty years? We greatly doubt the fact, as well as the existence of the symptoms which are adduced in proof of it. The last twenty years have, doubtless, been wonderfully fertile of crimes and miseries, and there have been some persons in this country who have hailed, with joy and praise, every step of that desolating tyranny, which threatened to spread over the world, and awakened in its progress all those strong emotions which are pronounced to be so delectable. But these persons were not very numerous, and certainly not legitimate arbiters of taste, or of poetical talent. In the whole remainder of the nation, we believe that the horrid realities, which passed before their eyes, did not raise any appetite for scenes of mimic terror; and if Mr Scott, Mr Southey, and Lord Byron have transported their readers to the ages of romance, to the wilds of America, or to the shores of Greece, we suspect that they all followed the impulse of their own studies or habits, without dreaming that they thus completed a poetical cycle, or ministered to any taste or appetite peculiar to the present age or country.

Without dwelling any longer on the general objections to this new and fanciful theory, we now proceed to the point immediately at issue. It is contended, on one hand, that for the purpose of suiting the poetical taste of the present times, 'the minds of the great agents must be unmasked for us—and all the anatomy of their throbbing bosoms laid open to our gaze.' We think, on the contrary, that this anatomical operation is essentially unpoetical; and that therefore Lord Byron, who is emphatically styled the 'searcher of dark bosoms,' is least attractive, and least popular, whenever he attempts to execute this special office. We do not mean to question the extent to which the analysis of mind, or of sensation, is capable of being carried, or to vilipend the delight attendant on such researches; we only contend that the pleasures of intellect are materially different from the pleasures of illusion, that the two are incompatible; and that the writer, who seeks to excite any emotion, will never effect this by attempting to analyse its nature and origin, but must content himself with describing its effects, because it is only with these that his readers can be supposed to be conversant. Every passion of the soul has its visible symptoms by which the correspondent feeling of the observer is instantly awakened; and it is only by the delineation of these symptoms, so correct as to be recognized by the simplest reader, and to produce a momentary illusion, and to call out, by means of the pictured image, the same train of sympathies as would have been excited by the reality, that the poet can possess himself of our imagination and become master of our emotions. The secret sensibility which lurks within our bosoms, which pervades the whole animated frame, and transmits through it the indications of joy or grief, of pleasure or pain, but of which the excess is suffocating and unutterable, cannot itself become the subject of description. To attempt such description is, we think, to exceed the legitimate pretensions of poetry, and to invade the province of metaphysics. On this ground we object to some passages in *The Corsair,* which are intended to represent the prison-thoughts of Conrad. On similar grounds we have more strongly objected to *The Giaour.*———But enough of this. We have stated our opinion, and leave the question for the decision of our readers.

—George Ellis, from his unsigned review of
The Corsair and *Lara, Quarterly Review,*
July 1814, issued Autumn 1814, XI, 428–457

HENRY CRABB ROBINSON (1813)

Known as a diarist, Henry Crabb Robinson (1775–1867) had studied in Germany for five years, becoming acquainted with renowned men of letters such as Goethe, Schiller, Herder, and Wieland. He also worked as a war correspondent during the Peninsular War and later studied law. A noted conversationalist, he collected his reminiscences of romantics such as Coleridge, Lamb, Blake, Wordsworth, and Byron in his *Diary, Reminiscences and Correspondence,* which was published in 1869.

[June 26, 1813] . . . Mrs Porden lent me this evening Lord Byron's *Giaour,* a Turkish tale (a fragment only). With a few energetic lines expressing a diseased state of feeling, the thing is as worthless and unmeaning as I should have expected, even from Lord Byron. A man must have a very mistaken notion of the importance of his writings who supposes that a few broken parts of a tale, wanting on that account the gross material interest of a story, and not having the recommendation of teaching any moral truth, or of exhibiting any picture delightful to the imagination or exciting the sympathy, can be in any way worth the attention of cultivated minds. For of the higher objects and views of poetry Lord Byron pretends not to entertain a notion.

[February 5, 1814] *The Corsair* displeases one less than *The Giaour* and *Childe Harold,* but I doubt whether its principal character does not present an incompatible combination: the "thousand crimes and single virtue" are not so combined as to impress on the reader the necessity or even the probability of their actual union. There are strong passages and a depth of passion which is sure to please those who are more accessible to impressions of strength than of delicacy. But the poem will not stimulate me to a frequent perusal.

[February 11, 1814] Read part of *The Bride of Abydos*—certainly a pretty poem; that is, full of flashy passages; and [liking] the irregular verse in which it is written, I read it with pleasure, though it has none of the higher excellencies of poetry.

[February 17, 1816] I went to Mr. Porden's. There I read aloud Lord Byron's *Siege of Corinth*—a story disgusting and horrid in its effects. . . . All is horror throughout, and a description of dogs eating up dead bodies surpasses in filthiness Lord Byron's usual style.

> —Henry Crabb Robinson, diary, in
> *Henry Crabb Robinson on Books and their Writers,*
> ed. Edith J. Morley, 1938, pp. 1, 129, 136, 137, 180

WALTER SCOTT (1813)

I am very much interested in all that concerns your *Giaour,* which is universally approved of among our mountains. I have heard no objection except by one or two geniuses, who run over poetry as a cat does over a harpsichord, and they affect to complain of obscurity. On the contrary, I hold every real lover of the art is obliged to you for condensing the narrative, by giving us only those striking scenes which you have shown to be so susceptible of poetic ornament, and leaving to imagination the says I's and says he's, and all the minutiae of detail which might be proper in giving evidence before a court of justice. The truth is, I think poetry is most striking when the mirror can be held up to the reader, and the same kept constantly before his eyes; it requires

most uncommon powers to support a direct and downright narration; nor
can I remember many instances of its being successfully maintained even by
our greatest bards.

—Walter Scott, extract from letter of
November 6, 1813, to Lord Byron, from
The Letters of Sir Walter Scott, III, p. 374

John Murray (1814)

John Murray (1778–1843), published the first two cantos of *Childe Harold*
and thereby established a connection that would last almost to the end
of Byron's life. The following extract is taken from his letter of February 3,
1814, in which he tells Byron of the incredible reception of *The Corsair.*

I am most happy to tell you that your last poem is—what Mr. Southey's is
called—a *Carmen Triumphale.* Never, in my recollection, has any work, since
the *Letter of Burke to the Duke of Bedford,* excited such a ferment—a ferment
which I am happy to say will subside into lasting fame. I sold, on the day of
publication—a thing perfectly unprecedented—10,000 copies; and I suppose
thirty people, who were purchasers (strangers), called to tell the people in
the shop how much they had been delighted and satisfied. Mr. Moore says it
is masterly—a wonderful performance. Mr. Hammond, Mr. Heber, D'Israeli,
every one who comes—and too many call for me to enumerate—declare their
unlimited approbation. Mr. "Ward was here with Mr. Gifford yesterday, and
mingled his admiration with the rest. Mr. Ward is much delighted with the
unexpected charge of the Dervis—

"Up rose the Dervis, with that burst of light",

and Gifford did what I never knew him do before—he repeated several
passages from memory, particularly the closing stanza,—

"His death yet dubious, deeds too widely known."
Indeed, from what I have observed, from the very general and unvarying
sentiment which I have now gathered, the suffrages are decidedly in
favour of this poem in preference to *The Bride of Abydos* and are even now
balancing with *The Giaour.* I have heard no one pass without noticing,
and without expressing regret at, the idea thrown out by your Lordship
of writing no more for a considerable time. I am really marking down,
without suppression or extension, literally what I have heard. I was

with Mr. Shee this morning, to whom I had presented the poem; and he declared himself to have been delighted, and swore he had long placed you far beyond any contemporary bard; and, indeed, your last poem does, in the opinion of almost all that I have conversed with. I have the highest encomiums in letters from Croker and Mr. Hay; but I rest most upon the warm feeling it has created in Gifford's critical heart. The versification is thought highly of indeed. . . . You have no notion of the sensation which the publication has occasioned; and my only regret is that you were not present to witness it.

—John Murray, quoted in Samuel Smiles,
A Publisher and His Friends, 1891, 1, pp. 223–224

Isaac Disraeli (1816)

Isaac Disraeli (1766–1848), author, and father of future prime minister Benjamin Disraeli, compares Byron's poetic powers, as displayed in *The Siege of Corinth,* to those of Homer in a letter to John Murray from December 1816.

I am anxious to tell you, that I find myself, this morning, so strangely affected by the perusal of the poem last night, that I feel that it is one which stands quite by itself. I know of nothing of the kind which is worthy of comparison with it. There is no scene, no incident, nothing so marvellous in pathos and terror in Homer, or any bard of antiquity. It impresses one with such a complete feeling of utter desolation, mental and scenical, that when Minotti touched that last spark which scattered its little world into air, he did not make it more desolate than the terrible and affecting energy of the poet's imagination. But Homer had not such a sort of spirit as the mistress of Alp—he had wolves, and vultures, and dogs; but Homer has never conveyed his reader into a vast Golgotha, nor harrowed us with the vulture flapping the back of the gorged wolf, nor the dogs: the terror, the truth, and the loneliness of that spot will never be erased from my memory. Alp by the side of the besieged wall; that ghost-like manner of giving him a minute's reflection by showing one of the phenomena of nature—that is a stroke of a spirit's character never before imagined, and can never be surpassed. And after the most sublime incident that ever poet invented, still to have the power to agitate the mind, by that eagle who flies nearer the sun, mistaking the cloud of destruction for night; in a word, I could not abstain from assuring you, that I never read any poem that exceeded in power this, to me, most extraordinary production. I do not know where I am to find any which can excite the same degree of emotion.

—Isaac Disraeli, letter to John Murray,
quoted in Samuel Smiles, *A Publisher and
His Friends,* 1891, I, 358

WILLIAM GIFFORD (1816)

William Gifford (1756–1826) was editor of the *Anti-Jacobin* from 1797 to 1798 and first editor of the *Quarterly Review.* Byron respected his judgment and submitted many of his works to his comment. The following note on *The Siege of Corinth* was sent to Murray.

It is a dreadful picture: Caravaggio outdone in his own way. I have hinted at the removal of one couplet: if its sense be wanted, it may be compressed into one of the other lines. Its powers are unquestionable; but can any human being deserve such a delineation? I keep my old opinion of Lord Byron. He may be what he will. Why will he not *will* to be the first of poets and of men. I lament bitterly to see a great mind run to seed, and waste itself in rank growth.

—William Gifford, letter to John Murray,
quoted in Samuel Smiles, *A Publisher and
His Friends,* 1891, I, pp. 357–358

JANE AUSTEN (1818)

The novelist Jane Austen (1775–1817) has captivated readers for almost two centuries with the realism, social commentary, and irony contained in her novels such as *Sense and Sensibility* (1811), *Pride and Prejudice* (1813), and *Northanger Abbey* (1818). The following extract is from her novel *Persuasion.*

While Captains Wentworth and Harville led the talk on one side of the room, and, by recurring to former days, supplied anecdotes in abundance to occupy and entertain the others, it fell to Anne's lot to be placed rather apart with Captain Benwick; and a very good impulse of her nature obliged her to begin an acquaintance with him. He was shy, arid disposed to abstraction; but the engaging mildness of her countenance, and gentleness of her manners, soon had their effect; and Anne was well repaid the first trouble of exertion. He was evidently a young man of considerable taste in reading, though principally in poetry; and besides the persuasion of having given him at least an evening's indulgence in the discussion of subjects, which his usual companions had probably no concern in, she had the hope of being of real use to him in some suggestions as to the duty and benefit of struggling against affliction, which had naturally grown out of their conversation. For, though shy, he did not seem reserved; it had rather the appearance of feelings glad to burst their usual restraints; and having talked of poetry, the richness of the present age, and gone through a brief comparison of opinion as to the first-rate poets, trying to ascertain whether *Marmion* or *The Lady of the Lake* were to be preferred, and how ranked *The Giaour* and *The Bride of Abydos;* and moreover, how *The Giaour* was to be pronounced, he shewed himself so intimately acquainted with all the tenderest songs of the one poet, and all the impassioned descriptions of hopeless agony of the other; he repeated, with such tremulous feeling, the various lines which imaged a broken heart, or a mind destroyed by wretchedness, and looked so entirely as if he meant to be understood, that she ventured to hope he did not always read only poetry; and to say, that she thought it was the misfortune of poetry, to be seldom, safely enjoyed by those who enjoyed it completely; and that the strong feelings which alone could estimate it truly, were the very feelings which ought to taste it but sparingly.

His looks shewing him not pained, but pleased with this allusion to his situation, she was emboldened to go on; and feeling in herself the right of seniority of mind, she ventured to recommend a larger allowance of prose in his daily study; and on being requested to particularize, mentioned such works of our best moralists, such collections of the finest letters, such memoirs of characters of worth and suffering, as occurred to her at the moment as calculated to rouse and fortify the mind by the highest precepts, and the strongest examples of moral and religious endurances.

—Jane Austen, extract from *Persuasion,* 1818,
in *Northanger Abbey and Persuasion,* ed. R. W.
Chapman, 3rd ed., 1933, pp. 100–101

MANFRED

After the failure of his marriage to Annabelle Milbanke, Byron lived in exile at the Villa Diodati in Switzerland. Most of the dramatic poem *Manfred* was written on a tour through the Bernese Alps in September 1816. The third act was rewritten in 1817. The Byronic protagonist of the drama suffers from a mysterious guilt, which has variously been interpreted as deriving from his incestuous love of his sister Astarte or from her murder-suicide. Manfred raises seven spirits, seeking forgetfulness, which they cannot give to him, because they have no control over the past. Manfred dies resisting the temptation of a redemption from sin offered by the abbot. The play was influenced by Goethe's *Faust*, a similarity that Goethe acknowledged. The drama was adapted musically by Robert Schumann in 1853, as well as by Peter Tchaikovsky in his Manfred Symphony. The religious unorthodoxy of Byron's original led to harsh criticism among conservative circles.

JOHN WILSON (1818)

The Scottish writer and critic John Wilson (1785–1854) shows his appreciation of Byron's *Manfred* in his review of the poetic drama in *Blackwood's Edinburgh Magazine* in 1817. He stresses the "morality" of the text and contextualizes it within a skeptical tradition.

It seems to us, that this exquisite sense of beauty has of late become still more exquisite in the soul of Byron. *Parisina*, the most finished of all his poems, is full of it to overflowing;—it breathes from every page of the *Prisoners of Chillon*;—but it is, in *Manfred* that it riots and revels among the streams and waterfalls, and groves, and mountains, and heavens. Irrelevant and ill-managed as many parts are of that grand drama, there is in the character of Manfred more of the self-might of Byron than in all his previous productions. He has therein brought, with wonderful power, metaphysical conceptions into forms,—and we know of no poem in which the aspect of external nature is throughout lighted up with an expression at once so beautiful, solemn and majestic. It is the poem, next to *Childe Harold*, which we should give to a foreigner to read, that he might know something of Byron. Shakspeare has given to those abstractions of human life and being, which are truth in the intellect, forms as full, clear, glowing as the idealized forms of visible nature. The very words of Ariel picture to us his beautiful being. In *Manfred*, we see glorious but immature manifestations of similar power. The poet there creates, with delight, thoughts and feelings and fancies into visible forms, that he may cling and cleave to them, and clasp them in his passion. The beautiful Witch of the Alps seems exhaled from the luminous spray of the Cataract,—as if the poet's eyes, unsated with the beauty of inanimate nature, gave spectral apparitions of loveliness to feed the pure passion of the poet's soul.

We speak of *Manfred* now, because it seems to us to hold a middle place between the *Tales of Byron*, and *Childe Harold*, as far as regards the Poet himself. But we likewise do so, that we may have an opportunity of saying a few words on the moral of this poem, and a few words on a subject that may scarcely seem to fall under the legitimate province of the critic, but which, in the case of this great writer, forms so profoundly-interesting a part of his poetical character—we mean, his scepticism.

The moral character of Byron's poetry has often been assailed, and we have ourselves admitted that some strong objections might be urged against it. But we think that his mind is now clearing up, like noon-day, after a stormy and disturbed morning;—and when the change which we anticipate has been fully brought about, the moral character of his poetry will be lofty and pure. Over this fine drama, a moral feeling hangs like a sombrous thunder cloud. No other guilt but that so darkly shadowed out could have furnished so dreadful an illustration of the hideous aberrations of human nature, however noble and majestic, when left a prey to its desires, its passions and its imagination. The beauty, at one time so innocently adored, is at last soiled, profaned and violated. Affection, love, guilt, horror, remorse and death come in terrible succession, yet all darkly linked together. We think of Astarte as young, beautiful, innocent—guilty—lost—murdered—buried—judged—pardoned; but still, in her permitted visit to earth, speaking in a voice of sorrow, and with a countenance yet pale with mortal trouble. We had but a glimpse of her in her beauty and innocence; but, at last, she rises up before us in all the mortal silence of a ghost, with fixed, glazed and passionless eyes, revealing death, judgement and eternity. The moral breathes and burns in every word,—in sadness, misery, insanity, desolation and death. The work is "instinct with spirit,"—and in the agony and distraction, and all its dimly imagined causes, we behold, though broken up, confused and shattered, the elements of a purer existence.

On the other point, namely, the dark and sceptical spirit prevalent through the works of this poet, we shall not now utter all that we feel, but rather direct the notice of our readers to it as a singular phenomenon in the poetry of the age. Whoever has studied the spirit of Greek and Roman literature, must have been struck with the comparative disregard and indifference wherewith the thinking men of these exquisitely polished nations contemplated those subjects of darkness and mystery which afford, at some period or other of his life, so much disquiet—we had almost said so much agony to the mind of every reflecting modern. It is difficult to account for this in any very satisfactory, and we suspect altogether impossible to do so in any strictly logical manner. In reading the works of Plato and his interpreter Cicero, we find the germs of all the doubts and anxieties to which we have alluded, so far as these are connected with the workings of our reason. The singularity is, that those clouds of darkness, which hang over the intellect, do not appear, so far as we can perceive, to have thrown at any time any very alarming shade upon the feelings or temper of the ancient sceptic. We should think a very great deal of this was owing to the brilliancy and activity of his southern fancy. The lighter spirits of antiquity, like the more mercurial of our moderns, sought refuge in mere "gaiete du coeur" and derision. The graver poets and philosophers—and poetry and philosophy were in those days seldom disunited—built up some airy and beautiful system of mysticism, each following his own devices, and suiting the erection to his own peculiarities of hope and inclination; and this being once accomplished, the mind appears to have felt quite satisfied with what it had done, and to have reposed amidst the splendours of its sand-built fantastic edifice, with as much security as if it had been grooved and rivetted into the rock of ages. The mere exercise of ingenuity in devising a system, furnished consolation to its creators or improvers. Lucretius is a striking example of all this; and it may be averred that, down to the time of Claudian, who lived in the 4th century of our era, in no classical writer of antiquity do there occur any traces of what moderns understand by the restlessness and discomfort of uncertainty as to the government of the world, and the future destinies of Man.

There are three only even among the great poets of modern times, who have chosen to depict, in their full shape and vigour, those agonies to which great and meditative intellects are, in the present progress of human history, exposed by the eternal recurrence of a deep and discontented scepticism. But there is only one who has dared to represent himself as the victim of these nameless and indefinable sufferings. Goethe chose for his doubts and his darkness the terrible disguise of the mysterious Faustus. Schiller, with still greater boldness, planted the same anguish in the restless, haughty and heroic bosom of Wallenstein. But Byron has sought no external symbol in which to embody the inquietudes of his soul. He takes the world and all that it inherits for his arena and his spectators; and he displays himself before their gaze, wrestling unceasingly and ineffectually with the demon that torments him. At times there is something mournful and depressing in his scepticism; but oftener, it is of a high and solemn character, approaching to the very verge of a confiding faith. Whatever the poet may believe, we his readers always feel ourselves too much ennobled and elevated even by his melancholy, not to be confirmed in our own belief by the very doubts so majestically conceived and uttered. His scepticism, if it ever approaches to a creed, carries with it its refutation in its grandeur. There is neither philosophy nor religion in those bitter and savage taunts which have been cruelly thrown out, from many quarters, against those moods of mind which are involuntary, and will not pass away;—the shadows and spectres which still haunt his imagination, may once have disturbed our own;—through his gloom there are frequent flashes of illumination;—and the sublime sadness which, to him, is breathed from the mysteries of mortal existence, is always joined with a longing after immortality, and expressed in language that is itself divine.

—John Wilson, *Edinburgh Review*, June 1818,
issued September 1818, XXX, pp. 87–120

FRANCIS JEFFREY (1817)

In his 1817 review, the co-founder and editor of the *Edinburgh Review* points at a connection between Christopher Marlowe's *Doctor Faustus* and Byron's *Manfred*, an affinity that Byron later denies: "Many thanks for the *Edinburgh Review* which is very kind about *Manfred*, and defends its originality, which I did not know that any body had attacked. I *never read*, and do not know that I ever saw, the *Faustus* of Marlow . . . , but I heard Mr Lewis translate verbally some scenes of Goethe's *Faust* (which were some good, and some bad) last summer;—which is all I know of the history of that magical personage; and as to the germs of *Manfred*, they may be found in the Journal which I sent to Mrs. Leigh. . . . The *Prometheus*, if not exactly in my plan, has always been so much in my head, that I can easily conceive its influence over all or every thing that I have written;—but I deny Marlow and his progeny." (Thomas Moore, *Life of Lord Byron. With His Letters and Journals*, IV, pp. 173–175).

This is a very strange—not a very pleasing—but unquestionably a very powerful and most poetical production. The noble author, we find, still deals with that dark and overawing Spirit, by whose aid he has so often subdued the minds of his readers, and in whose might he has wrought so many wonders. In Manfred, we recognize at once the gloom and potency of that soul which burned and blasted and fed upon itself—Harold, and Conrad, and Lara—and which comes again in this piece, more in sorrow than in anger—more proud, perhaps, and more awful than ever—but with the fiercer traits of its misanthropy subdued, as it were, and quenched in the gloom of a deeper despondency. Manfred does not, like Conrad and Lara, wreak the anguish of his burning heart in the dangers and daring of desperate and predatory war—nor seek to drown bitter thoughts in the tumult of perpetual contention—nor yet, like Harold, does he sweep over the peopled scenes of the earth with high disdain and aversion, and make his survey of the business and pleasures and studies of man, an occasion for taunts and sarcasms, and the food of an unmeasurable spleen. He is fixed by the genius of the poet in the majestic solitudes of the central Alps—where, from his youth up, he has lived in proud but calm seclusion from the ways of men, conversing only with the magnificent forms and aspects of nature by which he is surrounded, and with the Spirits of the Elements over whom he has acquired dominion, by the secret and unhallowed studies of Sorcery and Magic. He is averse indeed from mankind, and scorns the low and frivolous nature to which he belongs; but he cherishes no animosity or hostility to that feeble race. Their concerns excite no interest—their pursuits no sympathy—their joys no envy. It is irksome and vexatious for him to be crossed by them in his melancholy musings,—but he treats them with gentleness and pity; and, except when stung to impatience by too importunate an intrusion, is kind and considerate of the comforts of all around him.

This piece is properly entitled a dramatic Poem—for it is merely poetical, and is not at all a drama or play in the modern acceptation of the term. It has no action; no plot—and no characters; Manfred merely muses and suffers from the beginning to the end. His distresses are the same at the opening of the scene and at its closing—and the temper in which they are borne is the same. A hunter and a priest, and some domestics, are indeed introduced; but they have no connexion with the passions or sufferings on which the interest depends; and Manfred is substantially alone throughout the whole piece. He holds no communion but with the memory of the Being he had loved; and the immortal Spirits whom he evokes to reproach with his misery, and their inability to relieve it. These unearthly beings approach nearer to the character of persons of the drama—but still they are but choral accompaniments to the performance; and Manfred is, in reality, the only actor and sufferer on the scene. To delineate his character indeed—to render conceivable his feelings—is plainly the whole scope and design of the poem; and the conception and execution are, in this respect, equally admirable. It is a grand and terrific vision of a being invested with superhuman attributes, in order that he may be capable of more than human sufferings, and be sustained under them by more than human force and pride. To object to the improbability of the fiction is, we think, to mistake the end and aim of the author. Probabilities, we apprehend, did not enter at all into his consideration—his object was, to produce effect—to exalt and dilate the character through whom he was to interest or appal us—and to raise our conception of it, by all the helps that could be derived from the majesty of nature, or the dread of superstition. It is enough, therefore, if the situation in which he has placed him is *conceivable*—and if the supposition of its reality enhances our emotions and kindles our imagination;—for it is Manfred only that we are required to fear, to pity, or admire. If we can once conceive of him as a real existence, and enter into the depth and the height of his pride and his sorrows, we may deal as we please with the means that have been used to furnish us with this impression, or to enable us to attain to this conception. "We may regard them but as types, or metaphors, or allegories: But *he* is the thing to be expressed, and the feeling and the intellect of which all these are but shadows. . . .

There are great faults, it must be admitted, in this poem;—but it is undoubtedly a work of genius and originality. Its worst fault, perhaps, is, that it fatigues and overawes us by the uniformity of its terror and solemnity. Another is the painful and offensive nature of the circumstances on which its distress is ultimately founded. It all springs from the disappointment or fatal issue of an incestuous passion; and incest, according to our modern ideas—for it was otherwise in antiquity—is not a thing to be at all brought before the imagination. The lyrical songs of the Spirits are too long, and not all excellent. There is something of pedantry in them now and then; and even Manfred deals in classical allusions a little too much. If we were to consider it as a proper drama, or even as a finished poem, we should be obliged to add, that it is far too indistinct and unsatisfactory. But this we take to be according to the design and conception of the author. He contemplated but a dim and magnificent sketch of a subject which did not admit of more accurate drawing, or more brilliant colouring. Its obscurity is a part of its grandeur; and the darkness that rests upon it, and the smoky distance in which it is lost, are all devices to increase its majesty, to stimulate our curiosity, and to impress us with deeper awe.

It is suggested, in an ingenious paper, in a late Number of the *Edinburgh Magazine* that the general conception of this piece, and much of what is excellent in the manner of its execution, have been borrowed from *The Tragical History of Dr Faustus* of Marlow *[sic]*; and a variety of passages are quoted, which the author considers as similar, and, in many respects, superior to others in the poem before us. We cannot agree in the general terms of this conclusion;—but there is, no doubt, a certain resemblance, both in some of the topics that are suggested, and in the cast of the diction in which they are expressed. . . .

But . . . many . . . smooth and fanciful verses in this curious old drama, prove nothing, we think, against the originality of *Manfred*; for there is nothing to be found there of the pride, the abstraction, and the heartrooted misery in which that originality consists. Faustus is a vulgar sorcerer, tempted to sell his soul to the Devil for the ordinary price of sensual pleasure, and earthly power and glory—and who shrinks and shudders in agony when the forfeit comes to be exacted. The style, too, of Marlow, though elegant and scholarlike, is weak and childish compared with the depth and force of much of what we have quoted from Lord Byron; and the disgusting buffoonery and low farce of which his piece is principally made up, place it much more in contrast, than in any terms of comparison, with that of his noble successor. In the tone and pitch of the composition, as well as in the character of the diction in the more solemn parts, the piece before us reminds us much more of the *Prometheus* of Aeschylus, than of any more modern performance. The tremendous solitude of the principal person, the supernatural beings with whom alone he holds communion, the guilt, the firmness, the misery, are all points of resemblance to which the grandeur of the poetic imagery only gives a more striking effect. The chief differences are, that the subject of the Greek poet was sanctified and exalted by the established belief of his country, and that his terrors are nowhere tempered with the sweetness which breathes from so many passages of his English rival.

—Francis Jeffrey, *Edinburgh Review*, August 1817,
issued September 1817, XXVIII, 418–431

Johann Wolfgang von Goethe
"Byron's Manfred" (1820)

Goethe expresses his admiration for Byron's use of his own drama *Faust* as a source for and influence on the verse drama *Manfred*.

To me Byron's tragedy of *Manfred* was a wonderful phenomenon, touching me closely. This singular but highly gifted poet has absorbed my own *Faust* into himself, and, like a hypochondriac, drawn from it the strangest sort of nourishment. Those motives and ideas which suited his purposes he has made use of, but in his own original way, so that everything seems different; and for this reason I cannot wonder enough at his genius. This transformation affects the whole so intimately that highly interesting lectures could be given on the similarity and dissimilarity which his work bears to his pattern; but I do not deny that in the long run the dull glow of a boundless and profound despair becomes irksome to us. Yet in the dissatisfaction which one feels there are always interwoven both admiration and respect.

Thus we find in this tragedy quite uniquely the very quintessence of the feelings and passions of a remarkable genius, but a genius doomed from birth to suffering and anguish. The details of his life and the characteristics of his poetry hardly permit of a just and fair criticism. He has often enough confessed his anguish; he has repeatedly presented it in his verse, and it is difficult for any one not to feel real pity for the unbearable pain which he is forever working and gnawing over in his heart.

There are two women whose shadows follow him unceasingly, and who play a large role in his best-known works; one appears under the name Astarte, the other, without form or presence, simply as A Voice.

The following story is told of the tragic adventure which was his experience with the first. As a young, daring and highly attractive youth he won the love of a Florentine lady; her husband discovered it and murdered her. But the murderer was found dead that same night in the street, and there was nothing to throw suspicion upon a single soul. Lord Byron left Florence, but these apparitions haunted him throughout his whole life.

This romantic event appears in his poems in countless allusions, as for example where he, probably brooding over his own tragedy, applies the sad story of the king of Sparta to his own case. The story is as follows: Pausanias, the Lacedaemonian general, having won fame in the important victory at Plataea, later through arrogance, stubbornness, and cruel treatment, loses the affection of the Greeks, and, on account of a secret understanding with the enemy, loses also the confidence of his countrymen. He thus brings blood-guiltiness upon his head, which pursues him to a miserable end. For while in command of the fleet of the Greek allies in the Black Sea, he falls violently in love with a girl of Byzantium. After a long struggle he wins her from her parents; she is to be brought to him in the night. Filled with shame, she requests the servants to put out the light; this is done, but groping about in the room, she knocks over the lamp-stand. Pausanias awakes suddenly from sleep, suspects murder, seizes his sword and kills his beloved. The horrible vision of this scene never leaves him afterwards, its shadow pursues him unceasingly, so that he appeals in vain to the gods and to necromancers for aid and absolution.

What a sick heart the poet must have who would seek out such a story from the ancient world, appropriate it to himself, and burden himself with its tragic image! This will explain the following monologue, so laden with gloom and the despair of life; we recommend it to all lovers of declamation for aerious practice. Hamlet's monologue is here intensified. It will take considerable art especially to pick out the interpolations and yet keep the connection and the flow and smoothness of the whole. Besides it will be discovered that a certain vehement, even eccentric, expression is needed in order to do justice to the intention of the poet.

—Johann Wolfgang von Goethe,
"Byron's *Manfred*," 1820, *Literary Essays*,
tr. J.E. Spingarn, 1921, pp. 202–204

George Gordon, Lord Byron (1820)

When Byron sent the following letter to his publisher Murray, he expressed pride in Goethe's appreciation, stressing though that the Swiss alpine landscape exerted a greater influence than any literary model.

―――――

Enclosed is something which will interest you—(to wit) the opinion of *the* Greatest man of Germany—perhaps of Europe—upon one of the great men of your advertisements—(all "famous hands" as Jacob Tonson used to say of his ragamuffins) in short—a critique of *Goethe's* upon *Manfred*.—There is the original—Mr. Hoppner's translation, and an Italian one—keep them all in your archives—for the opinions of such a man as Goethe whether favourable or not are always interesting—and this is moreover favourable.—His *Faust* I never read—for I don't know German—but Matthew Monk Lewis in 1816 at Coligny translated most of it to me *viva voce*—& I was naturally much struck with it;—but it was the *Staubach* & the *Jungfrau*—and something else—much more than Faustus that made me write *Manfred*. The first Scene however & that of Faustus are very similar.

—George Gordon, Lord Byron,
letter to John Murray, June 7, 1820

Margaret Oliphant (1883)

Margaret Oliphant (1828–1897) was a Scottish novelist and historical writer, who contributed more than one hundred articles to *The Blackwood Magazine*. Her evaluation of *Manfred* dismisses the play as outmoded and half-forgotten among the Victorians.

―――――

Manfred has passed, we think, in great measure, from the mind of the reader. The number of students who read an author through, and know everything he has written, is always few. The greater part of the world makes instinctive selection of what is immortal, and leaves the rest, if not to perish, at least to freeze and crystallise, without any living soul of human remembrance to keep it fresh. But at the moment when these works are getting published, nobody can tell which it will be that posterity will choose; and when we read Jeffrey's awe-stricken applause and Wilson's enthusiastic appreciation, and find that even such an authority as Goethe declares Manfred's mouthings of mock despair to be an improvement on Hamlet's soliloquy, the extraordinary mistake takes away our breath. The one idea of

Byron's limited imagination had been worked hardly enough in the previous tales, which made no such claim upon the reader. Subdued and enshrined in the fine poetry of *Childe Harold,* it has been added to the permanent population of the world; but to place this conventional form among the mighty mountains, and to surround him, in emulation of greater witcheries, with the vapoury visions of an unseen rather more vague and pyrotechnic than himself, was a rash and unfortunate experiment. The subject is one which only the most exceptional merit in the poetry could make tolerable; and the poetry is not exceptional, but below the highest level of Byron's power. To compare his *diablerie* with that of Goethe, or the songs of the spirits whom Manfred evokes, with the melody of Shelley's responses in the *Prometheus,* is to put him at an extraordinary disadvantage.

—Margaret Oliphant, *The Literary History of England,* 1790–1825, 1882, vol. 3, pp. 72–73

JOSIAH ROYCE (1885)

Josiah Royce (1855–1916) was an American objective idealist philosopher who studied and taught at the University of California, Berkeley. Royce claimed that the apparently external world has real existence only as known by an ideal Knower and that this Knower must be actual rather than merely hypothetical. In *The Religious Aspect of Philosophy* (1885), he gives an interpretation of *Manfred* that views Manfred's defiance as being directed against the meaninglessness of the universe, which could only be rectified by labor and concentrated effort.

The only peace that can come to this world-weary spirit, Manfred expresses at the sight of a quiet sunset. The only freedom from eternal self-examination is found in an occasional glance at peaceful nature.

It will not last,

But it is well to have known it though but once; It hath enlarged my thoughts with a new sense, And I within my tablets would note down That there is such a feeling. The famous last words of Manfred,—

Old man, 't is not so difficult to die,

—coming as they do after all Manfred's vacillation upon just this point, indicate the final resolution of despair to brave all possible wretchedness from without for the sake of feeling within, in all its strength, though but for a moment, the fierce defiance of the rebellious Titan. Hungry for deeds, finding nothing to do, fearing the possible future life, and hating the present, the hero at last resorts to an untrue but stirring assertion of absolute personal independence of all the hateful universe here and hereafter:—

> Thou didst not tempt me, and thou couldst not tempt me.
> I have not been thy dupe, nor am thy prey—
> But was my own destroyer, and will be
> My own hereafter.

This is pessimism that overleaps itself. The outcome of self-analyzing romanticism is the determination to build afresh a world that shall be nobler than this poor world of decaying passive emotions. Feeling will not do. Manfred attains something by action, even though he first acts in the moment of death. Doing work of some kind is, then, that to which we are necessarily driven. But if the action of defiance can make death tolerable, why might not some kind of activity make life tolerable? Is not the worthy life then to be found, not in emotion, but in work? Is not the ideal state the ideal activity, not the ideal feeling? This suggestion had been at the foundation of the prototype of Manfred, the Faust of Goethe.

—Josiah Royce, *The Religious Aspect of Philosophy*, 1885, pp. 120–121

John Churton Collins "The Collected Works of Lord Byron" (1905)

John Churton Collins (1848–1908) reviews Byron's *Manfred* in his essay "The Collected Works of Lord Byron," which was published in the *Quarterly Review* in April 1905 in reaction to R.E. Prothero's edition of Byron's *Letters and Journals* and E.H. Coleridge's edition of the *Poetical Works*. Collins dismisses *Manfred* as a mere concoction of Byron's individual sources, not an original work of art.

Keats, with characteristic insight, once described Byron as "a fine thing in the worldly, theatrical, and pantomimical way"; and this description, with some modification, almost always applies to him when he attempts what he attempts, for example, in *Manfred*. That work may indeed be taken as a comprehensive illustration both of his falsetto and of what redeems that falsetto from contempt. The drama as a whole is mere fustian, a chaotic concoction from what has been suggested by other poets, with a substratum of the impressions really made on him by the scenery of Switzerland, recorded in his journal to Mrs. Leigh.

He was no doubt anxious to have it supposed that *Manfred* was drawn from himself, and that Manfred's crimes and remorse had their counterparts in his own; and this Goethe was induced to believe. But beyond a generic resemblance in certain superficial qualities, Manfred has no more resemblance to Byron than he has to any other human being. He is partly a poor copy of Goethe's *Faust*, with touches of Aeschylus's *Prometheus* and Milton's Satan, partly of Beattie's *Edwin* and Shelley's *Alastor*, partly of Schiller's Moor in *Die Räuber*, to which Byron had access either in a French version or in the English translation of 1795 partly of Southey's Ladurlad when under the curse, partly of Mrs. Radcliffe's *Schedoni*, and partly of Ahasuerus.

And as is the protagonist—a thing of shreds and patches—such is the whole drama. Resolved into its constituent parts, the opening scene, the machinery of Spirits, the incantation, the scenes with the Chamois Hunter, the soliloquies and their surroundings, the intervention of the Abbot, and Manfred's relations with him—there is no portion of it which cannot be traced to pre-existing poems or fictions. The drama has neither unity, soul, nor motive. Indeed, it is part of the falsetto that for intelligible motive is substituted juggling mystification, just as we find in Lara. In truth the motive, or what does service for it, appears to be to send curiosity on a quest after the secret of "the all nameless hour," the solution of which is, so it is insinuated, that Astarte was Manfred's sister, and that remorse for an incestuous union with her, coupled with the conviction that the sin was inexpiable, is the chief cause of his torture. But, as is usual with Byron's falsetto, the vigour of the rhetoric in the descriptions and soliloquies half disguises it. Every one must be arrested by the eloquence of the soliloquy which opens the second scene of the first act, by the impassioned appeal to Astarte, and by the impressive picture of the Coliseum. What is true of Manfred is true of the other metaphysical dramas. Byron was no philosopher, though he delighted to pose as one, and in all these works he illustrates what Goethe so truly said of him, that so soon as he began to reflect he was a child.

It is when we compare the dramas with *The Vision of Judgment* and *Don Juan*, and with such poems and such passages in poems as found their inspiration in what sincerely moved him, that we measure the distance between Byron the rhetorician and Byron the poet, between degrees of talent and the pure accent of genius. A large proportion, perhaps two-thirds, of Byron's poetry resolves itself into the work of an extraordinarily gifted craftsman, with a rhetorical talent as brilliant and plastic as Dryden's, working on the material furnished by an unusually wide experience of life, by sleepless observation, and by a marvellously assimilative and retentive memory, incessantly if desultorily adding to its stores. No English poet, not Ben Jonson, not Milton, not Gray, not Tennyson, owed more to reading than Byron, or had a mind more stored with acquired knowledge.

—John Churton Collins, from "The Collected
Works of Lord Byron," *Studies in Poetry
and Criticism*, 1905, pp. 107–123

BEPPO

Byron's satire *Beppo* marks a return, after the melancholy fourth part of *Childe Harold's Pilgrimage*, to his earlier humorous strain. Living in Venice, he had heard the story of the return of a husband, supposedly dead, to his wife, who had since become romantically involved with another man. Byron presents her dilemma, the choice among husband, lover, and a solitary life in a mock heroic satire written in *ottava rima*, an eight-line stanzaic form derived from Italian sources. John Hookham Frere's *Whistlecraft* (1817), which Byron had read in the same year, provided him with a model of a colloquial and digressive poem. He hoped to convince his readers with this work that he could also write cheerfully. Murray published *Beppo, A Venetian Story*, without Byron's name on the title page, on February 28, 1818, to immediate success. The *Monthly Review* of March 1818 found Byron's "satire, though at times a little tinged with vulgarity, ... usually good-humoured and often well pointed." In the issue of the *Edinburgh Review* from February 1818, Francis Jeffrey commended "the matchless facility" with which the "unknown writer" "cast into regular, and even difficult versification ... the most light, familiar, and ordinary conversations."

JOHN MURRAY (1818)

Byron's publisher informs the poet that John Hookham Frere, the author of the mock heroic poem *Whistlecraft*, has finally accepted Byron as the author of *Beppo*. Murray had sent the first two cantos of Frere's poem to Byron, who imitated its form, which was derived from Italian sources. Both *Beppo* and *Don Juan* show the influence of Frere's tale about monks, knights, and giants.

Mr. Frere is at length satisfied that you are the author of *Beppo*. He had no conception that you possessed the protean talent of Shakespeare, thus to assume at will so different a character. He, and every one, continues in the same very high opinion of its great beauties. I am glad to find that you are disposed to pursue this strain, which has occasioned so much delight. Do you never think of prose? . . . I have just put forth two more cantos of *Whistlecraft*—which the knowing ones think excellent, and of which the public think nothing, for they cannot see the drift of it. I have not sold 500 copies of the first parts yet; and of *Beppo*, I have sold six times that quantity in a sixth part of the time, and before, indeed, it is generally known to be yours.

—John Murray, extract from letter of June 16,
1818 to Byron, from Samuel Smiles, *A Publisher
and his Friends*, 1891, 1, pp. 393–394

Unsigned (1818)

The poem is of the burlesque kind, and were it not that it is licentious in its moral, occasionally vulgar and profane in its expressions, and rather tedious in its narrative, it might serve very well to laugh through after dinner. There is a happy whimsicality in some of the rhymes, and now and then a stroke of humour and of satire, which will succeed with the good natured reader, who has not adventured to read the poem aloud, nor set himself to read it through.

—Unsigned, from the *Eclectic Review*,
June 1818, N.S., IX, p. 555

Francis Jeffrey (1818)

Jeffrey shows his appreciation of Byron's ability to write in the comic manner in the following extract from an unsigned review that appeared in the Spring 1818 issue of the *Edinburgh Review*.

Though there is as little serious meaning or interest in this extraordinary performance, as can easily be imagined, we think it well entitled to a place in our fastidious Journal—and that, not merely because it is extremely clever and amusing, but because it affords a very curious and complete specimen of a kind of diction and composition of which our English literature has hitherto afforded very few examples. It is, in itself, absolutely a thing of nothing—without story, characters, sentiments, or intelligible object—a mere piece of lively and loquacious prattling, in short, upon all kinds of frivolous subjects,—a sort of gay and desultory babbling about Italy and England, Turks, balls, literature and fish sauces. But still there is something very engaging in the uniform gayety, politeness, and good humour of the author—and something still more striking and admirable in the matchless facility with which he has cast into regular, and even difficult versification, the unmingled, unconstrained, and un-selected language of the most light, familiar, and ordinary conversation. The French have always had a great deal of this sort of poetry—though with a very severe regard to the purity of the diction—and the Italians also, in a looser and more extravagant tone; but, in England, it seems never to have been naturalized. The nearest approach to it is to be found in some of the tales and lighter pieces of Prior—a few stanzas here and there among the trash and burlesque of Peter Pindar—and in several passages of Mr Moore, and the author of the facetious miscellany, entitled, *The Twopenny Post Bag.* Chaucer and Shakespeare had ease and gayety enough for the style of which we are speaking—but it belongs intrinsically to the silver, and not to the golden age of poetry; and implies the existence of certain habits of dissipation, derision, and intelligence in general society, and of a sort of conventional language, for the expression of those things, which were still to be formed in the days of these great masters.—It is scarcely necessary to add, except for our duller readers, that this same familiar, lively, conversational poetry is perfectly distinct both from the witty, epigrammatic and satirical vein in which Pope will never be surpassed—or equalled; and from the burlesque, humorous and distorted style which attained its greatest height in *Hudibras,* and has been copied abundantly enough by humbler imitators. The style of which we are speaking is, no doubt, occasionally satirical and witty and humorous—but it is, on the whole, far more gay than poignant, and is characterized, exactly as good conversation is, rather by its constant ease and amenity, than by any traits either of extraordinary brilliancy, or of strong and ludicrous effect. There must be a certain allowance of sense and sagacity—and little flying traits of picturesque description—and small flights of imagination—and sallies of naivete and humour—but nothing very powerful, and nothing very long. The great charm is in the simplicity and naturalness of the language,—the free but guarded use of all polite idioms, and even of all phrases of temporary currency that have the stamp of good company upon them,—with the exclusion of all scholastic or ambitious eloquence, all profound views, and all deep emotions.

The unknown writer before us has accomplished all these objects with great skill and felicity; and, in particular, has furnished us with an example, unique we rather think in our language, of about one hundred stanzas of good verse, entirely composed of common words, in their common places; never presenting us with one sprig of what is called poetical diction, or even making use of a single inversion, either to raise the style or assist the rhyme—

but running on in an inexhaustible series of good easy colloquial phrases, and finding them fall into verse by some unaccountable and happy fatality. In this great and characteristic quality it is almost invariably excellent. In some other respects it is more unequal. About one half is as good as possible, in the style to which it belongs; the other half bears perhaps too many marks of that haste with which we take it for granted that such a work must necessarily be written. Some passages are rather too foolish, some too snappish, and some run too much on the cheap and rather plebeian humour of out-of-the-way rhymes and strange sounding words and epithets. But the greater part is very pleasant, amiable, and gentlemanlike. . . .

This story, such as it is, occupies about twenty stanzas, we think, out of the ninety-five of which the poem consists. The rest is made up of digressions and dissertations at the author's discretion; and these form unquestionably by far the most lively and interesting part of the work. . . .

—Francis Jeffrey, *Edinburgh Review,*
XXIX, pp. 302–304, 306–307

UNSIGNED "LETTER TO THE AUTHOR OF *BEPPO*" (1818)

In his "Letter to the Author of *Beppo*," the anonymous author criticizes Jeffrey for his admiration of the style and tone of Byron's *Beppo* and identifies Byron with the madness and immorality of his protagonists. Byron later denied this easy equation: "the conclusion drawn was, that Childe Harold, Byron, and the Count in *Beppo*, were one and the same person . . . thereby making me turn out to be, as Mrs. Malaprop says, *like Cerberus, three gentlemen at once*" (LJ, IV, p. 475).

Your predecessors, in one word, my Lord, have been the friends—you are the enemy of your species. You have transferred into the higher departments of poetry (or you have at least endeavoured to transfer) that spirit of mockery, misanthropy, and contempt, which the great bards of elder times left to preside over the humbler walk of the satirist and the cynic. The calm respect which these men felt for themselves inspired them with sympathetic reverence for their brethren. They perceived, indeed, the foibles and the frailties of humanity, and they depicted, at least as well as you have ever done, the madness of the senses and the waywardness of the passions; but they took care to vindicate the original dignity of their nature, and contrasted their representations of the vice and weakness, which they observed in some, with the more cheering spectacle of the strength and the virtue, whose stirrings they felt within themselves, and whose workings they contemplated in others. Conscious of the glorious union of intellectual grandeur and moral purity within, they pitied the errors of other men; but they were not shaken from their reverence for the general character of man. Instead of raving with demoniacal satisfaction about the worthlessness of our motives and the nothingness of our attainments, they strove, by shewing us what we might be and what we had been, to make us what we should be. They drew the portraits of wrath, jealousy, and hatred, only that we might appreciate more justly the kindly feelings which these fierce passions expel from the rightful possession of our bosoms. They took our nature as it is, but it was for the purpose of improving it. . . .

In all your writings, how little is there whose object it is to make us reverence virtue, or love our country! You never teach us to despise earthly sufferings, in the hope of eternal happiness. With respect to all that is best and greatest in the nature and fate of man, you preserve not merely a sorrowful, but a sullen silence. Your poetry need not have been greatly different from what it is, although you had lived and died in the midst of a generation of heartless, vicious, and unbelieving demons. With you, heroism is lunacy, philosophy folly, virtue a cheat, and religion a bubble. Your Man is a stern, cruel, jealous, revengeful, contemptuous, hopeless, solitary savage. Your Woman is a blind, devoted, heedless, beautiful minister and victim of lust. The past is a vain record, and the present a fleeting theatre, of misery and madness: the future one blank of horrid darkness, whereon your mind floats and fluctuates in a cheerless uncertainty, between annihilation and despair.

The interest which you have found means to excite for the dismal creations of your poetry, is proof abundant of the vigour of your genius, but should afford small consolation to your conscience-stricken mind. You are a skilful swordsman; but you have made use of poisoned weapons, and the deadliness of your wound gives no addition to your valour. You have done what greater and better men despised to do. You have brought yourself down to the level of that part of our erring and corrupted nature, which it was their pride and privilege to banish from the recollection and the sympathy of those to whom they spake. In the great struggle between the good and the evil principle, you have taken the wrong side, and you enjoy the worthless popularity of a daring rebel. But hope not that the calm judgment of posterity will ratify the hasty honours which you have extorted from the passions of your contemporaries. Believe me, Men are not upon the whole quite so unprincipled,—nor Women quite so foolish,—nor Virtue so useless,—nor Religion so absurd,—nor Deception so lasting,—nor Hypocrisy so triumphant, as your Lordship has been pleased to fancy. A day of terrible retribution will arrive, and the punishment inflicted may not improbably consist of things the most unwelcome to a poet's view—the scorn of many, and the neglect of all. Even now, among the serious and reflective part of the Men and the Women of England, your poetry is read, indeed, and admired, but you yourself are never talked of except with mingled emotions of anger and pity. With what pain do the high spirits of your virtuous and heroic ancestors contemplate the degradation of their descendant. Alas! that the genius which might have ennobled any name, should have only assisted you *to* stamp a more lasting stain upon the pure, the generous, the patriotic, the English name of Byron.

Any other poet might complain with justice, should he see remarks of a personal nature mixed up with a criticism upon his writings. You, my Lord, can scarcely flatter yourself that you have any right to expect such forbearance. If the scrutiny of the world be disagreeable to you, either in its operation or in its effects, you need blame no one but yourself. We were well enough disposed to treat you with distant respect, but you have courted and demanded our gaze. You have bared your bosom when no man entreated you; it is your own fault if we have seen there not the scars of honourable wounds, but the festering blackness of a loathsome disease. You have been the vainest and the most egotistical of poets. You have made yourself your only theme; shall we not dare to dissect the hero, because, forsooth, he and his poet are the same? You have debased your nobility by strutting upon the stage; shall we still be expected to talk of you as of a private and unobtrusive individual? You must share the fate of your brethren, and abide the judgment of the spectators. . . .

You made your debut in the utmost dignity and sadness of the Cothurnus. You were the most lugubrious of mortals; it was the main ambition of your vanity to attract *to* your matchless sorrows the overflowing sympathies of the world. We gave you credit for being sincere in your affliction. We looked upon you as the victim of more than human misery, and sympathized with the extravagance of your public and uncontrollable lamentations. It is true that no one knew whence your sorrow had sprung, but we were generous in our compassion, and asked few questions, in time, however, we have become less credulous and more inquisitive; the farce was so often renewed, that we became weary of its wonders; we have come to suspect at last, that whatever sorrows you may have, they are all of your own creating; and that, whencesoever they may be, they are at least neither of so uniform nor of so majestic a character as you would fain have had us to suppose.

Under pretence of making us partakers in a fictitious or exaggerated grief, you have striven to make us sympathize with all the sickly whims and phantasies of a self-dissatisfied and self-accusing spirit. That you were, as you have yourself told us, a dissipated, a sceptical, and therefore, for there was no other cause, a wretched man, was no reason why you should wish to make your readers devoid of religion, virtue, and happiness. You had no right to taint the pure atmosphere of the English mind with the infectious phrenzies of the fever of debauch. Your misery was the punishment of your folly and your wickedness; why did you come to rack the eyes of the wise, the good, and the tranquil, with the loathsome spectacle of your merited torments? Could genius, a thousand times more splendid than yours, entitle the poor, giddy, restless victim of remorse, to make his art the instrument of evil,—to abuse the gifts of his God, by rendering them the engines of corruption and ruin among his fellow-men? For shame! my Lord, for shame upon your manhood! . . .

Visible, however, as was your apostacy, and mean your vengeance, there was still something about you to create respect, even in those who comprehended the best your vices and your errors. If you were an immoral and an unchristian, you were at least a serious, poet. Your pictures of depravity were sketched with such a sombre magnificence, that the eye of vulgar observers could gain little from surveying their lineaments. The harp of the mighty was still in your hands; and when you dashed your fingers over its loosened strings, faded as was the harmony, and harsh the execution, the notes were still made for their listening, who had loved the solemn music of the departed.

The last lingering talisman which secured to you the pity, and almost the pardon, even of those that abhorred your guilt,—with the giddiness of a lunatic, or the resolution of a suicide,—you have tossed away. You have lost the mournful and melancholy harp which lent a protecting charm even to the accents of pollution; and bought, in its stead, a gaudy viol, fit for the fingers of eunuchs, and the ears of courtezans. You have parted

With what permissive glory, since that fall,
Was left—

You have flung off the last remains of the 'regal port;' you are no longer one of 'the great seraphic lords,' that sat even in Pandemonium, 'in their own dimensions like themselves.' You have grown weary of your fallen grandeur, and dwarfed your stature, that you might gain easier access, and work paltrier mischief. You may resume, if you will, your giant-height, but we shall not fail to recognize, in spite of all your elevation, the swollen features of the same pigmy imp whom we have once learned—a lasting lesson—not to abhor merely, and execrate, but to *despise*. You may wish, as heretofore, to haunt our imaginations in the shadowy semblance of Harold, Conrad, Lara, or Manfred:

you may retain their vice, and their unbelief, and their restlessness; but you have parted irretrievably with the majesty of their despair. We see you in a shape less sentimental and mysterious. We look below the disguise which has once been lifted, and claim acquaintance, not with the sadness of the princely masque, but with the scoffing and sardonic merriment of the ill-dissembling reveller beneath it. In evil hour did you step from your vantage-ground, and teach us that Harold, Byron, and the Count of *Beppo* are the same.

—Unsigned, "Presbyter Anglicanus," from
"Letter to the Author of *Beppo*," in *Blackwood's
Magazine*, June 1818, III, pp. 323–329

DON JUAN

Byron's mock epic poem *Don Juan* is a long, digressive satire in *ottava rima*, based on the legend of the Spanish arch-womanizer Don Juan. Byron reverses the tradition by turning Don Juan into an inexperienced youth, who is easily seduced by various women, instead of seducing them. Beginning in 1818, Byron completed sixteen cantos, leaving a seventeenth unfinished before his death in 1824 and admitting that he did not know what would happen in the end. On August 12, 1819, he wrote in a letter to John Murray: "You ask me for the plan of Donny Johnny; I have no plan—I had no plan; but I had or have materials. . . . You are too earnest and eager about a work never intended to be serious. Do you suppose that I could have any intention but to giggle and make giggle?—a playful satire, with as little poetry as could be helped, was what I meant" (Thomas Moore, *Life of Lord Byron, With His Letters and Journals,* vol. IV).

When the first two cantos were published anonymously in 1819, the poem was criticized for its immorality, though it simultaneously acheived immense popularity. The poem was issued in parts, with long intervals of unequal duration between the parts, due to deferrals and delays by the publisher and discouragement from Byron's friends. There is no evidence that Byron knew Tirso de Molina's *El burlador de Sevilla y convidado de piedra* (*The Deceiver of Seville and the Stone Guest*), written in 1626, or Molière's *Dom Juan, ou le festin de Pierre*, produced in 1665. He had seen Carlo Antonio Delpini's pantomime, which was based on Thomas Shadwell's *Libertine*, and he may have seen, in Milan or Venice, a performance of Mozart's *Don Giovanni*.

The haphazard character of the composition of *Don Juan* is evident in another letter to John Murray: "The Fifth is so far from being the last of *Don Juan*, that it is hardly the beginning. I meant to take him the tour of Europe, with a proper mixture of siege, battle, and adventure, and to make him finish as Anacharsis Cloots in the French Revolution. . . . I meant to have made him a Cavalier Servente in Italy, and a cause for a divorce in England, and a Sentimental 'Werther-faced' man in Germany, so as to show the different ridicules of the society in each of these countries, and to have displayed him gradually gâté and blasé, as he grew older, as is natural. But I had not quite fixed whether to make him end in Hell, or in an unhappy marriage, not knowing which would be the severest." Both author and publisher remained anonymous in the earlier issues of the first five cantos as a means of precaution. *Don Juan* was praised, though, by Scott and Shelley, as well as by Goethe and Swinburne. Today, it is typically regarded as Byron's masterpiece.

LEIGH HUNT (1819)

As a political radical who fought against philistinism and religious conservatism, Leigh Hunt (1784–1859) gave his full support to Byron's *Don Juan* in the *Examiner*. His praise, however, did Byron a disservice, as he became even more closely associated by conservative reviewers with radicalism. Hunt argues against the common perception of *Don Juan* as immoral and stresses the humorous nature of the work.

Some persons consider this the finest work of Lord Byron,—or at least that in which he displays most power. It is at all events the most extraordinary that he has yet published. His other poems, with the exception of that amusing satire *Beppo*, are written for the most part with one sustained serious feeling throughout,—either of pathos, or grandeur, or passion, or all united. But *Don Juan* contains specimens of all the author's modes of writing, which are mingled together and push one another about in a strange way. The groundwork (if we may so speak of a stile) is the satirical and humourous; but you are sometimes surprised and moved by a touching piece of human nature, and again startled and pained by the sudden transition from loveliness or grandeur to ridicule or the mock-heroic. The delicious and deep descriptions of love, and youth, and hope, come upon us like the 'young beams' of the sun breaking through the morning dew, and the terrific pictures of the misery of man and his most appalling sensations, like awful flashes of lightning;—but when the author reverses this change, he trifles too much with our feelings, and occasionally goes on, turning to ridicule or hopelessness all the fine ideas he has excited, with a recklessness that becomes extremely unpleasant and mortifying. What, for instance, can be more beautiful and at the same time true to nature than where,—just after a very anti-pathetic description of the confusion of *Julia* at her husband's sudden appearance, and her contrivances and lovers' falsehoods to elude his search for the beloved youth, he says (speaking of their alarm at the expected return of the old gentleman)—

> Julia did not speak,
> But pressed her bloodless lip to Juan's cheek.
> He turn'd his lip to hers, and with his hand
> Call'd back the tangles of her wandering hair;
> Even then their love they could not all command,
> And half forgot their danger and despair.

What more calculated to 'harrow up one's soul' than the following stanzas, which come in the very midst of some careless jests on the abstract ludicrousness of the wretched shifts of starving sailors in a becalmed boat, surrounded by a boundless prospect of the ocean? The Italics are our own.

> The seventh day, and no wind—the burning sun
> Blister'd and scorch'd; and, stagnant on the sea,
> They lay like carcases! and hope was none,
> Save in the breeze which came not: *savagely*
> *They glared upon each other*—all was done,
> Water, and wine, and food,—and you might see
> The *longings of the cannibal arise,*
> *(Although they spoke not)* in their *wolfish* eyes.
> At length one whispered his companion, who
> Whispered another, and thus it went round
> And then into a *hoarser murmur* grew,
> An ominous and wild and desperate sound;
> And when his comrade's thought each sufferer knew,
> 'Twas but his own, suppress'd till now, he found:
> And *out they spoke* of lots for flesh and blood,
> And who should die to be his fellow's food.

... *Don Juan* is accused of being an 'immoral' work, which we cannot at all discover. We suppose that this charge more particularly alludes to the first canto. Let us see then on what foundation it rests. The son of a Spanish patrician, educated in the most prudish manner by a licentious, yet affectedly virtuous mother, falls in love with the young wife of an old man. She returns his affection, and their passion being favoured by opportunity, she gives way to her natural feelings, and is unfaithful to her marriage vows, the example (observe) being set her by this very husband's intrigues with *Juan's* mother. Now Lord

Byron speaks lightly of the effect of any scruples of conscience upon her, and of her infidelity; and this, it is said, has tendency to corrupt the minds of 'us youth', and to make us *think* lightly of breaking the matrimonial contract. But if to do this be immoral, we can only say that Nature is immoral. Lord Byron does no more than relate the consequences of certain absurdities. If he speaks slightingly of the ties between a girl and a husband old enough for her father, it is because the ties themselves *are* slight. He does not ridicule the bonds of marriage generally, or where they are formed as they should be: he merely shows the folly and wickedness of setting forms and opinions against nature. If stupid and selfish parents will make up matches between persons whom difference of age or disposition disqualifies for mutual affection, they must take the consequences;—but we do not think it fair that a poet should be exclaimed against as a promoter of nuptial infidelity because he tells them what those consequences are. In this particular case, too, the author does not omit some painful consequences to those who have sinned according to 'nature's law'. *Julia*, the victim of selfishness and 'damned custom', is shut up in a convent, where no consolation remains to her but the remembrance of her entire and hapless love; but even that was perhaps pleasanter to her than living in the constant irksomeness of feigning an affection she could not feel.

There are a set of prudish and very suspicious moralists who endeavour to make vice appear to inexperienced eyes much more hateful than it really is. They would correct Nature;—and they always over-reach themselves. Nature has made vice to a certain degree pleasurable, though its painful consequences outweigh its present gratification. Now the said prudes, in their lectures and sermons and moral discourses (for they are chiefly priests) are constantly declaiming on the *deformity* of vice, and its almost total want of attraction. The consequence is, that when they are found to have deceived (as they always are), and immoral indulgence is discovered to be not without its charms,—the minds of young persons are apt to confound their true with their false maxims, and to think the threats of future pain and repentance mere fables invented to deter them from their rightful enjoyments. Which then, we would ask, are the immoral writings,—those which, by misrepresenting the laws of nature, lead to false views of morality and consequent licentiousness?—or those, which ridicule and point out the effects of absurd contradictions of human feelings and passions, and help to bring about a reformation of such practices.

Of the story in the second canto it is unnecessary to say much, for these remarks will apply to both. We suppose there has been some sermonizing on the description of the delight arising from the 'illicit intercourse' *of Juan* and *Haidée*. People who talk in this way can perceive no distinctions. It certainly is not to be inculcated, that every handsome young man and woman will find their account in giving way to all their impulses, because the very violent breaking through the habits and forms of society would create a great deal of unhappiness, both to the individuals, and to others. But what is there to blame in a beautiful and affectionate girl who gives way to a passion for a young shipwrecked human creature, bound to her by gratitude as well as love? She exacts no promises, says the bard, because she fears no inconstancy. Her father had exposed her to the first temptation that comes across her, because he had not provided against it by allowing her to know more of mankind. And does she not receive, as well as bestow, more real pleasure (for that is the question) in the enjoyment of a first and deep passion, than in becoming the wife of some brother in iniquity to whom her pirating father would have trucked her for lucre?

The fact is, at the bottom of all these questions, that many things are made vicious, which are not so by nature; and many things made virtuous, which are only so by calling and agreement: and it is on the horns of this self-created dilemma, that society is continually writhing and getting desperate.

—Leigh Hunt, *Examiner,*
October 31, 1819, pp. 700–702

ROBERT SOUTHEY (1820)

Robert Southey (1774–1843), the historian and Lake Poet represents the voice of conservatism. In a letter to Walter Savage Landor, he attacks Byron's poem as an "act of high treason on English poetry."

A fashion of poetry has been imported which has had a great run, and is in a fair way of being worn out. It is of Italian growth,—an adaptation of the manner of Pulci, Berni, and Ariosto in his sportive mood. Frere began it. What he produced was too good in itself and too inoffensive to become popular; for it attacked nothing and nobody; and it had the fault of his Italian models, that the transition from what is serious to what is burlesque was capricious. Lord Byron immediately followed; first with his *Beppo,* which implied the profligacy of the writer, and, lastly, with his *Don Juan,* which is a foul blot on the literature of his country, an act of high treason on English poetry. The manner has had a host of imitators. The use of Hudibrastic rhymes (the only thing in which it differs from the Italian) makes it very easy.

—Robert Southey, letter to
Walter Savage Landor, February 20, 1820

Johann Wolfgang von Goethe
"Byron's *Don Juan*" (1821)

The German classic Johann Wolfgang von Goethe (1749–1832) regarded *Don Juan* as the work of a genius. He compares English comic writing with German modes of comedy and discusses the possibility of translating Byron's language.

Don Juan is a work of infinite genius, misanthropical with the bitterest inhumanity, yet sympathetic with the deepest intensity of tender feeling. And since we now know the author and esteem him, and do not wish him to be otherwise than he is, we enjoy thankfully what he dares with overgreat independence, indeed insolence, to bring before us. The technical treatment of the verse is quite in accord with the singular, reckless, unsparing content. The poet spares his language as little as he does his men, and as we examine it more closely we discover indeed that English poetry has a cultivated comic language which we Germans wholly lack.

The comic in German lies preeminently in the idea, less in the treatment or style. We admire Lichtenberg's abounding wealth; he has at his command a whole world of knowledge and relations to mix like a pack of cards and deal them out roguishly at pleasure. With Blumauer too, whose compositions in verse certainly possess the comic spirit, it is especially the sharp contrast between old and new, aristocrats and common people, the noble and the mean, that delights us. If we examine further we find that the German, in order to be amusing, steps back several centuries and has the luck to be peculiarly ingenuous and engaging only in doggerel rhyme.

In translating *Don Juan* there are many useful things to be learned from the Englishman. There is only one joke which we cannot imitate from him,— one that gets its effect by a singular and dubious accent in words which look quite differently on paper. The English linguist may judge how far the poet in this case has wantonly exceeded the proper limits.

It is only by chance that the verses inserted here happened to be translated, and they are now published not as a pattern but for their suggestiveness. All our talented translators ought to try their skill at least partly upon them; they will have to permit assonances and imperfect rhymes and who knows what besides. A certain laconic treatment will also be necessary, in order to give the full quality and significance of this audacious mischievousness. Only when something has been accomplished along these lines, can we discuss the subject further.

Possibly we may be reproached for spreading in translation such writings as these through Germany, thus making an honest, peaceful, decorous nation acquainted with the most immoral works that the art of poetry ever produced. But according to our way of thinking, these attempts at translation should not be intended for the press, but may serve as excellent practice for talented brains. Our poets may then discreetly apply and cultivate what they acquire in this way, for the pleasure and delight of their countrymen. No particular injury to morality is to be feared from the publication of such poems, since poets and authors would have to cast aside all restraint to be more corrupting than the papers of the present day.

—Johann Wolfgang von Goethe,
"Byron's *Don Juan*," 1821, *Literary Essays*,
tr. J.E. Spingarn, 1921, pp. 205–207

SAMUEL TAYLOR COLERIDGE (1824)

How lamentably the *art* of versification is neglected by most of the poets of the present day!—by Lord Byron, as it strikes me, in particular, among those of eminence for other qualities. Upon the whole, I think the part of *Don Juan* in which Lambro's return to his home, and Lambro himself, are described, is the best, that is, the most individual thing, in all I know of Lord B.'s works. The festal abandonment puts one in mind of Nicholas Poussin's pictures.

—Samuel Taylor Coleridge,
Table Talk, June 7, 1824

CAROLINE NORTON (1837)

Caroline Elizabeth Sarah Norton (1808–1877) was a promoter of women's legal rights and a well-known British society beauty, involved in a highly scandalous separation from her abusive husband. The granddaughter of playwright Richard Brinsley Sheridan and daughter of novelist Caroline Norton, she established herself as a hostess for literati such as Edward Bulwer-Lytton, Edward Trelawney, Fanny Kemble, and Benjamin Disraeli, among others. Deprived of contact to her own children by her husband, she campaigned for the rights of married and divorced women. In a letter to John Murray, she expresses a female or feminist perspective on Byron's *Don Juan*.

November 4th, 1837.
DEAR SIR,

I have received "Don Juan" and the October Quarterly. . . . In thanking you for the two volumes of Byron belonging to the present beautiful edition, I must tell you that I have never read "Don Juan," through before, which very few women of my age in England could say,—and which I do not mind owning, since it adds greatly to the pleasure with which I perused the poem. I am afraid, in spite of the beauty, the wit, and the originality of the work, I think, with the Guiccioli—"Mi rincrese solo che Don Giovanni non resti al inferno." It is a book which no woman will ever like, whether for the reasons given by the author, or on other accounts, I will not dispute. To me the effect is like hearing some sweet and touching melody familiar to me as having been sung by a lost friend and companion, suddenly struck up in quick time with all the words parodied.

I am in town for a short time, occupied with lawyers and law—as usual. I used to boast of my partiality for the Bar as a profession, but I begin to think it would be pleasanter to follow a marching regiment than to see the seamy side of this intellectual trade.

Who has sprung up as Mrs. Norton in Bentley's Miscellany! It is pretty cool of the lady taking the name and title of my husband's wife; and I do not much like the mistake, as I have been too ill to write for those to whom I was bound by the bond of hire.

Yours ever,
Caroline Norton

—Caroline Norton, letter to John Murray,
November 4, 1837, *A Publisher and His Friends:
Memoir of John Murray*, 1891, 2, pp. 414–415

James Northcote (1830)

The painter and author, a pupil of Sir Joshua Reynolds, is mainly known as a portrait painter, but he also wrote on historical subjects. Hazlitt's *Conversations of James Northcote, Esq. R.A.* was published in book form in 1830, collecting items published earlier. Whether these are an accurate record of Northcote's conversations or not remains difficult to determine, as Hazlitt makes it clear that much of the work was his own composition. The comments on *Don Juan* are from the sixteenth conversation, first published in the *Atlas* in April 1829.

（Northcote:) I cannot help thinking there are essences in Lord Byron that are not to be surpassed. He is on a par with Dryden. All the other modern poets appear to me vulgar in the comparison. . . . I do not mean to vindicate the immorality or misanthropy in that poem—perhaps his lameness was to blame for this defect—but surely no one can deny the force, the spirit of it;

and there is such a fund of drollery mixed up with the serious part. Nobody understood the tragicomedy of poetry so well. People find fault with this mixture in general, because it is not well managed; there is a comic story and a tragic story going on at the same time, without their having any thing to do with one another. But in Lord Byron they are brought together, just as they are in nature. In like manner, if you go to an execution at the very moment when the criminal is going to be turned off, and all eyes are fixed upon him, an old apple-woman and her stall are overturned, and all the spectators fall a-laughing. In real life the most ludicrous incidents border on the most affecting and shocking. How fine that is of the cask of butter in the storm! Some critics have objected to it as turning the whole into burlesque; on the contrary, it is that which stamps the character of the scene more than any thing else. What did the people in the boat care about the rainbow, which he has described in such vivid colours; or even about their fellow-passengers who were thrown overboard, when they only wanted to eat them? No, it was the loss of the firkin of butter that affected them more than all the rest; and it is the mention of this circumstance that adds a hardened levity and a sort of ghastly horror to the scene. It shows the master-hand—there is such a boldness and sagacity and superiority to ordinary rules in it!

> —William Hazlitt, *Conversations of James Northcote, Esq.,* 1830, *Complete Works,* ed. Howe, XI, pp. 279–280

Thomas Babington Macaulay (1849)

I passed some hours over Don *Juan,* and saw no reason to change the opinion which I formed twenty-five years ago. The first two cantos are Byron's masterpieces. The next two may pass as not below his average. Then begins the descent, and at last he sinks to the level of his own imitators in the magazines.

> —Thomas Babington Macaulay, *Journal,* August 3, 1849, cited in G. Otto Trevelyan, *The Life and Letters of Lord Macaulay,* 1876, vol. 2, p. 227

John Addington Symonds "Lord Byron" (1880)

The poet and cultural historian Symonds (1840–1893) gives a sensitive account of Byron's mode of composition. While he notes the haphazard, fragmentary nature of *Don Juan,* he also acknowledges an underlying unity.

In the year 1818 Byron began *Don Juan*. Until his death in 1824 he used it as the channel of expression for the varied reminiscences of past experience, and for the miscellaneous pictures of society and human life with which his mind was stored. It was a poem without a plan, and for this very reason well adapted to his purpose. Juan is a name: the fact that his parentage and earliest adventures are Spanish does not bring him into competition with the Don Juan of Spanish legend. He has but little in common with the hero of Moliere's play or Mozart's opera. Juan's biography is the thread on which Byron hangs descriptions, episodes, satirical digressions, and reflective passages of brilliant audacity. That *Don Juan*, as Byron began it in the extant sixteen cantos, should have arrived at a conclusion, seems inconceivable. It was therefore scarcely a misfortune that death cut the poet short, when he had closed the fourth chapter of his hero's adventures. Byron, it may be observed, was essentially an occasional poet. He needed some substratum of fact or personal emotion for his imaginative edifices, and wrote best when he was least hampered by self-imposed theories of art. *Childe Harold* and *Don Juan* may therefore be regarded as continuous poetic journals. He used them as receptacles for the ideas that every passing day suggested. 'If things are farcical,' he once said to Trelawny, during their voyage to Greece, 'they will do for *Don Juan*; if heroical, you shall have another canto of *Childe Harold*.' This accounts for the defect of structure in both poems. But while the change of style and tone in *Childe Harold* has been already pointed out, no such failure can be indicated in *Don Juan*. Within itself, and judged by the laws of its own nature, it is vigorously organised. The flux and reflux of contrasted incidents,—the balance of emotions between pathos and comedy, humour and satire,—the correspondence of voluptuous and piquant, sensual and tender, touches,—the passage from Donna Julia to Haidee and Dudu,—the siege succeeding to the shipwreck,—the picture of St. Petersburgh under Catherine followed by that of England ruled by Whig and Tory peers;—this counterpoise of interests, this rapid modulation from key to key, gives to *Don Juan*, fragment as it is, a fine artistic coherence.

—John Addington Symonds, "Lord Byron,"
The English Poets, ed. Thomas Humphry Ward,
1880, vol. 4, p. 250

ALGERNON CHARLES SWINBURNE (1866)

Swinburnes's account of *Don Juan* is taken from the introduction to his *Selections from the Works of Lord Byron* (1866).

From the beginning indeed he had much to fight against; and three impediments hung about him at starting, the least of which would have weighed down a less strong man: youth, and genius, and an ancient name. In spite of all three he made his way; and suffered for it. At the first chance given or taken, every obscure and obscene thing that lurks for pay or prey among the fouler shallows and thickets of literature flew against him; every hound and every hireling lavished upon him the loathsome tribute of their abuse; all nameless creatures that nibble and prowl, upon whom the serpent's curse has fallen, to go upon his belly and eat dust all the days of his life, assailed him with their foulest venom and their keenest fangs. And the promise given of old to their kind was now at least fulfilled: they did bruise his heel. But the heads of such creatures are so small that it is hard to bruise them in return; it would first be necessary to discern them.

That Byron was able to disregard and to outlive the bark and the bite of such curs as these is small praise enough: the man who cannot do as much is destructible, and therefore contemptible. He did far more than this; he withstood the weight of circumstances to the end; That his youth and his rank were flung in his face with vulgar insolence on the publication of his first little book it can hardly be necessary to remind any reader of Byron; but possibly even these offences might have been condoned in a scribbler whose work had given no offensive promise of greatness yet to be. In the verses on Lochnagar at least an ominous threat or presage of something new and splendid must have been but too perceptible to the discerning eye of criticism, not always without complaint, but always without misgiving. His glorious courage, his excellent contempt for things contemptible, and hatred of hateful men, are enough of themselves to embalm and endear his memory in the eyes of all who are worthy to pass judgment upon him. And these qualities gave much of their own value to verse not otherwise or not always praiseworthy. Even at its best, the serious poetry of Byron is often so rough and loose, so weak in the screws and joints which hold together the framework of verse, that it is not easy to praise it enough without seeming to condone or to extenuate such faults as should not be overlooked or forgiven. No poet is so badly represented by a book of selections. It must show something of his weakness; it cannot show all of his strength. Often, after a noble overture, the last note struck is either dissonant or ineffectual.

His magnificent masterpiece, which must endure for ever among the precious relics of the world, will not bear dissection or extraction. The merit of *Don Juan* does not lie in any part, but in the whole. There is in that great poem an especial and exquisite balance and sustenance of alternate tones which cannot be expressed or explained by the utmost ingenuity of selection. Haidée is supplanted by Dudù, the ship-wreck by the siege, the Russian court by the English household; and this perpetual change, this tidal variety of experience and emotion, gives to the poem something of the breadth and freshness of the sea. Much of the poet's earlier work is or seems unconsciously dishonest; this, if not always or wholly unaffected, is as honest as the sunlight, as frank as the sea-wind. Here, and here alone, the student of his work may recognise and enjoy the ebb and flow of actual life. Here the pulse of vital blood may be felt in tangible flesh. Here for the first time the style of Byron is beyond all praise or blame: a style at once swift and supple, light and strong, various and radiant. Between *Childe Harold* and *Don Juan* the same difference exists which a swimmer feels between lake-water and sea-water: the one is fluent, yielding, invariable; the other has in it a life and pulse, a sting and a swell, which touch and excite the nerves like fire or like music. Across the stanzas of *Don Juan* we swim forward as over "the broad backs of the sea"; they break and glitter, hiss and laugh, murmur and move, like waves that sound or that subside. There is in them a delicious resistance, an elastic motion, which salt water has and fresh water has not. There is about them a wide wholesome air, full of vivid light and constant Wind, which is only felt at sea. Life undulates and death palpitates in the splendid verse which resumes the evidence of a brave and clear-sighted man concerning life and death. Here, as at sea, there is enough and too much of fluctuation and intermission; the ripple flags and falls in loose and lazy lines: the foam flies wide of any mark, and the breakers collapse here and there in sudden ruin and violent failure. But the violence and weakness of the sea are preferable to the smooth sound and equable security of a lake: its buoyant and progressive impulse sustains and propels those who would sink through weariness in the flat and placid shallows. There are others whom it sickens, and others whom it chills; these will do well to steer inshore.

Cancel or select a leaf from these poems, and you will injure the whole framework equally in either case. It is not without reluctance that I have given any extracts from *Don Juan*; it is not without a full sense of the damage done to these extracts by the very act of extraction. But I could only have left them untouched with a reluctance even greater; and this plea, if it can, must excuse me. As fragments they are exquisite and noble, like the broken hand or severed foot of a Greek statue; but here as much is lost as there. Taken with their context, they regain as much of beauty and of force as the sculptured foot or hand when, reunited to the perfect body, they resume their place and office among its vital and various limbs. This gift of life and variety is the supreme quality of Byron's chief poem; a quality which cannot be expressed by any system of extracts. Little can here be given beyond a sample or two of tragic and serious work.

The buoyant beauty of surrounding verse, the "innumerable laughter" and the profound murmur of its many measures, the fervent flow of stanzas now like the ripples and now like the gulfs of the sea, can no more be shown by process of selection than any shallow salt pool left in the sand for sunbeams to drain dry can show the depth and length of the receding tide.

It would be waste of words and time here to enlarge at all upon the excellence of the pure comedy of *Don Juan*. From the first canto to the sixteenth; from the defence of Julia, which is worthy of Congreve or Molière, to the study of Adeline, which is worthy of Laclos or Balzac; the elastic energy of humour never falters or flags. English criticism, with a mournful murmur of unanimous virtue, did at the time, and may yet if it please, appeal against the satire which strikes home and approve the satire that flies abroad. It was said, and perhaps is still said, that the poem falls off and runs low towards the end. Those who can discover where a change for the worse begins might at least indicate the landmark, imperceptible to duller eyes, which divides the good from the bad. Others meantime will retain their belief that this cry was only raised because in these latter cantos a certain due amount of satire fell upon the false and corrupt parts of English character, its mealy-mouthed vices and its unsound virtues. Had the scene been shifted to Italy or France, we might have heard little of the poet's failing power and perverse injustice.

It is just worth a word of notice that Byron, like Fielding before him, has caught up a well-known name and prefixed it to his work, without any attempt or desire to retain the likeness or follow the tradition attached to it. With him Don Juan is simply a man somewhat handsomer and luckier than others of his age. This hero is not even a reduced copy of the great and terrible figure with which he has nothing in common but a name. The Titan of embodied evil, the likeness of sin made flesh, which grew up in the grave and bitter imagination of a Spanish poet, steeped in the dyes and heated by the flames of hell, appears even in the hands of Molière diminished, and fallen as it were from Satan to Belial; but still splendid with intellect and courage that tower above the meaner minds and weaker wills of women and of men; still inflexible to human appeal and indomitable by divine anger. To crush him, heaven is compelled to use thunder and hell-fire; and by these, though stricken, he is not subdued. The sombre background of a funereal religion is not yet effaced; but it tasked the whole strength of Molière, gigantic as that strength was, to grapple with the shadow of tins giant, to transfigure upon a new stage the tragic and enormous incarnation of supreme sin. As it is, even when playing with his debtors or his peasants, the hero of Molière retains always some feature of his first likeness, some shadow of his early shape. But further than France the terrible legend has never moved. Rigid criticism would therefore say that the title of Byron's masterpiece was properly a misnomer: which is no great matter after all, since the new Juan can never be confounded with the old.

—Algernon Charles Swinburne, *Essays and Studies*, 1875, pp. 242–243, 254–257

George Bernard Shaw
"Dedicatory Letter" (1903)

The Irish playwright George Bernard Shaw (1856–1950) was a socialist who was active in the Fabian Society, an intellectual movement whose aim was to promote socialist principles. Apart from his dramatic writings—such as *Pygmalion, Saint Joan,* and *Mrs. Warren's Profession*—he also wrote a vast amount of criticism on music, art, and literature. He was awarded the Nobel Prize for Literature in 1925. He mentions *Don Juan* in the dedicatory letter to his play *Man and Superman.*

Byron's hero [Don Juan] is, after all, only a vagabond libertine. And he is dumb: he does not discuss himself with a Sganarelle-Leporello or with the fathers or brothers of his mistresses: he does not even, like Casanova, tell his own story. In fact he is not a true Don Juan at all; for he is no more an enemy of God than any romantic and adventurous young sower of wild oats. . . . Byron was as little of a philosopher as Peter the Great: both were instances of that rare and useful, but unedifying variation, an energetic genius born without the prejudices or superstitions of his contemporaries. The resultant unscrupulous freedom of thought made Byron a greater poet than Wordsworth just as it made Peter a greater king than George III; but as it was, after all, only a negative qualification, it did not prevent Peter from being an appalling blackguard and an arrant poltroon, nor did it enable Byron to become a religious force like Shelley.

—George Bernard Shaw,
from the "Dedicatory Letter" to
Man and Superman, 1903

Paul Elmer More
"A Note on Byron's Don Juan" (1905)

Paul Elmer More (1864–1937) was an American critic and essayist. Educated at Washington University in St. Louis and at Harvard University, he edited the *The Independent* (1901–03) and the New York *Evening Post* (1903–09) and was editor of *The Nation* (1909–14). He was a proponent and representative of conservatism and Anglo-Catholicism and wrote extensively on Greek philosophy; his best-known work, *Shelburne Essays*, is an eleven-volume collection of articles and reviews culled from 1904 to 1921.

It has often been a source of wonder to me that I was able to read and enjoy Byron's *Don Juan* under the peculiar circumstances attending my introduction to that poem. I had been walking in the Alps, and after a day of unusual exertion found myself in the village of Chamouni, fatigued and craving rest. A copy of the Tauchnitz edition fell into my hands, and there, in a little room, through a summer's day, by a window which looked full upon the unshadowed splendour of Mont Blanc, I sat and read, and only arose when Juan faded out of sight with "the phantom of her frolic Grace—Fitz-Fulke." I have often wondered, I say, why the incongruity of that solemn Alpine scene with the mockery of Byron's wit did not cause me to shut the book and thrust it away, for in general I am highly sensitive to the nature of my surroundings while reading. Only recently, on taking up the poem again for the purpose of editing it, did the answer to that riddle occur to me, and with it a better understanding of the place of Don Juan among the great epics which might have seemed in finer accord with the sublimity and peace of that memorable day.

In one respect, at least, it needed no return to Byron's work to show how closely it is related in spirit to the accepted canons of the past. These poets, who have filled the world with their rumour, all looked upon life with some curious obliquity of vision. We, who have approached the consummation of the world's hope, know that happiness and peace and the fulfilment of desires are about to settle down and brood for ever more over the lot of mankind, but with them it seems to have been otherwise. Who can forget the recurring minynthadion of Homer, in which he summed up for the men of his day the vanity of long aspirations? So if we were asked to point out the lines of Shakespeare that express most completely his attitude toward life, we should probably quote that soliloquy of Hamlet wherein he catalogues the evils of existence, and only in the fear of future dreams finds a reason for continuance; or we should cite that sonnet of disillusion: "Tired with all these for restful death I cry." And as for the lyric poets, sooner or later the lament of Shelley was wrung from the lips of each:

Out of the day and night
A joy has taken flight:

Fresh spring, and summer, and winter hoar
Move my faint heart with grief, but with delight
No more—oh, never more!

This, I repeat, is a strange fact, for it appears that these poets, prophets who spoke in the language of beauty and who have held the world's reverence so long it appears now that these interpreters of the fates were all misled. Possibly, as Aristotle intimated, genius is allied to some vice of the secretions which produces a melancholia of the brain; something like this, indeed, only expressed in more recondite terms, may be found in the most modern theory of science. But more probably they wrote merely from insufficient experience, not having perceived how the human race with increase of knowledge grows in happiness. Thus, at least, it seems to one who observes the tides of thought. Next year, or the next, some divine invention shall come which will prove this melancholy of the poets to have been only a childish ignorance of man's sublimer destiny; some discovery of a new element more wonderful than radium will render the ancient brooding over human feebleness a matter of laughter and astonishment; some acceptance of the larger brotherhood of the race will wipe away all tears and bring down upon earth the fair dream of heaven, a reality and a possession for ever; some new philosophy of the soul will convert the old poems of conflict into meaningless fables, stale and unprofitable. Already we see the change at hand. To how many persons today does Browning appeal though they would not always confess it more powerfully than Homer or Milton or any other of the great names of antiquity? And the reason of this closer appeal of Browning is chiefly the unflagging optimism of his philosophy, his full-blooded knowledge and sympathy which make the wailings of the past somewhat silly in our ears, if truth must be told. I never read Browning but those extraordinary lines of Euripides recur to my mind: "Not now for the first time do I regard mortal things as a shadow, nor would I fear to charge with supreme folly those artificers of words who are reckoned the sages of mankind, for no man among mortals is happy." Θνητων γάρ ουδείς εστιν εύδαίμων, indeed!—would any one be shameless enough to utter such words under the new dispensation of official optimism?

It is necessary to think of these things before we attempt to criticise Byron, for *Don Juan*, too, despite its marvellous vivacity, looks upon life from the old point of view. Already, for this reason in part, it seems a little antiquated to us, and in a few years it may be read only as a curiosity. Meanwhile for the few who lag behind in the urgent march of progress the poem will possess a special interest just because it presents the ancient thesis of the poets and prophets in a novel form. Of course, in many lesser matters it makes a wider and more lasting appeal. Part of the Haidée episode, for instance, is so exquisitely lovely, so radiant with the golden haze of youth, that even in the wiser happiness of our maturity we may still turn to it with a kind of complacent delight. Briefer passages scattered here and there, such as the "'T is sweet to hear," and the "Ave Maria," need only a little abridgment at the close to fit them perfectly for any future anthology devoted to the satisfaction and the ultimate significance of human emotions. But, strangely enough, these disturbing climaxes, which will demand to be forgotten, or to be rearranged as we restore old mutilated statues, do, indeed, point to those very qualities which render the poem so extraordinary a complement to the great and accepted epics of the past. For the present it may yet be sufficient to consider Don Juan as it is with all its enormities upon it.

And, first of all, we shall make a sad mistake if we regard the poem as a mere work of satire. Occasionally Byron pretends to lash himself into a righteous fury over the vices of the age, but we know that this is all put on, and that the real savageness of his nature comes out only when he thinks of his own personal wrongs. Now this is a very different thing from the deliberate and sustained denunciation of a vicious age such as we find in Juvenal, a different thing utterly from the saeva indignatio that devoured the heart and brain of poor Swift. There is in Don Juan something of the personal satire of Pope, and something of the whimsical mockery of Lucilius and his imitators. But it needs but a little discernment to see that Byron's poem has vastly greater scope and significance than the Epistle to Dr. Arbuthnot or the spasmodic gaiety of the Menippean satire. It does in its own way present a view of life as a whole, with the good and the evil, and so passes beyond the category of the merely satirical. The very scope of its subject, if nothing more, classes it with the more universal epics of literature rather than with the poems that portray only a single aspect of life.

Byron himself was conscious of this, and more than once alludes to the larger aspect of his work. "If you must have an epic," he once said to Medwin, "there's Don Juan for you; it is an epic as much in the spirit of our day as the Iliad was in that of Homer." And in one of the asides in the poem itself he avows the same design:

> A panoramic view of Hell's in training,
> After the style of Virgil and of Homer,
> So that my name of Epic's no misnomer.

Hardly the style of those stately writers, to be sure, but an epic after its own fashion the poem certainly is. That Byron's way is not the way of the older poets requires no emphasis; they

reveled in the fancies of the time,
True Knights, chaste Dames, huge Giants, Kings
        despotic;
But all these, save the last, being obsolete,
I chose a modern subject as more meet.

Being cut off from the heroic subjects of the established school, he still sought to obtain something of the same large and liberating effect through the use of a frankly modern theme. The task was not less difficult than his success was singular and marked; and that is why it seemed in no way inappropriate, despite its occasional lapse of licentiousness, to read Don Juan with the white reflection of Mont Blanc streaming through the window. Homer might have been so read, or Virgil, or any of those poets who presented life solemnly and magniloquently; I do not think I could have held my mind to Juvenal or Pope or even Horace beneath the calm radiance of that Alpine light.

I have said that the great poets all took a sombre view of the world. Man is but *the dream of a shadow* said Pindar, speaking for the race of genius, and Byron is conscious of the same insight into the illusive spectacle. He has looked with like vision upon

        this scene of all-confessed inanity,
    By Saint, by Sage, by Preacher, and by Poet,

and will not in his turn refrain "from holding up the nothingness of life." So in the introduction to the seventh canto he runs through the list of those who have preached and sung this solemn, but happily to us outworn, theme:

    I say no more than hath been said in Dante's
    Verse, and by Solomon and by Cervantes.

It must not be supposed, however, because the heroic poems of old were touched with the pettiness and sadness of human destiny, that their influence on the reader was supposed to be narrowing or depressing; the name "heroic" implies the contrary of that. Indeed their very inspiration was derived from the fortitude of a spirit struggling to rise above the league of little things and foiling despairs. It may seem paradoxical to us, yet it is true that these morbid poets believed in the association of men with gods and in the grandeur of mortal passions. So Achilles and Hector, both with the knowledge of their brief destiny upon them, both rilled with foreboding of frustrate hopes, strive nobly to the end of magnanimous defeat. There lay the greatness of the heroic epic for readers of old, the sense of human littleness, the melancholy of broken aspirations, swallowed up in the transcending sublimity of man's endurance and daring. And men of lesser mould, who knew so well the limitations of their sphere, took courage and were taught to look down unmoved upon their harassed fate.

Now Byron came at a time of transition from the old to the new. The triumphs of material discovery, *"Le magnifiche sorti e progressive"* had not yet cast a reproach on the earlier sense of life's futility, while at the same time the faith in heroic passions had passed away. An attempt to create an epic in the old spirit would have been doomed, was indeed doomed in the hands of those who undertook it. The very language in which Byron presents the ancient universal belief of Plato and those others

Who knew this life was not worth a potato,

shows how far he was from the loftier mode of imagination. In place of heroic passion he must seek another outlet of relief, another mode of purging away melancholy; and the spirit of the burlesque came lightly to his use as the only available *vis medica*. The feeling was common to his age, but he alone was able to adapt the motive to epic needs. How often the melancholy sentimentality of Heine corrects itself by a burlesque conclusion! Or, if we regard the novel, how often does Thackeray in like manner replace the old heroic relief of passion by a kindly smile at the brief and busy cares of men. But neither Heine nor Thackeray carries the principle of the burlesque to its artistic completion, or makes it the avowed motive of a complicated action, as Byron does in *Don Juan*. That poem is indeed "prolific of melancholy merriment." It is not necessary to point out at length the persistence of this mock-heroic spirit. Love, ambition, home-attachments, are all burlesqued; battle ardour, the special theme of epic sublimity, is subjected to the same quizzical mockery:

There was not now a luggage boy, but sought
Danger and spoil with ardour much increased;
And why? because a little odd old man,
Stripped to his shirt, was come to lead the van.

In the gruesome shipwreck scene the tale of suffering which leads to cannibalism is interrupted thus:

At length they caught two Boobies, and a Noddy,
And then they left off eating the dead body.

The description of London town as seen from Shooter's Hill ends with this absurd metaphor:

A huge, dun Cupola, like a foolscap crown
On a fool's head and there is London Town!

Even Death laughs, death that "hiatus maxime deflendus," "the dunnest of all
duns," etc. And, last of all, the poet turns the same weapon against his own
art. Do the lines for a little while grow serious, he suddenly pulls himself up
with a sneer:

Here I must leave him, for I grow pathetic,
Moved by the Chinese nymph of tears, green tea!

I trust, however, it has been made sufficiently clear that *Don Juan* is something
quite different from the mere mock-heroic from Pulci, for instance, "sire of
the half-serious rhyme," whom Byron professed to imitate. The poem is in a
sense not half but wholly serious, for the very reason that it takes so broad a
view of human activity, and because of its persistent moral sense. (Which is
nowise contradicted by the immoral scenes in several of the cantos.) It is not,
for example, possible to think of finding in Pulci such a couplet as this :

But almost sanctify the sweet excess
By the immortal wish and power to bless.

He who could write such lines as those was not merely indulging his humour.
Don Juan is something more than

A versified Aurora Borealis,
Which flashes o'er a waste and icy clime.

Out of the bitterness of his soul, out of the wreck of his passions which,
though heroic in intensity, had ended in quailing of the heart, he sought what
the great makers of epic had sought, a solace and a sense of uplifted freedom.
The heroic ideal was gone, the refuge of religion was gone; but, passing to
the opposite extreme, by showing the power of the human heart to mock at
all things, he would still set forth the possibility of standing above and apart
from all things. He, too, went beyond the limitations of destiny by laughter,
as Homer and Virgil and Milton had risen by the imagination. And, in doing
this, he wrote the modern epic.

We are learning a new significance of human life, as I said; and the
sublime audacities of the elder poets in attempting to transcend the
melancholia of their day are growing antiquated, just as Byron's heroic
mockery is turning stale. In a few years we shall have come so much closer
to the mysteries over which the poets bungled helplessly, that we can afford
to forget their rhapsodies. Meanwhile it may not be amiss to make clear to

ourselves the purpose and character of one of the few, the very few, great poems in our literature.

—Paul Elmer More, "A Note on Byron's
Don Juan," *Shelburne Essays, Third Series,*
1905, pp. 166–177

R.E. PROTHERO "THE POETRY OF BYRON" (1924)

Rowland Edmund Prothero, first Baron Ernle (1851–1937), was a British scholar, author, and politician. A fellow at Oxford University's All Souls' College and a Member of Parliament representing Oxford, he published widely on farming in addition to issuing the seminal *Letters and Journals of Lord Byron* (1898–1901). His *Centenary Reflections on Childe Harold's Pilgrimage and Don Juan* (1924) gives a detailed account of Byron's sources.

By accident or by destiny, he found in the serio-comic Italian poets and in *Whistlecraft* the models that he wanted. So, in spite of the advice and even pleading of his friends, he persisted in the work which has most incontestably perpetuated his genius. The new vein produced three masterpieces—a light story, a personal satire, an epic of humanity, *Beppo* is, as Prof. Grierson truly says . . . 'our best and almost our only comic story in verse since Chaucer.' The same gaiety, blended with contemptuous scorn, makes 'The Vision of Judgment' the most effective personal satire in the English language. But the richest product of the vein is *Don Juan*, of which five Cantos had been finished before *The Vision of Judgment* was begun.

In *Don Juan*, Byron took as his master Pulci, the 'sire of the half-serious rhyme'. The 'Morgante Maggiore' has had an illustrious history. Written to amuse the mother of Lorenzo the Magnificent, recited before such an audience as Ficino, Politian, and Michaelangelo, it had been one of the inspirations of Ariosto. It had given hints to Milton. Now it offered suggestions for *Don Juan*. Apart from the humorous gravity with which the tale is told of Charlemagne and his Paladins, of wars and adventures, of giants, devils, and enchantments, Byron was fascinated by the medley of conflicting feeling. Digressing from his story in every direction, Pulci passes in a moment from pathos to laughter, from seriousness to drollery, from simplicity of faith to banter, from tender passion to cynical mockery, from piety to ribaldry. To men of the Italian Renaissance the poem was intelligible enough; but it is not surprising that to later critics it has been a riddle. Each of the twenty-eight Cantos of the 'Morgante Maggiore' begins with a pious invocation, and ends with an intimation to the audience that there is more to come. After his own fashion Byron follows his model, though at will he reduces the invocation to 'Hail, Muse! *et cetera*'. At the close of each Canto he drops his curtain so skilfully as to leave the reader expectant. Thus, Canto VI closes with the sack, and the Bosphorus, as the imminent doom of Juan and Dudu, and Canto XVI leaves Juan clasping the Duchess of Fitz-Fulke disguised as a ghostly Friar. The metre is also that of Pulci. But Byron has made the *ottava rima* his own. He handles it with consummate mastery and with an amazing facility of rhyming. In stanza after stanza of clear idiomatic English, as colloquial as metrical style will allow, the rhymes fall into their place without unnatural involutions of the sentences. In *Don Juan*, at any rate, Byron shows a very high degree of that skill in prosody in which he is sometimes alleged to be wanting.

To the contents of *Don Juan*, Pulci, it need scarcely be said, contributed nothing. No one but Byron could have written it, and even he at no other period. It expresses many sides of the man; it represents also the most important characteristic of the age. Of Byron himself the poem gives the least incomplete portrait. In it meet the vivacity, versatility, and amazing cleverness of the gay letter-writer; the knowledge and experience of the travelled, observant, loose-living, yet studious, man of the world; the firm grasp of actualities, the clear vision, merciless candour, and indignation of the satirist of contemporary life; the passionate intensity of feeling, tender as well as scornful, of the poet. It also represents a reactionary age which was chiefly remarkable for the accumulation of those destructive forces which prepared the way for reconstruction. Europe was settling down on its former foundations; rulers and politicians of the old school threatened once again to strangle the spirit of individual liberty. Byron's moral critics, Wordsworth, Southey, and Coleridge, were either dumb or they supported the governing classes. He himself took a bolder and less obsequious course. In *Don Juan*, as in many other passages in his poems, he satirises and ridicules the hypocrisies of aristocratic society, at home and abroad, the insincerity of their conventions, the sycophancy of their hireling supporters, the type of human nature which was moulded by their standards, fashions, and preoccupations. His outspoken protest is a finer record than the silence of his poetic rivals. For his service to the cause of liberty foreign nations forget his faults and reverence his name.

The poem is amazing in its intense vitality, vibrating with life in its multitudinous variety, as Byron saw it with clear disillusioned eyes. Without any vision of the future beyond the ideal of liberty, he knew no meaning or purpose in existence. With infinite art he conveys his own impression of the irrelevance of life by the rapidity of his shifting scenes and emotional changes, his sudden transitions, his digressions, musings, and reflexions, his juxtaposition of incongruous feelings. From this medley of apparent inconsequence stand out passages of exquisite beauty and of poetic power in many fields. They are made more effective by their setting. Detached from their context they lose much of their power. Imagine the diary of a citizeness of Paris during the Revolution, the record of her visits and her ailments, the purchase of her salads, cosmetics, and stockings, and, in the midst of the trifling details of commonplace life, the bare uncommented entry, *La veuve Capetienne a la guillotine*. The tragic force of such an entry is accentuated by the triviality of its surroundings. So in *Don Juan* the clash of contrast is skilfully used to heighten the effects, as when the tender scene of Haidee bending over the unconscious Juan on the shore follows hard on the grim almost revolting realism of the shipwreck; or as when the song of 'the Isles of Greece' soars above the fiddling and dancing, chatter and irresponsible gaiety of the feast in the garden and house of the pirate Lambro; or as when the solemnising beauty of the Ave Maria strikes across and interrupts the gay mockery of a brilliant literary digression.

Byron was at work on 'Don Juan' three weeks before his death at Missolonghi. In the manner of his end he proved the falseness of the sophistry of his own Lucifer. It is not by self-will but by self-sacrifice that a soul is ransomed.

Critics rightly prize artistic perfection, and Byron frequently falls below its highest standard. But he had, to an almost unrivalled degree, passion, strength, and energy. A great theologian would once have given all his learning for a tinker's power of reaching the heart. So too, perhaps, in the century that has passed since 1824, there may have been literary craftsmen who would have gladly exchanged their exquisiteness of artistic skill for Byron's power of swaying the feelings of ordinary men. The fastidious taste of cultivated minds might have been impoverished in the sources of its gratification. But the emotional life of the nation would have been beyond measure enriched.

—R.E. Prothero, "The Poetry of Byron,"
in *Quarterly Review,* CCXLI, 1924,
pp. 238–242, 250–253

MARINO FALIERO

Marino Faliero (1821) was published, with a dedication to Goethe, four years after *Manfred* and represents Byron's attempt at replacing the "wild old English drama" with a regular tragedy" that heeds the unities of time, place, and action (*BLJ*, VIII, p. 210). Set in Venice like *The Two Foscari*, the play expresses Byron's frustration at the reactionary political climate after the defeat of Napoléon at Waterloo and the reordering of Europe at the Congress of Vienna. Oppression, the corruption of empire, and the encroachment of the state on the private life of its citizens have a claustrophobic effect, which is enhanced by the neoclassical character of the tragedy.

Faliero, a character based on a real person, who was doge of Venice between 1354 and 1355, displays some similarities with Manfred in his isolation, yet he has striven to serve Venice in a long career as citizen-soldier. He is now to be rewarded with the position of doge, the head of the state, but as he realizes, the role is functionary, and he would be a mere puppet and "slave" to the aristocratic oligarchy. When his young and innocent wife is accused of adultery and the unfounded accusation goes unpunished, he agrees to lead a coup against the patricians, accepting the butchery of the entire elite as the price for revenge and political renewal. Faliero is isolated on all sides; he is planning to kill his former aristocratic friends, while not feeling a part of the "common ruffians" (I.ii.582) he conspires with. The doge's ineffectual attempt to revolutionize the corrupt state of Venice and his subsequent execution mirror Byron's frustration with the Carbonari, who tried to liberate Italy from Austrian rule. *Marino Faliero* was staged by Robert William Elliston at Drury Lane in 1821, against Byron's express wishes and despite the court injunction Murray had obtained on Byron's behalf. Byron was not surprised that the play ran only seven nights. "Murray writes that they want to stage the tragedy of *Marino Faliero*, more fools they, it was written for the closet" (*BLJ* VIII, p. 22). Critics of *Marino Faliero* have been concerned with the play's suitability or unsuitability for the stage, its technical flaws, historical accuracy, political message, and its imagery.

WILLIAM HAZLITT "LORD BYRON'S TRAGEDY OF MARINO FALIERO" (1821)

We cannot speak in terms of very enthusiastic praise of this historical play. Indeed, it hardly corresponds to its title. It has little of a local or circumstantial air about it. We are not violently transported to the time or scene of action. We know not much about the plot, about the characters, about the motives of the persons introduced, but we know a good deal about their sentiments and opinions on matters in general, and hear some very fine descriptions from their mouths; which would, however, have become the mouth of any other individual in the play equally well, and the mouth of the noble poet better than that of any of his characters. We have, indeed, a previous theory, that Lord Byron's genius is not dramatic, and the present performance is not one that makes it absolutely necessary for us to give up that theory. It is very inferior to *Manfred,* both in beauty and interest. The characters and situations there were of a romantic and poetical cast, mere creatures of the imagination; and the sentiments such as the author might easily conjure up by fancying himself on enchanted ground, and adorn with all the illusions that hover round the poet's pen, 'prouder than when blue Iris bends.' The more the writer indulged himself in following out the phantoms of a morbid sensibility, or lapt himself in the voluptuous dream of his own existence, the nearer he would approach to the truth of nature, the more he would be identified with the airy and preter-natural personages he represented. But here he descends to the ground of fact and history; and we cannot say that in that circle he treads with the same firmness of step that he has displayed boldness and smoothness of wing in soaring above it. He paints the cloud, or the rainbow in the cloud; or dives into the secret and subterraneous workings of his own breast; but he does not, with equal facility or earnestness, wind into the march of human affairs upon the earth, or mingle in the throng and daily conflict of human passions. There is neither action nor reaction in his poetry; both which are of the very essence of the Drama. He does not commit himself in the common arena of man; but looks down, from the high tower of his rank, nay, of his genius, on the ignobler interests of humanity, and describes them either as a dim and distant phantasmagoria or a paltry fantoccini exhibition, scarce worth his scorn. He fixes on some point of imagination or of brooding thought as a resting-place for his own pride and irritability, instead of seeking to borrow a new and unnecessary stimulus from the busy exploits and over-wrought feelings of others. His Lordship's genius is a spirit of necromancy or of misanthropy, not of humanity. He is governed by antipathies more than by sympathies; but the genius of dramatic poetry is like charity which 'endureth much, is patient, and by humbling itself, is exalted.' Lord Byron, for instance, sympathizes readily with Dante, who was a poet, a patriot, a noble Florentine, and exile from his country: he can describe the feelings of Dante, for in so doing, he does little more than describe his own: he makes nothing out of Marino Faliero, Doge of Venice, and cares nothing about him, for he himself is neither a warrior, a statesman, nor a conspirator. Lord Byron can gaze with swimming eyes upon any of the great lights of Italy, and view them through the misty, widespread glory of lengthening centuries: that is, he can take a high and romantic interest in them, as they appear to us and to him; but he cannot take an historical event in her annals, transport us to the time and place of action, give us a real, living interest in the scene, and by filling the mind with the agonizing hopes, and panic-fears, and incorrigible will, and sudden projects of the authentic actors in the world's volume, charm us out of ourselves, and make us forget that there are such half-faced fellows as readers, authors, or critics in existence. Lord Byron's page has not this effect; it is modern, smooth, fresh from Mr. Murray's, and does not smack of the olden time. It is not rough, Gothic, pregnant with past events, unacquainted with the present time, glowing with the spirit of that dark and fiery age: but strewn with the flowers of poetry and the tropes of rhetoric. The author does not try to make us *overhear* what old Faliero, and his young wife, and his wily, infuriated accomplices would say, but makes them his proxies to discuss the topics of love and marriage, the claims of rank and common justice, or to describe a scene by moonlight, with a running allusion to the pending controversy between his Lordship, Mr. Bowles, and Mr. Campbell, on the merits of the natural and artificial style in poetry. 'That was not the way' of our first tragic writers, nor is it (thank God) that of some of the last. 'One touch of nature makes the whole world kin:'—one line of Webster, Decker, or Ford (to say nothing of Shakspeare), is worth all the didactic and descriptive paraphrases of what would neither be seen nor felt by men in a state of strong agitation as they occur in this play. We cannot call to mind, after reading it, a single electric shock of passion; not a spark of genius struck out of the immediate occasion, like fire out of the flint; not one revelation of our inmost nature, forced from the rack of restless circumstance. But this is all that is truly dramatic in any tragedy or poem: the rest is but a form of words, an imposing display of ingenuity, or understanding, or fancy, which the writer (however excellent he may be in any of these respects) might as well or much better make in his own person. We think most highly of Lord Byron's powers 'on this side of idolatry'; but we do not think those powers are dramatic, nor can we regard the present work as a splendid exception to that general opinion.

—William Hazlitt, "Lord Byron's Tragedy of
Marino Faliero," London Magazine, May 1821

FRANCIS JEFFREY (1821)

Jeffrey is unusually critical of Byron's drama *Marino Faliero*. He regards it as artificial and views the characters as unnatural, despite the fact that the play is based on a historical source.

This piece has undoubtedly considerable beauties, both dramatic and poetical; and might have made the fortune of any young aspirant after fame. But the name of Byron raises expectations which are not so easily satisfied; and, judging of it by the lofty standard which he himself has established, we are compelled to say, that we cannot but regard it as a failure, both as a Poem and a Play. This may be partly accounted for, from the inherent difficulty of uniting these two sorts of excellence—of confining the daring and digressive genius of poetry within the forms and limits of a regular drama, and, at the same time, impartial its warm and vivifying spirit to the practical preparation and necessary details of a complete theatrical action. These, however, are difficulties with which dramatic adventurers have long had to struggle; and over which, though they are incomparably most formidable to the most powerful spirits, there is no reason to doubt that the powers of Lord Byron would have triumphed.

The true history of his failure, therefore, we conceive, and the actual cause of his miscarriage on the present occasion, is to be found in the bad choice of his subject—his selection of a story which not only gives no scope to the peculiar and commanding graces of his genius, but runs continually counter to the master currents of his fancy. His great gifts, as all the world knows, are exquisite tenderness and demoniacal sublimity—the power of conjuring up at pleasure those delicious visio-of Jove and beauty, and pity and purity, which melt our hearts within us with a thrilling and etherial softness—and of wielding, at the same time, that infernal fire which blasts and overthrows all things with the dark and capricious fulminations of its scorn, rancour, and revenge. With the consciousness of these great powers, and as if in wilful perversity to their suggestions, he has here chosen a story winch, in a great measure, excludes the agency of either; and resolutely conducted it, so as to secure himself against their intrusion;—a story without love or hatred—misanthropy or pity—containing nothing voluptuous and nothing terrific—but depending, for its grandeur, on the anger of a very old and irritable man—and, for its attraction, on the elaborate representations of conjugal dignity and domestic honour,—the sober and austere triumphs of cold and untempted chastity, and the noble propriety of a pure and disciplined understanding. These, we think, are not the most promising themes for any writer whose business is to raise powerful emotions—nor very likely, in any hands, to redeem the modern drama from the imputation of want of spirit, interest and excitement. But for Lord Byron to select them for a grand dramatic effort, is as if a swift-footed racer were to tie his feet together at the starting, or a valiant knight to enter the lists without his arms. No mortal prowess could succeed under such disadvantages. Amadis himself when he laid aside his enchanted sword and his helmet of proof, was only a very strong man, and no way fit for the encounter of giants bid dragons; and Lord Byron, without his bitters and his sweets, his softness and horrors, is only a very bold and clever writer—withal somewhat clumsy and verbose.

The story, in so far as it is original in our drama, is extremely improbable; though, like most other very improbable stories, derived from authentic sources: But, in the main, it is [un]original—being indeed merely another *Venice Preserved*, and continually recalling, though certainly without eclipsing, the memory of the first. Except that Jaffier is driven to join the conspirators by the natural impulse of love and misery, and the Doge by a resentment so outrageous as to exclude all sympathy—and that the disclosure, which is produced by love in the old play, is here ascribed to mere friendship, the general action and catastrophe of the two pieces are almost identical—while, with regard to the writing and management, it must be owned that, if Lord Byron has most sense and vigour, Otway has by far the most passion and bathos; and that, though his conspirators are better orators and reasoners than the gang of Pierre and Reynault, the tenderness of Belvidera is as much more touching, as it is more natural than the stoical and self-satisfied decorum of Angiolina. But lest some of our readers may not have read the play through, it may be as well to preface the rest of our remarks with a short abstract of it. . . .

This naked outline, we confess, gives no great information as to the merits of the piece; and it is fair, therefore, to let the reader a little more into its details. The first scenes represent, rather tediously, the Doge waiting impatiently for the sentence of the Senate, and raving very extravagantly at its lenity. We think all this part very heavily and even unskilfully executed; nor can it be at all surprising that ordinary reader should not enter into his Highness's fury; when it appears that even his nephew does not at first understand it. This dutiful person comments thus calmly on the matter, in a speech which, though set down by Lord Byron in lines of ten syllables, we shall take the liberty to print as prose—which it undoubtedly is—and very ordinary and homely prose too.

> *Ber. Fal.* I cannot but agree with you, the sentence is too slight for the offence. It is not honourable in the Forty to affix so slight a penalty to that which was a foul affront to you, and even to them, as being your subjects; but 'tis not yet without remedy: you can appeal to them once more, or to the Avogadori, who seeing that true justice is withheld, will now take up the cause they once declined,

> and do you right upon the bold delinquent. Think you not thus,
> good uncle? why do you stand so fixed?

... As a play, it is deficient in the attractive passions, in probability, and in depth and variety of interest; and revolts throughout, by the extravagant disproportion which the injury bears to the unmeasured resentment with which it is pursued. As a poem, though it occasionally displays great force and elevation, it obviously wants both grace and facility. The diction is often heavy and cumbrous, and the versification without sweetness or elasticity. It is generally very verbose, and sometimes exceedingly dull. Altogether, it gives us the impression of a thing worked out against the grain, and not poured forth from the fulness of the heart or the fancy—the ambitious and elaborate work of a powerful mind engaged with an unsuitable task—not the spontaneous effusion of an exuberant imagination, sporting in the fulness of its strength. Every thing is heightened and enforced with visible effort and design; and the noble author is often contented to be emphatic by dint of exaggeration, and eloquent by the common topics of declamation. Lord Byron is, undoubtedly, a poet of the very first order—and has talents to reach the very highest honours of the drama. But he must not again disdain love and ambition and jealousy—he must not substitute what is merely *bizarre* and extraordinary, for what is naturally and universally interesting—nor expect, by any exaggerations, so to rouse and rule our sympathies by the senseless anger of an old man, and the prudish proprieties of an untempted woman, as by the agency of the great and simple passions with which, in some of their degrees, all men are familiar, and by which alone the Dramatic Muse has hitherto wrought her miracles.

To this very long play there is subjoined, in the volume before us, but short Cantos of a larger projected poem, called *The Prophecy of Dante,* which seems to be written far more from the impulse of the author's soul, and with ten times more good will to the work, than the tragedy which stands before it. It is a very grand, fervid, turbulent, and somewhat mystical composition—full of the highest sentiments, and the highest poetry;—but disfigured by many faults of precipitation, and overclouded with many obscurities. Its great fault with common readers will be, that it is not sufficiently intelligible, either in its general drift or in particular passages;—and even those who are qualified to enter into its spirit, and can raise themselves to the height of the temper in which it is conceived, will be entitled to complain of the interminable periods and endless interlacings of the diction, and of the general crudity and imperfect concoction of the bulk of the composition. It is however, beyond all question, the work of a man of great genius; and if he would only digest his matter a little more carefully, and somewhat concentrate the potent spirit of poetry which he has here poured abroad so lavishly in its unrectified state, we have no doubt that he might produce something that would command universal admiration, and not merely confirm, but extend the great fame he has already acquired.

—Francis Jeffrey, from his unsigned review of
Marino Faliero, Edinburgh Review, July 1821,
issued September 1821, XXXV, pp. 271–285

Reginald Heber (1822)

Reginald Heber (1783–1826), a clergyman and man of letters, was appointed bishop of Calcutta in late 1822. Here, he attacks Byron's attempt to recreate a neoclassical drama.

Several years have passed away since we undertook the review of any of Lord Byron's Poetry. Not that we have been inattentive observers of that genius whose fertility is, perhaps, not the least extraordinary of its characteristics, of whose earlier fruits we were among the first and warmest eulogists, and whose later productions—though hardly answering the expectation which he once excited—would have been, of themselves, sufficient to establish the renown of many scores of ordinary writers. Far less have we been able to witness, without deep regret and disappointment, the systematic and increasing prostitution of those splendid talents to the expression of feelings, and the promulgation of opinions, which, as Christians, as Englishmen, and even as men, we were constrained to regard with abhorrence. But it was from this very conflict of admiration and regret;—this recollection of former merits and sense of present degradation;—this reverence for talent and scorn of sophistry, that we remained silent. The little effect which our advice had, on former occasions, produced, still further tended to confirm us in our silence,—a silence of which the meaning could hardly, as we conceived, be misunderstood, and which we wished Lord Byron himself to regard as an appeal, of not the least impressive kind,—to his hotter sense and taste and feelings. We trusted that he would himself, ere long, discover that wickedness was not strength, nor impiety courage, nor licentiousness warmheartedness, nor an aversion to his own country philosophy; and that riper years, and a longer experience, and a deeper knowledge of his own heart, and a more familiar acquaintance with that affliction to which all are heirs, and those religious principles by which affliction is turned into a blessing, would render him not only almost but altogether such a poet as virgins might read, and Christians praise, and Englishmen take pride in.

With these feelings we have altogether abstained from noticing those strange, though often beautiful productions, which, since the appearance of the Third part of his *Childe Harold,* have flowed on, wave after wave, redundant as that ocean which Lord Byron loves to describe, but with few exceptions, little less monotonous,—and stained, in succession, with deeper and yet deeper tokens of those pollutions, which, even in the full tide of genius, announce that its ebb is near. We knew not any severity of criticism which could reach the faults or purify the taste of *Don Juan,* and we trusted that its author would himself, ere long, discover, that if he continued to write such works as these, he would lose the power of producing any thing better, and that his pride, at least, if not his principle, would recall him from the island of Acrasia.

In this hope we have not been disappointed. Whatever may be the other merits of his tragedies, on the score of morals they are unimpeachable. His females, universally, are painted in truer and worthier colours than we have been accustomed to witness from his pencil, and the qualities which he holds up, in his other characters, to admiration and to pity, are entirely unmingled with those darker and disgusting tints, from which even *Childe Harold* was not free, and which he appears to have thought necessary to excite an interest in such characters as Manfred, Lara, Alp, and the Giaour. Even the *Mystery of Cain,* wicked as it may be, is the work of a nobler and more daring wickedness than that which delights in insulting the miseries, and stimulating the evil passions, and casting a cold-blooded ridicule over all the lofty and generous feelings of our nature: and it is better that Lord Byron should be a manichee, or a deist,—nay, we would almost say, if the thing were possible, it is better that he should be a moral and argumentative atheist, than the professed and systematic poet of seduction, adultery and incest; the contemner of patriotism, the insulter of piety, the raker into every sink of vice and wretchedness to disgust and degrade and harden the hearts of his fellow-creatures. The speculations of a Hume and a D'Alembert may be the objects of respectful regret and pity, while the *Pucelle* is regarded with unmingled contempt and detestation. The infidel *may* be, the adversary of good morals *cannot* be, under a mistake as to the tendency of his doctrines.

Nor is this our only motive for returning at length to the examination of Lord Byron's writings. In his *Cain* he professes to reason, (with how much or how little success is nothing to the purpose,) but his appeal is made to the reason as well as to the passions of his readers. To remove, in his own instance, the difficulties by which he is perplexed, would indeed be a triumph beyond our expectations, but now that, by circumstances which Lord Byron himself could not foresee,—those speculations which he designed for the educated ranks alone, are thrown open to the gaze of the persons most likely to be influenced by them, and disseminated, with remorseless activity, among the young, the ignorant, and the poor,—by the efforts of the basest and most wicked faction that ever infested a christian country,—we are not only-justified but compelled by every sense of duty and of charity, to unmask the sophisms which lurk under his poetical language; and to show how irrelevant to the truths of natural and revealed religion are those apparent irregularities in the present course of things, which he makes his objection to the being or the benignity of the Creator. With these feelings,—very different from each other, but either of which would be sufficient to warrant an interruption of our late silence,—we undertake the review of his Tragedies and his *Cain* . . .

Marino Faliero has, we believe, been pretty generally pronounced a failure by the public voice, and we see no reason to call for a revision of their sentence. It contains, beyond all doubt, many passages of commanding eloquence and some of genuine poetry, and the scenes, more particularly, in which Lord Byron has neglected the absurd creed of his pseudo-Hellenic writers, are conceived and elaborated with great tragic effect and dexterity. But the subject is decidedly ill-chosen. In the main tissue of the plot and in all the busiest and most interesting parts of it, it is, in fact, no more than another *Venice Preserved,* in which the author has had to contend (nor has he contended successfully) with our recollections of a former and deservedly popular play on the same subject. And the only respect in which it differs is, that the Jaffier of Lord Byron's plot is drawn in to join the conspirators, not by the natural and intelligible motives of poverty, aggravated by the sufferings of a beloved wife, and a deep and well-grounded resentment of oppression, but by his outrageous anger for a private wrong of no very atrocious nature. The Doge of Venice, to chastize the vulgar libel of a foolish boy, attempts to overturn that republic of which he is the first and most trusted servant; to massacre all his ancient friends and fellow-soldiers, the magistracy and nobility of the land. With such a resentment as this, thus simply stated and taken singly, who ever sympathized, or who but Lord Byron would have expected in such a cause to be able to awaken sympathy? It is little to the purpose to say that this is all historically true. A thing may be true without being probable, and such a case of idiosyncrasy as is implied in a resentment so sudden and extravagant, is no more a fitting subject for the poet than an animal with two heads would be for an artist of a different description. . . .

Nor is it in the plot only, thus curtailed and crippled of what would have been its due proportions, that we think we can trace the injurious effects of Lord Byron's continental prejudices and his choice of injudicious models. We trace them in the uniform and unbending severity of his diction, no less than in the abruptness of his verse, which has all the harshness though not all the vigour of Alfieri, and which, instead of that richness and variety of cadence which distinguishes even the most careless of our elder dramatists, is often only distinguishable from prose by the unrelenting uniformity with which it is divided into decasyllabic portions. The sentence of the College of Justice, in the first act, was likely indeed to be prosaic; and Shakspeare and our other elder tragedians would have given it as bona fide prose, without that affectation (for which however Lord Byron has many precedents in modern times) which condemns letters, proclamations, the speeches of the vulgar, and the outcries of the rabble and the soldiery, to strut in the same precise measure with the lofty musings and dignified resentment of the powerful and the wise. But Bertuccio Faliero might as well have spoken poetry; and it might have been hoped and expected that the Doge himself, in the full flood-tide of his passion and his wrongs, should express himself in more vigorous terms than these:

> I sought not, *wished* not, *dreamed* not the election,
> Which reached me first at Rome, and I obeyed,—
> But found on my arrival, that, besides
> The jealous vigilance which always led you
> To mock and mar your sovereign's best intents,
> You had, even in the interregnum of
> My journey to the capital, curtail'd
> And mutilated the few privileges
> Yet left the Duke.

One source of feebleness in the foregoing passage, and it is one of frequent occurrence in all Lord Byron's plays, is his practice of ending his lines with insignificant monosyllables. 'Of' 'to,' 'and,' 'till' 'but' 'from' all occur in the course of a very few pages, in situations where, had the harmony or vigour of the line been consulted, the voice would have been allowed to pause, and the energy of the sentiment would have been carried to its highest tone of elevation. This we should have set down to the account of carelessness, had it not been so frequent, and had not the stiffness and labour of the author's general style almost tempted us to believe it systematic. A more inharmonious system of versification, or one more necessarily tending to weight and feebleness, could hardly have been invented. . . .

On the whole the Doge of Venice is the effect of a powerful and cultivated mind. It has all the requisites of tragedy, sublimity, terror and pathos—all but that without which the rest are unavailing, interest! With many detached passages which neither derogate from Lord Byron's former fame, nor would have derogated from the reputation of our best ancient tragedians, it is, as a whole, neither sustained nor impressive. The poet, except in the soliloquy of Leoni, scarcely ever seems to have written with his own thorough good liking. He may be suspected throughout to have had in his eye some other model than nature; and we rise from his work with the same feeling as if we had been reading a translation. For this want of interest the subject itself is doubtless in some measure to blame, though, if the same subject had been differently treated, we are inclined to believe a very different effect would have been produced. But for the constraint and stiffness of the poetry, we have nothing to blame but the apparent resolution of its author to set (at whatever risk) an example of classical correctness to his uncivilized countrymen, and rather to forego success than to succeed after the manner of Shakspeare.

—Reginald Heber, from his unsigned review of
Marino Faliero, Sardanapalus, The Two Foscari,
and *Cain, Quarterly Review,* July 1822,
XXVII, pp. 476–524

JOHN NICHOL (1880)

The Scottish man of letters John Nichol (1833–1894) was, along with Swinburne and others, a founder of the Old Mortality Society, which promoted the discussion of literature. In 1862, he became professor of English literature at Glasgow University.

Byron seems to have been sincere in saying he did not intend any of his plays to be represented. We are more inclined to accuse him of self-deception when he asserts that he did not mean them to be popular; but he took sure means to prevent them from being so. *Marino Faliero,* in particular, was pronounced by Dr. John Watkins—old Grobius himself—"to be the dullest of dull plays;" and even the warmest admirers of the poet had to confess that the style was cumbrous. The story may be true, but it is none the less unnatural. The characters are comparatively commonplace, the women especially being mere shadows; the motion is slow; and the inevitable passages of fine writing are, as the extolled soliloquy of Lioni, rather rhetorical than imaginative. The speeches of the Doge are solemn, but prolix, if not ostentatious, and—perhaps the vital defect—his cause fails to enlist our sympathies. Artistically, this play was Byron's most elaborate attempt to revive the unities and other restrictions of the severe style, which, when he wrote, had been "vanquished in literature."

"I am persuaded," he writes in the preface, "that a great tragedy is not to be produced by following the old dramatists, who are full of faults, but by producing regular dramas like the Greeks." He forgets that the statement in the mouth of a Greek dramatist that his play was not intended for the stage, would have been a confession of failure; and that Aristotle had admitted that even the Deity could not make the Past present.

—John Nichol, *Byron*, 1880, pp. 138–139

CAIN

Byron's "closet play," *Cain, A Mystery* was published in 1822 and immediately labeled blasphemous by several critics. It was attacked even by Hobhouse and Blake, yet celebrated and admired by Sir Walter Scott and Thomas Moore. Readers often identified Lucifer as the mouthpiece of Byron and accused him of Manicheism: a dualistic religious system dealing with opposing forces of darkness and light. The play renders the story of Abel and Cain from the point of view of Cain and is strongly influenced by Milton's *Paradise Lost*, the defiance of Cain mirroring Lucifer's.

JOHN CAM HOBHOUSE (1821)

[28 October 1821] Return to Murray, the publisher, the proofs of *Cain,* a poem by Lord Byron. Burdett and I read this poem. I think it has scarce one specimen of real poetry or even musical numbers in it. He says in a letter to Kinnaird that it is written in his purest metaphysical manner. Some will call it blasphemous, and I think the whole world will finally agree in thinking it unworthy. Yet I hear T. Moore says it is the best thing Byron ever wrote.

[17 November 1821] I lately wrote a letter to Lord Byron remonstrating in the strongest terms against his publishing *Cain,* which appears to me a complete failure.

—John Cam Hobhouse, extracts from his diary,
Recollections of a Long Life, ed. Lady Dorchester,
1909–11, II, pp. 172–173

THOMAS MOORE (1821)

The Irish poet and author of the popular *Irish Melodies* and the poem *Lalla Rookh,* Moore (1779–1852) had become Byron's close friend. In a letter to Byron from September 30, 1821, he registers his enthusiasm for *Cain.*

I have read *Foscari* and *Cain*. The former does not please me so highly as *Sardanapalus*. It has the fault of all those violent Venetian stories, being unnatural and improbable, and therefore, in spite of all your fine management of them, appealing but remotely to one's sympathies. But *Cain* is wonderful—terrible—never to be forgotten. If I am not mistaken, it will sink deep into the world's heart; and while many will shudder at its blasphemy, all must fall prostrate before its grandeur. Talk of Aeschylus and his Prometheus!—here is the true spirit both of the Poet—and the Devil.

—Thomas Moore, *The Letters of Thomas Moore,*
ed. Wilfred S. Dowden, 1964, II, pp. 494–495

WALTER SCOTT (1821)

Scott accepts Byron's proposal to dedicate *Cain* to him and defends the author against the accusation of Manicheism.

My Dear Sir,—I accept with feelings of great obligation the flattering proposal of Lord Byron to prefix my name to the very grand and tremendous drama of *Cain*. I may be partial to it, and you will allow I have cause; but I do not know that his Muse has ever taken so lofty a flight amid her former soarings. He has certainly matched Milton on his own ground. Some part of the language is bold, and may shock one class of readers, whose tone will be adopted by others out of affectation or envy. But then they must condemn the *Paradise Lost,* if they have a mind to be consistent. The fiend-like reasoning and bold blasphemy of the fiend and of his pupil, lead exactly to the point which was to be expected—the commission of the first murder, and the ruin and despair of the perpetrator.

I do not see how any one can accuse the author himself of Manicheism. The devil takes the language of that sect, doubtless; because, not being able to deny the existence of the Good Principle, he endeavours to exalt himself—the Evil Principle—to a seeming equality with the Good; but such arguments, in the mouth of such a being, can only be used to deceive and to betray. Lord Byron might have made this more evident, by placing in the mouth of Adam, or of some good and protecting spirit, the reasons which render the existence of moral evil consistent with the general benevolence of the Deity. The great key to the mystery is, perhaps, the imperfection of our own faculties, which see and feel strongly the partial evils which press upon us, but know too little of the general system of the universe, to be aware how the existence of these is to be reconciled with the benevolence of the great Creator.

> —Walter Scott, extract from a letter of
> December 17, 1821, to John Murray,
> *The Letters of Sir Walter Scott*, VII, pp. 37–38

Unsigned (1821)

The anonymous reviewer in the supplement to the *Gentleman's Magazine* for July–December 1821 (XCI, ii, pp. 613–615), expresses his disgust at Byron's *Cain* and presents extracts under the headings of "Hideous Blasphemy" and "Twaddle and Nonsense."

This is unquestionably one of the most pernicious productions that ever proceeded from the pen of a man of genius. It is in fact neither more nor less than a series of wanton libels upon the Supreme Being and His attributes. If the slanderer of a fellow mortal deserve reprobation and punishment, what ought to be the penalty of the calumniator of his omnipotent Maker, the miserable traducer of his God. If any additional fame can attach to Lord Byron from this odious "Mystery", it can be none other than an immortality of infamy.

> —Unsigned, review from *Gentleman's Magazine*,
> July–December 1821, XCI, ii, pp. 613–615

Mary Shelley (1821)

Mary Shelley (1797–1851) was the wife of Percy Shelley and the author of *Frankenstein*. In a letter of December 20, 1821, she tells Maria Gisborne about the effect *Cain* had on her.

My Lord is now living very sociably, giving dinners to his male acquaintance and writing divinely; perhaps by this time you have seen *Cain* and will agree with us in thinking it his finest production—To me it sounds like a revelation—of some works one says—one has thought of such things though one could not have expresscd it so well—It is not this with *Cain*—one has perhaps stood on the extreme verge of such ideas and from the midst of the darkness which has surrounded us the voice of the Poet now is heard telling a wondrous tale.

> —Mary Shelley, *The Letters of Mary Shelley*,
> edited by Frederick L. Jones, 1944, University of
> Oklahoma Press, vol. I, p. 153, ll. 13–20

PERCY BYSSHE SHELLEY (1822)

Here, Shelley comments on Byron's play in various letters to John Gisborne.

January 12, 1822

What think you of Lord Byron now? Space wondered less at the swift and fair creations of God, when he grew weary of vacancy, than I at the late works of this spirit of an angel in the mortal paradise of a decaying body. So I think—let the world envy while it admires, as it may.

January 26, 1822

What think you of Lord Byron's last Volume? In my opinion it contains finer poetry than has appeared in England since the publication of *Paradise Regained*. —*Cain* is apocalyptic—it is a revelation not before communicated to man.

June 18, 1822

I write little now. It is impossible to compose except under the strong excitement of an assurance of finding sympathy in what you write. Imagine Demosthenes reciting a Philippic to the waves of the Atlantic! Lord Byron is in this respect fortunate. He touched a chord to which a million hearts responded, and the coarse music which he produced to please them disciplined him to the perfection which he now approaches.

—Percy Bysshe Shelley, ed. F.L. Jones,
1964, II, pp. 376, 388, 436

HENRY CRABB ROBINSON (1822)

I called at Aders's and came home early to read *Cain,* which I finished the next day. *Cain* has not advanced any novelties in the author's speculations on the origin of evil, but he has stated one or two points with great effect. The book is calculated to spread infidelity by furnishing a ready expression to difficulties which must occur to every one, more or less, and which are passed over by those who confine themselves to scriptural representations. The second act is full of poetic energy, and there is some truth of passion in the scenes between Cain's wife and himself. It is certainly a mischievous work calculated to do nothing but harm.

—Henry Crabb Robinson, extract from
diary entry for March 1, 1822, in *Henry Crabb
Robinson on Books and their Writers,*
ed. E.J. Morley, 1938, 1, 281

UNSIGNED (1822)

The anonymous reviewer of *Cain* and Southey's *Vision of Judgement* accuses Byron of infamy and morbidity.

He has summoned both fiction and falsehood to aggravate the philosophical difficulties which he, in this poem, has laboured to embalm in verse; difficulties new to a large proportion of his readers, and with which the young and inexperienced are ill able to grapple. These, this new apostle of infidelity has endeavoured to propagate in a shape the most adapted to make an impression on the imagination. In the very spirit of the fabled Sphinx, he propounds these dark enigmas, that those who fail to unravel them, may perish.

That this is a heinous offence against society, who will dare deny? It is an offence of the deepest dye.

—Unsigned, from *Eclectic Review,*
May 1822, N.S., XVII, pp. 418–427

OXONIENSIS (H.J. TODD) (1822)

As a bookseller, I conclude you have but one standard of poetic excellence;— the extent of your sale. Without assuming any thing beyond the bounds of ordinary foresight, I venture to foretell, that in this case you will be mistaken; the book will disappoint your cupidity, as much as it discredits your feeling and discretion. Your noble employer has deceived you, Mr. Murray; he has profited by the celebrity of his name to palm upon you obsolete trash, the very off-scourings of Bayle and Voltaire, which he has made you pay for, as though it were first rate poetry and sound metaphysics. But I tell you (and if you doubt it, you may consult any of the literary gentlemen who frequent your reading room) that this poem, this Mystery with which you have insulted us, is nothing more than a Cento from Voltaire's novels and the most objectionable articles in Bayle's Dictionary, served up in clumsy cuttings of ten syllables, for the purpose of giving it the guise of poetry. . . .

He seems to have been possessed of all the gifts of nature and fortune, only that he might prove how vain such possessions are to those who know not how to use them rightly.

He was gifted with the highest intellectual talents, but he has "profaned this God-given strength" to the worst purposes: he was born a Briton, and inherited the honours and privileges of a class to which the proudest might have been proud to belong, yet when does he allude to his country or her institutions, without an expression of scorn or hatred? He did not scruple to contract the most solemn obligations which society can impose, and which usually call into exercise the tenderest feelings of our nature; those feelings he has wilfully thrown from him, and trampled on the ties from which they sprung: and now at last he quarrels with the very conditions of humanity, rebels against that Providence which guides and governs all things, and dares to adopt the language which had never before been attributed to any being but one, "Evil be thou my good." Such as far as we can judge is Lord Byron.

—Oxoniensis (the Reverend H.J. Todd),
A Remonstrance addressed to Mr. John Murray,
respecting a Recent Publication, 1822,
pp. 9–10, 18–19

LEIGH HUNT "A LETTER ON CAIN TO THE READERS OF THE EXAMINER" (1822)

For the radical Leigh Hunt, the acceptance or rejection of *Cain* became a touchstone of liberal thought.

You must have been much edified by the sensation which this poem has made. The civil authorities would rather say nothing about it: the religious cannot say anything fairly; and the critical are exceedingly hampered betwixt the two. . . .

The truth is simply this: The Jews, like many other nations, in endeavouring to account for the difficulties in the government of the world, put forth some apologues; and because these apologues have been incorporated with the books which the Christians account sacred, the latter, though the very essence of their religion consists in going counter to the Jews, think it their business to uphold them in every particular, and to find in them nothing but morality, right reason, and perfection. When I speak thus of the apologues in question, I do not mean to undervalue them in some respects. On the contrary, some of them appear to me very beautiful, as a sort of imperfect illustration, particularly the account of the Fall of Man, of that loss of a sense of innocence, which is generated by the subtle and wise absurdity of finding guilt where there is none. There is a very deep sentiment in it. But the worst of this and of other apologues is, that they are not complete in all their members. They give the Supreme Being a part in them: *the God of the apologue becomes in time identified with the Great First Cause of all things;* and, at last, even in ages of extreme civilization, if you do not take the letter of the story for the very essence of the Divine Spirit and its intentions, you are thought guilty of a daring impiety. Whereas it may be your very piety that prevents you. For instance; the Goths were of opinion that God drank mead with you in heaven out of the sculls of your enemies. Now though the Divine Principle includes small as well as great in its operations, yet if the Goths were extant still in any other shape than those of the Allied Governments, and I could go among them with my present opinions, I could never be brought to think that it would concentrate and infinitely diminish itself into the likeness of a Vandal Chieftain, and sit at table with me over the above liquor. If this is thought an irreverend instance, it is the fault of those who force one to bring such incompatible ideas together. I mean no irreverence, or I could have put the thing in a much more ridiculous light. By the same rule, if I were a Turk or a Persian, nothing could induce me to persuade myself that the Divine Principle had had those personal conferences with Mahomet, and given him a written license to have more wives than any one else. If I were a Hindoo, I should more than doubt the celestial origin of the injunctions about paring my nails, cooking my rice, and turning to the south-east when I put on my clothes. And to return to the Jews, if I were a Jew, I should have an exceeding scepticism about the trouble which the Great First Cause took to regulate the ornaments of the ark and temple, settling how many knobs there should be on this and that piece of furniture, and taking other strange delights in the borders. All this, I grant, may have had its uses. The Great Being in question (if we must use human terms in speaking of its mode of action) has at all events permitted it. It has taken place. But so have thousands of other things and trifles. So has the Pagan religion: so have the bishops' wigs; but we are not bound to have faith in either. I once more deprecate the idea of willingly bringing together two such incompatible subjects of contemplation, as the Divine Mystery of the Universe, and these toys of priestly invention. And again I say it is not my fault. Not that I presume to judge of the Divine feelings by those of the petty authorities of this earth, and conclude, that because a king or a clergyman cannot put up with a jest, the Supreme Being is equally unable to afford it. There are other reasons, and much more reverential ones, why they should not drive us upon these ludicrous inconsistencies. But let the anti-judaical defenders of Judaism, and the believers in eternal punishment, think as they may, no man is more inclined than myself to be grave on the subject of that mighty and beneficent Power, which has been so much degraded by the self-love and bad passions of creeds and sects under the title of God; so much so indeed, that one wishes one could give it some other name without hurting the feelings of the truly pious. If I cannot help smiling, and if others cannot help a movement of indignation, when people attribute to it all their little fugitive tastes and their more pernicious bigotries, a third time I say the fault belongs solely to the latter. Men of my way of thinking would identify with it nothing but love and joy, and the beauties of nature, and the bringing of good out of stubborn materials, and the great principle (whatever it be) of universal motion, and those energies of the better part of mankind, which, for aught we know to the contrary, are only so many experiments of its very self, trying how far it can extend itself, and take our nature along with it. Why are these aspirations to be diverted by the petty dogmas of theologians and critics, who, under pretence of enlarging and settling one's notions of the Divinity, only narrow, and confuse, and barbarize them?

Why murder and other evils came into the world to disturb the otherwise beneficent results of our passions, is a great mystery. But if philosophy cannot explain it, otherwise than as a portion of the stubborn materials above mentioned, our passions themselves can still less explain it; and yet it was with nothing better that the Jews undertook to do so. Fontenelle, in one of those apparently profane speeches which have often more piety at bottom than some of our most orthodox sentiments, said, that if God had made man in his own likeness, man had returned the compliment by making him in his. Yet nothing can be more true. Nations have made their gods according to their own tempers: individuals continue to do the same. If we were suffered to regard the account of Cain and Abel as a mere apologue, or as one of those poetical traditions which might mingle with the early history of all nations, or even as what it really appears to be, a semi-barbarous, semi-philosophical attempt to account for part of the origin of evil, it would be all very well; but by confounding the God of an eastern fable with the God of the Universe, and attributing to him the half-reasoning passions and the crude notions of morality and punishment which belong to the first stages of civilization, we do a number of very foolish things. In the first place, we give no real explanation of the mystery at all, but merely make passions account for passions: secondly, we make God the merest of men, even in his notions of justice: thirdly, we encourage ourselves in our own false notions of it; and fourthly, when better opinions arise by dint of experience and enquiry, we enable the bigoted to oppose us, and hinder the timid from siding with us, by making piety itself appear impious;—that is to say, by making it appear an impious thing to shew the wide difference between the vulgar idea of God, and the nobler one.

If the Jews, in the story of Cain and Abel, merely intended to shew the unhappy consequences of envy and murder, they made a very affecting apologue; imperfect, it is true, as far as they introduced the Divine Being, but very touching nevertheless; and, if you could keep the imperfect part of it out of sight, very useful. But this is impossible as men grow wiser, and require more complete and consistent lessons of justice: and it becomes worse than impossible, if they are then to be told, that they are impious for not liking to see modes of jurisprudence attributed to God, which their experience and knowledge have taught them to consider as unworthy of men. If they are to have no medium between considering the God of the apologue and the Great Principle of all things as the same being, their next step is to ask how he could be perfectly omnipotent and perfectly good, and yet permit all these evils which he so heavily punished: and again, how he could partake of so many human passions himself: and again, why he did not mend Cain rather than perpetuate his misery, and confirm him in his sullen temper;—how he knew so little of human nature, as not to be aware that extreme punishment went counter to the only utility of punishment, which is improvement. I omit other questions equally obvious but they are all questions which it is impossible to get over, as long as the Deity is thus set on a level with ourselves: nay, they bring us round, in its blankest sense, to the most godless feeling of Atheism, tending to prove that there is no other Deity than what we find in our human nature, the bad parts as well as the good:—whereas, by not playing the hypocrite with those terms of Invisible and Incomprehensible, which we are so fond of using and contradicting, and by sincerely leaving the Divine Nature its mystery, its universality, and its tendency to make the most of the stubborn materials it has to work upon, we leave it in possession of all that renders it truly adorable, and at the same time keep ourselves in that patient and all-endeavouring frame of mind, which, as I observed before, is, for aught we know to the contrary, necessary to the divinest of its own operations among us, and made to carry us along with its very self into ages of we know not what divine improvement. If it is so, how do we not encumber ourselves with these old and half-informed beggings of the question? If it is not so, the belief is at least a good, kind, and patient one; unperplexed with all that worries other systems of religion; quite compatible with the goodness we all wish to believe in; and a promoter of that very spirit of endeavour, which is at all events one of the best principles of human action. . . .

[T]he Cainites, a sect who sprung up in the second century merely out of the perplexities of this single story, and who found it so contradictory to their ideas of justice, that they ran, out of resentment, into a great absurdity. They supposed the God of the Old Testament to be a real malignant principle, who had sown discord in the world, and a injected our nature to a thousand calamities; upon which they concluded, that it was their business to oppose him in every one of his injunctions; which must have brought them into some very ridiculous dilemmas. To 'commit adultery' out of resentment, is bad enough; but how they could have contrived to dishonour their father and mother upon a moral principle,—to steal, out of a virtuous preference,—and to bear false witness against their neighbour, from charity to all mankind,—are difficulties which I leave to those who can reconcile anything,—the theologians. However, it has been well observed, that the instincts of mankind soon contrive to elude the literal injunctions of their respective faiths, except where they are turned into a handle of worldliness. The Cainite, like his neighbour, would soon discover that the natural interests of society, as well as the orders of a religion which he opposed, required him not to be dishonest; and the sect would speedily have fallen to nothing at any time, not only (as it did then) because it ran so Diametrically opposite to all the received opinions, and certainly not because it was hostile to evil, but because not knowing how to separate the evil from the good, and acting in the very spirit to which it objected, it made its inconsistencies appear the greater by holding them up as opposed to inconsistency.

The only real fault to be found with productions like the one before us, is that the poet either compliments or disregards the understandings of his readers a little too much; and by leaving them to gather his actual opinions on the subject for themselves, gives occasion to the weak and the hypocritical to charge him with something of this Cainite spirit. People are led to imagine that he has no other ideas of the Divine Being than the one which his drama puts in so disadvantageous a light; and not being able to take the real meaning of his hint, and work out his conclusion for themselves, they pay their unlucky faith the most unfortunate compliments, and complain bitterly of the atrocious and fiend-like person, who after all only lays before them a vigorous statement of their own proposition. Doubtless, if the ruling Deity were such a being as the advocates of unjust systems and eternal punishment represent him, it would be the duty of every humane disposition and decent mind to be in the most glorious and most awful of all minorities. Their very consciousness of the existence of something nobler in their own hearts would be their warrant and their strength; *that itself* would be a diviner, if not a more powerful, Deity; and who should tell them, if a Heavenly Sovereign is thus to be made out of common despotic matter, that his sovereignty did not in like manner depend upon opinion; and that, in the process of time, the homage fading away, the lonely tyranny must cease? It would be a similar case in one respect, if the Deity were nothing but an imagination of men's minds, and depended entirely upon them for the greater or less divinity with which they invested it. But as the amount of good in the world, that is to say, of ordinary and pleasurable excitement, is much greater than the reverse, (though if it were not, it would take more than bigotry's absurdities to prove that good was not ultimately regarded)—and as it seems impossible for the human mind to get rid of a consciousness of something superior to matter and impulsive of motion, however theologians degrade it and deists are puzzled to define it,—it is desirable in those who would do away false notions of things human and superhuman, not that they should let people fancy them more perplexed on these points than they are, nor that in every instance they should let them draw their own conclusions (which a variety of circumstances may long prevent them from drawing to any good purpose); but that they should frankly state the amount of the common opinion and their own, contrast the two as forcibly and sincerely as possible, and then leave the reader to draw the united conclusions of his heart and understanding. One or two more of Lord Byron's pithy prefatory sentences would have done away every objection on this score, and left to his drama all the effect which it is so well calculated to produce. It is true, he may say that this is not his humour,—not the turn of his genius. I do not think the answer unanswerable; though genius may say a great deal for being left to its impulses. But at all events, if the genius is worth having its omissions supplied by others, others *(ecce signum)* will most likely be found to supply them.

And now to refresh ourselves after these polemics with a little of his Lordship's poetry. Oh the beauty and the benignity of poetry! How it survives all circumstance of discussion, and subject, and contingency, and remains lovely and divine for its own sake! The noble-mindedness which flashes through the darkest and most mistakable parts of this drama, and the character of Adah alone, who makes a god of her affection, would be sufficient to lead thinking and sensitive minds to higher notions of the Deity, than those furnished by an uncivilized people. Although the author's genius is not dramatic in the true sense of the word, that is to say, although he does not so much go out of himself to describe others, as furnish others out of himself, yet this is the most dramatic of all his productions. . . . The magnificent melancholy of the description of Lucifer, when Cain sees him first coming, is worthy of Milton.

—Leigh Hunt, "A Letter on *Cain* to the
Readers of the *Examiner*," *Examiner*,
June 2, 1822, pp. 338–341

WILLIAM BLAKE "THE GHOST OF ABEL" (1822)

The English poet, painter, and printmaker William Blake (1757–1827) was a Swedenborgian mystic and, despite his attacks on orthodox religion, a devout writer. In "The Ghost of Abel," which he dedicated to Byron, he attempts to take on the assertions contained in Byron's *Cain*, which attacked the justice of God.

⟫⟫⟫ ⟫⟫⟫ ⟫⟫⟫

The Ghost of Abel

A Revelation
In the Visions of Jehovah

Seen by William Blake

To LORD BYRON in the Wilderness

What doest thou here Elijah?
Can a Poet doubt the Visions of Jehovah? Nature has no Outline:
but Imagination has. Nature has no Tune: but Imagination has!
Nature has no Supernatural & dissolves: Imagination is Eternity

Scene. A rocky Country. Eve fainted over the dead body of Abel which lays near a Grave. Adam kneels by her Jehovah stands above

Jehovah—Adam!
Adam—I will not hear thee more thou Spiritual Voice
Is this Death?
Jehovah—Adam!
Adam—It is in vain: I will not hear thee
Henceforth! Is this thy Promise that the Womans Seed
Should bruise the Serpents head: Is this the Serpent? Ah!
Seven times, O Eve thou hast fainted over the Dead Ah! Ah!
Eve revives
Eve—Is this the Promise of Jehovah! O it is all a vain delusion
This Death & this Life & this Jehovah!
Jehovah—Woman! lift thine eyes
A Voice is heard coming on
Voice—O Earth cover not thou my Blood! cover not thou my Blood
Enter the Ghost of Abel
Eve—Thou Visionary Phantasm thou art not the real Abel.
Abel—Among the Elohim a Human Victim I wander I am their House
Prince of the Air & our dimensions compass Zenith & Nadir
Vain is thy Covenant O Jehovah I am the Accuser & Avenger

Of Blood O Earth Cover not thou the Blood of Abel
Jehovah—What Vengeance dost thou require
Abel—Life for Life! Life for Life!
Jehovah—He who shall take Cains life must also Die O Abel
And who is he? Adam wilt thou, or Eve thou do this
Adam—It is all a Vain delusion of the all creative Imagination
Eve come away & let us not believe these vain delusions
Abel is dead & Cain slew him! We shall also Die a Death
And then! what then? be as poor Abel a Thought: or as
This! O what shall I call thee Form Divine! Father of
Mercies
That appearest to my Spiritual Vision: Eve seest thou also.
Eve—I see him plainly with my Minds Eye. I see also Abel living:
Tho terribly afflicted as We also are. yet Jehovah sees him
Alive & not Dead: were it not better to believe Vision
With all our might & strength tho we are fallen & lost
Adam—Eve thou hast spoken truly. let us kneel before his feet.
The Kneel before Jehovah
Abel—Are these the Sacrifices of Eternity O Jehovah, a Broken Spirit
And a Contrite Heart. O I cannot Forgive! the Accuser hath
Enterd into Me as into his House & I loathe thy Tabernacles
As thou hast said so is it come to pass: My desire is unto Cain
And He doth rule over Me: therefore My Soul in fumes of Blood
Cries for Vengeance: Sacrifice on Sacrifice Blood on Blood
Jehovah—Lo I have given you a Lamb for an Atonement instead
Of the Transgres[s]or, or no Flesh or Spirit could ever Live
Abel—Compelled I cry O Earth cover not the Blood of Abel
Abel sinks down into the Grave. from which arises Satan
Armed in glittering scales with a Crown & a Spear
Satan—I will have Human Blood & not the blood of Bulls or Goats
And no Atonement O Jehovah the Elohim live on Sacrifice
Of Men: hence I am God of Men: Thou Human O Jehovah.
By the Rock & Oak of the Druid creeping Mistletoe & Thorn
Cains City built with Human Blood, not Blood of Bulls & Goats
Thou shalt Thyself be Sacrificed to Me thy God on Calvary
Jehovah—Such is My Will.
Thunders
that Thou Thyself go to Eternal Death
In Self Annihilation even till Satan Self-subdud Put off Satan
Into the Bottomless Abyss whose torment arises for ever & ever.

On each side a Chorus of Angels entering Sing the following
The Elohim of the Heathen Swore Vengeance for Sin! Then Thou stoodst
Forth O Elohim Jehovah! in the midst of the darkness of the Oath! All Clothed
In Thy Covenant of the Forgiveness of Sins: Death O Holy! Is this Brotherhood
The Elohim saw their Oath Eternal Fire; they rolled apart trembling over The
Mercy Seat: each in his station fixt in the Firmament by Peace Brotherhood
and Love.
The Curtain falls

—William Blake, "The Ghost of Abel"

Reginald Heber (1822)

Reginald Heber (1783–1826) had already rebuked Byron for "a strange
predilection for the worser half of manicheism," in a review of Henry Hart
Milman's *Fall of Jerusalem* (*Quarterly Review*, May 1820, XXIII, p. 225) and the
following review is in the same vein, which Byron rejected.

The drama of *Cain*, Lord Byron himself has thought proper to call a
'Mystery,'—the name which, as is well known, was given in our own country,
before the reformation, to those scenic representations of the mysterious
events of our religion, which, indecent and unedifying as they seem to
ourselves, were, perhaps, the principal means by which a knowledge of those
events was conveyed to our rude and uninstructed ancestors. But, except in
the topics on which it is employed, Lord Byron's Mystery has no resemblance
to those which it claims as its prototypes. These last, however absurd and
indecorous in their execution, were, at least, intended reverently. The
composition now before us, is, unhappily, already too famous for its contrary
character; a character to which we fear it is, in no small degree, indebted for
the celebrity which it has attained, and which, though it certainly is marked
with much of Lord Byron's peculiar talent, its inherent merits would hardly
have secured for it. Of this our readers will judge from the following sketch
on the plot, and from some of the finest and least offensive specimens which
we have been able to select of the poetry and the argument. . . .

To apply the severe rules of criticism to a composition of this kind would
be little better than lost labour. Yet it can hardly fail to strike the reader as a
defect in poetry no less than a departure from history, that the event which
is the catastrophe of the drama is no otherwise than incidentally, we may
say, accidentally, produced by those which precede it. Cain, whose whole
character is represented in scripture as envious and malicious rather than

impious;—this Cain, as painted by Lord Byron, has no quarrel with his brother whatever, nor, except in a single word, does he intimate any jealousy of him. Two acts and half the third are passed without our advancing a single step towards the conclusion; and Abel, at length, falls by a random blow given in a struggle of which the object is not *his* destruction but the overthrow of Jehovah's altar. If we could suppose a reader to sit down to a perusal of the drama in ignorance of its catastrophe, he would scarcely be less surprized by its termination in such a stroke of chance-medley, than if Abel had been made to drop down in an apoplexy, and Cain to die of grief over his body.

Nor is it easy to perceive what natural or rational object the Devil proposes to himself in carrying his disciple through the abyss of space, to show him that repository, of which we remember hearing something in our infant days, 'where the old moons are hung up to dry.' To prove that there is a life beyond the grave was surely no part of his business when he was engaged, in fostering the indignation of one who repined at the necessity of dying. And, though it would seem that entire Hades is, in Lord Byron's picture, a place of suffering, yet, when Lucifer himself had premised that these sufferings were the lot of those spirits who sided with him against Jehovah, is it likely that a more accurate knowledge of them would increase Cain's eagerness for the alliance, or that he would not rather have inquired whether a better fortune did not await the adherents of the triumphant side? At all events, the spectacle of many ruined worlds was more likely to awe a mortal into submission than to rouse him to hopeless resistance; and even if it made him a hater of God, had no natural tendency to render him furious against a brother who was to be his fellow-sufferer.

We do not think, indeed, that there is much vigour or poetical propriety in any of the characters of Lord Byron's Mystery. Eve on one occasion and one only expresses herself with energy, and not even then with any great depth of that maternal feeling which the death of her favourite son was likely to excite in her. Adam moralizes without dignity. Abel is as dull as he is pious. Lucifer, though his first appearance is well conceived, is as sententious and sarcastic as a Scotch metaphysician, and the gravamina which drive Cain into impiety are circumstances which could only produce a similar effect on a weak and sluggish mind, the necessity of exertion and the fear of death! Yet, in the happiest climate of earth and amid the early vigour of nature, it would be absurd to describe (nor has Lord Byron so described it) the toil to which Cain can have been subject, as excessive or burthensome. And he is made too happy in his love, too extravagantly fond of his wife and his child to have much leisure for those gloomy thoughts which belong to disappointed ambition and jaded licentiousness.

Nor, though there are, as we have already shown, some passages in this us drama of no common power, is the general tone of its poetry so excellent as to atone for these imperfections of design. The dialogue is cold and constrained. The descriptions are like the shadows of a phantasmagoria, at once indistinct and artificial. Except Adah, there is in no person in whose fortunes we are interested; and we close the book with no distinct or clinging recollection of any single passage in it, and with the general impression only that Lucifer has said much and done little, and that Cain has been unhappy without grounds and wicked without an object.

But if, as a poem, *Cain* is little qualified to add to Lord Byron's reputation; we are unfortunately constrained to observe that its poetical defects are the very smallest of its demerits. It is not, indeed, as some both of its admirers and its enemies appear to have supposed, a direct attack on Scripture and on the authority of Moses. The expressions of Cain and Lucifer are not more offensive to the ears of piety than such discourses must necessarily be, or than Milton, without offence, has put into the mouths of beings similarly situated. And though the intention is evident which has led the Atheists and Jacobins (the terms are convertible) of our metropolis, to circulate the work in a cheap form, among the populace, we are not ourselves of opinion that it possesses much power of active mischief, or that many persons will be very deeply or lastingly impressed by insinuations which lead to no practical result, and difficulties which so obviously transcend the range of human experience. But it is unhappily certain that, if Lord Byron has not attacked Moses, it is only because his ambition soars higher than to assail any particular creed. The sarcasms of Lucifer and the murmurs of Cain are directed against Providence in general; and proceed to the subversion of every system of theology, except that (if theology it may be called) which holds out God to the abhorrence of his creatures as a capricious tyrant, and which regards the Devil (or under whatever name Lord Byron may chuse to embody the principle of resistance to the Supreme) as the champion of all which is energetic and interesting and noble; the spirit of free thought and stern endurance, unbrokenly contending against the bondage which makes nature miserable.

This deification of vice; this crazy attachment to the worser half of Manicheism, we long since lamented to find (as it even then was tolerably conspicuous) in some of the most powerful lines which have proceeded from Lord Byron's pen; and he has thought proper to express, though in a tone of good tempered expostulation, a degree of displeasure at the freedom with which we then gave vent to our feelings.[1] "We certainly, therefore, did not expect, and were still further removed from *hoping* or *desiring* that he would himself, at length, so unequivocally express those sentiments of which he so much disliked the reputation: but, if we had been anxious to justify the language which we then employed, no further justification could be required than *Cain* has now afforded.

In one respect, it is true, Lord Byron misunderstood us. He supposed that we accused him of '*worshipping* the Devil.' We certainly had, at the time, no particular reason for apprehending that he *worshipped* any thing; and he has himself now taught us, on the best authority which the case admits of, how, by neglecting exterior service to *one* of the rival principles, the other may be virtually honoured. But seriously, if to represent, through three long acts, the Devil as sympathizing with the miseries of mankind and moralizing on the injustice of Providence; if to represent God as the unrelenting tyrant of nature; the capricious destroyer of worlds which he has himself created; the object of open flattery and of secret horror even to the celestial ministers of his will and minstrels of his glory; if this be not to transfer, from God to Satan and from Satan to God, the qualities by which, in the general estimation of mankind, they are most distinguished from each other, we must own ourselves very little skilled in the usual topics of praise or censure.

We should have done an essential wrong, however, to the most celebrated of ancient heretics, if we had designated this system as more than the worser half of the system of Manes. His followers,—though they imputed the prevalence of evil in the world to the inveterate and invincible obstinacy of that principle of darkness, which they supposed to share with God the empire of things, and to pervade and govern all material existence,—confessed, nevertheless, that the superior and supreme Intelligence was transcendantly wise and benevolent. They anticipated, in fullness of faith, the ultimate victory of this last over his malignant enemy, and looked forward to a future state of happiness and glory, where the souls of the good were to be delivered from the God of this world and the bondage of their corporeal prisons. But the theology of *Cain* is altogether gloomy and hopeless. His evil God is *the supreme:* his Hades exclusively a state of misery; the body of man is, on his system, ordained to nothing more than to labour, disease and death, and the soul is immortal only to be wretched.

It is idle to say that this statement is put into the mouth of one who is described in scripture as an evil being, and whose assertions are to be only understood as the ex-parte statement of an insidious enemy.

Of Lucifer, as drawn by Lord Byron, we absolutely know no evil: and, on the contrary, the impression which we receive of him is, from his first introduction, most favourable. He is indued not only with all the beauty, the wisdom and the unconquerable daring which Milton has assigned him, and which may reasonably be supposed to belong to a spirit of so exalted a nature, but he is represented as unhappy without a crime and as pitying our unhappiness. Even before he appears, we are prepared (so far as the poet has had skill to prepare us) to sympathize with any spiritual being who is opposed to the government of Jehovah. The conversations, the exhibitions which ensue are all conducive to the same conclusions, that whatever is is *evil,* and that, had the Devil been the Creator, he would have made his creatures happier. Above all, his arguments and insinuations are allowed to pass uncontradicted, or are answered only by overbearing force, and punishment inflicted not on himself but on his disciple. Nor is the intention less apparent nor the poison less subtle, because the language employed is not indecorous, and the accuser of the Almighty does not descend to ribaldry or scurrilous invective.

That the monstrous creed thus inculcated is really the creed of Lord Byron himself, we, certainly, have some difficulty in believing. As little are we inclined to assert that this frightful caricature of Deism is intended as a covert recommendation of that further stage to which the scepticism of modern philosophers has sometimes conducted them. We are willing to suppose, that he has, after all, no further view than the fantastic glory of supporting a paradox ably; of showing his powers of argument and poetry at the expense of all the religious and natural feelings of the world, and of ascertaining how much will be forgiven him by the unwearied devotion of his admirers. But we cannot, with some of our contemporaries, give him the credit of 'writing conscientiously.' We respect his understanding too highly to apprehend that he intended a benefit to mankind in doing his best to make them vicious and discontented; and we tell him, *'even more in anger than in sorrow,'* that the great talents which he has received are ill employed in writing a libel on his Maker, and that the dexterity which flings about firebrands in sport is no object of ambition to any but a mind perverted by self-opinion and flattery.

We return, however, to *Cain,* and it is some comfort to find that the argument, however plausibly put together, is as infirm and disjointed as poetic arguments are apt to be. It depends on the admitted fact that evil exists, and on the presumption that a wise and benevolent Deity would not have permitted its existence. And it is, consequently, levelled (as we have already observed, and as we must intreat the reader to bear in mind) not against the Mosaic account of the manner in which evil first appeared on earth, (for whenever and however evil manifested itself, the same objection would apply,) but against the God by whom the present frame of things was constituted. It is not the Jehovah only, of the Christian or the Jew, against whom it may be alleged that he has created men to toil, to sicken and to die. If we admit a Creator at all, we must admit that he sends us into the world under this necessity; and any man, with whatever religious opinions, who dislikes these accompaniments of life more than he likes life with its countervailing advantages, may plead with Cain,—

> I was unborn;
> I sought not to be born, nor love the state
> To which that birth has brought me!

To cut this knot, as the ancient Stoics attempted to do, by denying the existence of evil, was a measure of which the success was not likely to be equal to its hardiness or its motive. But, before we proceed with Lord Byron, from the mixture of evil and sorrow which the world presents, to infer a malevolent Creator, it may be well to inquire, first, whether *more* good than evil, *more* happiness than misery is not found, after all, in the world with which we are so much displeased; and, secondly, whether the good which exists is not, apparently, the result of direct *design,* while the evil is *incidental* only.

Both these positions have, we think, been proved by Paley, in a work too sensible, too philosophical, too accordant with the general feelings and general experience of our species, to be in much danger of overturn from a few well-pointed sarcasms, a few daring assertions, and a little poetic phantasmagoria of former worlds created and ruined. . . .

The origin of evil itself is among those secrets of Providence which, if they do not surpass our present faculties, are, at least, not as yet communicated to us. It is one of the many vulgar errors by which the subject has been encumbered, to suppose that such a communication is found in the Book of Genesis. All which Moses relates is the first *appearance* of that evil which must have previously existed, the first demonstration of those hateful passions and that aspiring pride which have made labour and death no more than necessary to the well-being of nature. Of the causes which may have induced the Almighty to create man peccable, to expose him to temptations, and to try him by suffering, our reason may conjecture, but our faith is uninformed; and it is a fact which may be advantageously recollected by those who, on these accounts, insult Christianity, that the difficulties of which they complain belong not to Christianity alone, but to every creed which admits the responsibility of man, and the power and goodness of his Maker. But though Christianity does not tell us the *cause* of our calamities, she has not failed to point out their *cure;* in fostering those amiable affections which enable us to bear our own sorrows best while they most dispose us to alleviate the sorrows of others, and in holding out to us a clearer and brighter prospect of that life where Love shall reap his harvest of enjoyment, and where the happy and benevolent inhabitant of a better world shall neither feel nor witness affliction!

—Reginald Heber, from his unsigned review of
Marino Faliero, Sardanapalus, The Two Foscari,
and *Cain, Quarterly Review,* July 1822,
XXVII, pp. 476–524

SAMUEL EGERTON BRYDGES (1824)

Sir Samuel Egerton Brydges (1762–1837) was a man of letters, genealogist, and editor specializing in Elizabethan texts. After hearing of Byron's death, he wrote his *Letters on the Character and Poetical Genius of Lord Byron.*

There is another extraordinary poem of which I have not spoken hitherto; because, I will confess, that I know not how to speak of it properly, yet something must be said of it.—*Cain* is a poem much too striking to be passed in silence. But its impiety is so frightful that it is impossible to praise it, while its genius and beauty of composition would demand all the notice which mere literary merit can claim. It is scarcely necessary to repeat the answer to the very futile defence which has been made for it, against the charge of its attack on the goodness of Province. It must be obvious to every intelligent reader that the example of *Milton* does not apply to the manner in which Lord Byron has executed his poem of *Cain.* Milton puts rebellious and blasphemous speeches into the mouth of *Satan;* but Milton never leaves those speeches unanswered: on the contrary, he always brings forward a *good angel* to controvert triumphantly all the daring assertions and arguments of the EVIL SPIRIT. Lord Byron leaves all which he ascribes to *Cain* and *Lucifer* in their full force on the reader's mind, without even an attempt to repel them.

It seems to me, that of all Lord Byron's poems this is that of which the ill tendency is most unequivocal, and for which no plausible excuse can be made;—and it is the more dangerous, because it is one of the best written.

—Samuel Egerton Brydges, *Letters on the
Character and Genius of Lord Byron,*
1824, pp. 264–265

JOHANN WOLFGANG VON GOETHE (1824)

Goethe's praise of *Cain* in February 1824 was reported by his secretary Eckermann: "Goethe then showed me a short critique, which he had written on Byron's *Cain,* and which I read with great interest."

"We see," he said, "how the inadequate dogmas of the church work upon a free mind like Byron's, and how by such a piece he struggles to get rid of a doctrine which has been forced upon him. The English clergy will not thank him; but I shall be surprised if he does not go on treating biblical subjects of similar import, and if he lets slip a subject like the destruction of Sodom and Gomorrah.'"

> —Johann Wolfgang von Goethe, *Conversations of Goethe with Eckermann and Soret,* trans. John Oxenford, 1850, I, pp. 129–130

This short critique was written in 1824:

This poet, whose burning spiritual vision penetrates beyond all comprehension into the past and the present and, in their train, also into the future, has now conquered new worlds for his boundless talent; and no human being can foresee what he will achieve with them.

> —Johann Wolfgang von Goethe, quotation in E.M. Butler, *Byron and Goethe,* 1956, p. 183

SARDANAPALUS

The verse tragedy *Sardanapalus,* published in 1821, was, after *Marino Faliero* and the *Two Foscaris,* Byron's third historical tragedy. Sardanapalus is a figure of unverifiable authenticity, who is supposed to have been the last king of Assyria and who perished in the flames of his palace after being conquered by his foes. He is depicted in a well-known painting by Delacroix, whose work was deeply influenced by Byron. Sardanapalus is characterized in Byron's source—Diodorus Siculus, a Greek historian of the first century—as a ruthless and debauched ruler. Byron's Sardanapalus, however, rises above his self-indulgent proclivities to attain greater stature by devoting himself to the preservation of his kingdom against overwhelming odds. His self-sacrificial death assumes heroic proportions and he is, in the relationship of the verse drama's personal and political considerations, perhaps an idealized self-portrait of the poet himself.

FRANCIS JEFFREY (1822)

It must be a more difficult thing to write a good play—or even a good dramatic poem—than we had imagined. Not that we should, *a priori,* have imagined it to be very easy; but it is impossible not to be struck with the fact, that, in comparatively rude times, when the resources of the art had been less carefully considered, and Poetry certainly had not collected all her materials, success seems to have been more frequently, and far more easily obtained. From the middle of Elizabeth's reign till the end of James's, the drama formed by far the most brilliant and beautiful part of our poetry,—and indeed of our literature in general. From that period to the Revolution, it lost a part of its splendour and originality; but still continued to occupy the most conspicuous and considerable place in our literary annals. For the last century, it has been quite otherwise—our poetry has ceased almost entirely to be dramatic; and, though men of great name and great talent have occasionally adventured into this once fertile field, they have reaped no laurels, and left no trophies behind them. . . .

. . . we think it is certain that his late dramatic efforts have not been made carelessly, or without anxiety. To us, at least, they seem very elaborate and hardwrought compositions; and this indeed we take to be their leading characteristic, and the key to most of their peculiarities.

Considered as Poems, we confess they appear to us to be rather heavy, verbose, and inelegant—deficient in the passion and energy which belongs to the other writings of the noble author—and still more in the richness of imagery, the originality of thought, and the sweetness of versification for which he used to be distinguished. They are for the most part solemn, prolix, and ostentatious—lengthened out by large preparations for catastrophes that never arrive, and tantalizing us with slight specimens and glimpses of a higher interest scattered thinly up and down many weary pages of pompous declamation. Along with the concentrated pathos and homestruck sentiments of his former poetry, the noble author seems also, we cannot imagine why, to have discarded the spirited and melodious versification in which they were embodied, and to have formed to himself a measure equally remote from the spring and vigour of his former compositions, and from the softness and inflexibility of the ancient masters of the drama. There are some sweet lines, and many of great weight and energy; but the general inarch of the verse is cumbrous and unmusical. His lines do not vibrate like polished lances, at once strong and light, in the hands of his persons, but are wielded like clumsy batons in a bloodless affray. Instead of the graceful familiarity and idiomatical melodies of Shakespeare, it is apt, too, to fall into clumsy prose, in its approaches to the easy and colloquial style; and, in the loftier passages, is occasionally deformed by low and common images that harmonize but ill with the general solemnity of the diction.

As Plays, we are afraid we must also say that the pieces before us are wanting in interest, character, and action:—at least we must say this of the two last of them—for *there is* interest in *Sardanapalus*—and beauties besides, that make us blind to its other defects. There is, however, throughout, a want of dramatic effect and variety; and we suspect there is something in the character or habit of Lord B.'s genius which will render this unattainable. He has too little sympathy with the ordinary feelings and frailties of humanity, to succeed well in their representation—'His soul is like a star, and dwells apart.' It does not 'hold the mirror up to nature,' nor catch the hues of surrounding objects; but, like a kindled furnace, throws out its intense glare and gloomy grandeur on the narrow scene which it irradiates. He has given us, in his other works, some glorious pictures of nature—some magnificent reflections, and some inimitable delineations of character: But the same feelings prevail in them all; and his portraits in particular, though a little varied in the drapery and attitude, seem all copied from the same original.

His Childe Harold, his Giaour, Conrad, Lara, Manfred, Cain, and Lucifer,—are all one individual. There is the same varnish of voluptuousness on the surface—the same canker of misanthropy at the core, of all he touches. He cannot draw the changes of many-coloured life, nor transport himself into the condition of the infinitely diversified characters by whom a stage should be peopled. The very intensity of his feelings—the loftiness of his views—the pride of his nature or his genius, withhold him from this identification; so that in personating the heroes of the scene, he does little but repeat himself. It would be better for him, we think, if it were otherwise. "We are sure it would be better for his readers. He would get more fame, and things of far more worth than fame, if he would condescend to a more extended and cordial sympathy with his fellow-creatures; and we should have more variety of fine poetry, and, at all events, better tragedies. We have no business to read him a homily on the sinfulness of pride and uncharity; but we have a right to say, that it argues a poorness of genius to keep always to the same topics and persons; and that the world will weary at last of the most energetic pictures of misanthropes and madmen—outlaws and their mistresses!

A man gifted as he is, when he aspires at dramatic fame, should emulate the greatest of dramatists. Let Lord B. then think of Shakespeare—and consider what a noble range of character, what a freedom from mannerism and egotism, there is in him! How much he seems to have studied nature; how little to have thought about himself; how seldom to have repeated or glanced back at his own most successful inventions! Why indeed should he? Nature was still open before him, and inexhaustible; and the freshness and variety that still delight his readers, must have had constant attractions for himself. Take his Hamlet, for instance. What a character is there!—how full of thought and refinement, and fancy and individuality! 'How infinite in faculties! In form and motion how express and admirable! The beauty of the universe, the paragon of animals!' Yet close the play, and we meet with him no more—neither in the author's other works, nor any where else! A common author, who had hit upon such a character, would have dragged it in at every turn, and worn it to very tatters. Sir John Falstaff, again, is a world of wit and humour in himself. But except in the two parts of *Henry IV* there would have been no trace of such a being, had not the author been 'ordered to continue him' in *The Merry Wives of Windsor*. He is not the least like Benedick, or Mercutio, or Sir Toby Belch, or any of the other witty personages of the same author,—nor are they like each other. Othello is one of the most striking and powerful inventions on the stage. But when the play closes, we hear no more of him! The poet's creation comes no more to life again under a fictitious name, than the real man would have done. Lord Byron, in Shakespeare's place, would have peopled the world with black Othellos! What indications are there of *Lear* in any of his earlier plays? What traces of it in any that he wrote afterwards? None. It might have been written by any other man, he is so little conscious of it. He never once returns to that huge sea of sorrow; but has left it standing by itself, shoreless and unapproachable. Who else could have afforded not to have 'drowned the stage with tears' from such a source? But we must break away from Shakespeare, and come at last to the work before us.

In a very brief preface, Lord B. renews his protest against looking upon any of his plays, as having been composed 'with the most remote view to the stage'—and, at the same time, testifies in behalf of the *Unities*, as essential to the existence of the drama—according to what 'was, till lately, the law of literature throughout the world, and is still so, in the more civilized parts of it.' We do not think those opinions very consistent; and we think that neither of them could possibly find favour with a person whose genius had a truly dramatic character. We should as soon expect an orator to compose a speech altogether unfit to be spoken. A drama is not merely a dialogue, but *an action:* and necessarily supposes that something is to pass before the eyes of assembled spectators. Whatever is peculiar to its written part, should derive its peculiarity from this consideration. Its style should be an accompaniment to action—and should be calculated to excite the emotions, and keep alive the attention, of gazing multitudes. If an author does not bear this continually in his mind, and does not write in the ideal presence of an eager and diversified assemblage, he may be a poet perhaps, but assuredly he never will be a dramatist. If Lord B. really does not wish to impregnate his elaborate scenes with the living spirit of the drama—if he has no hankering after stage-effect—if he is not haunted with the visible presentment of the persons he has created if, in setting down a vehement invective, he does not fancy the tone in which Mr Kean would deliver it, and anticipate the long applauses of the pit, then he may be sure that neither his feelings nor his genius are in unison with the stage at all. Why, then, should he affect the form, without the power of tragedy? He may, indeed, produce a mystery like *Cain,* or a far sweeter vision like *Manfred,* without subjecting himself to the censure of legitimate criticism; but if, with a regular subject before him, capable of all the strength and graces of the drama, he does not feel himself able or willing to draw forth its resources so as to affect an audience with terror and delight, he is not the man we want—and his time and talents are wasted here. Didactic reasoning and eloquent description, will not compensate, in a play, for a dearth of dramatic spirit and invention: and besides, sterling sense and poetry, as such, ought to stand by themselves, without the unmeaning mockery of a *dramatis personae.*

As to Lord Byron's pretending to set up the *Unities* at this time of day, as 'the law of literature throughout the world', it is mere caprice and contradiction. He, if ever man was, is *a law to himself*—'a chartered libertine;'—and now, when he is tired of this unbridled license, he wants to do penance within the *Unities!* This certainly looks very like affectation; or, if there is any thing sincere in it, the motive must be, that, by getting rid of so much story and action, in order to simplify the plot and bring it within the prescribed limits, he may fill up the blank spaces with long discussions, and have nearly all the talk to himself! For ourselves, we will confess that we have had a considerable contempt for these same *Unities,* ever since we read Dennis's *Criticism on Cato* in our boyhood—except indeed the unity of action, which Lord Byron does not appear to set much store by. Dr Johnson, we conceive, has pretty well settled this question: and if Lord Byron chuses to grapple with him, he will find that it requires a stronger arm than that with which he puts down our Laureates. We shall only add, that when the moderns tie themselves down to write tragedies of the same length, and on the same simple plan, in other respects, with those of Sophocles and Aeschylus, we shall not object to their adhering to the Unities; for there can, in that case, be no sufficient inducement for violating them. But, in the mean time, we hold that English dramatic poetry soars above the *Unities,* just as the imagination does. The only pretence for insisting on them is, that we suppose the stage itself to be, actually and really, the very spot on which a given action is performed;

and, if so, this space cannot be removed to another. But the supposition is manifestly quite contrary to truth and experience. The stage is considered merely as a place in which any given action *ad libitum* may be performed; and accordingly may be shifted, and is so in imagination, as often as the action requires it. That any writer should ever have insisted on such an unity as this, must appear sufficiently preposterous; but, that the defence of it should be taken up by an author whose plays are never to be acted at all, and which, therefore, have nothing more than a nominal reference to any stage or locality whatever, must strike one as absolutely incredible.

It so happens, however, that the disadvantage, and, in truth, absurdity, of sacrificing higher objects to a formality of this kind, is strikingly displayed in one of these dramas—*The Two Foscari*. The whole interest here turns upon the younger of them having returned from banishment, in defiance of the law and its consequences, from an unconquerable longing after his own country. Now, the only way to have made this sentiment palpable, the practicable foundation of stupendous suffering, would have been, to have presented him to the audience wearing out his heart in exile—and forming his resolution to return, at a distance from his country, or hovering, in excruciating suspense, within sight of its borders. We might then have caught some glimpse of the nature of his motives, and of so extraordinary a character. But as this would have been contrary to one of the unities, we first meet with him led from 'the Question,' and afterwards taken back to it in the Ducal Palace, or clinging to the dungeon-walls of his native city, and expiring from his dread of leaving them; and therefore feel more wonder than sympathy, when we are told, in a Jeremiad of wilful lamentations, that these agonizing consequences have resulted not from guilt or disaster, but merely from the intensity of his love for his country. . . .

Of *Cain, a Mystery* we are constrained to say, that, though it abounds in beautiful passages, and shows more *power* perhaps than any of the author's dramatical compositions, we regret very much that it should ever have been published. It will give great scandal and offence to pious persons in general— and may be the means of suggesting the most painful doubts and distressing perplexities, to hundreds of minds that might never otherwise have been exposed to such dangerous disturbance. It is nothing less than absurd, in such a case, to observe, that Lucifer cannot well be expected to talk like an orthodox divine—and that the conversation of the first Rebel and the first·Murderer was not likely to be very unexceptionable—or to plead the authority of Milton, or the authors of the old mysteries, for such offensive colloquies. The fact is, that here *the whole argument*—and a very elaborate and specious argument it is—is directed against the goodness or the power of the Deity, and against the reasonableness of religion in general; and there is no answer so much as attempted to the offensive doctrines that are so strenuously inculcated. The Devil and his pupil have the field entirely to themselves—and are encountered with nothing but feeble obtestations and unreasoning horrors. Nor is this argumentative blasphemy a mere incidental deformity that arises in the course of an action directed to the common sympathies of our nature. It forms, on the contrary, the great staple of the piece—and occupies, we should think, not less than two-thirds of it;—so that it is really difficult to believe that it was written for any other purpose than to inculcate these doctrines—or at least to discuss the question upon which they bear. Now, we can certainly have no objection to Lord Byron writing an Essay on the Origin of Evil—and sifting the whole of that vast and perplexing subject with the force and the freedom that would be expected and allowed in a fair philosophical discussion. But we do not think it fair, thus to argue it partially and *con amore,* in the name of Lucifer and Cain; without the responsibility or the liability to answer that would attach to a philosophical disputant—and in a form which both doubles the danger, if the sentiments are pernicious, and almost precludes his opponents from the possibility of a reply.

Philosophy and Poetry are both very good things in their way; but, in our opinion, they do not go very well together. It is but a poor and pedantic sort of poetry that seeks to embody nothing but metaphysical subtleties and abstract deductions of reason—and a very suspicious philosophy that aims at establishing its doctrines by appeals to the passions and the fancy. Though such arguments, however, are worth little in the schools, it does not follow that their effect is inconsiderable in the world. On the contrary, it is the mischief of all poetical paradoxes, that, from the very limits and end of poetry, which deals only in obvious and glancing views, they are never brought to the fair test of argument. An allusion to a doubtful topic will often pass for a definitive conclusion on it; and, clothed in beautiful language, may leave the most pernicious impressions behind. We therefore think that poets ought fairly to be confined to the established creed and morality of their country, or to the *actual* passions and sentiments of mankind; and that poetical dreamers and sophists who pretend to *theorise* according to their feverish fancies, without a warrant from authority or reason, ought to be banished the commonwealth of letters. In the courts of morality, poets are unexceptionable *witnesses;* they may give in the evidence, and depose to facts whether good or ill; but we demur to their arbitrary and self-pleasing summing up; they are suspected *judges,* and not very often safe advocates, where great questions are concerned, and universal principles brought to issue. But we shall not press this point farther at present. We do not doubt that Lord Byron has written conscientiously, and that he is of opinion that the publication of his sentiments will not be disadvantageous to mankind. Upon this, and upon other matters, we confess we think otherwise—and we too think it our duty to make public our dissent.

As to the question of the Origin of Evil, which is the burden of this misdirected verse, he has neither thrown any new light upon it, nor darkened the previous knowledge which we possessed. It remains just where it was, in its mighty, unfathomed obscurity. His Lordship may, it is true, have recapitulated some of the arguments with a more concise and cavalier air, than the old schoolmen or fathers; but the result is the same. There is no poetical road to metaphysics. In one view, however, which our rhapsodist has taken of the subject, we conceive he has done well. He represents the temptations held out to Cain by Satan as constantly succeeding and corresponding to some previous discontent and gloomy disposition in his own mind; so that Lucifer is little more than the personified demon of his imagination: And farther, the acts of guilt and folly into which Cain is hurried are not treated as accidental, or as occasioned by passing causes, but as springing from an internal fury, a morbid state akin to phrensy, a mind dissatisfied with itself and all things, and haunted by an insatiable, stubborn longing after knowledge rather than happiness, and a fatal proneness to dwell on the evil side of things, rather than the good. We here see the dreadful consequences of not curbing this disposition (which is, after all, perhaps the sin that most easily besets humanity), exemplified in a striking point of view; and we so far think, it is but fair to say, that the moral to be derived from a perusal of this Mystery is a valuable one.

—Francis Jeffrey, from his unsigned review of
Sardanapalus, The Two Foscari, and
Cain, Edinburgh Review, February 1822,
issued April 1822, XXXVI, pp. 413–452

John Gibson Lockhart (1822)

It would be highly ridiculous to enter, at this time of day, into any thing like a formal review, *here,* of Lord Byron's new volume. We have not happened to meet with any two individuals who expressed two different opinions about it and its contents. There is a great deal of power in *Sardanapalus* . . . but as a play, it is an utter failure; and, in God's name, why call a thing a tragedy, unless it be meant to be a play? What would people say to a new song of Tom Moore's, prefaced with an earnest injunction on man, woman, and child, never to think of singing it? A tragedy, *not meant to be acted,* seems to us to be just about as reasonable an affair as a song not meant to be sung. But even as *a poem, Sardanapalus* is *not* quite worthy of its author. Let any one just think, for a moment, of the magnificent story of Sardanapalus, and then imagine what a thing Lord Byron might have made of it, had he chosen the fiery narrative-pace *of Lara,* or *The Giaour*—instead of this lumbering, and lax, and highly *undramatic* blank-verse dialogue.—The *Foscari* is totally inferior to the *Sardanapalus.* It is a ridiculous caricature of some historical situations, in themselves beautiful and interesting. The true tragedy of the Foscari is to be read in the notes at the end of Lord Byron's tragedy bearing that name; and the public is much obliged to him, and so is M. Simonde de Sismondi, for these very pretty extracts. *Cain* contains, perhaps, five or six passages of as fine poetry as Lord Byron ever wrote or will write; but, taken altogether, it is a wicked and blasphemous performance, destitute of any merit sufficient to overshadow essential defects of the most abominable nature. The three plays, bound up together, we repeat, constitute a dullish volume—perhaps one of the heaviest that has appeared in the poetical world since the days of *Ricciarda, Tragedian.*

—John Gibson Lockhart, from an unsigned
review of *Sardanapalus, The Two Foscari,*
and *Cain, Blackwood's Magazine,*
January 1822, XI, pp. 90–91

Chronology

1788   George Gordon Byron born January 22 in London to Captain John Byron and his wife, formerly Catherine Gordon of Gight.

1790   Byron's mother, her fortune spent on her husband's lavish lifestyle, takes her son to Aberdeen.

1791   Captain Byron dies at the age of thirty-six in France.

1792   George Gordon attends day school in Aberdeen.

1798   He inherits the title of his granduncle, the fifth Lord Byron, and moves to Newstead Abbey, Nottinghamshire, the Byron family seat.

1798–99   Tutored in Nottingham; his foot deformity is unsuccessfully treated by an incompetent physician.

1799–1801   Attends boarding school at Dulwich, near London.

1801–05   Byron attends Harrow School and spends his vacations with his mother at Southwell.

1803   He has his first romance with Mary Chaworth of Annesley Hall, grandniece of Lord Chaworth, whom the fifth Lord Byron had killed in a duel.

1804   Begins correspondence with half sister, Augusta.

1805   He enters Trinty College at Cambridge University.

1806   *Fugitive Pieces,* his first collection of poems, is privately printed.

1807   *Hours of Idleness* is published. Byron is drawn into a Cambridge circle of young intellectually and political liberals.

1808   *Hours of Idelness* is attacked in the *Edinburgh Review.* Byron receives a master's degree at Cambridge in July and moves to London.

1809   Takes a seat, on March 13, in the House of Lords. Publishes *English Bards and Scotch Reviewers* in retaliation against the *Edinburgh Review;* Byron points to Alexander Pope and John Dryden as the standards for English poetry. With John Cam Hobhouse, he departs in July for a journey through Portugal, Spain, Albania, and Greece. Completes first canto of *Childe Harold* in Athens.

1810   Finishes the second canto of *Childe Harold* on March 28. Travels in Turkey and Greece, swimming the Hellespont on May 3 and continuing to live in Athens the rest of the year.

1811   Returns to England in July. His mother dies in August.

1812   He gives three liberal speeches at the House of Lords. *Childe Harold,* published in March, brings immediate fame to its author, and Byron becomes a popular figure in London social circles. He has an affair with Lady Caroline Lamb.

1813   He begins an affair in June with his half sister, Augusta Leigh. Publishes *The Giaour* and *The Bride of Abydos.*

1814   Publishes *The Corsair* and *Lara.* Becomes engaged in September to Anabella Milbanke.

1815   Byron marries Annabella Milbanke, January 12. He is frequently hounded by creditors. Daughter, Augusta Ada, is born December 10.

1816   Byron's wife leaves him on January 15; separation papers are formally signed April 21. Four days later, Byron leaves England for good and spends the summer in Switzerland with Percy Shelley, Mary Godwin, and Claire Clairmont, with whom he has an affair. He publishes *The Prisoner of Chillon* and canto III of *Childe Harold* and begins writing *Manfred.* Later in the year, he travels to Italy.

1817   Allegra, daughter of Claire Clairmont, is born January 12. Byron resides in Venice where he has an affair with Mariana Segati. He visits Florence and Rome, completes *Manfred,* and works on the fourth canto of *Childe Harold.* He experiments in *Beppo* with colloquial *ottava rima,* writing about Venetian life.

1818   He begins a romantic liaison with Margarita Cogni. *Beppo* is published in February, and the fourth canto of *Childe Harold* in April. He begins *Don Juan,* finishing canto I in September.

1819   Byron embarks on a relationship with the married Teresa, Countess Guiccioli in April. He spends the autumn with her at

La Mira and continues *Don Juan*. Thomas Moore visits Byron and is given the gift of Byron's memoirs. The first two cantos of *Don Juan* are published in July.

1820   Byron lives in Guiccioli palace in Ravenna and continues to write *Don Juan*. He writes his first verse drama, *Marino Faliero*. Teresa's application for separation from Count Guiccioli is granted by the pope in July. Byron visits Teresa at the Gamba family villa at Filetto; he comes involved in the revolutionary struggle led by the Carbonati in opposition to Austrian rule in Italy.

1821   The Carbonati movment is defeated. The Gambas, Teresa's family, are banished to Pisa. The outbreak of the Greek war for independence captures Byron's interest. *Don Juan* cantos III, IV, and V are published in August, and Byron promised Teresa he will not add to the work. In September, he writes *Vision of Judgment*. He joins the Gambas and Shelley in Pisa in November. *Cain* is published in December.

1822   The British outcry against *Cain* and *Don Juan* increases. With Teresa's consent, Byron resumes *Don Juan*. Leigh Hunt and his family stay in Byron's Pisa house. Shelley drowns in the Bay of Lerici. Byron joins the exiled Gambas in Genoa. He finds a new publisher in John Hunt.

1823   London Greek Committee enlists Byron's aid on behalf of Greece. Byron sails in July for Greece and becomes seriously ill after a strenuous excursion to Ithaca. He sets sail for Missolonghi on December 30. *Don Juan,* cantos VI through XIV, are published.

1824   Byron tries to form an artillery corps to attack the Turkish-held stronghold of Lepanto. Cantos XV and XVI of *Don Juan* are published in March. Byron falls ill on April 9. Doctors insist on repeated bleedings as treatment, and he dies on April 19. Regarded throughout Europa as "the Trumpet Voice of Liberty," he is buried July16 in Hucknall Torkard Church near Newstead.

Index

A

Adams, John Quincy, 51–52
Adonais (Shelley), xv
Alastor (Shelley), xvi
Albania, 3, 183
aristocracy, 92, 112, 242
Arnold, Matthew, 28–29, 84–92, 121
"At Lord Byron's Tomb" (Miller),
    35–37
Austen, Jane, 200–201

B

Beddoes, Thomas Lovell, 51
Bell, Peter, 70
Beppo (Byron), xvi, 6
    Jeffrey on, 215–217
    Murray on, 214–215
    opinions on, 214–221
    satire in, 99
biography, of Byron, 1–8
Blake, William, 265–268
Bloom, Harold, xi–xix
The Bride of Abydos (Byron), 4, 183,
    197
Brougham, Henry Lord, 2, 43–44
Browning, Robert, 105, 128
Brydges, Samuel Egerton, 274
Byron, Augusta Ada, xiii, 5
Byron, George Gordon Lord. *See also*
    specific works
    Arnold on, 84–92

biography of, 1–8
Bloom on, xi–xix
on *Childe Harold*, 159
compared with Goethe, 79–83
death of, 8, 17–18, 22, 60–61, 116
fame of, 109, 118, 177
friendship with Shelley, xii, xv–
    xix, 5, 178
Hazlitt on, 52–61
importance of, 124–126
influence of, 126
as man of his age, 71–72
on *Manfred*, 210
marriage of, xiii–xiv, 4–5, 12–13
originality of, 62–63
personal character of, 90, 94, 98,
    174, 217–221
personal remembrances on, 11–39
politics of, xiii, 4, 7, 20, 88–89,
    180
romances of, xiii, xvi–xvii, 1, 2,
    4, 7, 30
sexuality of, xi, xii, xiii, 1
Shakespeare and, xi
Shelley compared with, 95–97
sources for writings of, 241–243
temperament of, 22–25
travels of, 3–4, 6, 31–32
writing style, 55–56, 74–76, 127–
    128, 130–132, 190–193, 232
Byron, John "Mad Jack", xi–xii, 1

Byron, Lady Annabelle, xiii–xiv, 4–5, 12–13, 18–19

Byron in Love (O'Brien), xii

Byronic hero, 1, 5, 170–171

Byronism, 117–118

C

Cain (Byron), 7, 133–134, 251, 255
    Brydges on, 274
    Goethe on, 275
    Heber on, 268–274
    Hobhouse on, 255
    Hunt on, 260–265
    Mary Shelley on, 257
    Moore on, 255–256
    offensiveness of, 280–281
    Percy Shelley on, 258
    Robinson on, 258
    Scott on, 256–257

Carlyle, Thomas, 17–18, 51

Cavendish, Elizabeth, Duchess of Devonshire, 142

characters, 74, 97, 170

Chaworth, Mary, 1

Chesterton, G.K., 116–120

Childe Harold's Pilgrimage (Byron), xii, 3, 5, 6, 63
    appendix to, 153
    Collins on, 122–123
    criticism of, 114, 115–116, 144–146
    Ellis on, 146–154
    Hazlitt on, 56, 160–161
    hero in, 149–152, 163–164, 171–172, 182
    melancholy in, 181–182
    notes to, 152–153
    opinions on, 142–183
    parodies of, 154–155
    popularity of, 141, 142, 179–180
    publication of, 4, 141
    reaction to, 4
    Scott on, 21, 161–164
    self-reflection in, 182
    Shelley on, 174–175
    structure of, 75
    Swinburne on, 97–98
    Wilson on, 164–174
    writing style in, 148

Christianity, 273–274

Clairmont, Claire, 5

Clairmont, Clara Allegra, 5, 8

Clarke, Hewson, 11–12

Clermont, Jane, 38–39

Coleridge, Samuel Taylor, 16–17, 51, 70, 93, 96, 128, 227

Collins, John Churton, 120–126, 212–214

comedy, 99, 101, 121, 134, 226, 233

The Corsair (Byron), 183, 191–192
    heroic couplets of, 191
    objections to, 196
    reception of, 198–199
    Robinson on, 197

"Cui Bono?" (Smith and Smith), 154–155

The Curse of Minerva (Byron), 3

D

The Deformed Transformed (Byron), 8, 96

descriptive language, 75–76

Devil, 270, 271–272, 280–281

dialogue, 74–75, 97

Disraeli, Isaac, 199–200

Doctor Faustus (Marlowe), 205, 207–208

Don Juan (Byron), 6, 64, 121, 221–222
    Collins on, 123–124
    feminist perspective on, 227–228
    Goethe on, 226–227
    Hazlitt on, 58
    humor in, 101, 222, 233
    Hunt on, 222–225
    as immoral, 223–225
    More on, 234–241
    opinions on, 222–243
    satire in, 221, 222, 233, 237
    Scott on, 21
    Shelley on, xi

sources for, 241–243
structure of, 75, 230
Swinburne on, 94–95, 100–102,
    230–234
translation of, 226–227
writing of, 221–222
writing style in, 232
Dowden, Edward, 111–113
drama, 278–279
Dryden, John, 72, 191

E

Edelston, John, xii, 2, 4
Edgeworth, Maria, 12–14
Edinburgh Review, xii, 2, 142
egotism, 77–78, 168, 179
Eliot, George, 34–35
Eliot, T.S., 137–138
Ellis, George, 146–154, 194–196
English Bards, and Scotch Reviewers
    (Byron), xii, 2–3, 57, 65, 142
"English Literature of the Nineteenth
    Century" (Prescott), 67–69
evil, 271, 272–273, 281–282

F

Fabian Society, 234
Faust (Goethe), 208
The Feast of the Poets (Hunt), 44–45
Felix Holt (Eliot), 34–35
Flaubert, Gustave, 26
French Revolution, 180
Frere, John Hookham, 6, 214
Fugitive Pieces (Byron), 2

G

Galt, John, 61–64
Gamba family, 7, 8
Gardiner, Marguerite, Countess of
    Blessington, 26–27
Gerould, Katherine Fullerton,
    136–137
"The Ghost of Abel" (Blake), 265–
    268
The Giaour (Byron), 86–87

Collins on, 125
Jeffrey on, 192
reception of, 183
Robinson on, 196–197
Scott on, 197–198
Swinburne on, 99
Gifford, William, 2, 200
Godwin, Mary, 5, 271–273
Goethe, Johann Wolfgang von, 6, 90
    on Byron, 64–67, 125
    on *Cain*, 275
    compared with Byron, 79–83
    on *Don Juan*, 226–227
    Faust, 208
    on *Manfred*, 208–209, 210
Gordon, Catherine, 1
Graham, William, 38–39
Greece, xvii, 3, 8, 183
Greek Committee, 8
Guiccioli, Teresa, xvi–xvii, 7

H

Hazlitt, William
    on Byron, 46–47, 52–61
    on *Childe Harold*, 160–161
    *Conversations of James
        Northcote, Esq.*, 228–229
    on *Marino Faliero*, 244–246
Heaven and Earth (Byron), 96
Heber, Reginald
    on *Cain*, 268–274
    on *Marino Faliero*, 250–254
Hebrew Melodies (Byron), 5
Henley, William Ernest, 107–108
heoric couplets, 191
Hobhouse, John Cam, xii, 2, 3, 6,
    155–156, 255
homosexuality, 1, 2, 176
Hours of Idleness (Byron), xii, 2,
    43–44
Hugo, Victor, 97
human nature, 188, 189
humor, 134, 222, 233
Hunt, Leigh, 8
    on Byron, 22–25

on *Cain*, 260–265
on *Don Juan*, 222–225
The Feast of the Poets, 44–45

I

immorality, 223–225
incest, 4, 183
individuality, 79–83
insincerity, 121–122
The Island (Byron), 8
"The Isles of Greece" (Byron), 3
Italy, 7–8

J

Jeffrey, Francis, 2
on *Beppo*, 215–217
on *Childe Harold*, 144–146,
157–158
on *Manfred*, 205–208
on *Marino Faliero*, 246–250
on *Sardanapalus*, 276–282
on *Turkish Tales*, 184–194
Johnson, Lionel, 113–116
Julian and Maddalo (Shelley), xviii–
xix

K

Keats, John, xv–xvi, 92, 93, 96

L

Lake Poets, 48, 72
Lamb, Lady Caroline, xiii, 4, 11, 30
Leigh, Lady Augusta, xii, xiii, xiv,
1, 4
*The Liberal—Verse and Prose from
the South* (journal), 8, 22
literary career, 71
Lockhart, John Gibson, 282–283
"Lord Byron" (Symonds), 229–230
"Lord Byron's Poems" (Jeffrey),
157–158

M

Macaulay, Thomas Babington, 69–79,
229

Maginn, William, 48–51
Manfred (Byron), xvi, 5–6, 57,
201–214
Byron on, 210
character in, 178–179
Collins on, 212–214
Goethe on, 208–209, 210
Jeffrey on, 205–208
morality of, 202–203
Oliphant on, 210–211
originality of, 63
Royce on, 211–212
Wilson on, 202–205
writing of, 201
Manicheism, 256–257, 270–271
Marchand, Leslie A., xiii
Marino Faliero, Doge of Venice
(Byron), 7, 243–244
Hazlitt on, 244–246
Heber on, 250–254
improbability of, 248
Jeffrey on, 246–250
as neoclassical drama, 252–254
Nichol on, 254–255
setting of, 244
Marlowe, Christopher, 205, 207–208
Marx, Karl, xiii
Mazeppo (Byron), 6
Mazzini, Giuseppe, 79–83
Medora, Elizabeth, 4
Medwin, Thomas, 18–19
melancholy, 78, 119, 132–133, 162,
181–182, 204, 239
"Memorial Verses" (Arnold), 28–29
metaphysics, 196
Milbanke, Annabelle. *See* Byron,
Lady Annabelle
Miller, Joaquin, 35–37
Milton, John, 95, 274
Molière, 102
Moore, Thomas, 7, 255–256
"Moore's Life of Lord Byron"
(Macaulay), 69–79
More, Paul Elmer, 234–241
Murray, John, 4, 141

on *Beppo*, 214–215
on *Childe Harold*, 156–157
on reception of *Corsair*, 198–199

N

nature, 76, 96–97, 121–122, 173
Newstead Abbey, 1
Nichol, John, 254–255
Nightmare Abbey (Peacock), 175–176
Northcote, James, 228–229
Norton, Caroline, 227–228

O

O'Brien, Edna, xii, xiii, xiv, xvii
"Ode to the West Wind" (Shelley), 96
"Odeherty on Werner" (Magnin),
    48–51
Oliphant, Margaret, 210–211
optimism, 119
"The Optimism of Byron'
    (Chesterton), 116–120
originality, 62–63
Oxoniensis, 259–260

P

passions, 184–189, 194–195, 239
Peacock, Thomas Love, 175–176
Persuasion (Austen), 200–201
pessimism, 118–120, 132–133, 212
Philistinism, 88–89, 92
philosophy, 281
Poems on Various Occasions (Byron),
    2
poetic cycle, 184–187, 194–195
poetry, 281
Pope, Alexander, 2, 70, 191, 216
Prescott, William H., 67–69
The Prisoner of Chillon (Byron), 5
The Prophecy of Dante (Byron), 249
Prothero, R.E., 179–183, 241–243
Pulci, 241–242

R

Robinson, Charles, xv
Robinson, Henry Crabb, 196–197, 258

Rogers, Samuel, 29–30, 142–143
Rossetti, William Michael, 106
Rousseau, Jean-Jacques, 164–166,
    168, 169
Royce, Josiah, 211–212

S

Saintsbury, George, 109–111
Sardanapalus (Byron), 7, 73–74,
    275–283
Satanic School, 7, 48
satire, 99–100, 114, 121, 135, 221, 222,
    233, 237
scandals, 136–137
scepticism, 204
Schlegel, Friedrich von, 45–46
Scott, Sir Walter, 73–74
    on Byron, 19–22
    on *Cain*, 256–257
    on *Childe Harold*, 143, 161–164
    compared with Byron, 52–55, 59
    on *Giaour*, 197–198
    popularity of, 72, 109
Segati, Marianna, 6
Shakespeare, William, xi, 73, 125,
    128, 132, 277–278
Shaw, George Bernard, 234
Shelley, Mary, 257
Shelley, Percy Bysshe, 93
    Arnold on, 85–86
    Byron compared with, 95, 96–97
    on *Cain*, 258
    on Childe Harold, 174–175
    death of, 8
    on *Don Juan*, xi
    friendship with Byron, xii, xv–
        xix, 5, 178
    Trelawney on, 33–34
Shelley and Byron (Robinson), xv
Siege of Corinth (Byron), 197, 199–
    200
Smith, Horace, 154–155
Smith, James, 154–155
Smith, Sydney, 16
solitude, 167–168

sonnets, 98–99
Southey, Robert, 7, 48, 225
Spenser, Edmund, 95–96, 146,
    148–149
"Stanzas from the Grande
    Chartreuse" (Arnold), 28
Swinburne, Algernon Charles, 92–
    105, 230–234
Symonds, John Addington, 176–179,
    229–230
Symons, Arthur, 126–135

T
Ticknor, George, 14–16
Titanism, 121, 123
"To Thyrza" (Byron), 4
Todd, H. J., 259–260
Trelawney, Edward John, xvii, 31–34
Trinity College, 2
Turkish Tales (Byron), 183–184
        Jeffrey on, 184–194
        writing style in, 192–193

The Two Foscari (Byron), 7, 280

V
The Vision of Judgment (Byron),
    99–100, 121, 129
Voltaire, 72

W
Walpole, Horace, 182
Werner (Byron), 8
Whistlecraft (Frere), 6, 214
Wilde, Oscar, 37–38
Williams Edward Elliker, 18
Wilson, John
        on Byron, 164–174
        on Childe Harold, 159–160
        on Manfred, 202–205
Woolf, Virginia, 135
Wordworth, William, 70, 72, 84–87,
    91–93, 102, 122
writing style, 75–76, 127–128, 130–
    132, 148, 190–193